*f*P

FORGOTTEN HEROES

INSPIRING AMERICAN PORTRAITS FROM OUR LEADING HISTORIANS

· A SOCIETY OF AMERICAN HISTORIANS BOOK ·

EDITED BY

SUSAN WARE

WITH A FOREWORD BY

DAVID McCULLOUGH

THE FREE PRESS

NEW YORK   LONDON   TORONTO   SYDNEY   SINGAPORE

THE FREE PRESS
A Division of Simon & Schuster Inc.
1230 Avenue of the Americas
New York, NY 10020

Designed by Carla Bolte

Manufactured in the United States of America

10 9 8 7 6 5 4 3 2 1

Photo Credits on p. 363

Library of Congress Cataloging-in-Publication Data

Forgotten heroes : inspiring American portraits from our leading historians /
   edited by Susan Ware ; with a foreword by David McCullough.
        p.   cm.—(A Society of American Historians book)
   Includes bibliographical references and index.
     1. Heroes—United States—Biography.   2. United States—Biography.
I. Ware, Susan, date.   II. Series.
CT214.F67   1998
920'.073—dc21
     [B]   98-23878
                                                       CIP

ISBN 0–684–84375–7

Contents

Foreword

DAVID McCULLOUGH

HISTORIANS AND BIOGRAPHERS are forever encountering unsung heroes and often such figures enliven the work as little else can, for along with the delight of discovery comes the satisfaction of giving credit where credit may be long overdue. Naturally we each have our favorites.

From my own experience, I think of Emily Warren Roebling, about whom I knew almost nothing before embarking on a history of the Brooklyn Bridge. When her husband, Washington Roebling, the chief engineer, became stricken with the bends and was confined for years to a sickroom overlooking the project, she became his "strong tower," as he said: secretary, nurse, his all-important, if unofficial, first assistant, taking part in decisions of every kind, small and large, and representing him to the outside world. Without her, he would have been forced to give up. Without him, the project would have foundered.

Another who was there when needed, and who never received the acclaim deserved, was the great civil engineer John Stevens, whose courage and determination, quite as much as his professional ability, made all the difference in the grim early stages of the American effort to build a Panama canal. Few today know anything about him.

I think too of the first Theodore Roosevelt, the father of President Theodore Roosevelt, who had none of the burning need for attention and the love of glory that so characterized his namesake but whose good works, and many public and private kindnesses, combined with an unfailing sense of civic duty, set an example for a whole generation of New Yorkers. Seldom has a city had a better citizen.

Many of the most memorable stories of heroes past are of seemingly ordinary men and women who took on what appeared to be impossible tasks, and with astonishing results. The story of young Revolutionary War officer Henry Knox and the expedition to retrieve the guns of Ticonderoga, vividly told here by Tom Wicker, is one of the best I know, a true and authentically heroic adventure if ever there was.

Heroes are also often those who come to the rescue in moments of crisis, and among the unsung variety I am drawn particularly to another Revolutionary War stalwart, John Glover of Massachusetts. On August 29, 1776, under the cover of night and a fortuitous fog, John Glover and his Marblehead mariners rescued George Washington and his army from certain defeat and capture, ferrying them across the turbulent East River from Long Island to New York, a feat of exceptional bravery and nautical skill. Later it was Glover and his men who transported Washington across the Delaware to launch the surprise Christmas attack against the Hessians at Trenton. In Boston, a statue of Glover stands on Commonwealth Avenue, but probably not one passerby in a thousand has any idea who he was or how much is owed to him.

Consider Admiral Uriah Levy, one of the few Jewish naval officers of the last century, without whom Jefferson's Monticello would never have survived intact. When the sadly neglected old house went on the auction block in the 1830s, a decade after Jefferson died in bankruptcy, neither the federal government nor the state of Virginia, nor anyone else, stood ready to save it. Admiral Levy, an ardent admirer of Jefferson, stepped in, bought the house, and dedicated himself to its preservation.

Quite a few on my own list of unsung favorites were teachers. There was Jefferson's own professor of mathematics and metaphysics, William Small of the College of William and Mary, who had an infectious, irrepressible interest in almost everything and of whom Jefferson would later say, he "probably fixed the destinies of my life." Louis Agassiz, once the crown jewel of the Harvard faculty, his name a household word, transformed the teaching of the natural sciences in nineteenth-century America. Samuel David Gross, the brilliant Philadelphia surgeon, is remembered today, if at all, only as the central figure in the painting by Thomas Eakins called *The Gross Clinic*, done in 1875.

A man of humble origins, Dr. Gross became a commanding influence at Philadelphia's Jefferson Medical College. He was a pioneer of modern surgery, one of the greatest of all practitioners and innovators in a period of accelerating progress in medicine, and the author of several of the most important surgical treatises of the day, including a text on wounds of the intestines that was invaluable during the Civil War. In the Eakins painting, he is portrayed dramatically as the teacher as hero, and that he was. In his *Autobiography* he wrote, "I never enter the lecture room without a feeling that I have a solemn duty to perform—and that upon what I may utter during the hour may depend the happiness and misery of hundreds, if not thousands, of human beings."

But then, in their ways, all heroes are teachers, which is made evident again and again in the essays that follow and is among the prime reasons that this lively collection is of such immense value.

Timeline

1893   Florence Kelley is named Illinois' first Chief Factory Inspector to crack down on sweatshops

1898   Admiral Dewey destroys the Spanish fleet at Manila Bay

1901   Frederick Funston captures resistance leader Emilio Aguinaldo to end the War in the Philippines

1910   J. C. M. Hanson begins his reorganization of the University of Chicago library

1914   Labor organizer O. Delight Smith leads a major textile strike in Atlanta

1918   Margaret Anderson begins publishing James Joyce's *Ulysses* in the *Little Review* despite threats of censorship and criminal prosecution

1922   William Chandler Bagley speaks out against intelligence testing for sorting students

1923   Alice Paul drafts the Equal Rights Amendment

1926   Gertrude Ederle becomes the first woman to swim the English Channel

1930   Samuel Seabury opens his investigation into New York City corruption

1932   Alabama sharecropper Ned Cobb takes a stand against racial and class injustice

1942   Actor Lew Ayres stands on principle by seeking conscientious objector status during World War II

1943   John Basilone receives the Medal of Honor

1943   Carlo Tresca, impassioned opponent of both fascism and communism, is gunned down in Greenwich Village

1944   Caroline Ware joins her Howard University students in protesting Jim Crow

1949   Miriam Van Waters fights her dismissal as superintendent of the Massachusetts Reformatory for Women

1952   Sam Phillips establishes Sun Records

1961–63 Pauli Murray battles for her version of legal equality on the President's Commission on the Status of Women

1964   White Mississippian Hazel Brannon Smith wins the Pulitzer Prize for editorial writing for her support for civil rights

1966   Edward Prichard vindicates his conviction for ballot stuffing by his appointment to Kentucky's State Council on Higher Education

Introduction:
Historians' Forgotten Heroes

> The interest these fine stories have for us, the power of a romance
> over the boy who grasps the forbidden book under his bench at
> school, our delight in the hero, is the main fact to our purpose.
> All these great and transcendent properties are ours. . . .
> Let us find room for this great guest in our small houses.
>
> —Ralph Waldo Emerson, *On Heroism*

EVEN THOUGH it has only four letters, "hero" is a big word, overflowing with connotations of Greek warriors, Roman gods, medieval saints, revolutionary leaders, and larger-than-life individuals performing extraordinary deeds or acts of courage. Every culture, in every age, has had its heroes—men (and, less frequently, women) who lead by example and uplift us all in the process. Many of these heroes become deeply embedded in national mythology. What would America be without George Washington, Sacagawea, Daniel Boone, Abraham Lincoln, Sojourner Truth, Jane Addams, Babe Ruth, Charles Lindbergh, Douglas MacArthur, and so many more?

Historians have sometimes created heroes by well-wrought phrases and carefully chosen stories, but more often of late, scholars and writers have seemed intent on picking apart the reputations of once-revered Americans. The late twentieth century has been especially unkind to the celebration of national heroes. This debunking has even reached the general public. Who today can talk of Thomas Jefferson without mentioning his slaves, or John

Kennedy without speaking of his extramarital affairs? And yet our thirst for heroes continues unabated. The reasons are not hard to see. In May Sarton's memorable phrase, "One must think like a hero to behave like a merely decent human being." And as a sports-minded commentator put it once, "History is meaningless without heroes; there is no score before they come to bat." This book is an attempt to enlarge and uplift our past rather than just to question it.

Anyone who studies the past, whether a professional historian or a casual reader, knows the happy serendipity of discovering an unknown or little-understood character. Here, thirty-five of America's leading historians and writers, all members of the Society of American Historians, share their favorite stories of individuals who made a difference to their times and whose lives still stand as compelling models of heroism. Some of the characters were well known at the time and later forgotten; many never found popular recognition during their lifetimes. All have either dropped from the national collective memory or remain there only as caricatures or sketchy presences; all deserve far wider recognition than they have received. Covering the entire panorama of the American past, from settlement to the twentieth century, their stories offer a fresh way of thinking about America and its heroes, forgotten or otherwise.

At times it seems as if there are as many definitions of hero as there are heroic figures themselves. There are military heroes, political heroes, cultural heroes, folk heroes, and athletic heroes, and that doesn't begin to exhaust the list. A hero performs some extraordinary feat or brave deed, such as saving a child from a burning building or rescuing comrades in battle. A hero exercises moral, ethical, or political authority and definitively affects his or her times. A hero is a "great man" or "great woman." A hero represents what a society considers its best qualities at a given time, a model of behavior and character to which we aspire: "a jack—to lift people above where they would be without the model." As Dixon Wecter put it in an influential 1941 book, *The Hero in America: A Chronicle of Hero-Worship*, "The hero is he whom every American should wish to be. His legend is the mirror of the folk soul."

Why do heroes emerge when they do? The most often repeated truism is that heroes are created by popular need. In this view, the reception that greeted Charles Lindbergh after his 1927 transatlantic solo or the adulation that surrounded Babe Ruth reflected the needs and aspirations of 1920s America. Similarly, the elevation of George Washington to mythic stature spoke to the values and needs of the early years of the American Republic, with a little help from Parson Weems, author of all those legends like Washington's throwing the silver dollar across the Rapahonnock and his cutting down the cherry tree. But is that all? Are heroes merely puppets, built and manipulated by a needy public?

Clearly there is something more at work. In contrast to celebrities, who are merely famous (in Daniel Boorstin's deft formulation, "well-known for their well-knownness"), heroes have substance. They can be just as inspiring long after they have lived. We can peel away myths and still admire them. If any of the heroes in this book inspire you, ask yourself if the same could be said of other well-known figures of the past—the Jenny Linds, Andrew Carnegies, or William McKinleys—who were famous but not necessarily heroic. Heroes have a special kind of staying power.

As a general rule, it has proved easier to locate heroes in the past than to agree on who among contemporary figures is truly heroic. This is not to say that there is a lack of contemporary heroes. In fact, just the opposite is the case: there are too many. Perhaps out of an impulse to make people feel good about themselves, we anoint heroes constantly: the marine who eats bugs to stay alive for six days, the volunteer firefighter who rescues the little girl from the bottom of the well, the gymnast who ignores a painfully injured ankle to make the final vault for the gold medal. These are easy to spot but fleeting. Only rarely do leaders such as Václav Havel and Nelson Mandela so dominate their times that their stature as contemporary heroes seems destined to be confirmed posthumously by history. The task of figuring out whose lives among us are worth valorizing for the long haul is made even harder when an oversaturation of media images threatens to make us all candidates for our proverbial fifteen minutes of fame.

As we bestow the designation "hero" indiscriminately, the term threatens to become cheapened, almost debased. This in turn feeds into the often-heard lament that "heroes just aren't what they used to be." But it is wrong to pin this mood solely on our cynical times. Americans were saying the very same thing in the complacent 1950s, the debunking 1920s (which nonetheless had little trouble in instantly recognizing Charles Lindbergh as a hero), and the war-torn 1860s. As Dixon Wecter put it, "Today seems always less heroic than yesterday."

Many definitions of heroism set such high standards that only a tiny group of individuals could possibly meet them. (Abraham Lincoln comes to mind.) This book proposes a slightly more populist definition of an American hero, locating heroism and significance not just in political leadership or battlefield bravery (which are nevertheless well represented in the book) but also in the lives of ordinary individuals who made a difference to their times and our national history. That these contributions often went unrecognized does not diminish their heroic nature or significance.

In a 1943 book, *The Hero in History*, philosopher Sidney Hook surveyed the various meanings and manifestations of heroism over the ages. In an attempt to sort through the verbiage on the subject, Hook drew a distinction between the eventful man and the event-making man. (This being the 1940s, those were the terms he used.) The proverbial eventful man is the boy who puts his finger in the dike and saves Holland from the flood. It doesn't really matter so much whose finger it is: any number of Dutch citizens could have played the same role. The character is nonetheless eventful, for the action did change the course of future events. The event-making man, by contrast, takes a more active role in defining his place in history, and his contributions are more dependent on his specific talents and skills. The event-making man is self-directed, a take-charge kind of character, whose individual actions are the result of superior intelligence, will, and character. Through his unique talents, he leaves a large imprint on subsequent events. This book is full of event-making men and women, with a few eventful ones for good measure.

Having categorized heroes in that way, Hook warns against recognizing only a narrow range of excellence, if only because elevating so few so high makes the great mass of individuals appear as a "dull, gray average." He then proceeds to offer a formulation of heroes in history that comes closest to the spirit of this book: "If, however, we extend social opportunities so that each person's specific talents have a stimulus to development and expression, we increase the range of possibility of distinctively significant work. From this point of view, *a hero is any individual who does his work well and makes a unique contribution to the public good* [emphasis added]." Without going so far as to declare "Every Man a Hero," in this book we find heroism in acts of individual courage. We find it in acts of inspiring excellence. We find it in individuals whose political, cultural, or social actions truly did make a difference to their society at large.

One prominent category of forgotten heroes in this collection is individuals who took a principled stand, no matter what the consequences. These acts of conscience or deeply held belief varied widely, depending on the person and the historical moment. Sometimes the motivations were religious or ethical, such as Quaker Mary Dyer's defiance of Puritan authorities in 1660 or actor Lew Ayres's declaration of conscientious-objector status during World War II. Other times the motives remain lost to history, such as what made an obscure drummer in New Haven named Robert Basset speak out for his political rights in the 1650s. Often a specific event or moment in history called forth these principled stands, such as James Bayard's brokering of the 1800 electoral stalemate, Nicholas Trist's defiant negotiation of the treaty that ended the Mexican War in 1847, and John McLuckie's courageous stand in the Homestead strike of 1892. During the repressive climate of World War I, Margaret Anderson risked jail to publish portions of James Joyce's masterpiece, *Ulysses;* in the 1950s a crusading newspaper editor, Hazel Brannon Smith, supported the emerging civil rights movement even though it made her an outcast among her white Mississippi peers. Performed in vastly different historical periods and with very different results, each of these individual stands was in its own way heroic, then and now.

A somewhat overlapping category is what can best be called heroic or uplifting lives: that is, heroism that is not restricted to a single moment or act but resides in a lifelong commitment to an ideal. President John Quincy Adams lived such a heroic or exemplary life, although he has been overshadowed by other members of his illustrious family; so did John Chapman, better known as the legendary Johnny Appleseed. The daily, heroic struggles of African Americans for respect and dignity are well represented by former slaves Thomas Peters and Susie King Taylor, and sharecropper Ned Cobb. William Chandler Bagley never let criticism stop him from promoting his controversial views on American education; Samuel Seabury's devotion to public service culminated in investigations that brought down Tammany Hall in the early 1930s. Anarchist Carlo Tresca spoke out against fascism and communism; reformers Florence Kelley, Caroline Ware, and Pauli Murray dedicated their lives to social justice. So did New Dealer Edward Prichard (with one notable lapse). We learn from these heroic lives about the rewards (and costs) of single-minded devotion to a cause or a belief, of obstacles faced and not always overcome. These models of engaged commitment are compelling.

At first glance another group of characters included in this book may appear neither event-making nor eventful, but merely exemplary. Meriwether Lewis and William Clark are properly celebrated as American heroes, but what about some of the lesser-known men with the expedition? In the case of George Drouillard, he was probably thought of as heroic only by the few who knew him. Or, to take Stephen Jay Gould's touching example, what about Dummy Hoy, an early deaf baseball player of exceptional but overlooked talent? By traditional definition, he would not qualify as a hero since the sportswriters of the day chose not to elevate him to that status. But in these cases and others, such as librarian J. C. M. Hanson and southern record producer Sam Phillips, the contributors to this book put forth their own arguments for a previously unrecognized heroism that emerges when these characters are plucked from obscurity and their lives valued for qualities seen most clearly in retrospect or from a distance.

Then there is the category of female trailblazers and pioneers. While not all the women profiled in this book saw themselves as advancing the cause of women, they all had to buck or defy established gender definitions and expectations to do their life's work, which adds a heroic dimension to their successes and struggles. Myra Bradwell was a pioneering lawyer who saved Mary Todd Lincoln from incarceration in a mental institution, Victoria Woodhull spoke out for free love in the 1870s when such a subject was not considered fit for public discussion, and Emmeline Wells combined her devout Mormonism with support for woman suffrage and other reforms. In the early twentieth century, labor organizer O. Delight Smith battled the bosses while waging her own private battle for personal liberation, while Gerturde Ederle became a national hero for swimming the English Channel. Prison administrator Miriam Van Waters courageously defended her views when critics tried to dismiss her, and feminist Alice Paul soldiered on for the Equal Rights Amendment for more than five decades. These lives, along with the other women included in the book, confirm that an equal opportunity definition of heroism has much to offer.

Finally there is the category of military hero. The Revolutionary War contributed Henry Knox, the Spanish-American War George Dewey and Frederick Funston, and World War II the decorated combat veteran, Marine Sergeant John Basilone. Each served his country in time of war, won honor and recognition, but failed to maintain a hold on the collective national memory.

These military heroes remind us to pay attention to the other part of our title: Who gets forgotten, and why? Several of the stories present a fairly straightforward trajectory of the forgotten hero: sudden rise to fame and heroic stature, public acclaim and adulation, a cult of followers and fans, followed, sooner or later, by a falling out of public favor or disappearance from the public eye. The muddled attempts of Admiral George Dewey, hero of Manila Bay in the Spanish-American War in 1898, to translate his military fame into a political career led to the dramatic collapse of his popular following, to say nothing of his historical reputation. Gertrude Ederle came home in 1926 to a wildly enthusiastic ticker-tape parade but lived the rest of her life in obscurity. And the story of home-grown military hero Colonel Frederick Funston reminds us that some popularly acclaimed heroes whose reputations fall into eclipse are perhaps best left forgotten.

For the most part, though, the characters in this book were not well known in their times, nor are they in ours. In many respects, they are unsung or unrecognized heroes as much as forgotten ones. The reasons for their absence from the historical record vary. Some were marginalized in history because they were on the losing side or were pushed aside by better-known contemporaries; others were so controversial that they self-destructed and dropped from view. More to the point, until recently entire groups, such as women or African Americans, were not considered worthy of public acclaim except in highly exceptional situations.

Tastes in heroes change, and we cannot escape the fact that historians' anointing of heroes, just as the public's in general, is linked to the period in which we live A prime example is the large representation of women in this book—more than a third of the characters, some fourteen in all. This probably sets a record for the highest female participation in any comparable collection of heroes, a field whose very definitions and standards until recently were male. In an odd twist, it may be easier today to think of forgotten women heroes than to find equivalent men precisely because women were so unfairly excluded from consideration in the first place.

Recent trends in the writing of history, notably the rise of social history, women's history, and a broader commitment to integrating ethnic and other minorities into the American mosaic, help make this more expansive definition of heroism possible This contemporary approach, sometimes called "history from the bottom up," actually dates to the 1920s (cultural historian Caroline Ware, the subject of a chapter, was one of its early practitioners), but it found an especially receptive climate in the 1960s and 1970s. Social history is one, but by no means the dominant, branch of history included in this book. More traditional approaches, including a strong emphasis on political and diplomatic history, are also well represented. Politicians, diplomats, and military heroes remain respected parts of our national heritage. Here they are joined by a wider cast of characters who show heroism in all its diversity and heterogeneity over the centuries—old heroes and new, side by side, with neither supplanting the other.

Although every culture has its heroes, in the end there is something distinctively and wonderfully American about this collection. It is hard to imagine such an eclectic mix coming out of Germany's past, or China's, or India's. America is a constantly shifting, striving land of opportunities and second chances; the country's deep-seated tradition of individualism has supplied fertile ground for soloists to buck the tide and heroes to rise above the crowd. While it is sometimes said that democracies have trouble choosing heroes, the American tradition of celebrating the self-made man (and, later, the self-created woman) gives lie to this. The individuals in this book made things happen; things didn't just happen to them. They made a difference. America has always looked up to these kinds of heroes, the movers and shakers, the doers and do-gooders. Let's hope we always will.

John Chapman (Johnny Appleseed)

WILLIAM E. LEUCHTENBURG

John Chapman, better known as Johnny Appleseed, never reached quite the legendary status that Daniel Boone or Davy Crockett enjoy, but who can help but be charmed by his practice of sowing apple seeds as he roamed the Ohio Valley, seeds that had grown into young saplings by the time settlers arrived? Largely absent today from textbooks and standard historical accounts, Johnny Appleseed lives on as a hero in American literature and folklore.

I T MAY SEEM ODD to call John Chapman a forgotten hero, for almost
everyone has heard of him, though most likely by his more familiar
name: Johnny Appleseed, the vagabond planter of orchards in the Old
Northwest. Few know more than that single fact about him, and much that
has been written is altogether wrong. His appearance has been reported in
Arkansas and Kansas, even as far west as Oregon, thousands of miles beyond the range of his travels. A book published in 1894 asserted not only
that he was present at the Civil War battle of Lookout Mountain, nearly
two decades after his death, but also that he was quite likely still alive. So
intertwined is his life with legend that he has long seemed, as one historian
wrote, "no man born of sperm but of myth." He has come to appear, as his
most astute biographer, Robert Price, has stated, more "like a phantom
sprung from the moon or from an ancient sycamore along the Muskingum
or the Kokosing than someone begotten of the flesh."

What we truly know about John Chapman's beginnings is shrouded in
the meadow mists of the first mornings of the American republic. We can
say with confidence that he was born in apple harvest time on September
26, 1774, in Leominster, Massachusetts, son of a minuteman who would be
sent to Concord the following spring and of a Yankee woman whose first
cousin was the fabled Count Rumford, who would be knighted by George
III, head the regency in Bavaria, and gain international fame as a scientist.
But after John's birth was registered in the local Congregational church, all
traces of him disappear. During the next twenty-three years, this apparently
well-educated New Englander left nary a mark. Rare in the pantheon of
American heroes, he enters our line of sight full grown.

We first see him tramping along the crest of the Allegheny River
plateau in far northwestern Pennsylvania in November 1797, on the eve of
a hard snowfall. The following spring, he sowed the seeds for his first apple
nursery along the Big Brokenstraw, a tributary of the Allegheny. For the
next several years, he was to linger in northwestern Pennsylvania—staking
land claims, planting apple seeds gathered from cider presses to create tree
stock to be sold to the next wave of settlers, drifting about like many other
young men who had gone westering. In Vachel Lindsay's words:

He ran with the rabbit and slept with the stream . . . In the days of
President Washington.

By about 1800, he had moved on to the territory (soon to be a state) that was to be his home for most of the rest of his days: Ohio. In 1801, he hove into view at Licking Creek with a packhorse laden with burlap bags of apple seeds, which he planted in lands that had recently been the hunting grounds of the Delaware. He then vanished into the wilderness of bears and wolves and ferocious wild hogs and was not seen again for another five years. Always, he traveled alone. Some writers have conjured up a love interest, but so far as we know, there was none, and he was celibate. (If we are to believe one tale, two feminine spirits told him that if he did not marry, they would be his brides in the next world.)

In 1806, an early settler spotted him floating past Steubenville on the Ohio River in a strange craft: two canoes lashed together and bearing a cargo of rotting apples from which he procured seeds. He drifted with the current down the Ohio to Marietta, then made his way up the Muskingum to the mouth of White Woman Creek, and still farther up the Mohican into the Black Fork, only forty miles from Lake Erie, planting apple seeds at intervals on his voyage. When he came to a woodland glade along a stream, he would loosen the earth, sow his seeds, and weave a brush barricade to keep out the deer. Not the first to bring orchards to the West, or even the first to gain a livelihood from this activity, he was the first to spend a lifetime planting apple seeds in advance of the moving frontier, and he had an uncanny sense of where the routes of migration would be.

For the next forty years, John Chapman carried out his self-appointed task. By 1810, he had made Ashland County, where he lived at times with his half-sister in a cabin near Mansfield, his main base, but he was never in one place for long. He traversed the watercourses of Ohio, planting new orchards and nurturing old ones. "He sleeps with his head toward the setting sun," a passage in Howard Fast's *The Tall Hunter* (1942) says. "Westward he goes, and always westward. He walks before the settlers, so that the fruit of the tree will greet them." When the pioneers arrived, they found Johnny's seedlings, now grown into saplings, ready for them to transplant. They treasured the apples, for they provided fruit for the table (even in winter, since they stored well), apple butter preserves, cider (both as a beverage and for vinegar), and brandy. He sowed medicinal herbs too: catnip, mullein, wintergreen, hoarhound, pennyroyal, and, it is said, perhaps unfairly, the foul-smelling dog fennel, a prolific bane, in the mistaken notion that it was a cure for malaria.

Everyone who encountered him remarked on his appearance. Of medium height, spare but sinewy, with a weatherbeaten face and black (later gray) hair down to his shoulders, blue-eyed Johnny wore garb that even rough-hewn frontiersmen found peculiar. In latter-day pageants, he has been depicted clad only in an old coffee sack rent with holes for his arms and his head, with a mushpan as his headgear, giving an impression of a cross between the Scarecrow and the Tin Man in *The Wizard of Oz*.

In 1939, an Ohio writer observed: "Most of us know better than any schoolchild the story of the gaunt, bearded, long-haired man who wandered alone through the Middle West during its settlement, carrying a Bible, a staff, and a sack, dressed in burlap, with a rope round his waist and his cook-pan for a hat." In truth, there is no evidence he ever topped his head with a mushpan (though that is likely always to be an ineradicable part of Johnny Appleseed lore), but the rest of the characterization is accurate enough. He wore ragged garments, including a long, collarless coat that fell to his knees, and when not barefoot, as he often was, battered shoes with no stockings. Fast's novel got it about right: "His garb was a tunic of the roughest home-spun, gathered with a rope at the waist and falling to the knees. From the tunic, his bare arms and legs protruded, and he wore neither shoes nor moc-casins. . . . His hair was long and he wore a full beard. His skin was burned . . . dark . . . and his eyes were . . . blue."

To a degree, he may be thought of as a frontier entrepreneur, even as a kind of traveling salesman, for his business earned him enough cash so that, in the manner of other land speculators with their eyes on the main chance, he took title to more than a thousand acres. One of the few documents about his life that has come to light, a deed registered in 1828, reads:

John Chapman, to Jesse B. Thomas:

Know all men by these presents, that, I, John Chapman (by occupation a gatherer and planter of apple seeds), residing in Richland County, for the sum of thirty dollars, honest money, do hereby grant to said Jesse B. Thomas, late Senator from Illinois, his heirs and assigns forever, lot No. 145 in the corporation limits of the village of Mt. Vernon, State of Ohio.

Yet he lived primitively and frequently sold his seedlings for a trifle (a "fip-penny bit") or bartered them for food or castoff clothes. Sometimes he took a promissory note he did not bother to collect or just gave away bits of his precious cargo. His main fare was corn mush, and he dwelled in lean-tos or hollow trees. One pioneer, recording a visit by Chapman to his cabin, remembered: "When bedtime arrived, Johnny was invited to turn in, a bed being prepared for his especial accommodation, but Johnny declined the proffered kindness, saying he chose to lay on the hearth by the fire, as he did not expect to sleep in a bed in the next world, so he would not in this."

His religious views came from his study of the Swedish mystic Emanuel Swedenborg, who had spoken to spirits and angels and claimed to have had direct communication with God after the second coming of Christ, which he said had taken place in 1757. John Chapman was one of the very first American converts to Swedenborg's New Church, whose pitifully few members included a prominent Philadelphia publisher who had witnessed Benjamin Franklin's will, a judge who had clerked in the Edinburgh office of Sir Walter Scott's father, and a sculptor whose patron had been Frederick the Great. A zealous believer, he would tear Swedenborg's tracts into two or three parts and distribute them a segment at a time to the settlers, then exchange them for another portion on his next visit. After an arduous trek, he would fling himself down on the plank floor of a cabin, and, after asking his hosts whether they would like to hear "some news right fresh from heaven," recite to them from Swedenborg or the Bible. Years later, a woman recalled: "We can hear him read now, just as he did that summer day, when we were busy quilting upstairs, and he lay near the door, his voice rising denunciatory and thrilling—strong and loud as the roar of wind and waves, then soft and soothing as the balmy airs that quivered the morning-glory leaves about his gray beard."

His ascetic lifestyle lent conviction to the religious message he purveyed. In 1817, when Johnny was forty-two, a Philadelphian wrote to the Swedenborg headquarters in Manchester, England: "There is in the western country a very extraordinary missionary of the New Jerusalem. A man has appeared who seems to be almost independent of corporal wants and sufferings. He goes barefooted, can sleep anywhere, in house or out of house, and live upon the coarsest and most scanty fare. He has actually thawed the ice with his bare feet."

When at a revival meeting a smug, pretentious evangelist (sometimes said to have been the hellfire preacher Peter Cartwright) posed the daunting rhetorical question, "Where is the man who, like the primitive Christian, walks toward heaven barefoot and clad in sackcloth?" there emerged from the throng the ragged figure of Johnny Appleseed replying, "Here is your primitive Christian."

Unarmed in the savage wilderness, he came to be regarded as "a lay saint, a St. Francis of the frontier." He frowned upon hunting, for, a farmer he met recalled, "he maintained that God was the Author of all life" and hence "inasmuch as we could not give life to any creature, we were not at liberty to destroy life with impunity." He negotiated for maltreated horses and put them out to pasture. It was said, too, that he damped down a camp-fire because it attracted and then incinerated mosquitoes, and that he once expressed remorse over having killed a rattlesnake that had bitten him. He felt no threat from Indians, who admired his stoicism, and he, in turn, put the blame for "Indian troubles" on the white settlers. Rosemary and Stephen Vincent Benét later wrote:

> The stalking Indian,
> The beast in its lair
> Did no hurt while he was there.
>
> For they could tell
> As wild things can,
> That Jonathan Chapman
> Was God's own man.

Nonetheless, when Indians went on the warpath, he identified with the settlers.

During the War of 1812, Johnny Appleseed rode thirty miles through hazardous country at night from Mansfield, where a settler had been scalped, to the U.S. garrison at Mount Vernon, Ohio, to fetch help and warn settlers at remote homesteads in the woods along the way by sounding a powder horn and rapping on cabin doors. "Flee for your lives," he cried. "The British and Indians are coming upon you, and destruction followeth in their footsteps." According to another version, his words had a more biblical ring: "The spirit of the Lord is upon me, and he hath anointed me to blow the trumpet in the wilderness, and sound an alarm in the forest; for, behold, the tribes of the heathen are round about your doors, and a devouring flame followeth after them." In truth, the threat of a massacre was never so imminent as was feared, and he had earlier unwittingly sounded a false alarm, but the frightened farmers in the Mansfield blockhouse were relieved to see soldiers from Mount Vernon arrive by daybreak and grateful to Johnny for his heroics. (In later accounts, he was said to have run barefoot the whole way, or to have ridden silhouetted against the midnight light of blazing farm dwellings, both unlikely yarns.)

Toward the end of the 1820s, always ahead of the line of settlement, he moved into the cranberry bog country of the Shawnee in farthest northwestern Ohio, creating nurseries along the Maumee, the Auglaize, and the Saint Marys rivers. By 1830, he had crossed over into Indiana, where he was espied floating in a dugout with a cargo of apple seeds as he approached Wayne's fort. When the first settlers arrived at Fort Wayne and the hinterland of northeastern Indiana, there he was with his apple saplings awaiting them.

Each year, Johnny, now in his fifties, would spend autumn and winter in central Ohio, where he would gather apple seeds for his next journey, then, in harmony with the rhythm of the seasons, head west through the Lake Erie marshes in the spring for Indiana. A perpetual nomad, he has been likened to the Wandering Jew, "a being driven by some supernatural necessity to roam through the world, homeless, undying, compelled to show himself in certain localities on certain occasions, and then to resume his endless pilgrimage."

Early in 1845, he went once again to northern Indiana, this time to resurrect a failing orchard, and there, at a rude cabin on a snowy day in March, he succumbed to pneumonia. The *Fort Wayne Sentinel* reported: "Died in the neighborhood of this city, on Tuesday last, Mr. John Chapman, better known as Johnny Appleseed. The deceased was well known through this region by his eccentricity, and the strange garb he usually wore. He followed the occupation of nursery-man." Not many weeks later, a northern Indiana diarist recorded: "First apple blossoms."

When word of his death reached the floor of the U.S. Senate, Sam Houston said, "Farewell, dear old eccentric heart. Your labor has been a labor of love, and generations yet unborn will rise up and call you blessed." His final resting place is on an Indiana hillside where, one early writer noted, "In the spring the wild thorn-apple waves its boughs of pink and white above his unmarked grave." In an eloquent elegy, Robert Price has concluded, "He had walked more miles than any other recorded borderer of his generation— now he belonged to the American trails and rivers forever."

More than half a century after his death, when a monument was erected to him in Mansfield, a writer remarked of this authentic American hero: "The memory of his good deeds lives anew every springtime in the beauty and fragrance of the blossoms of the apple trees he loved so well." No one captured that sense more simply than the nineteenth-century abolitionist Lydia Maria Child, who also edited children's literature, when, in a poem published in the children's magazine *Saint Nicholas,* she wrote:

> Weary travelers, journeying west,
> In the shade of his trees find pleasant rest;
> And they often start, with glad surprise,
> At the rosy fruit that round them lies.
>
> And if they inquire whence came such trees,
> Where not a bough once swayed in the breeze,
> The answer still comes, as they travel on:
> "These trees were planted by Apple-Seed John."

John Chapman left America a distinctive legacy. Unlike Daniel Boone or Wyatt Earp, he carried no gun, and unlike the mythical Paul Bunyan, he won renown not by felling trees but by planting them. As the country's foremost historian of folklore pointed out, "Where Bunyan represents destructive power, Johnny Appleseed connotes sweet fertility." He embodies, a midwestern writer, Charles Allen Smart, declared on the eve of World War II, "the America that has . . . nurtured life instead of destroying it, and that has been sensitive to the beauty of this continent, and done something to create here a civilization. Johnny Appleseed stands for ourselves at our best."

Henry Knox's Wilderness Epic

TOM WICKER

*The battlefields of war often create national heroes, but some-
times contributions far distant from the fighting front produce
just as great dramas, and equal opportunities for heroism.
Henry Knox's charge—to bring captured British artillery from
Fort Ticonderoga to Boston in the dead of the winter of 1775–
1776—was a superhuman feat then, and it remains one today.
Most Americans have heard of Fort Knox, but the Revolutionary era hero for whom it was named remains largely forgotten.*

Gᴇɴᴇʀᴀʟ ɢᴇᴏʀɢᴇ ᴡᴀsʜɪɴɢᴛᴏɴ, commanding the ragtag American army besieging the British occupiers of Boston in 1775, issued to his troops a historic general order on December 12: "The honorable, the Continental Congress, having been pleased to appoint Henry Knox, Esq. Colonel of the Regiment of Artillery . . . he is to be obeyed as such."

From that start, Henry Knox was to become chief of artillery and the youngest major general in the Continental army, in the war that gave birth to the United States. But in December 1775, there were two problems with Washington's orders: his army—which then barely could be called an army—had no artillery for Henry Knox or anyone else to command. And the new colonel thought he was still a civilian, since he was far away in what was then the West, on one of the most remarkable missions in American military history.

Knox had been sent to recover a force of artillery available, at least in theory, at Fort Ticonderoga on the lower end of Lake Champlain—the long, narrow waterway pointing like an arrow from the Canadian border into the thirteen colonies, on what in later years would be the border between New York and Vermont. The redoubtable Ethan Allen and his Green Mountain Boys had captured the cannon from British forces on May 15, 1775, and the weapons had since been rusting away, unused, at Ticonderoga.

Henry Knox's problem was to transport this "noble train of artillery" (as he called it in a letter to Washington) hundreds of miles through a mostly roadless wilderness, over frozen rivers and lakes, through snow that sometimes turned to mud (a pattern still familiar to New Englanders), across mountains and through forests, with only oxen, horses, and human muscle for motive power.

The guns Knox found usable at Ticonderoga weighed 119,000 pounds altogether (almost 60 tons), but if the task was imposing, the need was even more so. Boston was the most powerful British outpost in America, an occupied city whose 17,000 inhabitants were suffering severely for lack of supplies and from the winter cold. Although the Continental army technically had bottled up the British forces in Boston, commanded by Sir William Howe, the Continentals numbered only about 14,000 raw and untrained troops to Howe's 13,500 redcoat regulars, 900 American Tories, and a formidable naval fleet.

Without artillery, Washington could not attack and drive the British out of Boston. He feared, moreover, that his cannonless army could be vulnerable to a British relief force sallying out from the city. The American commander badly wanted all those captured guns sitting unused at Ticonderoga; they would lend some powerful teeth to the relatively weak force with which he was "besieging" Boston.

Some sources assert that Benedict Arnold, later a celebrated traitor but then a much-admired patriot officer, first suggested that the Ticonderoga guns be brought to Boston. Be that as it may, when Henry Knox—a young Boston bookseller and patriot, whose energy and intelligence had attracted Washington—proposed to lead an expedition to secure the guns and bring them to Boston, the general promptly ordered him to go and get them.

"The want of them is so great," Washington concluded in his instructions to Knox, "that no trouble or expense must be spared to obtain them." A committee of the Continental Congress also directed Knox to go after the guns at Ticonderoga—but only after he already was on the way (which suggests that the first Congress was little more efficient than the current body).

Knox was young (twenty-five in 1775) and strapping (weighing about 250 pounds by contemporary accounts), energetic and imaginative—"one of those providential characters which spring up in emergencies as if formed by and for the occasion," Washington Irving later observed.

After stops in New York City and Albany and a long journey by horseback, Knox arrived at Ticonderoga in December 1775 to find about sixty of the guns the Green Mountain Boys had captured still usable—some as small as four-pounders, some as large as twenty-four-pounders (the Big Berthas of the day), and a number of mortars and howitzers. By his own reckoning, Knox set out for Boston with fifty-nine pieces, ranging from one to eleven feet in length and from one hundred to fifty-five hundred pounds in weight, plus a barrel of flints (those from the Ticonderoga area were highly valued) and twenty-three boxes of lead.

The sheer size and weight of this cargo, and the arduousness of the impending journey even for an unburdened party on horseback, would have intimidated most men, but one of the characteristics that attracted Washington to Knox was his ebullient optimism. His letters, diary, and reports of the time disclose not a hint of doubt that he could do the job.

On December 6, 1775, after a short portage (about twelve miles) from Lake Champlain to nearby Lake George, his men and animals loaded the artillery on a huge, flat-bottomed scow, sometimes termed a gondola (though nothing like the famed Venetian variety). They then sailed in freezing weather for Fort George, far away down Lake George. Ice lined the shores but did not extend far enough into the lake to block passage.

"Colonel" Knox, as he was soon to be, sailed ahead in a piragua, a two-masted, shallow-draft craft designed for lake cruising, and headed for Sabbath Point on the western shore of Lake George. The gun-laden scow, following behind, grounded on a submerged rock; when it was freed after much exertion, the wind had died, and the huge and unwieldy craft had to be rowed to Sabbath Point. By the time it arrived, Knox recorded, he and his advance party had dined well on roast venison provided by "some civil Indians who were with their ladies abed." But when the crew of the scow pulled in, they were too exhausted for anything but sleep.

Early the next day, the expedition sailed for Fort George at the foot of the lake, Henry Knox in his piragua again in advance. He covered the thirty-three miles to the fort in "six hours and a quarter of excessive hard pulling against a fresh, hard breeze." After many more anxious hours, however, the heavily laden scow with its invaluable cargo, the expedition's reason-for-being, had not arrived.

Knox sent a boat back from Fort George to investigate, only to learn that the scow and all 119,000 pounds of guns had sunk off Sabbath Day Point—doubly bad news. Not only was General Washington's expected artillery at the bottom of Lake George, and with it the means of driving the British from Boston, perhaps from the continent, but the scow had been commanded by Henry Knox's younger brother, William—presumably lost with the guns.

A lesser man than Henry Knox would have been crushed by the news; but however he might have been affected, the disaster was almost immediately denied in a note forwarded from William Knox. William not only had survived but reported that the scow had foundered and sunk "luckily so near the shore that when she sank, her gunnel was above water and yesterday we were able to bail her out."

Within two days, the scow came lumbering into Fort George with all the guns safe, and drying out in the cold winter wind. The hardest part of the journey still lay ahead: overland through New York and Massachusetts, across the Hudson River and over the Berkshires, on "roads that never bore a cannon before and never have borne one since."

From Fort George, in a letter dated December 17, the confident Knox informed General Washington: "I have had made 42 exceeding strong sleds, and have provided 80 yoke of oxen to drag them as far as Springfield, where I shall get fresh cattle to carry them to [Boston]. The route will be from here to Kinderhook [New York], from thence to Great Barrington [Massachussetts] and down to Springfield." Knox optimistically predicted he would deliver the guns "in 16 or 17 days." Little did he know that in fact it would be a biblical forty days and forty nights of hardship almost inestimable in this day of interstate highways and powerful truck-trailers before that "noble train of artillery" would be presented to George Washington—and the unsuspecting British.

Knox had estimated that the Ticonderoga expedition could be carried out for a thousand dollars, the sum fixed as his official budget. But then, as now, Americans had a sharp eye for profit, and the young leader soon found that few "patriots" wanted to accept his authorized payment of seven pounds per ton per sixty-two miles, or twelve shillings a day per span of horses. In the end, Knox had to submit a bill for about twenty-five hundred dollars (still cheap)—and the Continental Congress again showed kinship with its modern heir by taking its own good time to reimburse him.

At Fort George, however, in the icy December of 1775, at least the first leg of Knox's long journey was behind him. And with the considerable help of General Philip Schuyler of Albany, whose aid Washington had enlisted, and one Squire Palmer of Stillwater, New York, Knox soon had his strange convoy moving again, through the near-wilderness between Fort George and Albany. He also sought—then and in the later stages of the expedition—the assistance of local committees of safety along the route, urging them to provide food, shelter, and fresh horses and oxen. Sometimes they did.

The "noble train," with Henry Knox riding ahead to ensure a clear trail, passed through Glens Falls, skidded across the frozen Hudson, and pushed through a thick snow along the western shore of the great river to Saratoga, arriving on Christmas Eve. Exhausted horses and oxen carried them eight miles farther south to a night's camp, and on Christmas Day 1775, they plunged through two feet of snow to Lansingburg, nine miles above Albany.

December 26 was one of the hardest days on an incredibly hard journey. Only two miles beyond the Christmas night camp, the horses refused to struggle farther through the snow. Henry Knox, on foot, made "a very fatiguing march" through pathless woods to the house of a Squire Fisher, who provided breakfast and fresh horses for the remainder of the journey to Albany. There Knox visited pleasantly with General Schuyler. But the artillery train that was the purpose of his expedition was stalled miles farther back along the icy trail, on the other side of the Mohawk River (which flows into the Hudson north of Albany).

Schuyler and Knox went to work rounding up more men, horses, sleds, and oxen, again seeking the help of Squire Palmer. This time, the good squire demanded twenty-four shillings a day for two yoke of oxen. Schuyler, a tough haggler, would pay only eighteen and nine-pence, and ultimately had to break off the negotiation. Even so, by New Year's Day 1776, 124 pairs of horses with sleighs had been rounded up and sent to the snowbound caravan.

Knox and his men spent that day hacking holes in the ice near the confluence of the Mohawk and the Hudson. Water flooding up through the holes then froze, strengthening the existing icecap sufficiently to get the heavy guns across on sleds pulled by horses. A long rope was tied to the tongue of each sled, the other end fastened to the horses pulling the sled. A man with a sharp hatchet walked beside the rope, ready to cut it and save the horses if a sled carrying a big gun should crash through the ice.

Inevitably, one did—just as Knox, a renowned trencherman, was sitting down to dinner with General Schuyler, several miles distant in Albany. Knox unhappily abandoned his meal to hurry to the scene (near the present town of Waterford). On arrival he found that, as with the scow on Lake George, the eighteen-pounder had sunk to the bottom in fairly shallow water. It was recovered with considerable difficulty, but to have got that monstrous load of metal up from the river bottom and across the ice at all seems in retrospect almost superhuman.

At about this time, Henry Knox, like millions of Americans after him, yielded to the sightseer's impulse. He rode up the Mohawk to Cohoes Falls, recording in his diary that the eighty-foot drop was the "most superb and affecting sight" of his life. Such "stupendous works of nature" left him "not a little humbled by thoughts of my own insignificance." Later, taking in the view from a snow-covered peak in the Berkshires, he thought he could "almost have seen all the Kingdoms of the Earth."

The long line of guns reached Albany by January 5, 1776, exciting citizens who had never seen large cannon—certainly not in American hands.

Many were impressed enough to volunteer to help in the eastward crossing of the Hudson, which was made easier by a new freeze, solidifying the ice. Nevertheless, as the heavy sleds were incautiously allowed to follow in each other's tracks, the ice wore thin and the last sled broke through. Another big gun sank to the bottom—"drowned," Knox wrote in his diary.

So many Albany men helped raise the behemoth through a fourteen-foot hole in the ice—the job took all day after the accident—that Knox "christened" the piece "the Albany." And his exotic caravan headed south once again, over the Old Post Road to Kinderhook, thence to Claverack, and finally eastward toward Massachusetts.

On January 10, 1776, Knox led the way into the Berkshires over what is now Route 23, but which was then a difficult stretch of trail through a dense forest known as Greenwoods. Past Great Barrington and Otis, the long train of cannon-laden sleds, with their teams of horses and oxen, their profane and whip-cracking teamsters, encountered perhaps the most treacherous leg of the entire journey: mountain terrain through which there were no roads at all.

Steep precipices, deep chasms, forests, swamps, lakes, and streams had to be traversed or bypassed—hard enough for any traveler, seemingly impossible for a long string of horse- and ox-drawn sleds carrying the huge, squat cannon of the eighteenth century through a winter wilderness. The snow, moreover, began to thin out, and the sledding became harder, in a pattern of freeze-and-thaw all too common in upper New England in January.

It was, Knox wrote, "almost a miracle that people with heavy loads should be able to get up and down such hills as are here." Two hundred years later, it seems even more miraculous than it might have appeared at the time, though once it took Knox "three hours of persuasion" and the provision of two extra yoke of oxen to talk one group of teamsters out of quitting. And as hard as climbing was, going downhill was perhaps more dangerous; drag chains and poles had to be shoved under sled runners, and check ropes fastened to trees, to keep heavily laden sleds from plunging down on those in front.

A receipt signed by one Solomon Brown of Blandford on January 13, 1776, has survived. Its flat, spare language suggests the caravan's travails on this part of the journey: "Received of Henry Knox, 18 shillings of lawful money for carrying a cannon weighing 243 pounds from this town to Westfield, being 11 miles."

George Washington, meanwhile, was waiting eagerly. "I am in hopes that Colonel Knox will arrive with the artillery in a few days," he wrote Schuyler. "It is much needed."

As the train of sleds and guns emerged on the east side of the Berkshires, however, and reached Westfield, Massachusetts, new causes of delay were encountered. The townspeople, awed and excited by the cannon, crowded the road and blocked passage. They also brought out quantities of whiskey and cider, heartily welcomed by the teamsters who were parched from their herculean exertions in crossing the mountains. They soon were in no condition to go on.

Henry Knox himself, never one to pass up refreshments, joined in a convivial evening at the local tavern. To mark the occasion and reward the townsmen, he even had a twenty-four-pounder known as "The Old Sow" charged and fired, a thunderous form of celebratory fireworks much appreciated by the locals.

Eventually the procession moved on toward Springfield, along a road notorious even in the eighteenth century for terrible conditions. To make matters worse, the snow was melting, turning the frozen ground rapidly to mud, inhibiting passage of the sleds; worse, teamsters from New York, unhappy in a foreign state, had to be released to return to their homes. On the other hand, fresh oxen were obtained at Springfield, and Knox pushed on with fresher Massachusetts men manning the teams and sleds.

At Framingham, on January 25, the Revolutionary leader and future president, John Adams, who had recommended Henry Knox for his colonelcy, noted in his diary that he had seen "the train of artillery brought down from Ticonderoga by Colonel Knox." Probably leaving some of the guns at Framingham, Knox hurried on to Washington's headquarters at Cambridge, along a route renamed a century and a half later The General Knox Highway.

Washington greeted the young colonel with praise and good news: American forces had captured a British brigantine laden with three thousand round shot for twelve-pounders and four thousand for six-pounders. All those hungry maws Henry Knox had dragged so laboriously through the wilderness would not long be empty.

Losing no time, the commanding general mounted the new guns at Lechmere's Point, Cobble Hill, and Roxbury and secretly fortified Dorchester Heights, effectively surrounding and overlooking the British army in

Boston proper, with artillery as well as men. General Howe soon was forced to evacuate Boston by sea, transporting his army to Halifax—the real measure of Henry Knox's achievement.

With such a start, still a marvelous feat to soldiers and engineers who know about it, it is little wonder that Henry Knox went on to become "the father of American army artillery," improving the mobility and performance of what was essentially a makeshift artillery arm to the extent that the marquis de LaFayette said its progress was "one of the wonders of the Revolution." Knox also was an early advocate of and planner for the establishment of a military academy. As Washington's chief gunner, he further distinguished himself in the battles around New York City and at Trenton, Princeton, Brandywine, Monmouth, and Yorktown.

After independence was won, Henry Knox twice served as secretary of war: once under the Articles of Confederation, once under President George Washington. He worked mightily for Massachusetts's ratification of the new Constitution, helped suppress Shays's rebellion, and in 1794 retired to a prosperous private life in Maine. He died unexpectedly at age fifty-six, more than three decades after his extraordinary journey from Ticonderoga to Boston—and appropriately enough for a great gourmand, by choking on a chicken bone.

Mary Dyer:
Religious Martyr

PATRICIA U. BONOMI

There are few more heroic stories than that of Quaker Mary Dyer, who in 1660 defied Massachusetts Bay's Puritan authorities by refusing to abide by their decrees barring Quaker prose-lytizing. Banned from Boston and eventually expelled from the colony, Dyer kept returning to preach the message of the Society of Friends. She was fully aware of the consequences of her actions, death by hanging, and neither asked for nor received any mercy because she was a woman. Her "witness" (in the Quaker sense of the word) represents one of the most coura-geous stands for religious freedom and freedom of conscience in our country's history.

MARY DYER was notorious as a religious radical long before she disembarked at Boston on a rainy day in August 1659. A convert to the Society of Friends in England, Mary was the latest among a swarm of Quaker "fanatics" who recently had descended on the Puritan colony of Massachusetts Bay. No sooner had her ship arrived in Boston harbor than the nearly fifty-year-old Mary was "clapt up into a prison" though "wett to the skin [and] not a place to sit or lye upon but dust." So wrote Mary's husband William Dyer, an official of Rhode Island, to the Massachusetts magistrates as soon as he got word of his wife's arrest. William demanded that the Bay Colony cease its "merciless Crueltie" and end the "unjust molestation and detaynment of my deare yokefellow."

What Mary Dyer did not know when she arrived in Boston was that Massachusetts had lately tightened its laws against the Quakers, whom the magistrates viewed as an increasingly disruptive and "pernitious sect." Neither public whippings, ear croppings, nor burning of the letter H (for "heretic") into Quaker hands had stopped the invasion. Forced removal had proved equally futile as time and again the exiled Quakers returned to spread, as Governor John Endicott scornfully put it, their "malignant and assiduous . . . Doctrines directly tending to subvert both our Churches and State." Finally, the harassed magistrates had passed a law against future violators that invoked the ultimate penalty: death. Possibly because Mary Dyer had been ignorant of the recent legislation, she was on this occasion ejected from Massachusetts and forcibly transported to her family home in Rhode Island.

Yet one month later, in October 1659, this time fully aware of the potentially mortal consequences of her action, Mary Dyer returned to Boston. She was promptly arrested and jailed. On October 18, in company with fellow Quaker agitators William Robinson, a London merchant, and Marmaduke Stevenson, a Yorkshire plowman, Mary was haled before Governor Endicott and the General Court of Massachusetts Bay.

Each of the defendants had previously been banished from the colony and was indisputably in contempt of its authority. The court wasted little time disposing of their cases. One week hence, the three Quakers—Dyer, Robinson, and Stevenson—were to be handed over to Captain James Oliver and his company of one hundred soldiers "armed with pike, and musketteers with powder and bullett," who would "lead them to the place of execution, and there see them hang till they be dead." On hearing the sentence, an unrepentant Mary Dyer intoned: "The will of the Lord be done . . . yea, and joyfully I go."

On October 27 Dyer, Robinson, and Stevenson, guarded by the troop of soldiers and followed by a raucous multitude of locals (as was always the case with public executions), walked through the streets of Boston to the gallows. A Quaker later reported that the prisoners went "Hand in Hand, all three of them, as to a Weding-day, with great cheerfulness of Heart." A drummer beat a steady tattoo to drown out their final exhortations to the crowd.

Once they reached the hanging tree, Mary, her skirts tied about her ankles, was forced by order of the General Court "to stand upon the gallowes, with a rope about her necke" as sentence was carried out on her companions. First Robinson was hanged, then Stevenson. Just as "the Hangman was ready to turn [Mary] off, they cryed out Stop, for she was reprieved."

Mary may or may not have known that on the same day she was sentenced, her son had obtained a reprieve on the condition that he remove her from the colony within forty-eight hours. But the hairbreadth deliverance did not please Mary. "She was not forward to come down" from the scaffold but stood calmly, proclaiming to the crowd that she was prepared to suffer as her brethren had done unless Massachusetts voided its "wicked Law" against Quakers.

The Puritan leaders were obviously reluctant to execute their sentence against Mary Dyer. She was, after all, the wife of a man of estate. Another consideration was her sex, for women were seen as the weaker vessels in the seventeenth century, given to emotion over reason, and thus more susceptible to extreme behavior. And so Mary Dyer was once again banished from Massachusetts Bay to Rhode Island, to the enormous relief of her anguished husband and children.

What forces were at work in the mid-seventeenth century that brought Quakers and Puritans to such a melancholy confrontation? Their fatal encounter in Massachusetts is perhaps best understood within the overheated religious climate of that time. The seventeenth century was not only an age of belief but an age that saw religious sects proliferate, especially in England. The Puritans, only one century removed from the Protestant Reformation, had emerged by the 1630s as a faction within the Church of England determined to cleanse the established state church of all vestiges of Catholicism, to "purify" it of the lingering taint of its Romish origins. The majority of Puritans remained in England to carry out this mission, harrying bishops and king—some becoming martyrs to the cause—until both church and state were violently overthrown in the English Civil War.

A minority of Puritans, however, in obedience to their distinctive interpretation of God's command, withdrew to the wilderness of New England to build a holy commonwealth—the biblical city upon a hill—that would provide a model for the kingdom to come. It was this band of pious men and women that in 1630 established the colony of Massachusetts Bay.

Popular myth once portrayed these spiritual pioneers as seekers after religious liberty and founders of one of our most basic freedoms. This view was mistaken. The Puritan leadership had no intention of tolerating any person or group that might pose a threat to their utopian experiment. Like zealous sects before and after them, and certainly like those of their own time, the Puritans believed that they alone possessed the truth. They were a people chosen by God to establish his Zion in the wilderness. To permit disruptions to the formation and order of their saintly society was not only to fail one another but to fail in the eyes of God.

Yet disruptions there were. In an age when the best minds and most original imaginations were drawn to theology, it was improbable that harmony should long prevail. Even the Puritans did not see alike on all points of doctrine, and the colony of Massachusetts Bay was barely settled before discord flared.

The first troubler of Zion was the censorious perfectionist Roger Williams, who in the winter of 1635–1636 was banished through the heavy snows to Rhode Island. Then came, in the words of one exasperated Puritan minister, not only Presbyterians but "Familists, Antinomians, Anabaptists, and other Enthusiasts," all of whom he wanted gone "the sooner the better." But the most grievous disruption was precipitated by Anne Hutchinson, a devout and learned woman who in the spiritually exhilarating environment of New England fomented such serious divisions in Puritan society as to threaten its very existence—or so the Puritan leaders believed. And one of Anne Hutchinson's closest disciples was Mary Dyer.

Mary and her husband, William Dyer, a milliner in England, had immigrated in 1635 to Boston. Mary, probably born around 1610, married

William in 1633; a son was born to them two years later and four other sons followed. Pious Puritans that they were, the Dyers on arriving at Boston in 1635 had promptly joined the Reverend John Wilson's congregation. Within a year, the young but rapidly growing colony was shaken by a shrill debate between rival factions of the Puritan communion. The dispute, as old as Christianity itself, polarized around issues of faith versus reason, the world to come versus the here and now. Should the community focus its energies exclusively on seeking God's grace, or did its survival depend also on a more earthly concern for social order and even material advancement?

Anne Hutchinson and her followers argued for a faith-centered individualism that critics saw leading only to anarchy and the colony's certain demise. (Cotton Mather would later denounce Hutchinson's "Scandalous, Dangerous, and Enchanting Extravagancies.") Tagged as antinomians (opposers of the law), Hutchinson and her faction were defeated in the election of 1638, and Anne was cast out of Massachusetts Bay as "unsavory salt." She and her followers, including the Dyers, made their way to Rhode Island, now mocked by defenders of the Bay as "the latrina of New England."

William Dyer became a founder of the town of Portsmouth and in 1639 of the town of Newport. The Dyers prospered in the free air of Rhode Island, William being elevated to secretary and then attorney general of the colony. In 1652 William, accompanied by Mary, returned to England on business. When two years later William resumed his colonial post, Mary stayed behind, perhaps to bask in the more salubrious climate of Oliver Cromwell's republican commonwealth.

Another attraction for Mary may have been a newly formed religious community known as the Society of Friends. Here was a far more radical group than the Puritans, for the Friends rejected all of the Christian sacraments as well as the principle of a formal clergy. Equality of station was also a guiding precept, one that brought women into leadership roles unique for that day. And most important was the Friends' belief in the inner light, a ravishment of the soul in which God's grace was shed directly on the individual, a doctrine considered so abstract by more orthodox Christians as to verge on the mystical.

That Mary Dyer—who in the 1630s had been described by Governor John Winthrop of Massachusetts as "notoriously infected with Anne Hutchinson's errors . . . a proud spirit, and much addicted to revelations"—

would be drawn to the new sect was perhaps inevitable. In any case, Mary became a convert to the Society of Friends during her sojourn in England; she then joined the parade of Quakers, as they now were called in derision, seeking to save the souls of the Puritans of New England.

Therefore, when Mary Dyer returned to Boston in 1659, she came not as a stranger but as a known religious zealot and provocateur. After Mary was taken from the scaffold in October of that year and banished to Rhode Island for the second time as a Quaker incendiary, she rested but briefly in the sanctuary of her family. Described by contemporaries as a comely and grave woman of striking intelligence, Mary's character also drove her to act on her beliefs. Once having embraced the inner light, she was determined to spread the precious message of salvation to all lost souls.

The barriers raised against that message in the American colonies, especially in Massachusetts Bay, only spurred the more resolute Quakers to greater exertions. Some seemed to believe, like the ancient Christians before Rome, that martyrdom was the only way to gain the world's attention and light the path of righteousness.

Mary Dyer, fortified by the brief respite with her family, set forth again in the dead of winter. She traveled to Long Island, then to Shelter Island, and then to Narragansett and Providence, Rhode Island, staying no doubt with Quakers who had settled in those parts. In May 1660 she once again "had Movings from the Lord to go to Boston." Arriving there toward the end of the month, she was promptly jailed.

A revealing plea from Mary's husband to the governor and General Court of Massachusetts was dispatched a few days later. The tone of William Dyer's letter on the occasion of Mary's previous arrest had been angry and demanding. This time it was meek and supplicatory, suggesting that William fully realized the peril in which his wife had placed herself. He abjectly begged for his "deare wife's" life. He had not seen her for the past six months and could not say how she "was moved thus againe to runn so great a Hazard to her self and perplexity to me and mine and all her friends and well wishers." He deplored that on her "unhappy journey" north she had been succored by those prepared to risk lives "for I know not whatt end or to what purpose." He pleaded for the court's compassion for Mary's "inconsiderate maddnesse." William closed his letter: "Oh do not you deprive me of her . . . I shall be so much obliged for ever . . . pitty me, I beg itt with teares."

A 1661 petition from the London Society of Friends to the recently restored king, Charles II, reviewing the Quakers' history in Massachusetts
and urging the king's intervention relates what happened next.

Mary was brought before the Massachusetts General Court on May 30,
1660:

Governor Endicott: Are you the same Mary Dyer that was here before?

Mary Dyer: I am the same Mary Dyer that was here the last General
Court.

Governor Endicott: You will own your self a Quaker, will you not?

Dyer: I own my self to be so reproachfully called.

Governor Endicott [pronouncing sentence]: You must return to the
Prison from whence you came, and there Remain until tomorrow at Nine of
the Clock, then from thence you must go to the Gallows, and there be
hanged till you are Dead.

At this point, Mary cast aside decorum and denounced the Massachusetts laws against Quakers. "I came," said she, "in Obedience to the Will of
God." If Massachusetts refused to repeal its laws, "The Lord will send others
of his Servants to Witness against them." Moreover, "The Lord will overthrow both your Law and you, by his Righteous Judgements, and Plagues
[will be poured] Justly upon you." Governor Endicott demanded to know if
Mary claimed to be a prophet. Mary responded that she "spake the words
that the Lord spake in her." As she proceeded to expound on her spiritual
calling, Endicott reached the end of his patience. "Away with her," he exclaimed, "away with her."

The next morning Mary again walked the dismal mile to the gallows, a
drum beating all the way to drown any words she might speak to the accompanying crowd. When they reached the hanging tree, Mary was again
readied for execution, but as she was positioned, some in the crowd urged
her to repent and come down off the ladder. "Nay, I cannot," she answered,
"for in obedience to the Will of the Lord God I came; and in his Will I abide
faithful to the Death."

Captain John Webb, in charge of the execution detail, pointed out that
Mary's blood was on her own hands because she returned to Massachusetts
though under sentence of death. But Mary would not relieve the magistrates or their agents of responsibility for what they were about to do. "Nay,

I came to keep Blood-guiltiness from you," she rejoined; "therefore my Blood will be required at your hands, who willfully do it."

Next, the Reverend John Wilson, Mary's former minister at Boston, exhorted her: "Mary Dyer, O Repent, O Repent . . . be not so deluded . . . of the Devil." To Wilson, Mary answered, "Nay, man, I am not now to Repent." Others tried to persuade her; some simply mocked her. But Mary, now seemingly beyond the din of earthly voices, spoke only of "her Eternal Happiness." "And so," wrote a Quaker chronicler, "sweetly and chearfully in the Lord she finished her Testimony, and dyed a faithful Martyr of Jesus Christ."

Some hours after Mary's execution, a Boston magistrate—secure in the belief that the Puritans, not the Quakers, were the anointed of God— triumphantly observed: "She did hang as a Flag for [others] to take example by."

The death of Mary Dyer did not bring religious consensus to the Puritans of Massachusetts Bay. If many believed with the magistrates that Massachusetts was obligated to point the sword outward in self-defense, and the Quakers "willingly rushing themselves thereupon was their own act," others were profoundly moved by the heroism of Mary Dyer and her fellow Quaker martyrs. The hanging of Quakers was clearly in conflict with other of God's laws, and this contradiction encouraged ever more vocal disputes over how Massachusetts should deal with future dissidents.

Thus, the martyrdom of Mary Dyer marked a kind of threshold in colonial religious sensibility. To be sure, change came gradually, as notions of religious toleration, and finally of true religious liberty, slowly worked their way into the American grain.

There is a coda to this story. On July 9, 1959, the General Court of Massachusetts, perhaps in an act of atonement for the deeds of their forebears, erected a statue of Mary Dyer before the east wing of the Massachusetts statehouse. Dedicated to Mary as a defender of free speech and conscience, the statue stands as a sentinel looking out over the city of Boston.

Robert Basset:
A Drumbeat for Liberty

WILLIAM S. McFEELY

Just as Mary Dyer's story reminds us that the early colonies were far from the bastions of religious tolerance later national mythology implied, the story of Robert Basset demonstrates that the vaunted political democracy and liberty so dear to our national heritage was not at first a self-evident proposition. But that did not keep an obscure New Haven drummer, otherwise totally lost to history, from in 1654 demanding his political rights, specifically the right to vote. Robert Basset chafed against a hierarchy that deposited all power—civic and religious—in the hands of a small elite. In his opinion, he had just as much right to participate in government as they did. His small but heroic challenge to the prevailing order came to naught in the 1650s, but served as a harbinger of far-reaching political changes.

R OBERT BASSET began his career as a drummer boy. In seventeenth-
century America, it was a colorful and useful calling, but hardly one
that was heroic in the conventional sense. And yet his story deserves
telling. Unknown except in the New Haven Colony Records, he was an
early New Englander who stood up for his liberty.

Basset was a troublemaker. He sought not to destroy government but
to gain a voice in his governing. He spoke of rebellion, but his goal was not
to uproot his commonwealth; it was to change it. Basset demanded that he
and his fellows, who were not of the governing order in their New Haven
Colony be granted the vote. He failed, but Robert Basset was an early hero
of the long struggle by disenfranchised Americans to gain democratic
rights.

From the start, a sternness unique to the New Haven Colony set it
apart from two of its fellow Puritan colonies, Massachusetts Bay and Connecticut. Its founders, John Davenport, a clergyman with a deep grasp of
theology, and Theophilus Eaton, a successful London merchant, arrived in
the Bay Colony from England in 1636. They were ill prepared to defer to
their fellow Puritans in Massachusetts, and so they quietly set out to found
their own holy commonwealth.

They chose land on the New England shore of the Long Island Sound,
and called the settlement New Haven. The sixty-three original planters established a government in which only a small fraction of them would vote.
Meeting in Robert Newman's new barn, they did the bidding of John Davenport, their strong-willed, strong-minded minister, who sought a government fit to rule a truly godly community. Since a godly community can only
be run by godly men, the Fundamental Order, the colony's governing docu-
ment, opens with the principle that "none shall be admitted free
burgesses . . . but such free planters as are members of some or other of the
approved churches."

Becoming a member of a church was no small matter. The free planters
(free men) and their wives who were not church members were expected to
attend church (and were assigned seats). Their hope was that somehow
they might receive a sign that they were of the elect, could publicly confess
to having attained faith, and become members. Although some women
were church members, it was assumed that the burgesses, the voters, would
be male communicants, or, as they were regularly referred to, saints. For the
men, however, it was not simply a matter of stating that faith had arrived.

Davenport "used," as Cotton Mather put it, "a more than ordinary Exactness in Trying, those who were Admitted unto communion of the Church." The result was that the entire electorate in 1639 consisted of sixteen men.

When the colony expanded to include five new towns along the Long Island Sound, men and women new to those towns who had been church members elsewhere were, to the irritation of long-time residents, accorded the same status in the New Haven Colony. Men among them could vote. But though numbers are lacking, it is certain that those voting were still a small minority of all the adult male residents. One of the new towns, Stamford, on the western edge of the colony adjacent to Dutch New Amsterdam, had only five, or perhaps seven, church members, and, hence, only they had votes, had voices that registered in their neighbors' governance.

It was in Stamford that dissent arose, with Robert Basset the most vocal protestor. Basset is interesting precisely because he was not a man rising to eminence. Nothing in the facts of his life leads one to imagine him becoming one of the elected members of the colony's governing General Council, and it is far from certain that he would have been a wiser ruler than those whom Davenport deemed worthy of governing. But there was no certainty in New Haven in the seventeenth century that an exclusive government would ensure wisdom, as there has not been since.

Basset was marked off from his betters not so much by class lines but by the kind of man he was. His voice, which got him into so much trouble, won him a good many listeners. But nothing in the earthy and human qualities of the man makes one want to see in him a solemn prophet of later political philosophies.

Basset posed a dangerous threat to Davenport's principle that those who were not in full communion with their God should not—indeed, could not—make responsible governing decisions. To Davenport, any challenge to the rule of these saints revealed only the corruption of the rest of humanity. He was a forerunner of those of the nation's founding fathers a century and a half later who sought to curb the threat of the mob. To Basset, the saints were people, and he saw their job as choosing between alternatives that he, Basset, could evaluate at least as accurately as they.

Robert Basset, probably born in England in the late 1620s, was the son of John and Margery Basset of New Haven. His father, an illiterate indentured servant, was a carpenter, a lucrative trade in a new town. By 1646, the elder Basset had discharged his bond by paying his passage money; in the same year, he bought a house and land. Two years before, he and his son had taken the oaths of fidelity required of all men living in the colony, and he and his wife had both been assigned seats in the meetinghouse.

Robert followed his father into the carpentry business in New Haven, working with him on town jobs and serving on the committee of carpenters, which was called to advise on the repair of the meetinghouse. He was also a shipbuilder, an occupation that sometimes interfered with his other regular job. Robert Basset was the town drummer.

Before bells took over, drums were used as a means of official proclamation to the townspeople. They were sounded each night at sundown, before services on Sunday, prior to judicial court sessions, as well as on days the General Court met. The drummer also had to summon the various squadrons for military drill on training days. In short, Robert Basset's job of drummer put him on the scene of all the public events of the town.

In 1648, Robert Basset bought a house. The house and lot cost thirty pounds; to finance it, he made an annual payment in "corne, cattle or wamppome." The purchase of the house probably coincided roughly with his marriage, for he had a wife and child in 1648. Another child was born in March 1649, but lived only nine days. In all he had at least four children.

Basset's job as carpenter, his duties as town drummer, and his domestic responsibilities and troubles do not reflect all of his interests. In August 1648, he and two sailors were in jail as the result of a handsome drunk. The bout began after sundown (which was supposed to end all the day's activities) in Basset's house and quickly became a brawl involving men from the crews of both a visiting ship and a local craft, along with the shipwrights working on a third. The "noyse and oathes being heard to the otherside of the creeke," the watch came to break it up, but not before a good portion of the town had arrived to see the closing chapters.

Basset was on bail when he appeared in town court a few days later. His case was argued on the point of his having sold the strong wine—legally if sold wholesale to neighboring plantations or to New Haven residents, illegally if he sold it in individual portions ("much less to use his house or cellar as a taverne").

Court cases arising from drinking disorders were not rare in the seventeenth century, but Basset's episode was epic if we are to credit its exhaustive, detailed coverage in the colony's records. Found guilty, Basset was given the heavy fine of five pounds (an eighth of the cost of his house and lot).

Drunkenness was not enough to disgrace anyone in New Haven permanently; Basset served on the meetinghouse repair committee later that fall. However, he had a propensity for peripheral enterprises such as running the impromptu tavern and the posting of bail (undoubtedly at a good rate of return) for some of the more flagrant New Haven offenders. In general, he had not gotten his feet on the ground. He resisted making payment on his fine, and by the following summer he had defaulted on all but five pounds in his payments on his house.

In April 1650, he quit as town drummer; he had had trouble in that job too, failing, on occasion, to appear to call the squadrons out for training. His resignation was accepted by the General Court (which made sure he turned in the drums before giving him his pay). Having lost his house, he moved to Stamford, where he may have run an inn.

If Basset found Stamford more congenial to his way of life than New Haven, his activities in his new town in time came to be of more serious concern to the government of the colony than had his previous lapses in conduct. At the November 1653 meeting of the General Court, Governor Eaton made public an unsigned letter calling on the men of the colony "to stand for their libberties, that they may all have their votes and shake of the yoake of government they have bine under in this jurisdiction." Ostensibly, Basset was the recipient of the letter, but a summons was issued so that Basset could be questioned as to whether, instead, he was in fact the author of what sounded like a call for insurrection.

This inquiry was delayed until the following spring, but that winter, Stamford's town's deputies asked the General Court to conduct a trial to hear charges against John Chapman, a New Haven freeman who had moved to Stamford and, like Basset, was a dissenter. Deputy Governor Stephen Goodyeare and Magistrate Francis Newman were appointed commissioners to travel from New Haven to Stamford to hear this case. They set out toward the west; between Fairfield and Norwalk they ran into Robert Basset and John Chapman, who were on a trip to urge support for an attack on the Dutch in neighboring New Amsterdam.

How much Goodyeare or Newman knew about what the two were up to we do not know, but in any case they returned the two to Stamford. On reaching the town, Chapman refused to allow his trial to be held, insisting that it be conducted by the full magistrates' court of the colony. His claim to this right was honored. The commissioners did not hold a local trial; instead, they called a town meeting.

Despite the fact that only a handful of men who went to town meeting in the New Haven Colony towns could vote, all the townsmen could have their say. In this stormy session, the two New Haven magistrates got an earful. In addition to taxes and the expenses of defense, the Stamford men complained of not having "their free vote in the choice of civill officers."

The magistrates took cover. They cited a letter written by a committee of Parliament that gave the New Haven General Court clear jurisdiction over all its people. For the moment, the discontent was reduced to grumbles, but the commissioners' rebuke did not silence Basset. In the spring of 1654, he stood up at Stamford's annual election town meeting and angrily attacked the principle of governing under which he lived. The meeting had been called to choose the town's two deputies to the next day's session of the General Court in New Haven.

Practicing considerable overkill, Basset called on the majority not only to deny the voting provision of the Fundamental Order of the Colony, but also to threaten the General Court with a move to put New Haveners under the direct authority of Cromwell's government in England: "Let us have England's lawes, for England doe not prohibbitt us from our votes and liberties, and here wee are, and wee are cut of from all appeales to England, and wee can [have] no justice here. . . . [We are] made asses of."

If his understanding of the voting practices in England was inaccurate (he could have found better precedents for liberal suffrage right in New England), Basset nevertheless made his point. Asked if he were willing that the General Court of the Colony should hear these charges, Basset did not back down: "I will say it againe, is that authority just that makes what lawes they please, and never so much as give them a reason. . . . [We are] not so much neighbours, but bondmen and slaves." He was not asking to enfranchise bondsmen (indentured servants), but he was objecting to a government run by a minority of the freemen. Basset, it must be said, spoke not for all the disenfranchised. It was he and those like him who should be voting: "[There] must be bond-men or free-men, for their [is] no medium."

Basset was brought to trial not only for his seditious speech but also for challenging the colony's foreign policy. Other New Englanders, with England's silent support, were engaged in a border war with the Dutch in New Amsterdam. New Amsterdam had grown increasingly uneasy not only over the presence of the New Haven people in Stamford on its eastern border, but also by both Connecticut and New Haven settlers in new towns in eastern Long Island. In addition, the Dutch feared attacks on their ships competing for trade with the English along Long Island Sound, which they used for the passage to New Amsterdam. The anxiety was well founded; Connecticut had begun active armed incursions into the Dutch colony.

The New Haven Colony chose to be neutral in this international conflict, but restless, expansion-minded men in Stamford were anxious for the reluctant New Haven General Court to enter the undeclared war. At his trial, Basset was questioned about a conference he had attended in the ordinary in New Haven, where, it was alleged, he had deplored the failure of New Haven to pursue its offensive against the Dutch. He had asked the meeting what their response would be if an English captain were to attack the Dutch, and asked the New Haven men if they were loyal to England in its war or to New Haven. There were four witnesses to Basset's having posed this question.

The judges, perhaps not wanting to challenge England's authority in foreign affairs, concerned themselves less with Basset's warmongering than his challenge to New Haven's governing principles. Basset was accused of using advocacy of participation in the war as a guise for raising an insurrection within the colony: "A Malignant p[ar]ty wch hee hoped would rise, to overthrow churches and commonwealths."

With this accusation, Basset's courage failed him; he became contrite and denied any insurrectionist intentions. He admitted not only having received, if not having written, the seditious unsigned letter that called for a "stand for their liberties, that they may have their vote and shake of the yoake of government . . .," but also not having notified the magistrates of its contents, as his oath of fidelity required. He pleaded guilty, asked forgiveness, and even implicated others: John Youngs, the rebellious son of the minister in Southold, and a Captain Easor, who had been staying with Basset earlier. Youngs was by now a prisoner of the Dutch; Easor was a war-provoking English privateer. In addition Basset named three Stamford men as also advocating defiance of New Haven authority: John Chapman, Jeremiah Jagger, and William Newman.

Chapman, Jagger, and Newman were then tried, found guilty, and condemned for using the encouragement of the war as a cover for their insurrectionist intentions. The General Court was giving solemn warning that New Haven would sustain its independent jurisdiction over its citizens. Threatened with the death penalty, the four instead received relatively light punishment. Chapman, one of New Haven's original freemen and a member of the colony's first General Court, received heavy censure and a fine of ten pounds. Jagger was fined twenty pounds; Basset and Newman were not fined at all. All four had to post large bonds to ensure future good conduct. Governor Eaton and the court had reinforced their authority; they had secured Davenport's rule of the saints.

Robert Basset's political voice had been silenced. He fell from the historical record, and it would seem likely that he gave up on the commonwealth whose ways he had failed to change. He had lost his chance to make New Haven truly his own.

The New Haven Colony itself did not have a bright future. A decade later, it lost its independence, at about the time that its Dutch neighbors were forced to cede the rule of their colony to the English. The irony of this coincidence cannot have been lost on John Davenport. Just as what had been thought of as a major obstacle to New Haven's independence—the proximity of a foreign power—was removed, the colony was absorbed into Connecticut.

New Haven's demise as an independent colony was caused chiefly by the changes in England attendant on the ending of the Puritan Commonwealth and the return of the Stuart monarchy, but there was another factor. In the 1660s, the men of the colony, unlike their predecessors back in Newman's barn in 1639, no longer cared as much about how best to build a kingdom of Christ on earth as they did about how they themselves would fare in this world. They spoke as Robert Basset might have spoken. The minority General Court lost crucial support with which to resist Connecticut's annexation of New Haven in 1665. Godly rule was abandoned.

Worse than the loss of independence for Davenport was this falling away of the faith. At the establishment of the New Haven Colony, Davenport had triumphed when he brought the planters to see that their prime concern of life, the obligation to serve God, could best be met if they were governed by men whose relationship to God had met the sternest standards of the Puritan world. There have been many Americans since who have thought government by the best would ensure the best of governing. There have been more who have been willing to risk the participation of the Robert Bassets.

Basset defied the court in a language that was not economic or military, despite its wartime context, or even, in a kingdom of Christ, religious, but rather in terms of political injustice. But he was made to express his contrition—his sinfulness—in John Davenport's words of religious atonement. There is something moving in the long report of his statement of repentance. He "is convinced that the way of govermt here setled is according to God, wch he hath not honnored as he ought," and he "hopes that as he hath bine an instrumt of dishonor to God in that place so he desires to be an instrumt of His honor here."

Robert Basset bowed to the saints. But the conflict between the Robert Bassets and the John Davenports went on not only in Puritan New Haven and New England, but, in secular terms, in the America that was in the making. In the end, the Bassets by their very ordinariness beat their betters.

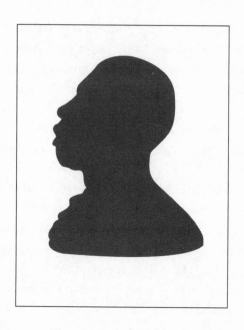

Thomas Peters:
Millwright and Deliverer

GARY B. NASH

Thomas Peters, a slave who used the Revolutionary War to se-cure his own freedom, took Robert Basset's call for liberty several giant leaps forward. His struggle spanned three decades and three continents, starting when he was kidnapped and sold into slavery in Africa and culminating with his return to Sierra Leone as a free man at the end of his life. Seizing the rhetoric employed by the American colonists against their British oppressors, Peters in 1776 cast his lot with the British forces, won his freedom from slavery, and then accepted resettlement in the British territory of Nova Scotia after the war. With this dramatic blow for freedom, Peters proved himself just as compelling a hero of the American Revolution as George Washington or any of the other founding fathers, although he fought on the other side.

HISTORIANS CUSTOMARILY portray the American Revolution as an epic struggle for independence fought by several million outnumbered but stalwart white colonists against a mighty England. But the struggle for "life, liberty, and the pursuit of happiness" also involved tens of thousands of black and Native American people residing in the British colonies of North America. One among the many remarkable freedom fighters whose memory has been lost in the fog of our historical amnesia is Thomas Peters.

In 1760, the year in which George III came to the throne of England and the Anglo-American capture of Montreal put an end to French Canada, Thomas Peters had not yet heard the name by which we know him or suspected the existence of the thirteen American colonies. Twenty-two years old and a member of the Egba branch of the Yoruba tribe, he was living in what is now Nigeria. He was probably a husband and father; the name by which he was known to his own people is unknown to us. In 1760 Peters was kidnapped by African slave traders and marched to the coast. It was Peters's lot to be sold to the captain of a French slave ship, the *Henri Quatre*, destined for Louisiana. We can imagine that he saw all of the brutality customarily imposed on the Middle Passage to create a climate of fear that would stifle any insurrectionist tendencies.

On his way to the New World, the destination of so many aspiring Europeans for three centuries, Peters lost not only his Egba name and his family and friends but also his liberty, his dreams of happiness, and very nearly his life. Shortly after, he started his own revolution in America because he had been deprived of what he considered to be his natural rights. He needed neither a written language nor constitutional treatises to convince himself of that, and no amount of harsh treatment would persuade him to accept his lot meekly. This personal rebellion was to span three decades, cover five countries, and entail three more transatlantic voyages. It reveals him as a hero of as great a stature as many famous white founding fathers of the Revolutionary era.

Peters never adapted well to slavery. He may have been put to work in the sugarcane fields in Louisiana, where heavy labor drained life away from plantation laborers with almost the same rapidity as in the Caribbean sugar islands. Whatever his work role, he tried to escape three times from the grasp of the fellow human being who presumed to call him chattel property. Three times, legend has it, he paid the price of unsuccessful black rebels:

46

whipped severely, then branded, and finally shackled. But his French master could not snuff out the yearning for freedom that seemed to beat in his breast. At length he may have simply given up trying to whip Peters into being a dutiful, unresisting slave.

Sometime after 1760 his Louisiana master sold the troublesome Peters to an Englishman in one of the southern colonies. Probably it was then that a new owner assigned the name Peters would carry for the remainder of his life. By about 1770 he had been sold again, this time to William Campbell, an immigrant Scotsman who had settled in Wilmington, North Carolina, located on the Cape Fear River, where the economy was centered on the production of timber products and naval stores—pine planking, barrel staves, turpentine, tar, and pitch. In all likelihood, it was in Wilmington that Peters learned his trade as millwright, for many of the slaves (who made up three-fifths of the population) worked as sawyers, tar burners, stevedores, carters, and carpenters.

The details of Peters's life in Wilmington are obscure; nobody recorded the turning points in the lives of slaves. Because slaves in urban areas were not supervised as strictly as on plantations, Peters may have gained a measure of autonomy. Wilmington masters even allowed slaves to hire themselves out in the town and keep their own lodgings. Peters appears to have found a wife and to have begun to build a new family in North Carolina at this time. His wife's name was Sally, and to this slave partnership a daughter, Clairy, was born in 1771. Slave owners did not admit the sanctity of slave marriages, and no court in North Carolina would give legal standing to such a bond. But this did not prohibit the pledges African Americans made to each other nor did it prevent their creation of families. What was not recognized in church or court had all the validity it needed in the personal commitment of the slaves themselves.

In the 1770s, Peters, then in his late thirties, embarked on a crucial period of his life. Pamphleteers all over the colonies were crying out against British oppression, British tyranny, British plans to "enslave" the Americans. Such rhetoric, though designed for white consumption, often reached the ears of black Americans, whose own oppression represented a stark contradiction of the principles that their white masters were enunciating in their protests against the mother country. Peters's own master, William Campbell, had become a leading member of Wilmington's Sons of Liberty in 1770. Thus Peters witnessed his own master's personal involvement in a rebellion to secure for himself and his posterity those natural rights that were called inalienable. If inspiration for the struggle for freedom was needed, Peters could have found it in the household of his own slave master.

By the spring of 1775 dread of slave uprisings swept through North Carolina and South Carolina. In May, just north of Wilmington, a local committee of safety warned that "there is much reason to fear, in these times of general tumult and confusion, that the slaves may be instigated, encouraged by our inveterate enemies, to an insurrection." Peters undoubtedly heard of the slave insurrection planned for July 8, 1775. White Wilmingtonians, discovering the plot hours before its scheduled rising, nipped it in the bud. A frenzied roundup of slaves brought severe punishments and a redoubling of patrols to smother any further plots. Peters watched and waited. Perhaps he heard in August of the South Carolina plot of the free black fisherman and river pilot Thomas Jeremiah, who planned to guide the royal navy approaching Charleston over a treacherous sandbar and to help slaves gain their freedom. Convicted of sedition by provincial judges, Jeremiah was hanged and burned to death on August 18, 1775.

Over the rest of the summer, the Cape Fear region trembled with rumors. For slaves such as Peters, it was becoming clear that the old tug-of-war between masters and slaves was turning into a three-way struggle with the intrusion of the British, encouraging the slaves to think of them as a savior and opening up a whole new set of possibilities. In July, tension mounted as the British commander of Fort Johnston, at the mouth of the Cape Fear River below Wilmington, gave "encouragement to Negroes to elope from their masters" and offered protection to those who escaped. Local authorities imposed martial law when slaves began fleeing into the woods outside town, and the word spread that the British had promised "every Negro that would murder his master and family that he should have his master's plantation." For Thomas Peters the time was near.

In November 1775, Lord Dunmore, the royal governor of Virginia, issued his famous proclamation offering lifelong freedom for any American slave or indentured servant "able and willing to bear arms" who escaped his master and made it to the British lines. White owners and legislators threatened dire consequences to those who were caught stealing away. Attempting to squelch bids for freedom, they vowed to take bitter revenge on the kinfolk left behind by fleeing slaves. Among slaves in Wilmington the news must have caused a buzz of excitement, for as, in other areas, the belief now spread that the emancipation of slaves would be a part of the British war policy. Yet for Peters, the time was not yet ripe; 250 miles of pine barrens, swamps, and inland waterways separated Wilmington from Norfolk, Virginia, where Lord Dunmore's British forces were concentrated. Between Wilmington and Norfolk, dozens of white patrols kept a lookout for escaping slaves.

In March 1776, Peters struck his blow for freedom. On February 9, Wilmingtonians fled as word arrived that the British sloop *Cruizer* was proceeding up the Cape Fear River to bombard the town. A month later, twenty British ships arrived from Boston, including several troop transports under Sir Henry Clinton. For the next two months, the British controlled the river, plundered the countryside, and set off a wave of slave desertions. Peters now seized the moment, broke the law of North Carolina, redefined himself as a man instead of a piece of William Campbell's property, and made good his escape.

Captain George Martin, an officer under Sir Henry Clinton, organized the escaped slaves from the Cape Fear region into the company of Black Pioneers. For the rest of the war, Peters fought with Martin's company, which became known as the Black Guides and Pioneers. He witnessed the British bombardment of Charleston, South Carolina, in the summer of 1776 and then moved north with the British forces to occupy Philadelphia in the fall of 1777. He was wounded twice during subsequent action and at some point during the war was promoted to sergeant, which tells us that he had already performed valiantly among his fellow escaped slaves in what amounted to the first large-scale rebellion of American slaves.

At the end of the war, Peters, his wife, Sally, twelve-year-old Clairy, and a son born in 1781 were evacuated from New York City by the British along with some three thousand other African Americans who had joined the British during the course of the long war. Peters understood that to remain in the United States meant a return to bondage, for even as the articles of peace were being signed in Paris, southern slave owners were traveling to New York in hopes of identifying their escaped slaves and seizing them before the British could remove them from the city.

But where would England send the American black loyalists? Its other overseas possessions, notably the West Indian sugar islands, were built on slave labor and had no place for a large number of free blacks. England itself wished no influx of ex-slaves, for London and other major cities already felt

themselves burdened by growing numbers of impoverished blacks demanding public support. The answer to the problem was Nova Scotia, the easternmost part of the frozen Canadian wilderness that England had acquired
at the end of the Seven Years' War. Here, amid the sparsely scattered old
French settlers, the remnants of Indian tribes, and the more recent British
settlers, the American blacks could be relocated.

Peters and his family were among the 2,775 blacks evacuated from New
York for relocation in Nova Scotia in 1783. Late fall gales blew Peters' ship
off-course, obliging the captain to seek refuge in Bermuda for the winter.
Not until the following spring did the sojourners set forth again, reaching
Nova Scotia in May, months after the rest of the black settlers had arrived.
Peters found himself leading his family ashore at Annapolis Royal, a small
port on the east side of the Bay of Fundy that looked across the water to the
coast of Maine. The whims of international trade, war, and politics had destined him to pursue the struggle for survival and his quest for freedom in
this unlikely corner of the earth.

In Nova Scotia the dream of life, liberty, and happiness turned into a
nightmare. The refugee ex-slaves found that they were segregated in impoverished villages, given scraps of often untillable land, deprived of the
rights normally extended to British subjects, forced to work on road construction in return for the promised provisions, and gradually reduced to peonage by a white population whose racism was as congealed as the frozen
winter soil of the land. White Nova Scotians were no more willing than the
Americans had been to accept free blacks as fellow citizens and equals. Discouraged at his inability to get allocations of workable land and adequate
support for his people, Peters traveled across the bay to St. John, New
Brunswick, in search of unallocated tracts. Working as a millwright, he
struggled to maintain his family, find suitable homesteads for black settlers,
and ward off the body snatchers, who were already at work reenslaving
blacks whom they could catch unawares, selling them in the United States
or the West Indies.

By 1790, after six years of hand-to-mouth existence in that land of
dubious freedom and after numerous petitions to government officials, Peters concluded that his people would have to find a way to escape from
semislavery and achieve real independence elsewhere in the world. Dep-
utized by more than two hundred black families in St. John, New
Brunswick, and Digby, Nova Scotia, Peters composed a petition to the

secretary of state in London and agreed to carry it personally across the Atlantic, despite the fearsome risk of reenslavement that accompanied any free black on an oceanic voyage. Sailing from Halifax that summer, Peters reached the English capital with little more in his pocket than the plea for fair treatment in Nova Scotia or resettlement "wherever the wisdom of government may think proper to provide for [my people] as free subjects of the British Empire."

Peters had arrived in London at a momentous time. English abolitionists—Granville Sharp, Thomas Clarkson, and William Wilberforce—were bringing to a climax four years of lobbying for a bill in Parliament that would abolish the slave trade forever, and the ex-slave was on hand to observe the parliamentary struggle. The campaign was unsuccessful in 1791 because the vested interests opposed to it were still too powerful. But it was followed by the introduction of a bill to charter the Sierra Leone Company for thirty-one years and to grant it trading and settlement rights on the African coast. That bill passed. The recruits for the new colony, it was understood, were to be the ex-slaves from America then living in Nova Scotia. After almost a year in London, working out the details of the colonization plan, Peters took ship for Halifax. He was eager to spread the word that the English government would provide free transport for any Nova Scotian blacks who wished to go to Sierra Leone and that on the African coast they would be granted at least twenty acres per man, ten for each wife, and five for each child. John Clarkson, the younger brother of one of England's best-known abolitionists, traveled with him to coordinate and oversee the resettlement plan.

This extraordinary mission to England, undertaken by an uneducated, fifty-four-year-old ex-slave, who dared to proceed to the seat of British government without any knowledge that he would find friends or supporters there, proved a turning point in black history. Peters returned to Nova Scotia not only with the prospect of resettlement in Africa but also with the promise that England's secretary of state would instruct the provincial government to provide better land for those black loyalists who chose to remain and an opportunity for the veterans to reenlist in the British army for service in the West Indies. It was the chance to return to Africa that captured the attention of most black Canadians.

Peters arrived in Halifax in the fall of 1791. Before long, he understood that the white leaders were prepared to place every obstacle they could devise in his way. Despised and discriminated against, the black Canadians would have to struggle mightily to escape the new bondage into which they had been forced. Governor John Parr adamantly opposed the exodus for fear that if they left in large numbers, the charge that he had failed to provide adequately for their settlement would be proved. The white Nova Scotians were also opposed because they stood to lose their cheap black labor, as well as a considerable part of their consumer market.

Try as they might, neither white officials nor white settlers could hold back the tide of black enthusiasm that mounted in the three months after John Clarkson and Thomas Peters returned from London. Working through black preachers, the principal leaders in the Canadian black communities, the two men spread the word. The return to Africa soon took on overtones of the Old Testament delivery of the Israelites from bondage in Egypt. On October 26, 1791, some 350 blacks from the settlement of Birchtown trekked through the rain to hear their blind and lame preacher, Moses Wilkinson, explain the Sierra Leone Company's terms. Pressed into the pulpit, the English reformer remembered that "it struck me forcibly that perhaps the future welfare and happiness, nay the very lives of the individuals then before me might depend in a great measure upon the words which I should deliver. . . . At length I rose up, and explained circumstantially the object, progress, and result of the embassy of Thomas Peters to England." Applause burst forth at frequent points in Clarkson's speech, and in the end the entire congregation vowed its intent to make the exodus out of Canada to the promised land.

Before Clarkson and Peters finished their labors, about twelve hundred black Canadians had chosen to return to Africa—a majority of those who were well enough to go. By the end of 1791, the prospective Sierra Leoneans were making their way to Halifax, the port of debarkation. Escaping their captors, a group from Annapolis made their way around the Bay of Fundy through dense forest and snow-blanketed terrain, finally reaching Halifax after covering 340 miles in fifteen days.

In Halifax, as black Canadians streamed in from scattered settlements in New Brunswick and Nova Scotia, Peters became John Clarkson's chief aide in preparing for the return to Africa. Together they inspected each of the fifteen ships assigned to the convoy, ordering some decks to be removed, ventilation holes to be fitted, and berths constructed. Many of the 1,196 voyagers were African born, and Peters, remembering the horrors of his own Middle Passage thirty-two years before, was determined that the return trip would be of a very different sort.

On January 15, 1792, under sunny skies and a fair wind, the fleet weighed anchor and stood out from Halifax harbor. We can only imagine the emotions unloosed by the long-awaited start of the voyage that was to carry so many ex-slaves and their children back to the homeland. Crowded aboard the ships were men, women, and children whose collective experiences in North America described the entire gamut of slave travail. Included was the African-born ex–Black Pioneer Charles Wilkinson with his mother and two small daughters. Wilkinson's wife had died after a miscarriage on the way to Halifax. Also aboard was David George, founder of the first black Baptist church to be formed in America by slaves in Silver Bluff, South Carolina, in 1773. George had escaped a cruel master and taken refuge among the Creek Indians before the American Revolution. He had reached the British lines during the British occupation of Savannah in 1779, joined the exodus to Nova Scotia at the end of the war, and become a religious leader there. There was Moses Wilkinson, sightless and crippled, since he had escaped his Virginia master in 1776. Now forty-five years old, Wilkinson had become another preacher of note in Nova Scotia. Eighty-year-old Richard Herbert, a laborer, was also among the throng, but he was not the oldest. That claim fell to a woman whom Clarkson described in his shipboard journal as "an old woman of 104 years of age who had requested me to take her, that she might lay her bones in her native country." And so the shipboard lists went, inscribing the names of young and old, African born and American born, military veterans and those too young to have seen wartime service. What they had in common was their desire to find a place in the world where they could be truly free and self-governing. This was to be their year of jubilee.

The voyage was not easy. Boston King, an escaped South Carolina slave who had also become a preacher in Nova Scotia, related that the winter gales were the worst in the memory of the seasoned crew members. Two of the fifteen ship captains and sixty-five black émigrés died en route. The small fleet was scattered by snow squalls and heavy gales, but all reached the African coast after a voyage of about two months. They had traversed an ocean that for nearly three hundred years had carried Africans, but only as shackled captives aboard ships crossing in the opposite direction, bound for the land of their misery.

Legend tells that Thomas Peters, sick from shipboard fever, led his ship-mates ashore in Sierra Leone singing, "The day of jubilee is come; return ye ransomed sinners home." He died less than four months later. His family and friends buried him in Freetown, where his descendants live today.

His final months were ones of struggle also, in spite of the fact that he had reached the African shore. The provisions provided from England until the colony could gain a footing ran short. Fever and sickness spread. The distribution of land went slowly, and the white councilors sent out from London to superintend the colony acted capriciously. Racial resentment and discontent followed, and Peters, who was elected speaker-general for the black settlers in their dealings with the white governing council, quickly became the focus of the spreading frustration. There was talk about replacing the white councilors appointed by the Sierra Leone Company with a popularly elected black government. This incipient rebellion was avoided, but Peters remained the head of the unofficial opposition to the white government until he died in the spring of 1792.

Peters lived for fifty-four years. During thirty-two of them he struggled heroically for personal survival and for some larger degree of freedom beyond physical existence. He crossed the Atlantic four times. He lived in French Louisiana, North Carolina, New York, Nova Scotia, New Brunswick, Bermuda, London, and Sierra Leone. He worked as a field hand, millwright, ship hand, casual laborer, and soldier. He struggled against slave masters, government officials, hostile white neighbors, and, at the end of his life, even some of the abolitionists backing the Sierra Leone colony. He waged a three-decade struggle for the most basic political rights, social equity, and human dignity. His crusade was individual at first, as the circumstances in which he found himself as a slave in Louisiana and North Carolina dictated. But when the American Revolution broke out, Peters merged his individual efforts with those of thousands of other American slaves who fled their masters to join the British. They made the American Revolution the first large-scale rebellion of slaves in North America. Out of the thousands of individual acts of defiance and heroism grew a legend of black strength, black struggle, black vision for the future.

Once free of legal slavery, Peters and hundreds like him waged a collective struggle against a different kind of slavery, one that while not written in law still circumscribed the lives of blacks in Canada. Their task was nothing less than the salvation of an oppressed people. Though he never learned to write his name, Thomas Peters articulated his struggle against exploitation through actions that are as clear as the most unambiguous documents left by educated persons.

James A. Bayard:
Savior of the Constitution

JAMES M. BANNER, JR.

*James Bayard seized an eventful moment, and his actions dra-
matically shaped the course of future events. As a member of
the House of Representatives in 1801, Bayard played the critical role in brokering a compromise to avoid the constitutional
crisis caused by the contested election of Thomas Jefferson as
the country's third president. The Constitution was barely a
decade old, and might not have survived if partisan discord prevented the designation of the next president. The fate of the
young American Republic was in the hands of this obscure congressman from Delaware. What would James Bayard do?*

CONTESTS FOR the presidency mark the seasons of American public life. Most of them end peacefully enough and with a certain clear finality. Only one, the election of Abraham Lincoln in 1860, has ended in violence. Yet three times in our history—in 1801, 1824, and 1877—the results of election balloting, in which no candidate received a majority of electoral college votes, have been inconclusive, and the presidential election has had to be decided in the House of Representatives. From two of these, the elections of 1801 and 1877, a constitutional crisis ensued, and the very integrity of American constitutional government was put in doubt. And of these two, the earlier crisis was the graver, for it occasioned the first serious threat to the nation's infant and still untested constitutional regime. It was also the only one to be ended by the act of a single man.

That man was James Ashton Bayard (1767–1815), sole congressman from the state of Delaware, then the least populous and, as it remains, the second smallest state in the continental United States. It was by virtue of the distinctive federal components of the very constitution Bayard was sworn to preserve that a representative from such a tiny jurisdiction found himself at the center of a constitutional storm. Yet it was owing to the man's character that he quieted it as he did.

The son of a doctor from an old Delaware family who died when he was three, Bayard grew up in the Philadelphia home of an uncle. Schooled there and then graduating second in his class from the College of New Jersey (now Princeton University), he was too young to have participated in the American Revolution. After legal study with some of Philadelphia's leading lawyers, he soon established a prosperous law practice and became an attorney of note. It did him no harm to marry and start a family of six children with Ann Bassett, the daughter of Richard Bassett, one of Delaware's most distinguished public servants. Yet it seems to have been Bayard's natural political skills and his moderate political views, rather than his links to the Philadelphia and Wilmington gentry, that ingratiated him with his legal clients and the voters of his tiny state. In 1796, at the age of twenty-nine, he won election to the U.S. House of Representatives as a member of the Federalist party.

That party—then in its infancy, like its opposing Democratic-Republican party—had been born out of growing debates about the direction of national policy under the new Constitution. We now recognize the necessary role of political parties in implementing constitutional government, but contemporaries considered them illegitimate and a threat, because of the discord they seemed to symbolize and create, to the very fabric of the nation and its young political system. Their very novelty—that they were the first of their kind in the Western world in the world's first constitutional republic—made them seem more alarming.

Bayard thus entered the House of Representatives at the dawn of party government, when the very existence of partisan division was widely feared. In the House, however, he characteristically earned a reputation for moderation and independence rather than for unquestioning and unbroken party loyalty. Not surprisingly, he adopted most conventional Federalist stances, backing, for instance, the notorious Alien and Sedition Acts (which severely restricted free speech and the rights of alien immigrants) and supporting the nation's undeclared naval war with France in 1798. But he worked to moderate the worst features of the Sedition Act and backed President John Adams when the latter, to much opposition within his own party, sent a peace mission to the European nation.

Yet mere moderation would not have earned Bayard an enduring place in history, nor was mere legislation likely to have called on his inner strength. What did that was his epicentral role in resolving the deep constitutional crisis that erupted in the wake of the presidential election of 1800, the first in which two parties openly and forcefully contested the chief magistracy of the land.

As a result of the voting in the sixteen individual states in November of that year, Thomas Jefferson, standard-bearer of the Democratic-Republican party, had narrowly edged out incumbent John Adams, a Federalist, in electoral college votes, seventy-three to sixty-eight, after one of the vilest and most scurrilous campaigns in the nation's history. As then provided in the Constitution, Jefferson was due to be inaugurated president on March 4, 1801. However, because of an oversight by the managers of Jefferson's campaign, the Democratic-Republicans had submitted an equal number of electoral votes for Jefferson and New York's Aaron Burr, assumed to be the party's candidate for vice president. Since the Constitution did not establish a mechanism to ensure that electoral votes for presidential and vice-presidential candidates be clearly distinguished (as they were subsequently required to be by the Twelfth Amendment, adopted in 1804 precisely to avoid a recurrence of such an electoral tie), Jefferson and Burr had seventy-three votes apiece. According to a provision of the Constitution, the tie had to be broken—the selection of a president made—by the House of Representatives.

Even though the new Seventh Congress, elected with Jefferson, was solidly Democratic-Republican, by constitutional provision (also later altered by amendment) that Congress was not to convene until the fall of 1801. Consequently, the holdover Sixth Congress had to choose the next president, and the Sixth was in Federalist hands. Congressional Federalists were thus in the position of having to choose between two leaders of the opposition. While they could not alone elect Burr, they might be able to make the New Yorker president if they could attract some Democratic-Republican defections. And at the very least, they might deny Jefferson—or, in fact, anyone else—the election by formally stalemating the vote in the House.

In contrast to his Federalist brethren who saw the situation in these delicious, mischief-making partisan terms, Bayard had a deeper apprehension of what was at stake. To him the tie vote was not just a partisan opportunity; it was a constitutional crisis. It was one thing, he believed, that the members of one party had an opportunity to thwart the popular will and exploit factional divisions within the opposing party. It was another entirely that only twelve years after the Constitution's ratification, there was a distinct chance that, due to partisan stalemate, a chief executive could not be chosen at all. If that proved to be the case, who could say what would become of the young constitutional regime?

Bayard knew that some of those who had opposed the Constitution in 1788 hoped to use the crisis as a chance to scuttle the Constitution entirely so that, as they had long sought to do, they might convene another convention to write another frame of government. Moreover, it was entirely possible that the southern states, all but South Carolina solidly Democratic-Republican, would leave the Union were the Virginian not allowed to assume the presidency. Rumors had even begun to circulate by January that the Democratic-Republican governors of Virginia and Pennsylvania were gathering militia troops to enforce Jefferson's election and that Democratic-Republicans were discussing a "uniform plan of acting" if the election were stolen from the Squire of Monticello. An electoral stalemate might result in civil war.

Comprehending the crisis in its constitutional dimensions, Bayard sought a role in working toward its solution. Named a member of the House committee appointed to establish the rules under which the chamber's members would vote to resolve the electoral tie, he worked first to immunize the proceedings against external pressure and delay. This was achieved by closing them to public view (a precedent established at the constitutional convention in Philadelphia in 1787) and suspending all other House business until a president was elected. To be sure, in promoting these rules he was not actuated solely by concerns that the election process be orderly and fair. He also understood his own potentially pivotal role in the outcome. Since votes in the House to break the tie would be by states rather than by individual congressmen, Jefferson, who needed the votes of nine states in order to be elected, could not become president if Delaware's single House vote—Bayard's—were not added to those of the eight firmly Democratic-Republican states.

On the other hand, his vote could decide the contest in favor of the Virginian, whose politics and character Bayard deeply mistrusted. The congressman therefore intended, he wrote in early January 1801, "to make the most of the occasion by giving the strongest impression it will enable me of the importance of the state." How did he intend to do that? By remaining as long as he could, he wrote, "inflexibly silent." He also believed that the longer the outcome was in doubt, the more likely it would be that the "current of public sentiment" would make itself felt and force the election of Jefferson or Burr. Constitutional government would then emerge unaffected.

No doubt savoring his position while keeping the Constitution in view, Bayard watched and waited. Throughout January and early February, everyone, Federalists and Democratic-Republicans alike, came courting his vote. "Perhaps no one," he wrote on the first day of February, "has been more in the secret of the whole business than myself." What blandishments the members of both parties offered Bayard, what was whispered in whose ear, we cannot now say with any certainty. Yet "the whole business" of which Bayard wrote no doubt concerned the respective advantages that might accrue to each party should either Jefferson or Burr gain the presidency. Hard partisan bargaining unquestionably took place.

Balloting to break the tie began on February 11, 1801, and the pressures on Bayard intensified. After the electoral vote was made official by the Senate at noon that day, the House got down to work. The votes of a majority, or nine, of the sixteen states being necessary for election, it was clear that Jefferson could not count on an early decision. On the first ballot, as expected, one short of the necessary nine states voted for Jefferson, six voted for Burr, and the delegations of two were equally divided, thus rendering their votes irrelevant to the immediate outcome. And thus it went for another thirty-four ballots over six grueling legislative days—the same results each time: successive votes, much like a modern filibuster, without interruption through the night (twenty-eight ballots without a break between early afternoon on the first day and noon the next); House members slumbering in nightcaps and on pillows until roused for the next vote—until February 17, sixteen days before the next president was scheduled to be inaugurated on March 4. Finally, shortly after noon on February 17 on the thirty-sixth ballot, two states handed in blank ballots (signifying that their votes were not to be counted) and ten voted for the Virginian, while the remaining four stuck with Burr. Thomas Jefferson was elected third president of the United States. What had occurred?

Among House members, Bayard had grown most deeply anxious about the consequences of a continued deadlock. If a president were not elected and a government could not form, the Constitution in effect would be a nullity. Just before the final vote, he wrote that "it was admitted on all hands that we must risk the Constitution and a civil war or take Mr. Jefferson." And in his view, it was "the New England gentlemen," his Federalist colleagues from the Northeast, who by holding out for Burr were forcing that risk on the nation. As much as he mistrusted Jefferson and his policies, by February 16 and no doubt earlier, despite the risk to his party standing, Bayard was trying to find a compromise by which the Virginian could be elected.

Whether Bayard and some Democratic-Republicans came to some sort of arrangement about the actions Jefferson would or would not pursue in exchange for his election has been debated ever since and is unlikely ever to be known. While Jefferson forever denied having come to any agreement with the Federalists, implicit or otherwise, some sort of tacit understanding no doubt allayed the concerns of a few moderate Federalists that Jefferson would overturn Federalist policies wholesale (which, once president, he did not do). While Bayard's own later statements cannot be confirmed, he always alleged that he had received assurances through an intermediary that Jefferson would not disturb (as, in fact, he did not) the Federalists' principal financial practices, assurances that Jefferson always resolutely denied. Moreover, the Federalists' major figure, Alexander Hamilton, though long out of public office, had also made clear his distaste for Burr and his view that his longtime political rival Jefferson was "by far not so dangerous a man" as the New Yorker.

Yet while Burr steadfastly disavowed a desire for the presidency, he never stated that he would refuse the office if elected. Thus even after thirty-five votes, he was keeping alive Federalists' hopes that something might break in their favor. And so, as Bayard wrote, he decided to act on his own, not in Hamilton's or others' shadow, and be "responsible for the issue."

He did so after having gotten the agreement of a few other Federalists to act in concert with him. With Burr refusing to commit himself and nothing remaining "but to appoint a President by law, or leave the government without one," Bayard later wrote, "I came out with the most explicit and determined declaration of voting for Jefferson" and thus putting nine states in the Virginian's column. Breaking his inflexible silence, Bayard made his views known to his fellow Federalists in caucus on February 14. For this, not surprisingly, he was "much abused," despite the fact that all agreed that "nothing but desperate measures remained." "The clamour was prodigious. The reproaches vehement." He told his copartisans that he had "an inflexible intention to run no risk of the constitution" and that "if necessary I had determined to become the victim of the measure. They might attempt to direct the vengeance of the Party against me but the danger of being a sacrifice could not shake my resolution." He was convinced that the Democratic-Republicans would be undeterred in their efforts for Jefferson, even if that meant leaving the country without a president "and, consequently, without a government." Even worse, it could mean civil war. Bayard could not allow himself, he wrote later, "to exclude Jefferson at the expense of the Constitution."

In effect, Bayard meant to save constitutional government from both parties. Consequently, he precipitated a conclusion on the thirty-sixth ballot by arranging that he would submit a blank ballot—one, because it had no name written on it, that did not count as the vote of a state—another delegation would do the same, and a Federalist in another delegation would withdraw, thus throwing that delegation into the Virginian's column. The arrangement allowed Jefferson to become president with the vote of ten states.

To outgoing president John Adams, Bayard wrote shortly after Jefferson's election to defend himself against charges of "impure motives." "Representing the smallest State in the Union, without resources which could furnish the means of self protection, I was compelled by the obligation of a sacred duty so to act as not to hazard the constitution upon which the political existence of the State depends." He acted, he said, out of "imperious necessity."

Bayard thus knew that he ran a severe political risk by taking matters into his own hands. Considered by many a "deserter of the party," he feared that he might be dropped as a candidate in Delaware or be made to pay some other political price. And in a modest measure he paid one. Although confirmed by the Senate on outgoing John Adams's nomination as ambassador to France, he chose not to accept the post because Jefferson's retention of him might seem a reward for his having been instrumental in the president's election. Defeat followed principled self-denial. In 1802 he lost his House seat in a closely divided election in his always closely divided state. Yet Bayard suffered no further penalties for his action. In fact, few contemporaries outside the Delaware Valley were even aware of his role in settling the nation's first serious constitutional crisis. Soon regaining his hold on Delaware, he was reelected to the House in 1804 and then almost immediately appointed by the state legislature to an unexpired term in the U.S. Senate, where he served, after reelection in 1805 and 1811, until 1813.

No doubt because of his support of the vigorous prosecution of the War of 1812, whose declaration he had opposed, President James Madison named Bayard in 1813 to the peace commission sent to Ghent to conclude a treaty of peace with Great Britain. After playing only a minor part in the negotiations, then declining the embassy to Russia, and in failing health, he returned home in 1815 and died shortly thereafter in Wilmington of some infection of the chest, perhaps cancer. Bayard was only forty-eight years old.

No doubt in part because he represented a small, closely divided mid-Atlantic state, Bayard could afford to be unwavering in his nationalism and constitutionalism and never yield wholly to either partisanship or ideology. But it was his deeply held beliefs that fueled his actions. He opposed his party's more radical members and consequently endangered his political well-being for what he considered greater ends. If political heroism is in part the application of power toward the solution of great public issues in such an unprecedented manner that a political culture is permanently altered—in this case, by the permanent victory of Jeffersonian liberal democracy—then Bayard's principles mark his acts as both exceptional and historic.

These acts, which Bayard always characteristically portrayed in modest terms, had consequences that are with us still and retain their world historical significance. Although the prospect of the political transformation that his action ensured was anathema to him, Bayard made possible the modern world's first peaceful transfer of power between opposing political parties, an example of the smooth transition between administrations that has proved difficult to achieve anywhere else, especially in young nations under young constitutions. Moreover, that a Federalist ensured the election of a Democratic-Republican made impossible the charge that the election was illegitimate because it was the triumph of party. Instead, Bayard's action implied that the outcome was creditable to constitutional methods and the rules of fair play. In addition, by putting the preservation of constitutional government, rather than the welfare of party or the continuation of policy, ahead of all else, Bayard's decision was arguably the first and perhaps greatest act of pure constitutionalism in the nation's history. When two infant institutions, the Constitution and political parties, collided, it was Bayard's genius to save both and thus ensure the continuity of constitutional government in the United States, at least until 1861.

Bayard's decision to forgo party obligations so as "not to hazard the Constitution" depended on his shrewd understanding that the Constitution had already gained a kind of talismanic standing in American culture. Guessing that many others would feel about the preservation of the young Constitution the same way and thus stand behind him, he could risk his standing with an unsurpassed act. That act, while depending on the confidence that his fellow Americans had already come to place in their young Constitution, thus reciprocally deepened Americans' reverence for their instrument of government and lent strength to those who, in the 1860s, would have to defend it. Bayard's was an act, as the sociologist Max Weber once described the acts of similar figures, that arose from "inner determination and inner strength." It was also an act, as Albert Gallatin, an older contemporary and secretary of the treasury under Jefferson, later put it, of "pure patriotism."

John Quincy Adams:
The Failed President Whose Real
Triumphs Should Be Known

ALFRED KAZIN

*John Quincy Adams may at first glance seem an unlikely can-
didate for a book on forgotten heroes. After all, he came from
one of America's most illustrious families, served as the country's sixth president, and has recently been portrayed in a major
motion picture, Amistad (1997). But his four years as president were the least noteworthy part of his political career, one
that began in the early days of the Republic and culminated in
Adams's final impassioned stand against slavery as a member
of the House of Representatives in the 1830s and 1840s. His
heroism was not of a single moment, but of an entire life.*

J OHN QUINCY ADAMS (1767–1848) is officially remembered because he was president of the United States (1825–1829) for just one term. He was a failure as president, unlucky from his first day in the White House to his last. This was due as much to his rigid, misanthropic character and his great but unavailing intellectual vision as to the general suspicion that Henry Clay had maneuvered Adams into the presidency over Andrew Jackson. Adams is supposed to have promised Clay the Department of State, which he duly got.

Adams's presidency was not only unhappy; it was the least significant, least characteristic portion of one of the most extraordinary and effective public careers in the history of the United States as diplomat, Harvard professor, lawyer, and secretary of state under James Monroe. He actually ended his career as a mere congressman from Massachusetts fighting (and triumphing over) the aggressive power in Congress of the slaveocracy. It is impossible to imagine any other ex-president "going down" to a career in Congress.

But he was an Adams, in some respects the most many-sided and brilliant (if privately unstable) member of the only American family that the British founder of eugenics, Sir Francis Galton, put into his pioneer study, *Hereditary Genius* (1869).

It was once of the highest importance to be an Adams. John Quincy Adams was not allowed to forget this when he married Louisa Johnson, a sensitive and seemingly fragile southern lady of "Maryland background," as her grandson Henry Adams jeeringly described her alien presence in his stiff New England family. Adams suffered because of all that was expected of him, but his extraordinarily varied public career was launched from childhood on because he was an Adams.

John Quincy Adams was the son of John Adams (1735–1826), second president of the United States, a leader of the struggle for independence, a founder of this country—and the first in his family to go to college. John Quincy Adams was in turn the father of Charles Francis Adams (1807–1886), whose firmness as minister to Great Britain during the Civil War helped to keep Britain from recognizing the Confederacy. He was the grandfather of Henry Adams (1838–1918), the most imaginative and irreverent of the great American historians.

John Quincy's own story is so much the story of his remarkably purposeful but understandably proud family that typically his defects seem the excess of his virtues. His formidable mother, Abigail Adams, was the great domestic influence on his life. His parents required and expected him to be the perfect son, and he was often devastated by his failure to oblige them and John Calvin's Puritan God, this in a Massachusetts still determined to hasten and chasten his own.

We must now recognize this emotional, truly frustrated, often misanthropically brilliant man as the greatest Adams of them all. No other American statesman of his time so clearly anticipated the Civil War and fought disunion with so much passion. President John Adams, a leading figure in America's struggle for independence and the greatest constitutional lawyer of our early era, had an unfortunate presidency entangled in the Napoleonic wars. His problems were not eased by his growing conservatism, pomposity of manner, and inability to handle opposition. His great-grandson Henry, the historian, came to despise a democracy not up to his gifts. John Quincy Adams, a would-be philosopher-king who did not realize his dream of physically uniting his country under the inspiration of modern science, succeeded on specific local issues. Near the end of his life, the lawyer who had once declined an appointment to the Supreme Court successfully pleaded before that Court for the release of West African blacks being transported into slavery on the vessel called the *Amistad*. They had been arrested for taking over the vessel.

The vision and energy Adams brought to his many services to the United States are utterly astonishing. Though ineffective as president, under President Monroe (1817–1825), Adams was the greatest secretary of state in our history. "His accomplishments during the 1814 to 1828 era," Walter LaFeber notes in *John Quincy Adams and American Continental Empire* (1965), "mark that decade and a half as the Golden Age of American diplomacy." Adams was the central figure when the United States signed the peace treaty concluding the War of 1812, issued the Monroe Doctrine, strengthened its maritime power through an agreement with England to clear the Great Lakes of warships, and obtained rights to fish the rich banks of Labrador and Newfoundland. Adams was more responsible than anyone else for getting Florida away from Spain, removing Russian influence from the southwestern coast of North America, getting Britain to establish the American-Canadian boundary from the Great Lakes to the Rockies, and staking U.S. claims to the Pacific coast. In the midst of all this, he single-handedly wrote a classic report on weights and measures and kept up the famous diary that is the longest, fullest personal record of public affairs ever kept by an American of such prominence.

Adams's career as an American diplomat and his other careers are equally astonishing. At ten years of age, in the midst of the Revolutionary War in 1778, the boy who three years before had sat on the grassy slopes of Penn's Hill to hear the sounds emanating from the battle of Bunker Hill now accompanied his father to Europe. John Adams was one of three commissioners appointed by Congress to negotiate a treaty with France. His son attended school in Paris until the father was able to return the next year. From 1781 to 1782, he was secretary to Francis Dana, the minister to Russia, and then joined his father in the Netherlands, with him went on to England after John Adams signed the Treaty of Paris in September 1783.

John Quincy graduated from Harvard in 1787 and began law practice in 1790 in Newburyport. In Europe as President Washington's minister to Holland, Adams met his future wife, the half-English daughter of a Maryland merchant in England who had taken refuge in France during the Revolutionary War. President John Adams appointed his son minister to Prussia. In 1803 he was elected to the Senate from Massachusetts, but he became so unpopular with his own party, the Federalists, for supporting Jefferson's Embargo Act of 1807 that he resigned in 1808.

Never at a loss for occupation, this marvelously gifted man had already been serving as Boylston Professor of Belles-Lettres at Harvard since 1806. A minor but determined poet who published collections of his verse, Adams was a translator of German literature, highly proficient in French, and so valued literature that he reproved the editor of the *Democratic Review*, saying, "Literature is always aristocratic." Now minister to Russia, he declined his nomination to the Supreme Court. He was right to admit that he lacked the judicial temperament, but his real reason was that he did not want to leave the cosmopolitan atmosphere he encountered in St. Petersburg.

In Russia from 1809 to 1814, Adams was flattered by the Emperor Alexander I's invitation to join him in walks along the Neva. Alexander, that most enlightened (and mysterious) of Russia's last czars, was happy to have Minister Adams enlighten his imperial majesty on that little-known republic country far off in the West. Few pages in Adams's self-conscious diary are so easy and light-hearted as his account of his walks and talks (in French, of course) with the czar. Two fellow diplomats in St. Petersburg were particularly interesting to him. On January 25, 1811, Adams noted in his diary, "General Pardo, a Spaniard, and Count Maistre, a Savoyard, are the only two persons of the Corps Diplomatique who have any interesting literary conversation . . . The Count asked me if we had any theaters or dramatic poets in America; and we talked about Shakespeare, and Milton and Virgil."

De Maistre was a Frenchman and ultra-Catholic whose whole life and thought expressed his violent reaction against the French Revolution and republicanism. If Adams ever learned Joseph de Maistre's real political views, he never let on. De Maistre was a remarkable writer and amusing gossip—*Les Soirées de Saint-Petersbourg*. He originated the saying, "Every country gets the government it deserves." What was most remarkable about him was his conviction that the world should be ruled absolutely by the pope as spiritual ruler, with no temporal ruler having independent authority. An executioner should always be on hand to keep order.

In 1824, Adams as secretary of state dearly wanted to succeed Monroe as president of the United States. The biggest obstacle was Andrew Jackson from the Tennessee frontier, who was born the same year as Adams, but was so unlike Adams in background, education, personal character, physical appearance, and quality of mind that they were obviously destined to hate and oppose each other. Adams said Jackson was "a barbarian who couldn't write his own name." Jackson actually owed Adams a debt. Adams the far-seeing nationalist alone in the Monroe cabinet had supported Jackson when, with his usual impulsive rage, Jackson had hanged two Englishmen in Florida for inciting the local Indians. Spain threatened military action, but the affair passed without war.

Adams, as New England's candidate for the presidency in 1824, was opposed by Henry Clay, as well as by Jackson and another southerner. Since none of the candidates commanded the electoral majority required by the Constitution, the election was decided by the House of Representatives, each state casting one vote. Clay threw his support to Adams, who was then elected over Jackson. When Adams made Clay his secretary of state, the angry Jackson accused Adams of having made "a corrupt bargain" with Clay. Adams was never to hear the last of this. His administration was a calamity to him from beginning to end.

The problem was partly Adams himself, who was not a political animal like Jackson. Jackson was actually not the leader of the democratic revolution that took over when he overwhelmingly defeated Adams the second time around, in 1828. He was a frontier rough whose personal vehemence appealed to Americans on the frontier stormy. Adams was "the last of the old order," said Richard Hofstadter. Jackson and Adams had both come out of the eighteenth century, but Jackson was the soldier who as a boy had experienced the Revolutionary War, and in the War of 1812 had won the Battle of New Orleans for America. Adams even as a New Englander was too conservative for the great new energy stemming from transcendentalism. He heavily denounced Ralph Waldo Emerson as a libertine in religion and blamed him for the moral downfall of his son George.

Adams entered the presidency without popular support and sympathy, and as a theorist showed that he had no gift for enlisting the public. His crucial "fault" (to his everlasting credit) was his everlasting vision, as the most far-seeing nationalist of his time, of a nation united by "internal improvements." The major changes were to be great federal highways stemming from Washington, which in Adams's view would be more than the administrative capital it was now. It would become the moral and intellectual command post of the country, supported by a great national university.

Adams would have liked Alfred North Whitehead's calling the nineteenth "the century of hope" because it was the century of inventions. These would liberate people from exhausting physical tasks and leave them free to pursue truth in science. Not always the firm believer in Christianity he wanted to be, Adams believed that astronomy was the key to all future scientific investigation. Astronomy disclosed the wonders of the original creation and would disclose the will of God himself. This led Adams to promote observatories, which he called "lighthouses of the skies."

This phrase added to Adams's undoing as president. Menaced in his own cabinet by secret adversaries and defied at every turn by political enemies in Congress, the president of the United States was derided for projecting a view of American unity forged by American science and technology. Adams the friend of science makes us think of American power today, not of the slave-ridden country that as early as the 1820s was heading toward civil war. Adams was thinking less of material power than of mass enlightenment. With Jefferson, his was the last eighteenth-century vision of the new country as the republic of reason. John Adams said that his son was intellectually as much Jefferson's son as his own—Jefferson he called "the great orderer." And "order" leading to a grand national renewal of American energies was at the center of John Quincy's thought. His grandson Brooks Adams wrote in 1920 that "the Presidency was the tragedy of our grandfather's life because it injected into his mind the first doubt as to whether there was a God, and whether this life had a purpose."

All Adamses, up to and including Henry the skeptical historian, identified themselves wholly with the republic that John Adams had been among the first to create. This in itself explains the great place of the Adams family in American history. But John Quincy brought so much moral intensity and personal suffering to the presidency because he was actually unsure of the God who was supposed to be protecting and furthering the American cause. Referring to the many places he had served as an American diplomat, he proudly wrote, "I have said the Lord's Prayer before retiring every night of my life. And have never mumbled it once." It was not only American disunion that John Quincy saw in the encroaching power of southern slavery; it was the seeming end of Christian love for one's neighbor.

Only John Quincy Adams, ex-president of the United States, would have returned to Washington as a mere congressman. Only John Quincy Adams, unpopular as president, would have become a national hero, "Old Man Eloquent," as he hurled all his moral force and literary eloquence to defy and defeat the southern gag bill prohibiting discussion of slavery in the House of Representatives. Only John Quincy Adams, having after years of struggle finally achieved the end of the gag bill, would thereupon have collapsed in the House and died in an antechamber—but not before stoically saying, "This is the last of earth." What drama! What symbolism!

John Quincy Adams's last great battle in the House of Representatives was a perfect end to such an arduous life. But there was an earlier, equal glory when as chairman of the House Committee on Foreign Affairs, he caused the resignation of all southern members of the committee by defending slaves who had gained their freedom by capturing the vessel *Creole*. When fifty-four slaves, members of the Mende tribe in Africa, revolted on the *Amistad* and were arrested, it was John Quincy Adams who argued for their freedom before the Supreme Court and won. In gratitude, the Mendes gave Adams several books, including a Bible that was once stolen from the Adams National Historical Site and later recovered.

Such services to the humblest and most easily victimized people on earth in his day were typical of John Quincy Adams. This "failed President" deserves to be remembered as the last great representative of the Enlightenment in America. Though he failed there politically, no other president (with the possible exception of Thomas Jefferson) had such hopes for his country, so noble a vision of our future.

Nicholas Trist:
The Disobedient Diplomat

THOMAS FLEMING

Nicholas Trist is another individual who played a key role in a major event in American history—in his case, the settlement of the Mexican War in 1847—and was later forgotten. In the complicated swirl of national politics in the 1840s, where every political leader seemed on the verge of declaring for the presidency, Trist was that rare bird—an idealist, out only to serve his country, although always on his own terms. To do so he had to disobey a president and the secretary of state. Like John Quincy Adams, he deserves to be remembered as a man of principle and conscience in mid-nineteenth-century political life.

IN THE FALL of 1847, Nicholas Trist defied a president, double-crossed a secretary of state, and infuriated a horde of lesser politicians to negotiate a treaty of peace with Mexico that stabilized relations with the United States for a century. Trist did the unpopular courageous thing—and in a way that virtually guaranteed that he would get no credit for it. All in all, it was a bitter fate for a man who began his career with dreams of fame as a disciple of Thomas Jefferson and James Madison.

Part of the almost total obscurity that Trist achieved can be attributed to his personality. Born in Charlottesville, Virginia, in 1800, he was imbued from birth with those characteristics southerners summed up in the phrase "high-toned." His grandmother, Elizabeth Trist, had run a boardinghouse in Philadelphia at which Thomas Jefferson, James Madison, and other notable Virginians stayed in the 1780s while serving in the Continental Congress. Jefferson appointed Trist's father, Hore Brose Trist, as collector of the District of Mississippi a few months after the United States acquired the Louisiana Territory. The father died the following year, when Nicholas Trist was only four, but Jefferson retained a strong interest in the family.

With Jefferson's help, Trist obtained an appointment to West Point. On his way to the military academy, the eighteen-year-old Trist stopped at Monticello and fell violently in love with Jefferson's granddaughter, seventeen-year-old Virginia Jefferson Randolph. All concerned except the lovers were aghast and persuaded Trist to restrain his ardor and continue his journey to West Point. He was not a promising cadet. Six feet tall but weighing only 120 pounds, he found the weather abominable and the discipline intolerable. In spite of his unhappiness, he made a valuable friend: Andrew Jackson Donelson, nephew of the hero of New Orleans.

Resigning from the academy in 1821, Trist resumed his pursuit of Virginia Jefferson Randolph. Perhaps aware that the entire Monticello enterprise was on the brink of financial collapse, she suggested he get a law degree first. In 1824 he returned from three years of reading for the law in Louisiana, and they were married on September 11, 1824.

Trist became the eighty-one-year-old Jefferson's secretary and companion for the last two years of his life. He helped him answer his letters and listened to his memories of the Revolution and his views on the great issues of the republic as they rode and walked about Monticello and its neighborhood. The young man became almost as close to Jefferson's best friend, James Madison.

Trist was at Jefferson's bedside when he died on July 4, 1826, and he became the chief administrator of his bankrupt estate. Martha Jefferson Randolph, his mother-in-law, soon came to rely on him for virtually everything from cash to how to deal with her erratic husband, Thomas Mann Randolph, who was also bankrupt and seriously depressed. The desperate woman wrote to Secretary of State Henry Clay, wondering if he could give Trist a job. He obliged with a $2,000-a-year clerkship in the Department of State.

Although he took the job in the last year of President John Quincy Adams's administration, Trist stayed on the federal payroll under President Andrew Jackson, thanks to Andrew Jackson Donelson, who came to Washington, D.C., as Jackson's secretary. Soon Trist and his wife were prized guests at the White House. Old Hickory was fascinated by their reminiscences of Jefferson, a politician to whom he paid public deference but had privately disliked. For his part, Trist became an ardent Jackson admirer, something his grandfather-in-law never was. As one historian put it, Trist became a link in the nonexistent friendship between the two Democratic titans.

During the nullification crisis of 1832, when South Carolina threatened to secede from the Union, Trist was a vital link between James Madison and Andrew Jackson. Madison wrote Trist numerous letters deploring and refuting nullification and denying that Jefferson ever intended to see it applied à la John C. Calhoun. Trist passed the letters on to Jackson, who appreciated this backing from the Father of the Constitution.

As proof of his gratitude, the reelected Jackson sent Trist to Havana in April 1833 as American consul. Here he should have prospered. Although a consul received no salary, he could invest and profit from funds left with him and charge fees for acting as a notary and intermediary for American businessmen and ship captains. But Trist lost a lot of money on an ill-fated sugar plantation and had difficulty keeping his head above financial water.

Trist also revealed the dark side of his character: a determination to justify his every action and defend his most minute judgments with an avalanche of verbiage. His letters to Washington regularly ran thirty or forty pages, and one to the Senate Committee on Finance hit fifty-two. Americans who passed through Havana found him difficult, and complaints piled up until a congressional committee investigated him.

The committee exonerated Trist of serious wrongdoing but amassed enough evidence of problematic performance to give Whig Secretary of State Daniel Webster an excuse to remove the Virginia Democrat in 1841. Trist soon proved to have, if not nine, at least three political lives. He returned to the State Department as chief clerk when "Young Hickory," James K. Polk, won the presidency in 1844. Old Hickory, still running the Democratic party from his deathbed, urged Polk to give Trist the job. Although the title sounds trivial to our twentieth-century ears, Trist was the second-ranking man in the department, and when Secretary of State James Buchanan was out of town, he performed many of the duties of his office.

The diminutive Polk entered the White House with orders from the Hermitage to bring Texas into the Union and extend the national domain to the Pacific. Texas proved to be no problem. President John Tyler, with the already elected Polk's not very secret backing, persuaded Congress to invite the Lone Star State to join the republic by a majority vote.

Mexico had warned that annexing Texas meant war. Although the country was bankrupt, the Mexicans spurned Polk's envoys, who offered as much as $30 million for California and everything between it and Texas. With a thirty-two-thousand-man army toughened by service in their numerous revolutions, the Mexicans thought they could handle the seventy-two-hundred-man U.S. regular army, which had fought no one but a few defiant Indians in the previous thirty years.

In the spring of 1847, the Mexicans boldly offered battle to General Zachary Taylor and a thirty-two-hundred man force that Polk had ordered to the Rio Grande to call their bluff. Taylor's outnumbered army clobbered them. The Mexicans failed to reckon with a new ingredient in the American military machine: the roughly one thousand young men who had graduated from the U.S. Military Academy that Thomas Jefferson had founded in 1802. They gave the Americans an immensely superior officer corps to lead both the regulars and the volunteer army that Polk created.

In spite of spectacular military successes, the war was a political disaster for the Polk administration. The president committed the first and worst blunder. He sent Antonio Lopez de Santa Anna, the exiled former president, back to Mexico on a promise that he would negotiate peace. Santa Anna immediately seized power and called for all-out resistance against the gringos, making Polk look like a fool. General Taylor turned into a presidential candidate who wrote savage criticisms of Polk's conduct of the war and leaked them to the newspapers. David Wilmot, a Pennsylvania Democratic congressman, attached a rider to an appropriation bill, mandating that slavery would be barred from any and all territory acquired by the war.

The Wilmot proposal set off a battle in Congress that infuriated southerners and threatened to split the Democratic party. In 1846, disenchanted voters gave the Whigs a majority in the House of Representatives. An early, victorious peace now became the Democratic party's only hope of salvation. To force the Mexicans to the negotiating table, Polk gave General Winfield Scott another army and ordered him to invade Mexico via Vera Cruz. Scott captured the heavily fortified port city with amazingly light casualties and smashed the Mexican army at Cerro Gordo. The Mexicans still declined to sue for peace, and Scott began a march on Mexico City.

An increasingly desperate Polk decided to gamble on a diplomatic initiative. He chose Nicholas Trist for the job because, as he put it in his White House diary, he could not give the assignment to any of the half-dozen leading Democrats who wanted it without arousing mortal jealousies. Trist's fluency in Spanish was another point in his favor. But Polk totally misjudged Trist's character. He looked on him as an unillusioned political operator like himself. He did not realize he was appointing an idealist.

Trist has left a scornful account of his final interview with the president, who told him that if he brought back a swift, satisfactory peace, his political future would be golden. Trist loftily replied that all he desired was a chance to serve his country. This response left Polk, hounded day and night by office seekers, almost derisive.

Things started going wrong even before Trist got to Mexico. He had barely left Washington when the *New York Herald* printed a story that, in the words of the outraged Polk, "disclose[d] with remarkable accuracy and particularity" the details of Trist's mission. Whigs, abolitionists—there were plenty of candidates for the probable leaker, including Polk's slippery secretary of state, James Buchanan.

Arriving in Vera Cruz on May 6, 1847, Trist did further damage to his mission. Instead of meeting with General Scott, who was halfway to Mexico City, Trist sent him a sealed copy of the draft treaty without giving him a clue to its contents. Trist unceremoniously ordered Scott to forward the treaty to Mexico City.

General Scott angrily returned the sealed packet, claiming that only he should decide whether to continue or discontinue hostilities. Trist responded with a scathing eighteen-page letter in his inimitably prolix style, rebuking Scott for failing to obey the orders of his commander in chief. He followed this up with a thirty-five-page epistle that Scott called "a farrago of impudence, conceit and arrogance." Trist told his wife that Scott was "decidedly the greatest imbecile that I have ever had anything to do with."

The general and the diplomat reported their mutual outrage to Washington, and the president became disgusted with both of them. He was receiving confidential reports from his former law partner, volunteer Major General Gideon Pillow, who was doing his utmost to put Scott in a bad light. While the president fumed, Scott achieved an unexpected rapprochement with Trist. When the diplomat fell ill, the general sent him a jar of guava jelly and a sympathetic note. Trist replied in a temperate tone, and the two men soon shook hands. Within a week they agreed that Polk—and his man Pillow—were less than great Americans.

A reinforced Scott invaded the Valley of Mexico and won two more battles, putting his army at the gates of Mexico City. President Santa Anna proposed an armistice and peace negotiations. Trist eagerly responded, but the Mexican counterproposal was wildly unrealistic. Without having won so much as a skirmish, they demanded that the Americans evacuate Mexico as well as New Mexico and California, already seized by Polk-dispatched forces—and pay Mexico for the costs of the war. They also tried to fish in Wilmot-proposal waters, insisting on a ban against slavery in any ceded territory.

In an attempt to keep the negotiations alive, Trist violated his instructions and offered to set the Texas boundary on the Nueces River rather than the Rio Grande. The Mexicans were unimpressed, and Gideon Pillow lost no time reporting this gaffe to Polk. Fighting resumed, and on September 14, 1847, Scott's army successfully stormed and occupied Mexico City. Santa Anna fled, and the government of Mexico more or less evaporated.

The country was prostrate—and back home the American mood was undergoing a drastic change. The Polk administration had previously said the goal was "to conquer a peace." By all the rules of supposedly civilized warfare, they had done that. The Mexicans had no army left in the field. Still they declined to negotiate.

In May 1847, the editor of the *New York Sun*, Moses Y. Beach, who had gone to Mexico as a secret Polk negotiator before hostilities began, suggested a new way to end the war in an editorial entitled, "Mexico Annexed to the United States." Within two months, "All-Mexico" became a movement backed by such large and influential papers as the *New York Herald,* the *Philadelphia Public Ledger,* and the *Baltimore Sun.* Senator Lewis Cass of Michigan, already running for the Democratic nomination in 1848, and the looming "Little Giant," Senator Stephen A. Douglas of Illinois, climbed aboard the bandwagon.

In Polk's cabinet, the powerful secretary of the treasury, Robert J. Walker of Mississippi, became an outspoken advocate. So did Polk's vice president, George M. Dallas, who declared Americans should not "shrink from subjugating implacable enemies." Secretary of State Buchanan, forever sniffing the political wind, joined the parade. Except for a handful of southerners around Senator John C. Calhoun, who had opposed the war from the start because of his hatred for Andrew Jackson and his putative successor, Polk, the South was already enthusiastic. All-Mexico had the makings of a mass movement.

As the All-Mexico clamor grew in size and volume, Polk began to view it with wary favor. It gave him a chance to make a spectacular leap beyond his original war aims and declare a military triumph worthy of Old Hickory in his pugnacious prime. When Polk heard from Pillow that Trist was "acting unwisely," he decided to get rid of his diplomatic representative. On October 6, 1847, he ordered Buchanan to recall him.

Significantly, Polk did not appoint a replacement. He was practically telling the Mexicans he no longer cared what they thought about a peace treaty. Buchanan's letter of recall was another strong indication of the shift in the administration's attitude. The secretary of state told Trist that a new situation had emerged since he had been appointed in April. Thousands more Americans had died, and more millions of American dollars had been spent because of Mexican intransigence.

It took five weeks for this recall letter to reach Trist. He consulted with James Freaner, a correspondent for the *New Orleans Delta,* who had become a close friend. Freaner was probably well informed about the All-Mexico movement. One of its chief voices was the rival *New Orleans Picayune.* Trist's correspondence with his wife, who was his intellectual partner, was another likely source of information on this oncoming political juggernaut. Deepening Trist's perplexity was the news that the Mexicans were finally moving toward peace negotiations. The treacherous Santa Anna had resigned as president. The head of the supreme court, long an advocate of peace, had been appointed in his place.

What to do? Freaner urged him to stay and negotiate a treaty, ignoring his recall. So did the British chargé, Edward M. Thornton, who had been acting as an intermediary between the Americans and the Mexicans. Trist asked Scott's opinion, and he made the same suggestion. He had recently turned down an offer by a group of Mexican politicians to make him dictator of Mexico for six years. He wanted to end the war and go home and run for president.

Trist wrote Secretary of State Buchanan a sixty-five-page letter, explaining he had decided to stay and negotiate a treaty. He saw the situation as a crisis for both countries. If All-Mexico succeeded and Mexico became a conquered province, Trist was convinced it would eventually corrupt and destroy America's free institutions.

By the time this letter wended its way to Washington, Polk had delivered his annual message to Congress, in which he said not a word about peace negotiations. Instead he called for more troops for the army in Mexico City. He was obviously contemplating the possibility of a prolonged occupation. When he saw Trist's sixty-five-page dispatch (one doubts he actually read it) the thunderstruck president dispatched orders to throw the deposed diplomat out of army headquarters and inform the Mexican government that he had no authority to speak for the United States.

By the time this draconian decree arrived in Mexico City five weeks later, Trist was deep in negotiations with the Mexicans. He clung to his post with Scott's support, telling the Mexicans that he was still the de facto American spokesman because no replacement had arrived. The Mexicans, who had their own sources of information in the United States, may have realized that Trist was rapidly becoming their one hope of preserving their country's independence. They abandoned their manifestos and bargained realistically for the best deal they could hope to get.

On February 2, 1848, Trist and the Mexicans signed the Treaty of Guadalupe Hidalgo (the town near Mexico City where they negotiated). The Mexicans ceded Texas to the Rio Grande and all of New Mexico and California down to a few miles below San Diego. Polk had wanted Lower California too, but the Mexicans clung to it as a point of pride. Trist shaved the original American offer of $30 million to $15 million by way of telling the Mexicans they should have come to the peace table sooner. But he agreed to assume over $3.25 million in claims against Mexico by American citizens.

Correspondent James Freaner rushed the peace treaty to Washington, D.C., in a breathless seventeen days. With it came another of Trist's interminable letters, defending it as honorable and just. Polk was enraged by Trist's insubordination, but he realized he was in a political bind. If he refused to accept the treaty, Freaner would tell the country about it. The Whigs had made a specialty of calling Polk a warmonger. They would shred him and the Democratic party if he rejected a treaty that contained the peace terms he had originally sought.

Polk decided to send the treaty to the Senate with a note recommending they debate it on its merits, without reference to Trist's insubordination. Secretary of State Buchanan opposed this decision. So did Secretary of the Treasury Walker. Their opposition did not augur well for the treaty's chances.

The Senate had been arguing about annexing Mexico since Polk's annual message in December. They soon got their hands on a copy of the treaty, and a preliminary head count showed a heavy majority against it. Foreign Relations chairman Ambrose Sevier of Arkansas told Polk his committee would recommend rejection. Numerous other Democrats opposed it for various reasons. Senator Daniel Webster led his Whig party in denouncing "this Trist paper" because it won more territory than America needed or wanted.

On February 23, 1848, the day Polk sent the treaty to the Senate, eighty-one-year-old ex-president John Quincy Adams died. He had collapsed at his desk in the House of Representatives two days earlier. Both houses of Congress adjourned, and for two days Washington was absorbed in Adams's funeral. During this interlude, a remarkable change took place in the temper of the Senate. Many senators began to think Trist's treaty was not as bad as it had looked at first.

Public opinion of Polk had sunk so low that Democrats fretted about the possibility that the Whigs might win the presidency in 1848 on a no-territory platform. When the Senate reconvened, a new realistic mood prevailed. Instead of rejecting the treaty, the Foreign Relations Committee passed it on to the full Senate without comment. After another eleven days of debate, the solons confirmed the treaty, thirty-eight to fourteen. But they revealed their All-Mexico yearnings by adding to their approval a preamble damning the "irregularities" of Nicholas P. Trist.

When Trist returned to the United States on May 17, 1848, he confronted an enraged president. Polk insisted that Trist's salary ceased on the day he received his letter of recall on November 16, 1847, and refused to pay any of his expenses in Mexico. His job at the State Department, needless to say, was gone forever. Not a politician in Congress raised a finger to help him. Moving to West Chester, Pennsylvania, Trist was forced to work as a clerk for the Wilmington and Baltimore Railroad Company, while his wife and her two sisters ran a girls' school, which soon went bankrupt.

Abandoned by the Democrats, Trist became a Republican on the eve of the Civil War. He published an article in the *New York World* quoting Jefferson and Madison as opposed to secession. Among the few friends who remained loyal was Winfield Scott, who vainly tried to get Trist a job with the Lincoln administration.

Not until 1870 did a politician speak out on Trist's behalf. That year, the Radical Republican Senator Charles Sumner of Massachusetts hailed him for rescuing the nation from All-Mexico and urged the Senate to pay Trist the money that the U.S. government owed him. The Senate voted Trist $14,559.90, his unpaid salary and expenses, plus twenty-three years of interest.

Sumner prevailed on President Ulysses S. Grant to appoint Trist postmaster of Alexandria, Virginia. After four more years on the government payroll, Nicholas P. Trist died in 1874, his idealism unblemished, his contribution to America known to only a small circle of family and friends.

George Drouillard:
Mountain Man

ROBERT M. UTLEY

The frontier has given America many heroes, from Johnny Appleseed to Daniel Boone to Kit Carson to Annie Oakley. Some of the most colorful frontier heroes were the mountain men who helped explore the great expanse of land between the Mississippi and Missouri rivers and the Pacific coast. George Drouillard was a valued member of the Lewis and Clark expedition of 1804–1806, where in addition to his trapping and hunting skills he served as an interpreter when dealing with the various Indian tribes the expedition encountered. Unfortunately his contributions have been overshadowed by the better-known exploits of fellow mountain man John Colter.

GEORGE DROUILLARD did not consider himself a hero. But he was—a hero of the Lewis and Clark expedition of 1804–1806, a hero of the formative years of Rocky Mountain beaver trapping in 1807–1810, and a hero of the first halting steps toward demythologizing the cartographic depiction of the American West. His name is inseparably linked with that of John Colter, another of Lewis and Clark's "Corps of Discovery," another beaver trapper, and another explorer of western wilds. Colter is remembered for incredible exploits of wilderness survival and Indian fighting. Drouillard is remembered hardly at all, yet he made the more significant contribution to history.

Both Drouillard and Colter demonstrated their mettle in the Lewis and Clark expedition, which sprang from the inquiring mind of President Thomas Jefferson. Even before concluding the Louisiana Purchase, the president had commissioned his private secretary, Captain Meriwether Lewis, to examine the western half of the North American continent. To share the command, Lewis turned to an old army comrade, William Clark. Leading some forty men, the two captains ascended the Missouri River, wintered at the Mandan Indian villages, crossed the Rocky Mountains, wintered again on the dank Pacific shore at the mouth of the Columbia River, then trekked and boated back to St. Louis.

Through the vast fantasy land that the Far West formed in the learned mind of 1804, the Lewis and Clark expedition blazed a narrow corridor of geographical reality. The little band of explorers discovered the true character of the Missouri's headwaters, so different from the prevailing notion. They learned the magnitude and complexity of the northern Rockies. They dashed forever the idea of navigation to the Pacific by way of the Missouri. They revealed a continent much wider than anyone supposed. This and much more to revise the conventional understanding they reported to Thomas Jefferson on their return in 1806. In this historic venture, Drouillard and Colter played conspicuous parts.

In his voluminous journals, Meriwether Lewis never got George Drouillard's name right. But "Drewyer" turns up often enough to certify him high in the esteem of the captain, who termed him "this excellent man." The offspring of a French-Canadian father and a Shawnee Indian mother, Drouillard exhibited enough learning to qualify as literate. But to Lewis and Clark, his critical value lay in mastery of the Indian sign language and awesome performance as a hunter. They signed him on as a civilian interpreter, not, like Colter and the others, as an enlisted soldier in the U.S. Army. A robust man in his late twenties, he proved himself vigorous, decisive, courageous, resourceful, and completely reliable.

In the continental crossing of Lewis and Clark, both Colter and Drouillard ranged widely as hunters, and both frequently received special assignments. It was Drouillard, however, whose talents proved more in demand and in the end more important to the success of the expedition.

More prolific and dependable than any of the other hunters, Drouillard performed prodigies of hunting. Grizzly bears seemed to offer a personal challenge. Huge, belligerent, swift, deadly, and exceptionally hard to kill, they roamed the plains and mountains in large numbers and posed a constant danger to the corps. Confronting a grizzly, Drouillard behaved as aggressively as the beast itself, rushing to the attack despite the risk or the state of his weaponry.

Although he brought in literally tons of meat for the sustenance of the corps—bear, bison, elk, deer, pronghorns—Drouillard's pivotal role lay not in hunting but in the duty for which he had been hired: Indian interpreter. As the explorers canoed up the Missouri River and then the Jefferson in the summer of 1805, they ran out of navigable water. Horses had to replace canoes, and these could be obtained only from Shoshone Indians.

Not only had the Shoshones to be found, which proved difficult, but they had to be communicated with. In one of history's beguiling coincidences, communication did not depend solely on Drouillard's signing. Accompanying the expedition was a Shoshone woman, Sacagawea, captured years earlier by Hidatsa Indian raiders and sold to a French trader, Toussaint Charbonneau, residing at the Mandan and Hidatsa villages on the upper Missouri. Here Lewis and Clark had hired Charbonneau as an interpreter and had allowed him to take along his young wife and infant son. Charbonneau did not speak Shoshone. His wife did. Her story would flourish as legend in the American imagination, but her contribution to history was genuine.

Drouillard and two others formed the advance party that under Lewis at last made contact with Shoshones, in the Lemhi River valley just west of the continental divide. When the entire corps had been reunited, Sacagawea discovered the Shoshone chief to be her brother. She helped the captains communicate with him, although awkwardly at best. She translated her brother's words from Shoshone to Hidatsa, her husband translated Hidatsa to French, and another rendered the French into English. Here and later, Drouillard's sign language provided a supplementary, if not a better, means of interpretation.

From the Shoshones the corps obtained horses. From the Shoshones too, and later from the neighboring Flatheads, Lewis and Clark gained important information about the mountain barrier that lay ahead. With Drouillard facilitating the exchange, the chiefs constructed relief maps on the ground, piling dirt to represent mountains and gouging troughs with sticks to represent rivers. From these models, the captains drew rough sketch maps that recorded the Indians' understanding of the geography of their homeland and provided important data for the engraved map that ultimately traced the route of the expedition.

Across the Bitterroot Mountains on the treacherous, wintry Lolo Trail, down the Clearwater, the Snake, and the Columbia by canoe, and during the wet winter at Fort Clatsop, George Drouillard continued to perform important services. He helped deal with each Indian group along the way and, through the winter months, with the unpredictable neighbors around Fort Clatsop. His unerring rifle proved critical to stocking the larder during these hungry months.

On the way back in the spring of 1806, Drouillard's signing skills again came into play. The previous autumn, the whites had made friends with the Nez Percé Indians, who lived on the Clearwater River at the western end of the Lolo Trail. Now, as the explorers waited for the spring thaw to unclog the trail, they again camped with the Nez Percés. Among them a Shoshone lad turned up who made possible another chain of oral communication through Sacagawea and her French husband: from Salish (the Nez Percé language) to Shoshone to Hidatsa to French and finally to English. Again, Drouillard employed the sign language to speed words and meaning through this cumbersome system. Drouillard also proved instrumental in recruiting reluctant Nez Percé guides to help the travelers across the Bitterroots.

East of the mountains, Drouillard was a player in a portentous drama. Both westbound and eastbound, Lewis and Clark had conveyed to their Indian friends the words of President Thomas Jefferson, their new "Great Father." He wanted peace with and among all tribes. In return, he would send men among them with goods to trade, including guns and ammunition. Thus innocently did Jefferson and his two captains trigger a quake whose tremors would shake and reorder the Indian world and its relationship to the white world. Shoshones, Flatheads, and Nez Percés, virtually without firearms, suffered grievously from Blackfeet and Hidatsas equipped with muskets by British traders. More than traditional hospitality motivated the helpful reception the mountain tribes extended to the American expedition. They wanted guns and ammunition to even the odds of war.

Neither Lewis nor Drouillard perceived these nuances as they set forth from the Great Falls of the Missouri with Joseph and Reuben Field to check the upper reaches of the Marias River, which Lewis thought might reach far enough north to tap the British beaver grounds of the Saskatchewan River. By July 25, 1806, the men had ascended high enough to see that the river issued from the mountains far south of where Lewis had thought. Next day they turned back for the Missouri, only to meet a group of eight Piegan Blackfeet warriors.

The meeting occurred with so little warning that both sides had to react with wary civility. That night they camped together. In an improvised hide shelter, with Drouillard interpreting, they held a council. From what the Indians said, Lewis glimpsed the extent of Blackfeet trade relations with the British. From what Lewis said, repeating the standard speech to western tribes, the Indians extracted an ominous message: the Americans intended to provide guns and ammunition to the Shoshones, Flatheads, and other enemies of the Blackfeet.

Whether that thought or simply temptation motivated what followed, the whites awoke the next morning to find the warriors stealing their rifles. Before the victims had even roused themselves from sleep, they had three rifles and were sprinting for cover. Reuben Field gave chase, overtook one of the Indians, and plunged a knife into his chest. He staggered some fifteen steps and fell dead.

Drouillard, meantime, had pounced on another Piegan. "Damn you, let go of my gun," he shouted as he wrested the weapon free.

His shout awakened Lewis, who joined the pursuit with a pistol, cornered the Indian who had his rifle, and forced him to lay it on the ground. The Field brothers rushed up and wanted to kill the thief, but Lewis refused. He also turned down Drouillard's plea to dispatch the Indian he had subdued.

Now the Piegans tried to make off with the whites' horses. Drouillard and the Field brothers went after one group. Lewis, alone and on foot, pursued two men running off with his own horse. Gasping for breath, he came close enough to shout at the Indians and aim his rifle. One turned and pointed his musket at Lewis, who fired. The ball hit the man in the stomach. He fell to his knees, then turned, partly raised on an elbow, and sent a ball at Lewis, who "felt the wind of his bullet very distinctly." The fatally injured warrior crawled behind a rock to join his companion. With his shot pouch back in camp, Lewis prudently withdrew.

The captain and his comrades had decisively routed their assailants, killed two, and recovered their rifles. They had lost two of their six horses but more than made up for them with thirteen horses the Indians had left behind. Hastily, they saddled and packed seven of the best horses and embarked on a forced march to get out of the area as quickly as possible. Before leaving, they burned most of the Indian possessions. At the first meeting, Lewis had given one Indian an American flag and another a medal. Now he retrieved the flag but "left the medal about the neck of the dead man that they might be informed who we were."

Whether or not they needed to be informed, the event marked the first violent encounter between Blackfeet and Americans. There would be many more.

Although the contributions of Lewis and Clark to geography and science would not be published for eight years, their reports of a vast new land rich in fur resources circulated swiftly. The first to respond was St. Louis entrepreneur Manuel Lisa. By the autumn of 1807, he had a trading post in place where the Bighorn River empties into the Yellowstone. Among his men were veterans of the Lewis and Clark expedition, including George Drouillard and John Colter.

From Lisa's fort, he sent men to let the Crow Indians know about the new trading post. One was John Colter, who alone, with rifle and thirty-pound pack, trudged through five hundred miles of snow-choked mountain wilderness. It was an incredible feat of persistence and endurance, qualifying Colter as the first known white man to gaze on the Grand Teton and the canyons and thermal wonders along the eastern fringe of what would become Yellowstone National Park.

Another of Lisa's messengers was George Drouillard. He followed some of Colter's trails, but covered less daunting country to the east, along the upper reaches of the Bighorn, Tongue, and Rosebud, and past the hilltop overlooking the Little Bighorn where George Armstrong Custer would die sixty-eight years later.

Repeated and embellished in the mountain man fraternity, Colter's feat soared into history and folklore. Less dramatic, Drouillard's slid into obscurity.

When Lisa returned to St. Louis in the summer of 1808, Drouillard went along. Colter remained, to aggravate Blackfeet animosity by fighting against them beside Crows and Flatheads and to add astonishing exploits to an already spectacular record.

The most astonishing occurred on the Jefferson River in the autumn of 1808, when he and John Potts fell captive to Blackfeet warriors. They killed Potts, butchered the corpse, and flung the limbs in Colter's face. Then they stripped Colter naked and sent him fleeing across a cactus-studded plain in a race for life, a howling mob in pursuit. A powerful man and swift runner, Colter gradually outdistanced all but one, who kept close on his heels. Suddenly stopping and turning, Colter confronted his adversary, who rushed forward with a spear. Colter seized it and threw the man off balance. The spear broke, leaving the head and part of the shaft in Colter's hands. The Indian fell on his back, and Colter rammed the spearhead through his body. Retrieving the weapon and grabbing the dead man's blanket, Colter resumed his dash and at last, after five punishing miles, plunged into the Madison River and found refuge beneath a raft of driftwood. The Blackfeet pursuers searched for several hours, without success. Naked except for a blanket, his feet shredded by cactus, weaponless except for the spear point, Colter made his way over two hundred miles of wilderness to Lisa's fort, which he reached, more dead than alive, eleven days later.

Meanwhile, Drouillard had taken with him to St. Louis an enlarged understanding of western geography and the explorer's keen desire to pass on what he had learned. Although lacking the grounding in contemporary literature and cartography of his officers, he had crossed the continent twice with the Corps of Discovery and acquired his own conception of its geography. He had scouted great tracts of country unseen by either Lewis or Clark. In the five months before he turned back to the mountains, Drouillard conferred often with the two explorers, now high federal officials in Missouri. A rough sketch map of the lands he and Colter had covered out of Lisa's fort was either drawn by Drouillard himself or by Lewis and Clark with Drouillard's participation.

On April 3, 1810, on a tongue of land at the confluence of the Jefferson and Madison rivers, a company of men began building a log stockade as a base for trapping and, if possible, opening trade with the Blackfeet. Led by Andrew Henry and Pierre Menard, the men represented a renewed effort by Manuel Lisa to exploit the rich beaver streams Lewis and Clark had reported. Among them, once again, were George Drouillard and John Colter.

While the stockade rose, some of the men trapped down the Missouri and others up the Jefferson. On April 12, only ten miles up the Jefferson, Blackfeet fell on eighteen trappers. By the time help arrived, two had been slain and mutilated, and three others were missing. Gone too were traps, skins, ammunition, and horses.

John Colter had been with the party scattered by Blackfeet. He escaped and found his way into the post. He had once promised his Maker to leave this country, he declared, hurling his hat to the ground, and "now if God will only forgive me this time and let me off I *will* leave the country day after to-morrow—and be damned if I ever come into it again." And leave he did, never to return.

Although discouraged, Henry and Menard hung on. In May the trappers resolved to endure constraint no longer. In a party of thirty, kept together for self-defense, they worked their way back up the Jefferson. This proved unwieldy and inefficient, so they divided into groups of four: two men to tend camp, two to work the traps. Garnering more pelts and observing no Indian sign, all grew bolder.

George Drouillard, who should have known better, began to venture out alone. Others protested, but he turned them aside. "I am too much of an Indian to be caught by Indians," he answered. Twice his solitary quests met with success. "This is the way to catch beaver," he exulted.

On the third morning he left again, followed by two Shawnee deer hunters. The main party shortly took the trail. Soon they overtook the two hunters, "pierced with arrows, lances and bullets and lying near each other." Beyond some 150 yards they found Drouillard and his horse, Drouillard (according to one who was there) "mangled in a horrible manner; his head was cut off, his entrails torn out and his body hacked to pieces." From the position of his body and the marks on the ground, he had skillfully maneuvered his horse to serve as a shield, riding in a circle and defending himself with rifle, pistol, knife, and tomahawk.

The Blackfeet had slain Drouillard as they had almost slain Colter, and as they would slay scores of trappers in the next thirty years. As the fur trade declined in the late 1830s, done in by silk hats and stubborn economic forces, so too did the Blackfeet, done in by smallpox.

Drouillard's death, capping a train of setbacks, ended for more than a decade efforts to trade with the Blackfeet or trap their country. Fortunately for geographic knowledge, however, George Drouillard had made his contribution in 1808. John Colter made his in 1810, when he worked with William Clark to perfect the great map that traced the Corps of Discovery's historic trek across the continent and back. When at last printed as part of the Lewis and Clark report in 1814, it bore witness to the travels of Drouillard and Colter and their contributions to its final form.

Neither George Drouillard nor John Colter ever saw the engraved rendering of the map. Colter, farming a Missouri homestead near Daniel Boone's, had died of jaundice a year earlier, not yet forty. Even so, this historic map stands as a modest monument to two great mountain men, prototypes of a generation to come.

Posterity records and marvels at the deeds of John Colter. Similar recognition of George Drouillard is long overdue.

Susie King Taylor:
A Black Woman's Civil War

CATHERINE CLINTON

*The life of Susie King Taylor displayed not just one but many
moments of determined heroism: her struggle for an education
even though it was illegal for slaves to learn to read, her service
as a nurse (now liberated from slavery) bravely confronting
disease and death among Civil War soldiers, her campaign as a
clubwoman to win respect for the contributions African Americans made to that war, and her witness against the insidious
racism that poisoned late-nineteenth-century American life.
Hers was a heroism anchored in the struggles of everyday life
but also fearless in demanding that the country live up to its
promises to blacks as they journeyed from slavery to freedom.*

SUSIE KING TAYLOR (1848–1912) was born into bondage on a Georgia plantation during the high tide of southern slavery. She ended her life a respected clubwoman and author among the ebony brahmins of Boston. The story of her triumph over circumstances is a heartening tale, but the fact that so few know about the Susie King Taylors of the past remains an ongoing tragedy of American history.

The key to Taylor's contribution lies within her great gift to posterity, her memoir, *Reminiscences of My Life in Camp, with the 33rd United States Colored Troops Late 1st South Carolina Volunteers* (1902). This vibrant and vital account contains not only the insightful and riveting record of Taylor's Civil War experiences, but her troubling and perceptive analysis of postwar struggles among freed people.

Taylor underscored the amnesia too many Americans develop when it comes to African American valor and accomplishment. She testified to black heroism and sacrifice, and her eyewitness account stands as rebuke to those who would forget this significant chapter of Civil War history.

Although Taylor had humble origins by nineteenth-century standards, she also had pride of family, especially her matrilineal ancestry. Born in Georgia on August 5, 1848, she was the first child of Hagar Ann Reed, a slave, and Raymond Baker. Her mother's mother, Dolly Reed, played a formative role in Susie's upbringing, telling her granddaughter stories about her own mother, Susannah Simons (who bore twenty-four children: twenty-three daughters and one son), and her grandmother, who lived to be 120 years old. Dolly Reed lived in Savannah, a slave who hired out her time under the supervision of a guardian. She remained close to her six surviving children and drove a wagonload of goods four times a year to the Isle of Wight in Liberty County (nearly forty miles away) to visit her daughter Hagar. In 1856 Reed was able to convince Hagar's owners to send seven-year-old Susie and two younger siblings to live in Savannah with her.

Savannah offered Susie the opportunity for education. Dolly Reed sent her grandchildren to a clandestine school run by a free black woman, Mary Woodhouse, whose house on Bay Lane became a haven for her thirty pupils. The children had to wrap their books in laundry or newspapers to disguise their destinations as they carried texts back to school every morning; teaching slave children was a crime. This charade persisted when Susie and her brother continued their studies at Mary Beasley's elementary school as well.

By 1860, twelve-year-old Susie had outgrown the black underground schools and begged a white neighbor, Katie O'Connor, her childhood play-mate, to give her lessons. O'Connor agreed, but only if her tutoring remained a secret, from even her parents. She tutored Susie for four months, until O'Connor entered a convent. Next, Dolly Reed secured the help of her landlord's son, James Blouis, who also offered Susie lessons—until April 1861, the firing on Fort Sumter. When Blouis went to the front with the Savannah Volunteer Guards, Susie's formal education ended.

When the war erupted, blacks in Savannah engaged in an even more dangerous underground: Susie was drafted to write false passes, forging the name of her grandmother's guardian, and other clandestine activities. When her grandmother was arrested in a raid on a church, the fourteen-year-old was sent back to her mother in Liberty County in April 1862.

When Fort Pulaski fell, the presence of federal troops nearby encouraged Taylor and members of her family to flee to St. Catherine's Island, one of the northernmost of Georgia's Golden Isles—the barrier islands stretching from South Carolina to the Florida border along the Atlantic coast. Union commanders protected this band of refugees and within a fortnight transported Taylor and two dozen other runaways to safety on St. Simon's Island, farther down the coast.

The commander in charge of the evacuation discovered Taylor was literate, articulate, and mature beyond her fourteen years. After landing at St. Simon's, he drafted her to run a school for contrabands on the island. Taylor had approximately forty young children in her classes and taught adults at night. The experiment lasted until the late fall of 1862, when Taylor was relocated to Beaufort, South Carolina, where the First South Carolina Volunteers were gathered at Camp Saxton.

When General David Hunter was put in charge of Union troops along the coast of South Carolina, Georgia, and Florida, he realized the enormous strategic impact black soldiers might have. On May 9, 1862, he declared slaves in the three occupied regions "forever free." Lincoln repealed this order ten days later. Hunter's unofficial band, denied uniforms and pay, eventually were forced to disband. However, they reassembled in mid-October under the supervision of General Rufus Saxton, the recently appointed supervisor of contraband affairs. This followed Lincoln's announcement of the preliminary Emancipation Proclamation in the wake of northern "victory" at Antietam in September 1862. These former First South Carolina Volunteers officially joined the fight, reconstituted as Company E, the Thirty-third regiment of the United States Colored Troops (USCT) in 1863.

Blacks were committed to the Union cause as a means of liberation, as a path to expanding rights. Frederick Douglass donated two of his own sons to a regiment in Massachusetts and proclaimed: "Let the black man get upon his person the brass letters 'U.S.'; let him get an eagle on his button and a musket on his shoulder and bullets in his pocket. . . . There is no power on earth which can deny that he has earned the right to citizenship in the United States."

Susie King Taylor's contributions to the Union effort were enormous. Although the army assigned her duties as a laundress when she landed in South Carolina, Taylor took on much more. She became a prized member of the regiment, respected and revered by black infantry and white officers alike.

Taylor devoted herself to the men of the Thirty-third. Her uncles and cousins joined up, as did a young carpenter from Georgia, whom Susie had known before the war, Edward King. King had escaped his master to volunteer for the Union. After his arrival in Beaufort, Susie and King became close and eventually married. The exact date is unknown, but sometime late in 1862 or early in 1863 they were wed.

The fifteen-year-old bride took on enormous responsibilities with Company E; she saw the need and became a nurse. Disease was more deadly during the Civil War than battle; three out of five enlisted men died from illness. Further, although less than 2 percent of black soldiers were killed in combat (compared with 6 percent of white soldiers), death from disease was nearly 20 percent for black troops, double the white rate.

The surgeons found her a skilled assistant, as she switched from washing bandages to applying them. When Clara Barton arrived at Beaufort in the summer of 1863, Taylor found her a stalwart compatriot. The two tended the wounded following the heroic assault on Fort Wagner in July, where the fallen Captain Robert Gould Shaw was buried alongside scores of his men, after he led the charge with the Massachusetts Fifty-fourth. Taylor appreciated the older woman's company, and commented: "Miss Barton was always very cordial toward me, and I honored her for her devotion and care of those men." The black southern teenager and the middle-aged Yankee spinster, working side by side, showed the way in which wars commingled diverse elements into one strong and unified force.

Both women confronted hardship, isolated from civilization and anchored on islands facing adversity and challenge. Taylor seemed to thrive under these hardy conditions and reported, "I learned to handle a musket very well while in the regiment and could shoot straight and often hit the target. I assisted in cleaning the guns and used to fire them off, to see if the cartridges were dry, before cleaning and reloading each day." Taylor also offered sober reflection on the challenges: "How we are able to see the most sickening sights, such as men with their limbs blown off and mangled by the deadly shell, without a shudder; and instead of turning away, how we hurry to assist in alleviating their pain, bind up their wounds and press the cool water to their parched lips."

Life in camp was fraught with danger, as Taylor recalled wartime's nightly disruptions: "Many times I would dress, not sure but all would be captured. Other times I would stand at my tent door and try to see what was going on, because night was the time the rebels would try to get into our lines." Once when crossing from Hilton Head Island to Port Royal by water, Taylor was caught in a terrible storm. The boat, manned by a Union soldier, capsized a little after eight o'clock at night, spilling into the sea the terrified women and children aboard, including Taylor. An infant died while being clutched by her mother, and the soldier-navigator drowned as well, but the rest were rescued shortly before midnight. It was a harrowing experience for Taylor—one that haunted her in later life, especially when she was involved in two subsequent steamboat accidents. Adrift and endangered, Taylor was given a strong dose of the dread and fear her male comrades endured.

Taylor described alarming challenges when black soldiers poured into Charleston on February 28, 1865. In the wake of Confederate army evacuation, flames threatened to raze the entire town. Taylor described the chaos and contempt: "It was a terrible scene. For three or four days the men fought the fire, saving the property and effects of the townspeople whenever possible, yet these white men and women could not tolerate our black Union soldiers, especially those known to them as former slaves. These brave men risked life and limb to assist residents of the 'Cradle of Secession' in their distress, enduring the fact that men and even women would sneer and molest them whenever they met up." The fierce white Charlestonians resisting help from black firefighters is a vivid image, symbolic of African Americans' Civil War struggles.

In contrast, Taylor frequently commented on the cordial attitude of the Yankee officers and northern ladies with whom she came in contact: the quartermaster's wife who was warm and friendly; Colonel Charles Trowbridge, who always brought northern visitors to the camp to meet Taylor; Lieutenant Parker, who told Taylor the stories of his home state, Massachusetts, which he called the "Cradle of Liberty." Many recognized Taylor's talents and appreciated her fine qualities. Taylor confessed, "I gave my services willingly for four years and three months without receiving a dollar."

On the subject of soldiers' pay, Taylor was less charitable. It was galling to her as well as her regiment that the army attempted to pay African American soldiers less than their white counterparts. Taylor supported the protest for fair pay that soldiers initiated; they finally achieved their goal of equal wages after over a year without pay. She proudly recalled, "I was the wife of one of those men who did not get a penny for eighteen months for their services, only their rations and clothing." These militant black soldiers broke the will of the U.S. Army with dignity and courage that surpassed many of their military leaders. Their heroics off the battlefield as well as on only recently have been heralded.

Taylor's volume chronicles the exploits of these valiant black soldiers, as any regimental history might. But her book is much more; she also rebukes the age in which she published, the turn of the twentieth century—a time that one scholar of the African American experience has labeled the "nadir" of race relations. Her not-so-gentle scolding is aimed at several audiences.

Certainly Taylor was disheartened that the enormous courage and sacrifice of USCT were not given wider recognition. She had much higher hopes for memorialization. When her regiment was mustered out, their commander believed that Fort Wagner would become a shrine, "Where in future your children's children will come on pilgrimages to do homage to the ashes of those who fell in this glorious struggle." (She hung on to a copy of this speech and kept it with her for the rest of her days.)

In reality, although the assault on Fort Wagner was celebrated, Colonel Robert Gould Shaw, the white commander, garnered the lion's share of honor. Shaw's heroism was celebrated in bronze when a St. Gaudens statue was dedicated in 1897 on the Boston Common. It was not until much later that a wider appreciation of the role of the black soldier in the Civil War was launched. Finally, in 1996 in Washington, D.C., a memorial to the black soldiers of the American Civil War was established.

In 1902, as the old soldiers were dying, Susie King Taylor was right to be disheartened. It was remarkable that Taylor triumphed over the hardships of her postwar experience. She and her husband, Sergeant Edward King, returned to her childhood home of Savannah. He was unable to get work as a carpenter due to racial bias, and took on contracts as a longshoreman, loading and unloading on the bustling docks. Savannah dockworkers protested low wages and formed the Union League to employ mutual help to fight against racism among Savannah's white employers. For her part, Taylor set up an independent academy in her home, charging her twenty pupils a dollar a month each.

Tragedy struck when her husband was killed in an accident in September 1866, leaving Taylor a pregnant widow. In December the American Missionary Association established a free school, the Beach Institute. Several black schools, Susie King's included, were forced to close. After her son was born in 1867, she tried to run a school in Liberty County. Eventually Taylor brought her baby back to Savannah to try to reestablish her academy. Taylor received $100 for King's army pension, but lost most of the money when the Freedman's Bank, where she had invested her savings, collapsed in 1874.

Impoverished and devoid of alternatives, Taylor left her son with her widowed mother and went into domestic service, even accompanying the Green family, for whom she worked in Savannah, on their vacation to a summer resort outside Boston in Rye Beach, New Hampshire. Her exposure to the North was thrilling, eye opening, and had a permanent impact. She wangled a way back to Boston and held a series of jobs there beginning in 1874. In 1879, she left domestic service to marry Bostonian Russell Taylor. Her remarriage allowed her to flourish. She organized a women's auxiliary to the Grand Army of the Republic chapter in Boston, serving in several capacities and finally as president in 1893. In 1896 she compiled a list of war veterans living in Massachusetts, which enabled old comrades to link up with one another.

In 1898 she received a summons from her son, an actor with a traveling theater company, who was desperately ill in Shreveport, Louisiana. Her journey to help him and the obstacles she faced form a dramatic ending to her reminiscences. Taylor's southern journey was jarring, unsentimental, disfigured by racism's ugly face. She was forced to sit in a smoking car, as blacks were relegated to separate and unequal accommodations. She could not get her son a sleeping car to take him back with her to Boston, and was forced to nurse him, and finally bury him in Shreveport. She witnessed a lynching in Clarksdale, Mississippi, on the sad road home and was nerved to express her wrath: "In this 'land of the free' we are burned, tortured, and denied a fair trial, murdered for any imaginary wrong conceived in the brain of the negro-hating white man" She vented her anger over the hollow mockery of the notion of "one flag, one nation."

But rather than sinking into bitter despair, Taylor remained optimistic. She dreamed of the day when justice for African Americans would arrive in the South. She declared that not all Caucasians should be blamed for the "few of the race" who are guilty of hatred and racism. She was grateful for those who lent her a helping hand. She employed biblical language, comparing blacks with the children of Israel and invoking images of Christian redemption. Her testimonial contains poetic and powerful prose.

Despite hopeful high notes, a pervasive air of melancholy envelops Taylor's memoir. We know she was able to escape southern racism to make a new life for herself in the North. We know she outlived her two husbands and her only child, but took comfort from her kinship with the many surviving members of her wartime regiment. But Taylor resented that "the war of 1861 came and was ended, and we thought our race was forever free from bondage, and that the two races could live in unity with each other, but when we read almost every day of what is being done to my race by some whites in the South, I sometimes ask, 'Was the war in vain?'"

For Susie King Taylor, it would not be in vain if only America would honor its covenant with those black men who fought and died. She modestly added that "noble women as well" participated and even lost their lives during Civil War struggles. And so her book attests not only to the deeds of valor and glory of soldiers, but to the talents and energies of black women who joined with Yankee allies to save the Union, perhaps even to create a more perfect Union—one free of slavery forever more, a union of black and white working together toward a common goal.

The choices facing Susie King Taylor may have been limited by the constraints of race and gender, but the heroism she demonstrated during wartime led to a lifelong vocation. Taylor kept the memories and hope alive. Her memoir was a poignant testimonial, "before the last comrades pass away."

Myra Colby Bradwell:
Champion of Women's Legal Rights

JEAN HARVEY BAKER

The battle for women to win access to the professions was a long and difficult one, the result of actions by unsung pioneers like Myra Bradwell who refused to be shut out of practicing law solely because of their gender. Despite a Supreme Court ruling against admitting her to the Illinois bar in 1873, Bradwell remained an active and respected member of the Chicago legal community through the Chicago Legal News, which she and her husband published. In 1890, at the age of fifty-nine, she was finally admitted to the practice of law in Illinois. But it was a heroic act of friendship and sisterhood fifteen years earlier— saving the widowed Mary Todd Lincoln from false incarceration on the grounds of mental incompetence—that turned Bradwell into a crusader for women's rights.

MYRA BRADWELL (1831-1894), America's first woman lawyer, was no stranger to public controversy. In 1875 she heroically won Mary Todd Lincoln's freedom from unjust confinement in a mental institution. In the 1880s and 1890s she campaigned for temperance and woman suffrage. But her first public battle was simply to try to win women the right to participate in the profession of law, which culminated in the famous case of *Bradwell v. Illinois* (1873). The Supreme Court ruled against Bradwell's petition, as had a lower court in Illinois, but that did not stop her from having a major impact on her profession as a champion of the legal rights of women and an inspiration for other aspiring women lawyers who followed in her footsteps.

In mid-nineteenth-century America, the profession of law was closed to women, either informally by custom or, in some states, by statute. When Myra Bradwell began her quest to practice law, her home state, Illinois, had not yet ruled on whether women could enter the legal profession. This silence, along with the fact that a college professor, Arabella Mansfield of Iowa, had passed that state's bar exams, encouraged Bradwell to pursue her dream. Also encouraging Bradwell was her lawyer husband, James Bradwell, who wholeheartedly shared his wife's commitments throughout their marriage in what was an unusual partnership for the times. So in her husband's office and with his blessing, Myra Bradwell began to read law, working her way through torts, civil procedures, and common and constitutional law, making use of his excellent legal library, which eventually became one of the largest in the state.

Myra Colby had met James Bradwell in Elgin, Illinois, while she was attending the Female Seminary and he was passing through the small town on business. The ensuing courtship was opposed by Myra's family, perhaps because James was the penniless son of English immigrants who had worked his way through college and his legal studies doing manual labor. They were married in 1852 when she was twenty-one years old. Her original intent to study law was nominally in keeping with the conservative view of wives as helpmates to their husbands. Bradwell was determined to read law, she later informed the *Chicago Tribune*, so that she could help her husband with his growing practice and so that she and James could work "side by side." In 1869 Myra passed the Illinois bar exam with high honors and petitioned the court for a license.

At this point her surviving children (two others had died in childhood) were thirteen and eleven, and her earlier civic activities, such as nursing

Civil War soldiers and raising money for the Union cause through the sanitary fairs, had ended. The energetic Bradwell was ready for more than housekeeping in an affluent home staffed by servants. Now she intended to work in the profession she had learned so thoroughly over the years.

Within the year, the Illinois courts had rejected Bradwell's petition—not on the basis of her gender, but on the surprising grounds of coverture. As a married woman whose legal existence the court considered suspended during her marriage, Myra Bradwell suffered what the court highlighted as "The Marital Disability." As Mrs. James Bradwell, she could not undertake the necessary contractual arrangements binding lawyers and clients, or so argued the court.

An angry Bradwell responded by likening the court's opinion, in its annhilation of the political, civic, and contractual rights of married women, to the *Dred Scott* decision, which in 1857 had denied any citizenship rights to American blacks. Faced with such a reactionary judgment, Bradwell carefully gathered precedents of successful challenges to the doctrine of coverture in Illinois statute law and presented a second brief. This time the rejection came on more expansive grounds: in 1869 the Illinois Supreme Court ruled that Bradwell could not practice because she was, irredeemably, a woman.

Undeterred by this second rejection, Bradwell took her case to the U.S. Supreme Court, retaining the well-known constitutional lawyer, Wisconsin senator Matthew Carpenter. Carpenter based his argument on the citizenship clause of the Fourteenth Amendment, a new and untested weapon adopted in 1868. But to the irritation of the leaders of the nascent woman suffrage movement, he separated Bradwell's constitutional right to practice law from any right of women to vote under the first section of the Fourteenth Amendment. The first might possibly be accepted by the Court; the second, he reasoned, was so revolutionary as to imperil his client's chances. Using the Fourteenth Amendment's privileges-and-immunities clause, Carpenter argued that Myra Bradwell was a citizen of the United States and that her privilege to practice her profession could not be abridged by the state of Illinois. In her own passionate plea published in the *Chicago Legal News*, Bradwell wrote, "One half of the citizens of the United States are asking—Is the liberty of pursuit of a profession ours, or are we slaves?"

The Supreme Court's answer was soon clear. In 1873 the Court upheld the Illinois statute hastily passed the year before that excluded women from practicing law on the grounds of their sex, ruling that federal courts could not interfere with a state statute. The Court further ruled that the right to practice law in state courts was not a privilege or immunity guaranteed to any citizen of the United States. But the Court did not stop there, ensuring that Myra Bradwell would go down in history as the subject of one of the most reactionary statements of any Supreme Court. In the paternalistic obiter dicta of Justice Joseph Bradley, "The natural and proper timidity and delicacy which belongs to the female sex evidently unfits it for many of the occupations of civil life. . . . The paramount destiny and mission of woman are to fulfill the noble and benign offices of wife and mother. This is the law of the Creator."

In the aftermath of the Court's decision, Bradwell found herself criticized as a female agitator by the press and no hero to the women's rights movement either. But that did not stop her public crusades: fighting for the right of women to be notary publics, justices of the peace, and school board members in Illinois. Bradwell also continued in her role as the influential editor and publisher of *Chicago Legal News*, a position she eventually held for over twenty years. But she had yet to confront the larger themes of injustice for all women or to consider what might be done about them. Like many other pioneers of women's advancement she thought in terms of individuals, not in terms of her sex.

In 1875 Bradwell entered a legal controversy that ultimately radicalized her perceptions of women's issues and moved her from a narrow agitator for women's occupational rights to a powerful activist for a whole range of feminist demands. This time it was not her own liberties that were being violated, but rather those of her friend and former Chicago neighbor, Mary Todd Lincoln. Ultimately the lack of protections for the vulnerable widow Lincoln exposed Bradwell to the systematic sex discrimination experienced by all American women and transformed a narrowly focused careerist into a leader of the women's movement.

Mary Lincoln's incarceration in a mental institution had begun without warning, after the convening of a kangaroo court in Cook County orchestrated by her eldest and only surviving son, Robert Todd Lincoln, in May 1875. At the time, Illinois law, in what was considered a form of protection of the basic rights of women, required a jury trial in all proceedings in which the defendant was charged with the condition of non compos

mentis. In practice, the Illinois system was easily manipulated by male rela-
tives intent on controlling disorderly women. Unlike women, men knew
the law or had friends who did. Unlike women, men knew the superinten-
dents of the new asylums that had increased in number so dramatically after
the Civil War.

Mary Lincoln's trial proved a perfect example of the deficiencies of the
Illinois system. That morning in May, Mrs. Widow Lincoln (as she was officially known) had no warning of her impending trial until an old friend of
her husband's appeared at her hotel room door along with two policemen
with a writ for her arrest. Her son, by this time a prominent, well-connected
attorney in Chicago who would soon be a candidate for a cabinet post, had
already hired her defense lawyer, Isaac Arnold. An old family friend in
Springfield, Arnold had always found Mary Lincoln difficult because of her
ambition and outspokenness, so he was hardly a strong advocate of her
cause. At the trial he offered no defense as a parade of witnesses recruited
and paid by her son marched to the stand to testify that Mary Lincoln was a
spiritualist, that she spent too much (of her own) money, and that at times
she seemed confused. Five doctors, none of whom had examined her, testified to her lunacy. In fact, her strange behavior could have been explained,
had Mary Lincoln been called to testify or had Arnold contested the issue
of her insanity. Without any defense mounted by her lawyer, the jury of six
men quickly found a stunned Mary Lincoln insane.

The next day Mary Lincoln was taken to a mental institution in
Batavia, Illinois, under an indefinite sentence. Most of the inmates of the
private Bellevue Place asylum (which was advertised by its owner, Dr.
Robert Patterson, as "for genteel women") stayed for long periods of time.
And so, it appeared, would Mary Lincoln. That certainly was the intention
of her son. With the superintendent of Bellevue controlling her food, her
reading material, even any travel off the premises and reporting any
changes in her behavior to Robert, Mary Lincoln was a prisoner.

Mary Lincoln prudently advertised her normalcy through her seeming
acceptance of her circumstances, and after two months she received permission to take carriage rides supervised by the attendants of the institution. Somehow in a visit to the tiny town of Batavia, she smuggled a letter
addressed to Myra Bradwell past the tight security that required all her letters be sent to and screened by Robert. Although its exact contents remain

unknown (Robert's lawyers later bought and destroyed the letter), in her cry for help Mary Lincoln begged the only (though still unlicensed) woman lawyer in the United States to obtain her release from Bellevue.

These two women had become friends when they were neighbors in Chicago's Union Square district, where Mary Lincoln had settled in 1865 after her husband's assassination. They found much in common: educated in excellent female seminaries, both were well read and shared a stylish elegance in dress and home. Both had married against the wishes of their families—Bradwell had eloped, Mary Lincoln had been married not in her father's Lexington, Kentucky, home, but at the home of her sister in Springfield. Both had, most tellingly, lost children (Mary Lincoln three sons; Myra Bradwell her namesake, Myra, at seven and a son at two) to the untreatable diseases of childhood. As a result, Myra Bradwell and Mary Lincoln were attracted to the doctrine of spiritualism so popular in the United States after the Civil War.

Despite Robert Lincoln's influence and the possible damage to her husband's legal career, Bradwell never hesitated in her efforts to help Mary Lincoln. The issue was not whether to help, but how best to aid a widow who had been railroaded by her assassinated husband's influential friends and her only surviving son into an institution where she did not need to be.

By August, Bradwell had a plan. Given Robert's control of his mother's legal and financial affairs as her court-appointed conservator, she could not invoke any legal protections. Instead she had to try to embarrass Robert publicly. She would visit Mary Lincoln, bringing reporters from the Chicago newspapers to Bellevue for interviews with the rational Mary Lincoln; she would persuade Mary's older sister to provide a home after her release so that Robert could not complain that his mother had nowhere to go; she would, in her capacity as the editor and publisher of the influential *Chicago Legal News*, write about injustices to women in the area of mental health; she would send well-timed "communications" to papers throughout the United States in a campaign to expose Robert and the superintendent of Bellevue; and she would, through her husband's auspices, threaten a writ of habeas corpus. With Myra's urging, James Bradwell agreed to accuse Dr. Patterson of trying to drive Mrs. Lincoln and others insane and to keep these women in an institution he ran for a profit.

By August "this irate lady" (as Robert and the superintendent called Myra) had set the stage for Mary's release. Papers beyond Illinois carried

Bradwell's telling commentary on Mrs. Lincoln's fate: "She is no more insane than I am"; "Is the widow of President Lincoln a prisoner?" "The whole country will rejoice at Mrs. Lincoln's freedom." In September, with Robert's grudging permission, Mary Todd Lincoln left Bellevue for her sister's home in Springfield and the freedom she might never have obtained without the intercession of her advocate. Later Mary Lincoln moved to France, where she lived independently until shortly before her death in 1882.

While Mary Lincoln remained the most compelling individual example of Myra Bradwell's effectiveness as an advocate for women's rights, many other women benefited from Bradwell's reform efforts. She helped rewrite Illinois statutes that limited to men a series of political appointments; she drafted bills ensuring married women's control over their earnings. (Fortuitously, her husband was a representative in the Illinois state legislature in the 1870s, and he introduced the bills.) She promoted temperance, a reform that through its leader, Frances Willard, had become linked to improvements in the circumstances of abused wives and children; she fought for suffrage, at first by gaining offices for Illinois women, who then, in Bradwell's logic, as elected officials could not be denied the right to vote, and in another tactic by appealing for suffrage for "the devoted wives and mothers." For over ten years she served on the executive committee of the Illinois Suffrage Association.

Unlike some other suffragists, Bradwell moved beyond the vote to take up a variety of women's causes, which she promoted in the pages of the *Chicago Legal News*. Her work in developing a statute to give mothers equal rights to the custody of their children and to allow married women to keep their own earnings affected far more Illinois women than her campaign for the release of Mary Lincoln. Still, Bradwell's interest in reform was sharpened as a result of that case, which laid bare the degree to which adult women were unprotected by the law. In one of her final crusades, Myra Bradwell fought vigorously against a retrogressive effort by the Illinois legislature to send private patients to state institutions on the certification of two doctors without a court hearing.

Barred from practicing the profession for which she had so arduously studied, Myra Bradwell, wife and mother, instead turned her efforts toward improving conditions for women. Despite her personal disappointment, she kept the motto *Lex Vincit* ("The law will conquer") at the masthead of her *Chicago Legal News*. By 1879 she could report that twenty-six females in the

United States (including her daughter, Elizabeth Bradwell Helmer, in 1882) had been admitted to the bar, although thirty of the Union's then thirty-seven states still barred women from the practice of law. Her own interest in women's issues had emerged from a personal struggle to do no more than that for which she was qualified. Her involvement with Mary Lincoln had sharpened her understanding of the range of dangerous discriminations against her sex.

When Bradwell died from cancer in 1894 at the age of sixty-three, she was saluted by the legal fraternity of Chicago as the able and effective editor of the *Chicago Legal News* on which every Illinois lawyer depended for an understanding of state law as well as available positions. Thousands of Illinois women who never knew her name were the beneficiaries of a struggle for the most basic of rights; Myra Bradwell's impact on their lives and those of their children was significant and invisible. Consistent and effective, this forgotten hero was an outspokenly courageous opponent of gender prejudice in Illinois. "Nothing save a blast from Gideon's trumpet can dispel these life-long prejudices," Myra had once said, and knowing that, she delivered several blasts.

Victoria Woodhull:
Free Love in the Feminine,
First-Person Singular

HELEN LEFKOWITZ HOROWITZ

If Myra Bradwell courted controversy in her battles for women's rights, she was nonetheless respectable and, from today's perspective, fairly mainstream in her steadfast belief in the role of law. Free love advocate Victoria Claflin Woodhull was something else entirely. Some of her opinions were on the "right side of history," but many were not. As a champion of political and economic rights for women, she accomplished a great deal in a brief period of time, only to self-destruct because of her outspokenness about controversial issues like sexual expression and free love and her highly unconventional personal life. Victoria Woodhull proves that heroism can be less than total, and that many heroes are driven by demons for both good and ill. Indeed, the same character traits can be both flaws and the raw ingredients for heroism.

ON NOVEMBER 20, 1871, to a crowd of over three thousand in New York's Steinway Hall, Victoria Woodhull broke through her prepared text, "The Principles of Social Freedom," to announce, "Yes, I am a free lover." It was a bold declaration by a heroic woman.

Victoria Woodhull made a powerful impact on American society beginning in 1870, the year that she (and her sister) broke the gender barrier to gain a seat on the New York Stock Exchange, declared herself a candidate for president of the United States, and presented a memorial to the U.S. Congress asserting that as citizens, women already held the right to vote. Woodhull cannot, however, be contained by this women's rights litany. She was a vivid woman who insisted that women and men had the right to sexual expression unconstrained by law and public opinion. She fought against hypocrisy and the double standard. She denied notions of women as passionless, and she affirmed that women own their own bodies.

Her most daring act came when she testified to these rights not in the abstract but in the concrete—for herself as a woman. Up to the point in her 1871 Steinway Hall speech when she announced herself a free lover, she had been enunciating the generalities and wordy prose supplied by reformer and writer Stephen Pearl Andrews. But as she addressed her critics, she turned to herself, and the language she used, though still elevated, moved closer to ordinary speech. "I have an inalienable, constitutional and natural right to love whom I may, to love as long or as short a period as I can; to change that love every day if I please, and with that right neither you nor any law you can frame have any right to interfere."

Neither the concept nor the words were new in 1871. For four decades, there had been intense debate about sex between free thinkers, health reformers, utopians, medical writers, and advocates of contraception on the one hand and evangelical Christians and moralists on the other. Sexual experimentation played an important role in a number of utopian experiments. John Humphrey Noyes's colony of perfectionists at Oneida, New

York, believed in "complex marriage," where each member of the community was a potential sexual partner of every adolescent and adult of the opposite sex. Within the emerging Spiritualist community, the notion of spiritual affinity led some to reject their husbands and wives to take new temporal as well as spiritual lovers. From American communities founded on the notions of French philosopher Charles Fourier emerged some colony members eager to extend the notion of "passional affinity" to a new dimension. On Long Island, Stephen Pearl Andrews's settlement, Modern Times, attracted secular as well as Spiritualist free lovers. Stretching from Long Island to Berlin, Ohio, loosely knit free love communities emerged, their members disseminating their ideas in journals throughout the nineteenth century.

What made Victoria Woodhull different in 1871 was that while utopians, Spiritualists, and free lovers were writing and speaking before specialized, like-minded assemblies, she addressed a general audience drawn by her fame. Most daring of all for a woman, she broke through abstractions and universals and claimed sexual rights for herself.

It was a heroic act. Yet, at the same time, it was laced with egotism and opportunism. In recovering Victoria Woodhull as a forgotten hero, we must recall her in her ambiguity and complexity. In 1871 Victoria Woodhull understood the power of personality. Already she was "The Woodhull." This was the source of her strength and ultimately of her downfall.

The years immediately following the Civil War introduced a new era in the culture. Vying for readers, newspapers and magazines competed with each other for news, and Victoria Woodhull made good copy. She hit New York not unlike the burlesque troupe of Lydia Thompson and the British blondes. She could hardly object. In this world of fluid opportunity, her three enterprises—a brokerage business, the lecture circuit, and a weekly newspaper—rested on her renown. Victoria Woodhull, the "bewitching lady broker," was most of all a celebrity. It is this circumstance that stands in the way of understanding her. Because of Woodhull's carefully nurtured public persona and the extent that others wrote the articles and speeches carrying her name, we can never fully know who she was or what she thought.

Victoria Claflin Woodhull had an early life that Mark Twain might best describe. Born in 1838 in Homer, Ohio, the seventh child of an improvident father and religious mother, she married at age fifteen, went on the San Francisco stage, and emerged as a Spiritualist healer. In the late 1860s

Victoria Woodhull arrived in New York with second husband James Harvey Blood, sister Tennie C. Claflin, and a plan. Relying on Tennie's sexual allure, the two sisters allied themselves with Cornelius Vanderbilt, known in the Spiritualist world for his efforts to reach his deceased mother and son. Although other women have been able to use sex to gain access to wealth and power, Woodhull and Claflin were unique in that they parlayed Tennie's sexual liaison into becoming the first women on the New York Stock Exchange. From a launching pad as a stockbroker, Victoria Woodhull set her sights on running for the presidency of the United States.

Propelling her were soaring ambition and a sense of personal power. Her handicaps, rationally evaluated, were great. The past pursued this woman in her thirties, burdening her with untidy kin, an alcoholic former husband, and two children, one of them mentally defective. One overlooked nicety was her age, below the constitutional minimum for the presidency. Her greatest advantage was her physical presence: radiant beauty, sexual magnetism, and a quiet simplicity in manner that disarmed opposition. Essential to her efforts in these years was her second husband, Colonel Blood, a former Union officer in the Civil War, who was willing to remain in the shadows and assist her ascent as adviser, bookkeeper, and amanuensis. America's home-grown anarchist Stephen Pearl Andrews and radical women's rights advocates gave her ideas and arguments.

Backed by Vanderbilt, Woodhull, Claflin & Company was initially a success. The sisters leased a great house at 15 East Thirty-eighth Street on Murray Hill. To it they welcomed not only Colonel Blood but also their parents, Victoria's two children, and her ailing first husband. If that were not enough for scandal, Stephen Pearl Andrews moved in as Victoria's teacher and probably as her lover. Soon emanating from the house were Andrews's pronunciamentos establishing Woodhull's political philosophy.

Woodhull lent her name to a series of Andrews's position papers. In May 1870, with Vanderbilt's backing, she established *Woodhull and Claflin's Weekly*. It was an important newspaper. Not only did it publish the wide-ranging radical ideas of Andrews and his circle, often under one of the sister's names, it also offered the first American printing of the English translation of Karl Marx's *Communist Manifesto*.

In the fall of 1870 Woodhull went to Washington and set herself up as a lobbyist for women's rights. In this capacity she shone. In the year preceding, she had quietly attended the Washington convention of the National

Woman Suffrage Association, remaining in the shadows to observe and learn. There she heard articulated the position that the proposed Sixteenth Amendment, granting women the right to vote, was unnecessary because the Constitution already guaranteed that right to women as citizens. Taking this position as her own, she gained the support of Massachusetts senator Benjamin Butler. Under his aegis, she presented a memorial to Congress and, in January 1871, addressed the House Judiciary Committee. Thrilled by what they heard, leaders of the National Woman Suffrage Association, present at the hearing and simultaneously in convention in Washington, had her repeat her address to the women's suffrage meeting.

By 1871 conflicts between those who sought a separate path for women's suffrage and those continuing to accommodate Reconstruction Republicanism led to a divided women's rights movement. The National, based in New York City, was headed by the more radical Elizabeth Cady Stanton and Susan B. Anthony. In these years, as Stanton and Anthony recruited a constituency, their publication *The Revolution* championed a range of causes, including reform of divorce laws. The American Woman Suffrage Association, spearheaded by Lucy Stone and Henry Blackwell, sought a more genteel tone, appropriate to its Boston setting. Agreeing with Republican legislators that this was "the Negro's hour," it cooperated in seeking passage of constitutional amendments guaranteeing the rights of former slaves. Henry Ward Beecher, pastor of Brooklyn's Plymouth Church and one of America's best-loved preachers (and brother of Catharine Beecher and Harriet Beecher Stowe), served as the American's titular head.

Although the Boston camp was impervious to Woodhull's legendary charm, members of the New York wing were drawn to her. Isabella Beecher Hooker—sister of Henry, Catharine, and Harriet—was immediately attracted to Woodhull, as were other women's rights supporters with Spiritualist sympathies. As Woodhull echoed many of their arguments in speeches and memorials, she got the attention of the press. Moreover, she had money to spend on an impoverished, small movement: in 1871 she offered $10,000, and it seemed like a godsend.

In seizing the spotlight in 1871, Woodhull initially feared that Isabella Hooker might snub her. As she later recounted, when she walked into a Washington gathering, a man said to her, "It would ill become these women, and especially a Beecher, to talk of antecedents or to cast any smirch upon Mrs. Woodhull, for I am reliably assured that Henry Ward

Beecher preaches to at least twenty of his mistresses every Sunday." What lay behind those words was a private sexual scandal swirling beneath the surface of the women's rights movement, the rumors that the pastor had an adulterous affair with Elizabeth Tilton, one of his congregants and the wife of his co-worker and champion, the writer and reformer Theodore Tilton, an active supporter of the National Woman Suffrage Association.

Beginning in the spring of 1871, the great undertow of celebrity began to suck Victoria Woodhull down. Her mother lodged a complaint in court against Colonel Blood, accusing him of threatening her with violence. A court reporter for the *New York Herald,* realizing that he had a story, took down the testimony, and over subsequent days New York readers learned of the curious marital history and irregular domestic arrangements of Victoria Woodhull. In the comic novel *My Wife and I,* serialized in the spring of 1871, Harriet Beecher Stowe turned her pen against Woodhull in the character Audacia Dangyereyes, a jaunty newspaperwoman who says to a new male acquaintance, "I claim my right to smoke, if I please, and to drink if I please; and to come up into your room and make you a call, and have a good time with you, if I please, and tell you that I like your looks, as I do. Furthermore, to invite you to come and call on me at my room."

Victoria Woodhull knew how to fight back, and she had her own access to publicity. Her knowledge of Henry Ward Beecher's affair was an obvious recourse. On May 22, 1871, she wrote a long letter to the editor of the *New York Times* defending her life and her household by writing provocatively that she knew of "a public teacher of eminence who lives in concubinage with the wife of another public teacher of almost equal eminence," hypocrites all, and she was willing to risk a libel suit to expose them. This statement frightened Beecher. At this moment he had enlisted Theodore Tilton in trying to ward off a disgrace that would publicly expose Elizabeth Tilton's sexual indiscretions. Beecher and Tilton believed that they must silence Woodhull by winning her as an ally. Tilton began writing a celebratory biography of Woodhull and by some accounts became another of her lovers.

At this point fate seemed to be turning against Victoria Woodhull. Accompanying the taint of notoriety was financial distress. Woodhull, Claflin & Company made some bad moves in a risky stock market and lost their fortune and their clients. Radical statements in *Woodhull and Claflin's Weekly* caused Cornelius Vanderbilt to withdraw his support. Needing a way to gain income to finance her household and many dependents, Victoria Woodhull turned to the lecture circuit. As she cast about for topics that could fill a hall, she discovered that she could turn her mother's court suit to her advantage. What had been suggestions of scandal now became declarations of right. Free love captured the crowds. Stephen Pearl Andrews was at her side to encourage her and provide her with text. He had long searched for an audience for such words. Spoken by the glamorous Woodhull, these words now reached crowds clamoring to hear them.

Thus on November 20, 1871, Victoria Woodhull prepared to give the address "The Principles of Social Freedom," her term for free love. She had hoped to enliven the evening by an introduction from Beecher, threatening to expose the scandal if he declined. Wilier even than she, he kept her in suspense until the last minute. When he refused, Theodore Tilton, adept at appeasement and an able lecturer, offered the introduction. Woodhull temporarily put off her decision to reveal Beecher's secrets and stepped to the podium.

She began the address with the fact of prostitution. Society cannot allege moral purity when scores of thousands of women are prostitutes serving hundreds of thousands of men. She slid into a demand for a single sexual standard for men and women. Men who frequented prostitutes should also be called by that name "since what will change a woman into a prostitute must also necessarily change a man into the same." She then insisted on the right to speak about sexuality. Because healthy birth was so important, "Are not these eminently proper subjects for inquiry and discussion . . . in a dignified, open, honest, and fearless way?"

She took the free love position known among Spiritualists that romantic love was a union of souls. Marriage was when two souls "meet and realize that the love elements of their nature are harmonious, and . . . they blend into and make one purpose of life." Sexual relations leading to reproduction are marriage, according to "nature." To be united by nature is to be united by God. Marriage happens when "true, mutual, natural attraction be sufficiently strong to be the dominant power." Unlike most other female Spiritualists, who believed in one ordained true union, Woodhull took a "varietist" position, allowing for many lovers. What comes can also leave: "Suppose after this marriage has continued an indefinite time, the unity between them departs, could they any more prevent it than they can prevent the love?" Law should have nothing to do with this natural process. "To love is a right higher than Constitutions or laws." The state should have nothing to do with love "since in its very nature it is forever independent of both constitutions and laws, and exists—comes and goes—in spite of them."

Behind the changes in sexual relations, she asserted, must come the shift in power relations between women and men that women's rights advocates and Spiritualists were demanding. "Women must rise from their position as ministers to the passions of men to be their equals. Their entire system of education must be changed. They must be trained to be like men, permanent and independent individualities, and not their mere appendages or adjuncts." Women should control the decision to have a child. "It should be theirs to determine when, and under what circumstances, the greatest of all constructive processes—the formation of an immortal soul—should be begun." She described with melodramatic language the careful and tactful suitor transformed into the drunken husband, a "beast in the shape of a man, who knows nothing beyond the blind passion with which he is filled, and to which is often added the delirium of intoxication." To prepare for their lives as wives, girls should be given knowledge about their bodies and sexual matters. "I deem it a false and perverse modesty that shuts off discussion, and consequently knowledge upon these subjects." She denounced as "barbarous the ignorance which is allowed to prevail among young women about to enter those relations which, under present customs, as often bring a life-long misery as happiness."

In the 1871 Steinway Hall speech written by Andrews, everything that Woodhull enunciated was familiar to moral reform, women's rights, Spiritualist, and free love audiences. The text used language carefully, employing euphemisms when necessary. As with the works of Spiritualist predecessors, it changed the meaning of common words. Love is marriage. A sexual relationship without love is adultery. And sexual intercourse accompanied by loathing is prostitution, "whether it be in the gilded palaces of Fifth Avenue or in the lowest purlieus of Greene Street."

Despite these often-used rhetorical devices, Woodhull was treading on dangerous ground. Her audience was no group of like-minded souls: they were paying customers who filled the hall to hear a show. As she declared, "Yes, I am a free lover," they got what they came for. Yet to claim for herself full sexual rights outside marriage before a general audience in 1871 was more than just good theater. It was a courageous act.

Victoria Woodhull was thus that wonderful American combination—heroic and opportunistic all at once. Was she also foolhardy? Later, yes; but not in November 1871. The following year, when she chose finally to expose Beecher in *Woodhull and Claflin's Weekly*, she breached some kind of limit. To claim a right for oneself is one thing; to expose the hypocrisy of the country's most beloved preacher turned out to be another. These written words called forth the wrath of Anthony Comstock, America's most dangerous opponent of free speech between the Civil War and World War I, just beginning his career of vice hunting. He had her arrested on the charge of sending obscene material through the mails. Unwittingly, Victoria Woodhull's outspokenness in unmasking Beecher fed the conservative opposition as it sought to limit sexual discussion. But that was 1872, not 1871.

Soon Woodhull's own life swerved in a new direction that removed her from these issues. In the trials that followed, she ultimately won the legal battle, but she was weakened by the conflict and emerged with diminished support. In 1876 she divorced Colonel Blood and the following year left for England, where as a lecturer on eugenics she gained an established London banker for a husband. At her death in 1927, Victoria Woodhull Martin was the mistress of a country estate in Worcestershire, more than half a century and an ocean away from her Steinway Hall address.

Heroic, opportunistic, foolhardy—in the early 1870s Victoria Woodhull was all of these. Perhaps as this disillusioned century ends, we can allow our heroes the humanity of mixed motives and muddled results.

Emmeline B. Wells:
Mormon Feminist and Journalist

LEONARD J. ARRINGTON

In the eyes of many nineteenth-century Americans, Mormons were just as controversial as free love advocates because of their practice of plural marriage or polygamy. But Mormon women did not consider themselves debased or oppressed by polygamy, and the full and active life led by Emmeline B. Wells suggests how central Mormon women were to their communities and indeed to national political movements like woman suffrage. Emmeline Wells's was a quiet but effective heroism that manifested itself in her commitment to the cause of women as part of her Mormon faith.

BECAUSE SHE WAS a woman and a Mormon, Emmeline B. Wells is a forgotten hero in American history. The important role of women in American history has only recently been appreciated, and the accounts of Mormon history are filled with the activities of men. Yet Emmeline Wells, who lived through the age of the steamboat, stagecoach, and buckboard wagon, and endured long enough to have motion pictures taken of her when she was in her nineties, was a prime mover in the successful drive to give Utah women the vote in 1870. For almost forty years she edited the *Woman's Exponent* (for many years the only magazine by and for women west of the Mississippi), served as an officer of the National Woman Suffrage Association and the International Congress of Women, and was influential in the cultural and political life of Utah and other areas where Mormons lived. For eleven years, she was general president of the powerful women's auxiliary of the Church of Jesus Christ of Latter-day Saints (Mormon). A woman of brilliant intellect, talented writing and editorial skills, determination, and perseverance, her efforts on behalf of Mormons were extensive; equally extensive were her efforts on behalf of women. She was important not only in Mormon and Utah history, but also American history generally.

Emmeline Blanch Woodward was born in Petersham, Massachusetts, in 1828, the seventh of nine children of descendants of early Puritan settlers. Her grandfather had fought in the Revolutionary War and the War of 1812. A precocious child, Emmeline attended local schools and then was sent off to a select boarding school in New Salem. During her absence, her mother joined the Church of Jesus Christ of Latter-day Saints (Mormon). When Emmeline returned from school in 1842, she accepted Latter-day Saint beliefs and was baptized in an ice-covered pool on their farm on her fourteenth birthday. She taught school for a year in Orange, Massachusetts, and then, at the urging of her mother, who worried that she might succumb to the pressure of her friends and superiors to give up Mormonism, Emmeline married James Harris, the son of the local Mormon leader. They moved to the Mormon headquarters in Nauvoo, Illinois, arriving aboard a Mississippi River steamboat in March 1844.

Emmie, as she was called at the time, taught grade school and Sunday school in Nauvoo, and she gave birth to a son, who died within a month. Shortly after, her husband left her, intending to earn a quick income, but never to return. Many years later, Emmeline learned that James Harris never remarried and that he had died in 1859 in Bombay, India, while working on a whaling vessel. He had written many letters to her but made the mistake of mailing them to his mother, who did not forward them to Emmeline. At this time of personal crisis, Emmeline was befriended by Elizabeth Ann Whitney, wife of Newel K. Whitney, presiding bishop of the church. Elizabeth and her husband took Emmeline into their household, and Emmeline became the plural wife of Bishop Whitney in 1845. He was fifty; she was sixteen.

In 1846 the Whitneys joined the thousands of other Mormons who were forced to leave Nauvoo. After a trek with several hundred others across the Great Plains, they arrived in the Salt Lake Valley in October 1848, and a month and a half later Emmeline's eldest daughter was born. Emmeline had one other child by Bishop Whitney before he died in 1850.

With Bishop Whitney's death, Emmeline suffered anguish. Four years later she wrote to one of Bishop Whitney's close friends, Daniel H. Wells, and asked him to consider her lonely state. Wells married her as a plural wife, and Emmeline had three additional daughters by him. Wells, a prominent Salt Lake City businessman, superintendent of public works, mayor, and later a counselor to Brigham Young in the First Presidency of the Mormon church, was able to provide her a home and some income, paid for the education of her five daughters, and allowed her to concentrate on her reading, writing, and public speaking, as well as affording her a prominent place in the community. While her children were small, however, Emmeline devoted herself almost exclusively to her home and family. She worked in her garden, sang in the choir of the Old Tabernacle in Salt Lake City, wrote verses, and visited with friends.

Emmeline was a small woman, barely five feet tall and weighing about one hundred pounds. Refusing to wear black dresses or a veil over her face, she wore pastel colors and soft scarves at her neck. She had a supreme will. As a contemporary wrote, "Emmeline was little and delicate, and great-minded, and she walked softly, but she had a fierce independence." Emmeline expressed her lifetime goal as follows: "I desire to do all in my power to help elevate the condition of my people, especially women . . . to do those things that would advance women in moral and spiritual, as well as educational work and tend to the rolling of the work of the Lord upon the earth."

In 1869, Emmeline began to serve as the private secretary of Eliza R. Snow, general president of the newly established Women's Relief Society in

Utah. Founded in 1842 as the women's auxiliary of the Mormon church, the Relief Society was revived in 1868 by Brigham Young; each local congregation had its own organization and officers. Overseeing the entire society and supervising the organization of local societies were a general president and two "counselors," who directed the women in many programs, including charity, health and hospitalization, handicrafts instruction, cultural refinement, spiritual revitalization, and even political activity. Holding the position of Snow's assistant for six years, Emmeline absorbed the spirit and wisdom of Eliza, an organizational genius.

As the wife of the presiding bishop and then of president Wells, Emmeline formed close friendships with leading Latter-day Saint women, all of whom shared a developing interest in the cause of women. Emmeline read national newspapers and magazines and watched with mounting interest the formation of a female reform movement aimed at social, educational, economic, and political equality with men. Emmeline had read *Vindication of the Rights of Woman* (1792) by the English author Mary Wollstonecraft, and she also knew of the efforts of Massachusetts women, particularly Abigail Adams, who agitated for women's rights in the federal Constitution. She had read Margaret Fuller's American feminist statement, *Woman in the Nineteenth Century* (1845), and was aware of the first women's rights convention organized by Elizabeth Cady Stanton in 1848 in Seneca Falls, New York, which launched the woman's suffrage movement.

As Emmeline knew, there were good reasons for these women's movements. Women could not vote, hold office, sit on juries, or, if married, own property unless by special dispensation. Women were not expected to hold high positions in church, go to college, practice law, or speak in public. Emmeline rejoiced when Utah women, partly because of her influence, were given the vote in 1870 and eagerly exercised her prerogatives. She became a member of the Central Committee of the People's Party, the Mormon church's political party; was a member of several constitutional conventions when Utah was attempting to become a state; and was nominated for the territorial legislature in 1872 but was forced to withdraw when it was not clear from the constitution that women could hold elective office. In 1879 she experienced firsthand discrimination when she was denied the office of Salt Lake City treasurer because she was a woman.

In 1872, when the *Woman's Exponent*, a semimonthly publication by and for Mormon women, was founded by Louisa Lula Greene, Emmeline submitted material for it, often using the pen name Blanche Beechwood. Many of her articles dealt with women's issues: equal pay for equal work, even equality in athletic programs. On the political side, in 1874 Emmeline became vice president for Utah of the National Woman Suffrage Association, the suffrage group associated with Elizabeth Cady Stanton and Susan B. Anthony.

After Lula Greene married Levi Richards and began to have children, her work on the *Woman's Exponent* slackened, and Emmeline stepped forward as assistant editor. In 1877 she became editor, a position she held until 1914, when the *Exponent* was replaced by the *Relief Society Magazine*. If it happened to women, whether locally, nationally, or overseas, Emmeline reported it in the *Exponent*, believing that Mormon women "should be the best-informed of any women on the face of the earth, not only upon our own principles and doctrines but on all general subjects."

Through the *Exponent*, Emmeline set out to replace the widely held belief that Mormon women were debased and suppressed. She projected on the pages of the publication a positive image of intelligence, boldness, competence, and self-assurance. For more than twenty years, the masthead carried the motto, "For the Rights of Women of Zion and All Nations." Emmeline campaigned against "the cult of true womanhood" and called on husbands to respect their wives for more than their housekeeping skills. She also strongly supported equal educational opportunities for men and women. If women were given the same opportunities for work and for education as men, Emmeline insisted, they would demonstrate that they were as smart as men, as able as men to exercise leadership in social, religious, and business activities. The desirable goal was for men and women to work together, to be united, to share both responsibilities and ideas.

Emmeline was not contending that women should neglect their children in seeking to do "public work," however. She had a close relationship with her own daughters—Belle, Mellie, Emmie, Annie, and Louie—mentioning them almost daily in her diary. But she insisted that women should also be free to assume responsibilities outside the home in church, in the community, and in the world of business: "That motherhood brings into a woman's life a richness, zest and tone that nothing else ever can I gladly grant you, but that her usefulness ends there, or that she has no other individual interests to serve I cannot so readily concede." Living up to her philosophy, Emmeline juggled family and personal challenges with her work with the *Woman's Exponent*, the women's suffrage movement, and the Relief Society.

Two specific assignments given to Emmeline in the late 1870s evolved into lifetime responsibilities. In 1876 Brigham Young asked her to lead a churchwide grain storage program. The women gleaned from the fields, built their own granaries, and distributed grain to thousands of poor families to eat, and gave feed to livestock. Supplies were also shipped to victims of national disasters and war in San Francisco, China, Turkey, and elsewhere. The program continued until World War I, when the 100,000 bushels they had accumulated were sold to the U.S. government for distribution overseas at the end of the war. President Woodrow Wilson, on a brief visit to Salt Lake City, personally visited Emmeline in her apartment in the Hotel Utah and thanked her for this contribution to the American war effort.

In 1870 Mormon leaders encouraged Emmeline and Zina Young Williams to attend the meeting of the National Woman Suffrage Association in Washington, D.C.. Over the years Relief Society leaders took an active role in that organization, although the other branch of the suffrage movement, the Boston-based American Woman Suffrage Association, led by Lucy Stone and Henry Stone Blackwell, refused to work with Mormon women because of the controversial issue of polygamy. Tensions lessened somewhat when the two sides reunited as the National American Woman Suffrage Association in 1890, and when polygamy was outlawed that same year.

Emmeline formed close friendships with national women leaders such as Frances Willard, Anna Howard Shaw, Julia Ward Howe, and Clara Barton, but was especially close to Susan B. Anthony. Emmeline wore a gold ring Anthony gave to her, declaring, "It is a symbol of the sympathy of two great women for one great cause." On Anthony's eightieth birthday, Wells presented her with a black brocaded dress made from Utah silk.

At the World's Congress of Women, held in Chicago at the Columbian Exposition in 1893, Wells presided at one of the important council meetings. May Wright Sewall, national chairman of the Congress of Women, arranged for her to give papers on "Western Women in Journalism" and "The Storage of Grain." Wells also edited two books exhibited in the Utah Pavilion: *Charities and Philanthropies: Woman's Work in Utah* and *Songs and Flowers of the Wasatch*, both published in 1893 by a Salt Lake City firm.

In the years that followed, Emmeline Wells attended suffrage conventions and women's congresses across the country and internationally. At the National Council held in Washington in 1895, she read "Forty Years in the Valley of the Great Salt Lake," a paper that was reproduced in many leading newspapers and magazines. At the Atlanta convention held later that year, she delivered such a well-received address that at its conclusion the auditorium resounded with tumultuous applause, and Susan B. Anthony came forward on the rostrum and embraced her. In 1899 her suffrage activism took her abroad, where, as an officer of the National Council of Women, she spoke at the International Council of Women held in London.

Regarded as a devout Mormon, Emmeline also advanced in responsibility on the church scene, becoming in 1888 general secretary and a member of the general board of the Relief Society. On October 3, 1910, Emmeline was called to be the fifth general president of the organization. She continued as president until 1921, when she was ninety-two. Belying her age, under her dynamic leadership she standardized and systematized the work of the Relief Society, instituted the *Relief Society Magazine*, began the first uniform course of study, and adopted the still-current slogan, "Charity Never Faileth." Welfare work became more methodical, and she coordinated Relief Society work with those of civic and county agencies.

In recognition of her many efforts and achievements in literature, Brigham Young University (BYU) conferred upon Emmeline the honorary degree of Doctor of Letters on her eighty-fourth birthday in 1912. She was the second person to receive the honor and the first woman. BYU would wait forty-four years before honoring another woman in this way.

At that time Susa Young Gates wrote of her:

> Emmeline's mind is keen, her intellect sure, and her powers unbending. She possesses a rarely beautiful spirit, and is affectionate, confiding, and exquisitely pure. She is an eloquent speaker, a beautiful writer, a true friend, and a wise counselor. She is beloved by all who dwell in the Church, and by all who know her, and their name is legion. . . . She is sensitive without smallness, wise without narrowness, and religious without bigotry. She is tender, a loving link between the women of the Church and those without, both of whom reverence and love her for the good she has done. . . . She is an inspiration to her friends, a thorn to her envious associates, and a "companion of princes" in her own right.

When Emmeline turned ninety, a party was given for this widely acknowledged heroine at the Hotel Utah. In honor of the occasion, a moving picture was made of her and other pioneers who had been living in Nauvoo during the time Joseph Smith was alive. More than a thousand people attended her ninety-second birthday party in the Hotel Utah. Shortly after her release from the presidency of the Relief Society in 1921, Emmeline died, age ninety-three, and her funeral was held in the Tabernacle in Salt Lake City, the second funeral ever held in that Temple Square facility for a woman.

On her hundredth anniversary, seven years after her death, the women of Utah placed a bust of Emmeline Wells in the rotunda of the Utah State Capitol Building. The brief inscription reads, "A fine soul who served us."

The Amazing Dummy

STEPHEN JAY GOULD

Dummy Hoy was an early baseball player who was also deaf. He deserves inclusion in a book about forgotten heroes not because he played with a disability but because of his skill as a player and the exemplary manner in which he conducted his life on the field and off. Did his deafness then make no difference to his baseball career? Only in limiting the publicity he received, because sportswriters couldn't be bothered to write out their questions in order to interview the player instead of talking with him in the clubhouse.

THE SOCIETY OF MALES, especially when bonded by a shared physical activity, often promotes a distinctive and curious form of camaraderie, neatly balanced on a fulcrum between near cruelty and ferocious loyalty. The nicknames given to professional athletes stand as telling testimony to this important social phenomenon. The press, particularly in earlier times of more leisurely and flavorful prose, may have christened Joltin' Joe DiMaggio as the Yankee Clipper or Babe Ruth as the Sultan of Swat. But ballplayers themselves usually favored the pungent and the derogatory. Ruth, to his peers, was often "Niggerlips."

We should interpret this apparent harshness as a badge of acceptance into a special sort of guild, with membership strictly limited by both the skills needed to play and the toughness required to brave the daily struggle. If you can't take a nasty name without an eyeblink ("like a man," as folks of my gender tend to say), how will you survive the fastball thrown at your head next time you crowd the plate, or the spikes aimed at your calf the next time you cover second base on a force play?

These derogatory names were often fixed on the particular mishaps or weaknesses of individuals. Thus, Fred Merkle, first baseman for the New York Giants during the early years of the century, remained "Bonehead" throughout his distinguished career, thanks to a stupid mistake in a crucial contest of his sophomore season (1908), when he forgot to touch second base on his teammate's supposedly game-winning single. But my greatest sympathy goes to H. S. Cuyler—Hall of Fame outfielder of the 1920s and 1930s—but known only as "Kiki" because he stuttered badly and frequently tripped over his own last name (pronounced Ki-ler).

Another, and more common, class of nicknames uses the tactic of the ethnic slur by labeling individuals with a pejorative name for their group—as in numerous short players called "Stump," or "Specs" for players with eyeglasses. In the early days of baseball, all Indian players were "Chief" (with Philadelphia pitcher Chief Bender and New York catcher Chief Meyers as the leading stars), while naifs from the farm became "Rube" (with Hall of Fame pitchers Rube Marquard and Rube Waddell as most notable bearers of the label).

Early baseball did dispense an odd form of rough justice based on the elite but democratic premise that all men who could stand the heat and hazing would be named for their weakness but judged only by their play. (Let us not, however, descend into maudlin romantic reverie about these times, for we need only remember the restrictive covenant applied to such "democracy": black men could not play, whatever their talent.) Several deaf men also played major league baseball during the game's early years—and every last one of them bore the name "Dummy." (As another linguistic cruelty by extension, the etymology of "dumb" refers only to muteness, not stupidity—as in the old phrase "deaf and dumb" for people who could neither hear nor speak. These men played at a time when few deaf people learned to vocalize and when signing was not yet regarded as true language. To the hearing world, therefore, they did not speak, and were consequently regarded as mute or dumb—hence "Dummy" in a world of derogatory nicknames.)

Two deaf players of baseball's early years stand out for excellence of performance: Luther Haden (Dummy) Taylor, a fine pitcher who won 112 games for the New York Giants between 1900 and 1908, and, the subject of this essay, William Ellsworth (Dummy) Hoy, a superb center fielder with a lifetime .288 batting average for six teams in four major leagues between 1888 and 1902. The career of Dummy Hoy—and I will, without apology, use this name throughout my essay, because Mr. Hoy bore it with pride and dignity throughout his career and later life—also offers us great insight into the history of American sports by virtue of Hoy's keen intelligence through such a long life, for he died in December 1961 at age ninety-nine, just five months shy of his hundredth birthday. (He was, at the time, the longest lived of all major league players. Since then, one man has slipped past the century boundary by a mere eight days—an unknown pitcher named Ralph Miller, who compiled an undistinguished record of five wins and seventeen losses in a two-year career from 1898 to 1899. So Dummy Hoy remains the most longevitous major leaguer of note.)

Note a central paradox and irony in the career of Dummy Hoy, a peculiarity that would have appealed to his wry sense of humor. We are drawn to this man because his disability, as recorded in a nickname now regarded as cruel, attracts our attention in an age of greater sensitivity toward human diversity. But when we study his career, we discover that he stands out not for his unusual deafness (which he regarded as largely irrelevant to his profession and, at most, a nuisance), but rather because he was such an exemplary performer and human being—in other words, because he occupies a pinnacle of excellence in the ordinary activities of his chosen life and career.

Dummy Hoy's biography typifies baseball's early history, when the game reigned supreme as a national pastime, but drew professional players almost entirely from the proletarian population of agricultural and industrial workers. Knowledge of this background remains essential for understanding many key features of baseball's social and organizational ways, including the paternalism of wealthy owners (and their horror and confusion at the successful unionization of players during our generation), and the structure of advance that leads from minor to major leagues, rather than from college teams to professional leagues, as in sports that became popular later, including basketball and, especially, football (which began as an elite college sport).

Dummy Hoy was a farmboy from the tiny rural hamlet of Houckstown, Ohio. He was born on May 23, 1862, and became deaf at age three following an attack of meningitis. He did not attend school until his parents learned about the Ohio School for the Deaf in Columbus. Beginning at age ten, but advancing rapidly, he finished both primary and high school, learned the trade of a cobbler, and graduated as valedictorian of his class at age eighteen. Hoy recalled that his father gave his sister a cow and a piano for a legacy when she turned eighteen, and then provided a suit of clothes, buggy, harness, and saddle to each of his brothers at age twenty-one. When Dummy Hoy reached majority, however, his father gave him just the suit and free board until age twenty-four, for the family had decided that, due to his deafness, Hoy should remain at home and become a cobbler.

He began as an assistant to the local Houckstown shoemaker but eventually saved enough money to buy his boss out. Hoy recalled, "I got the goodwill for nothing, but the leather, lasts, tools, and sewing machine cost me about $100." The rest of the recorded story smacks a bit of bucolic mythology and was no doubt more complicated; but as Hoy told the tale: Rural people went barefoot in the summer and business became slow. Hoy therefore encouraged the local kids to gather around his shop and play ball. Hoy recalled in a 1947 interview:

> This went on for years until one day a citizen from Findlay, Ohio, nine miles away passed through the town. He paused to watch the fungo hitting for a while, then accosted me. Disappointed at finding I was a deafmute he continued on his way. The next day he passed through the town and again stopped to watch players, me in particular. Taking out a pad and pencil he wrote me asking me if I would accompany him to Kenton, Ohio, a town some twelve miles further on and play for its team against its bitter rival

from Urbana. . . . I hit so well against them that it gave me an idea. The following spring I set out for the great Northwest and caught on with Oshkosh, Wis. That was in 1886. I stuck to baseball for 18 years, retiring at the end of 1903.

Hoy signed his first contract (with Oshkosh of the minor Northwest League) for $75 per month, with a stipulation that he could leave at the beginning of August because work was piling up at his cobbler's shop. But Oshkosh offered him $300 to finish the remaining two months of the season, and Hoy never looked back. He starred in his sophomore season at Oshkosh (following an indifferent rookie year), hitting .367, stealing sixty-seven bases, and leading his team to a pennant. He was then promoted to Washington in the major National League, where he enjoyed a fine rookie season in 1888, batting .274 and stealing a league-leading eighty-two bases. (Steals were defined differently and more generously in baseball's early years, so we cannot compare this figure with modern records. For example, a player was awarded a stolen base when he reached third from first on a single that, in the scorer's judgment, would usually advance a man only one base.)

Dummy Hoy followed a peripatetic career thereafter, although his play remained consistently excellent. After two seasons with Washington, he cast his lot with baseball's first prominent revolt and joined the Players League, organized by New York Giants captain John Montgomery Ward in hopes of winning fairer pay and working conditions, especially freedom from the peonage of the "reserve clause" that bound players to their owning teams (and did not fall until the legal battles of our current generation). But Hoy landed with the particularly inept Buffalo team in 1890, and the league failed in any case. In a letter written at age ninety-three, Hoy recalled this season in writing to thank a journalist for sending him a photograph of the 1890 Buffalo club:

> I recall those three clubowners. I thought they were good people to have behind the club, but that they were unlucky. . . . It was the poor playing of the team that caused them to lose money. One day the leading members . . . called a meeting of the team. It was suggested that, as the club was in financial difficulties, each player should be assessed a certain sum and share in the profits, if any. The majority, including myself, after due deliberation, decided to let the ship "sink" and go home, rather than throw good money after the bad.

In 1891, Hoy therefore moved to St. Louis in the American Association (then a major league), and thence back to the National League, where he played for Washington (1892), Cincinnati (1894), and Louisville (1898). But he bolted again to join the fledgling (but this time successful) American League in 1901. After the 1902 season, he could have continued in the majors, but decided to see another part of the country, and played all 211 games for Los Angeles in the minor Pacific Coast League in his last season of 1903.

Dummy Hoy may not have stood in the very first rank of players, but he was certainly a major star of the game's early history. He played 1,798 games, nearly all as center fielder, in fourteen seasons, and compiled an excellent lifetime batting average of .288. But his greatest skills lay in three other areas: his speed and superior base-running abilities (with 597 lifetime steals), his acknowledged intelligence and savvy understanding of the game's subtleties, and his excellent fielding, particularly his rifle arm. In his most famous single achievement, Hoy once threw three players out at home plate—from the outfield, of course—in a single game in 1888.

Dummy Hoy accomplished all these feats under an additional disadvantage potentially more serious than his deafness: he was one of the smallest men in the major leagues, even in these early days of lower average height for the general population. Hoy stood between five feet four inches and five feet five inches (sources differ) and weighed about 145 pounds.

On the more universally human side of our admiration, Hoy's later life remained a rare model of prosperity and apparent contentment. Hoy saved his money and bought a dairy farm in his native Ohio upon retirement. He married Anna Lowery, a teacher of the deaf (and a deaf woman herself), late in his career, and had three surviving children, two daughters (both of whom taught in schools for the deaf) and a son (who became a distinguished judge in Ohio). Hoy also left seven grandchildren and eight great-grandchildren when he died in 1962.

After selling his farm in 1924, Hoy worked as a personnel director for deaf employees at the Goodyear Rubber Company in Akron, and then for the Methodist Book Concern in Cincinnati until his retirement. (Hoy read lips with great proficiency and did learn some rudimentary, if inefficient, vocalization.) He maintained a home and continued to walk at least five miles a day, until his wife died during his early nineties. He then lived with his son until his death. As a wonderful last baseball hurrah, Dummy Hoy, at age ninety-nine, threw out the first ball both on opening day, and at one of the World Series games, for the 1961 Cincinnati Reds, the principal team of his own career (1894-1897, and again in his last major league season of 1902). Dummy Hoy had a truly wonderful life.

In addition to what one might call his more generic excellence, Dummy Hoy commands our attention (and commends our study) for at least three particular reasons that illuminate the history of American sports, and our social history in general.

His deafness. One cannot (and should not) fail to recognize the defining feature that gave Dummy Hoy his baseball name. First, as all aficionados of the game will instantly recognize, Dummy Hoy played center field—and center fielders must serve as generals of the outfield by calling which balls they will catch and which should be handled by the right or left fielder. How could a mute player express such leadership (while the very role, needless to say, serves as testimony to the acceptance and respect that Hoy commanded among his fellow players)? Wahoo Sam Crawford (from Wahoo, Nebraska), one of the game's early stars, played with Hoy in the outfield and provided personal testimony in his interview for Lawrence S. Ritter's wonderful 1966 book, *The Glory of Their Times*, an oral history told by the few survivors of baseball's early years:

> We played alongside each other in the outfield with the Cincinnati club in 1902. He had started in the Big Leagues way back in the 1880's, you know, so he was on his way out then. But even that late in his career he was a fine outfielder, a great one. I'd be in right field and he'd be in center, and I'd have to listen real careful to know whether or not he'd take a fly ball. He couldn't hear, you know, so there wasn't any sense in me yelling for it. He couldn't talk either, of course, but he'd make a kind of throaty noise, kind of a little squawk, and when a fly ball came out and I heard this little noise I knew he was going to take it. We never had any trouble about who was to take the ball.

But you did have to be tough to survive in these rough and tumble days. Tommy Leach, another early player, told this anecdote to Ritter about his first day with Louisville in 1898:

> My own bat hadn't arrived yet, so I just went over and picked one out I liked and went up to hit. After I was through, I hardly had time to lay the

bat down before somebody grabbed me and I heard this strange voice say something like, "What are you doing with my bat?" Scared the dickens out of me. I looked up, and it was a deaf mute. We had a deaf mute playing center field, Dummy Hoy. . . . I roomed with Dummy in 1899, and we got to be good friends. He was real fine ballplayer.

Leach later became friendly with Hoy's wife as well, and he recalled their styles of communication:

They could read lips so well they never had any trouble understanding anything I said. They could answer you back, too, in a little squeaky voice that usually you could understand once you got used to it. We hardly ever had to use our fingers to talk, although most of the fellows did learn the sign language, so that when we got confused or something we could straighten it out with our hands.

Hoy also won the appreciation of fans as well as players. Sportswriter Vincent X. Flaherty heard about Hoy's play as a child, and wrote an appreciation for Hoy's ninetieth birthday:

But perhaps none of these gilded facets of his all-around ability impressed me nearly as much as the fact that he was a deaf-mute. In a kid's mind, that made him unique. It set him apart from all others, and made him something special.

Several witnesses remembered Hoy's popularity among fans. When Hoy made a good hit or fielding play, the fans would stand up and wave their arms, hats, and handkerchiefs in easily visible appreciation. They called him "The Amazing Dummy."

But it would be dishonest and unfair to gild a reality with the claim that deafness did not matter, or even proved more of an advantage for the appreciation thus engendered than a detriment for jeers received or possibilities foreclosed. One has only to read standard press accounts of the time to get a flavor of old-style political incorrectness (a good antidote against too glib a dismissal of current ameliorations, whatever the absurdity of their extent or overblown claims for importance). Consider the following 1892 report on a salary dispute under the headline, "'I Won't Sign,' Says Hoy": "Wagner [the club owner] offered to split the difference and raised his figure to $3250, but the dummy wouldn't sign and the matter was dropped."

But the practices of journalism usually worked to Hoy's great disadvantage by the opposite route of silence. Press coverage did not matter as much then as now, but players' popularity and reputations still correlated strongly with journalistic attention. Few reporters ever bothered to interview Hoy at all, even though he was probably the smartest player in baseball at the time—the main reason for his unjust status as a *forgotten* hero. They were discomfited, didn't know how, or just didn't want to bother with the extra time needed to read and write answers. Disability then carried no cachet, and not a single reporter ever followed Hoy or interviewed him extensively. In the revealing letter quoted earlier, written when he was ninety-three, Hoy recalled with a particularly poignant final line, the origin of official confusion about his age:

> I was 28 with that club [Buffalo in 1890] and 93 on my last birthday—May 23, 1955. Why do not the records tally with those figures? I will tell you and go bail on the correctness of my figures—they were copied from the family Bible: One rainy day in the Spring of 1886, the Oshkosh (Wis.) players were assembled in the club house getting ready for the opening day. A newspaper man, representing the local press, entered to take down the age, height and weight of each player. When it came to my turn to be interviewed he omitted me because I was a deaf mute. Also because he had not the time to bother with the necessary use of pad and pencil. When I read the write-up the next day I saw where he had me down as 20 years old. He had made what he considered a good guess. Now, during my school days I had been taught to refrain from correcting my elders. Then, too, he had *whiskers*. After thinking the matter over I decided to let his figures stand. Later, the Associated Press copied them. In this way, I became known as the twenty-year-old Oshkosh deaf-mute player. Thus, I got along fine by telling all inquirers that I had my birthday last May 23 and that I was past the age in question. My looks satisfied them, too, as I was always looking younger than my real age. What would you have done if you had been in my place?

Journalist Robert F. Panera cites the following anecdote—a story that deserves to be true and might even be accurate—in an article for the *Rochester* (New York) *Democrat and Chronicle*:

> The first few months were difficult for Hoy, being unable to hear or speak. Often he was the butt of ridicule by his fellow players. But Hoy persisted

and let his play speak for itself. . . . He soon showed that he was not only literate but also had a keen sense of humor. Using pad and pencil to communicate with a reporter during an interview, he wrote, "What is your name?" The reporter, taken aback, voiced to those standing nearby, "Oh, I didn't know he could write!" Proving he could lipread too, Hoy snatched back the pad and wrote, "Yes, but I can't read."

Finally, we must acknowledge the contingent good fortune that gave Hoy a chance to develop his playing skills at all. Luckily, Hoy attended the Ohio School for the Deaf, and luckily his school became the first of its kind to institute baseball, sometime around 1870. In 1879, several players of the Ohio School organized the first semiprofessional deaf club, the Ohio Independent Baseball Team. They barnstormed through several eastern states, playing town clubs and even some National League teams. Major league baseball's other deaf star, pitcher Dummy Taylor, also graduated from the Ohio School for the Deaf.

His intelligence, independence, and education. Hoy played at a time when most players were semiliterate and lacked much formal education. Very few had ever attended college. (The great pitcher Christy Mathewson spent a few terms at Bucknell but never graduated. Still, and to this day, neither standard baseball prose nor Bucknell's promotional office will ever let you forget this tidbit.) Hoy never progressed beyond high school either, but his unusual literacy shines forth in the few letters, most written during his nineties, that the Hall of Fame Library in Cooperstown holds in its files. (One has to be familiar with the awkward and utterly ungrammatical prose of most early players to appreciate what a rare jewel these letters—and Hoy's equally articulate spontaneous testimonies—represent.)

But we needn't rely only on these documents. Contemporary accolades from Hoy's teammates and fans tell the same story. Thomas Lonegran, a St. Louis baseball historian, watched Hoy play throughout the 1891 season and remarked:

Hoy is one of the brainiest ballplayers I ever saw. . . . Hoy was as swift as a panther in the field. . . . I have seen balls hit for singles that would have been doubles or triples with other players fielding them. With men on bases, Hoy never threw to the wrong spot. No player ever returned a ball faster from the outfield. . . . Hoy was a "Cobb" on the bases. I never saw him picked off base. . . . Hoy, a deaf mute, didn't bother about coaches. He did his baserunning on his own. There'll never be another like him.

In an interview for his ninetieth birthday, Hoy recalled how he had used his own intelligence to make up for clues usually supplied by others:

> As to the yelling of my own coaches, that meant nothing to me. They meant well but I could not take my eyes off the ball in play to watch them. So I had to go solo. I was always mentally figuring in advance all possible plays on the bases and in the field.

I also wonder if Hoy's intelligence and pride (as well as his understanding of loneliness and the unfairness of labeling) can help to explain his restlessness in frequent moves between clubs, particularly his willingness, twice in his career, to jump from the established National League to "outlaw" groups (the Player's League, as defined by owners!) or "upstart" organizations (the American League at its inception in 1901). We do know that Hoy was one of the few early players willing to contest his tendered salary in public and to withhold signing in hopes for negotiation of a higher wage (in his age of limited options when the reserve clause forced a player to sign with his own club or not to play at all).

The success and prosperity of Hoy's later life also reflect his unusual intelligence and integrity. I was particularly touched by a small story told by Wahoo Sam Crawford about their post-baseball friendship:

> Another interesting thing about Dummy Hoy was the unique doorbell arrangement he had in his house. He had a wife who was a deaf mute too, and they lived in Cincinnati. Instead of a bell on the door, they had a little knob. When you pulled this knob it released a lead ball which rolled down a wooden chute and then fell off onto the floor with a thud. When it hit the floor they felt vibrations through their feet, and they knew somebody was at the door. I thought that was quite odd and interesting, don't you?

Above all, I love the wit and clarity of Hoy's letters over so many years. To cite just two examples from mid- and late life, Hoy wrote to the owner of the Cincinnati Reds in 1925, responding to an invitation sent to former players to join a celebration for the club's fiftieth anniversary: "Your invitation . . . is accepted with pleasure. Like all young players on the eve of a spring training trip, I am 'raring to go.'" After the event, Hoy wrote (and I quote his witty, if formal, note in full):

I wish to express to you and the Red directors my thanks and appreciation for the handsome manner in which you entertained us "oldtimers" yesterday.

The chance which the occasion afforded in the renewing of old acquaintances and the forming of new ones did us all much good, I assure you.

It was a good game we saw. It resulted in a win because we brought you good luck—probably.

We sure were surprised at the fine dining room you have up in the grand stand. Most of us did not know it existed. And the eats and drinks, and the smokes! As a host you have the job down fine and we take our hats off to you.

If the Reds would only play as well on the diamond as you entertain in the dining room, the pennant would be Cincinnati's easily.

On the day of his ninety-ninth birthday, May 23, 1960, Dummy Hoy wrote to his journalist friend J. M. Overfield:

Only a few days ago I decided to carry a walking stick, a stick I have been treasuring for 74 years, which I never used except the year it was presented to me by a bunch of Oshkosh baseball fans. Just why a walking stick was selected for a present is understandable because in the year 1886 the craze in the U.S. was the carrying by young people of slender bamboo sticks, priced at ten cents and up. They were put in cylinder containers, placed on the sidewalk in front of shops for the passerby to stop, select one, go inside and pay for his choice. Mine was and is a gold square-handled ebony cane, suitably engraved. The presentation ceremony was published in the Oshkosh newspapers of the period. I imagine the sporting editor of whatever paper it was would be surprised to learn that the centerfielder of the 1886 Oshkosh baseball club began his 99th year by carrying that same treasured stick for real aid in his walking.

His legends and their history. Standing in the way of history, but reflecting something precious about human foibles, legends inevitably arise about old-timers from supposedly golden ages, particularly players remembered for their excellences or eccentricities. Two particular legends both dog and surround Dummy Hoy—and I end with a short recitation in order to make an explicit point.

First, he did throw three runners out at the plate from the outfield in a single game in 1888—and only a handful of other players have ever accomplished this feat. We should, of course, mention and even highlight this peculiarity of genuinely superior fielding skills combined with the luck of odd circumstances in a single game. (Outfielders, no matter how good, rarely get three opportunities even to try for such long-distance assists in a single game.) But we make a terrible mistake—though the stuff of legends directs our focus to such oddly heroic events—when we write endlessly about single grand moments (partly fueled by luck) and neglect the daily grind of consummate play over many years. Who remembers Bill Wambsganss, a fine infielder over many seasons, for anything but his execution—an entirely automatic result of a purely lucky, but extremely rare, circumstance in this case—of an unassisted triple play in the 1920 World Series?

Second, nearly all popular sources state that Hoy initiated a ubiquitous, if minor, tradition of baseball practice ever since: the hand signals used by umpires to call balls and strikes. I suppose that the pathways of legend must conjure up stories to render the oddly contingent both purposeful and anecdotally touching—in short, to vest the origin of a general practice in a sensible and particular source. We should therefore always be wary of tales that sound so right. Perhaps the story is true, but best evidence indicates that the first umpire to use such signals did not enter baseball until 1905, two years after Hoy's retirement (although Hoy's teammates probably did signal him from the dugout, and perhaps with the same signs eventually adopted by umpires).

I stress these legends, and urge a proper placement in one case and a refutation in the other, in order to make a plea. Hoy's file in the Hall of Fame Library includes an extensive set of testimonials surrounding a campaign, still continuing, to persuade the Veteran's Committee to vote Dummy Hoy into the Hall of Fame. Most of these testimonials come from organizations of and for the deaf (Gallaudet College, among others) and—to put the matter diplomatically, but honestly—were obviously not written by people steeped in baseball history or current knowledge of the game. These letters continually emphasize the two "legendary" features of Hoy's career: his three putouts in one game and his role in inspiring the use of umpires' hand signals. One letter even states that Hoy belongs in the Hall solely because he initiated, however unwittingly, this custom that now occupies a space (albeit small) in the cultural knowledge of millions of Americans.

A real baseball fan, told that Hoy should be in the Hall of Fame for one great day or for possibly instigating one item of cultural history, will rightly laugh and dismiss the argument. Athletes belong in the Hall for sustained excellence in play—for career performance, not momentary happenstance. Citing a legend only obscures the real point—or even suggests (to folks who do not consult the actual records) that the player in question fails to pass muster by the proper criterion. But Dummy Hoy belongs in the Hall of Fame by sole virtue of his excellent, sustained play over a long career. His case seems undeniable to me. A dozen players from Hoy's time have been elected with records no better than the exemplary statistics—particularly the great fielding and savvy base running, not to mention the more than adquate hitting—of Dummy Hoy.

I have tried not to stress Hoy's deafness in citing his virtues throughout this essay, but one final point about his disability does underscore the un-kindest cut of all: his absence from the Hall of Fame. I suspect that Hoy's deafness did deprive him of a necessary tool for the later renown that gets men into the Hall by sustained reputation. As mentioned earlier, Hoy never received much press coverage. Journalists refrained from interview-ing him, even though he was the smartest and most articulate player in baseball. So Hoy was forgotten after he left the field, and his fierce pride prevented any effort at self-promotion. His inbuilt silence abetted the un-just silence of others.

I therefore end with one last example of Hoy's wit—again from the let-ter written on his ninety-ninth birthday:

> I am finding it harder and harder to write, to think, to decide on anything, or to act properly. In short, I am rapidly slowing up.

Let us therefore decide on one thing, and thereby enshrine Dummy Hoy for whatever eternity means in baseball. Dummy Hoy belongs in the Hall of Fame for his playing skills alone (while his inspirational dignity, keen intelligence, sparkling wit, and sustained courage should place him in the first rank of any pantheon devoted to forgotten heroes). Only then will we break the circle of silence that still surrounds this savvy, wonderfully skilled, and exemplary man who also happened to be deaf, while devoting his life to a sport never well played by ear.

John McLuckie: Burgess of Homestead

DAVID BRODY

Homestead, Pennsylvania, in 1892 was a town under siege, and John McLuckie, the town's burgess (or mayor), was at the center of the swirling conflict. On one side was the Amalgamated Association of Iron and Steel Workers, a union to which McLuckie belonged and which had the strong support of the predominantly working-class community. On the other was the steel baron Andrew Carnegie and his second in command, Henry Clay Frick, both determined to break the union. In the end, the working people of Homestead were no match for the combined power of the Carnegie Steel Corporation and the state militia. In retrospect, their defeat at Homestead marked the beginning of the end for trade unionism in the iron and steel industry. For John McLuckie, the personal costs of his heroic stand were high.

PITTSBURGH SITS at the confluence of the Allegheny and Monongahela rivers, where they join to form the Ohio River. The Monongahela runs southeasterly from the city's point, and there, for twenty miles along its banks, Pittsburgh's famed steel district once flourished. Today almost nothing remains of the blast furnaces and rolling mills, just miles of rubble-strewn fields waiting for the developers. But a hundred years ago the great mills—Homestead, the Edgar Thomson, Duquesne—exemplified American industrialism at its mightiest, capable of producing half as much steel as all of Great Britain and so profitable that they made Andrew Carnegie's immense fortune.

At one of those mills, in 1892, there occurred an extraordinary labor strike. The word *strike* does not quite capture the event, since the dispute took on the character of civil war, pitting the town of Homestead against America's most powerful corporation and the great Commonwealth of Pennsylvania. In that contest, Homestead was bound to be crushed, and it was. Also crushed was the resolute man who served as the town's mayor, the burgess of Homestead, John McLuckie.

McLuckie was forty years old in 1892. He was born in Elizabeth, a Monongahela river town, and probably never got beyond grade school. He became a miner, working in the mid-1870s at Turtle Creek, in the hills above Duquesne. He then went into the steel mills, first the Edgar Thomson in Braddock, then Bellaire, Ohio, and, in 1887, back to Homestead. He advanced there no higher than semiskilled hand in the converting mill; he testified that he earned between sixty and sixty-five dollars a month. In Homestead, where home ownership was common, McLuckie and his wife rented. But there was more to McLuckie than his work history.

A surviving photograph shows him somberly attired, with winged collar, wire-rim glasses, carefully barbered, for all the world an American bourgeois. And that, indeed, was how McLuckie meant to be taken—not as a worker, but as a citizen, and as good as anyone else. This was the essence of what historians have labeled labor republicanism, and it supplied McLuckie with the language of protest that infused his life. He was forever bent on fighting the evil forces that sought "to deprive the workingmen of their rights under the constitution of this government—those of life, liberty and the pursuit of happiness."

The politics of labor republicanism swept him up at an early age. In 1876 he ran (unsuccessfully) for the state legislature on the Greenback ticket, and was never after absent from the labor reform movements roiling the steel district. He helped organize the great Pittsburgh demonstration of 1882 that became Labor Day, ran (hopelessly) for the state senate that year, took part in the Knights of Labor, and was a Bellaire city councilman. But unlike so many of his fellow labor reformers, McLuckie had no eye for the main chance. He was not one to make a timely party switch, or parlay his popularity into a patronage job, or profit at all from his politics. He made his living in the mills. That fact was not lost on the citizens of Homestead. "Honest John," they called him when they elected him burgess—the town's governing official—in 1890, and again, in 1892.

That a worker might serve as burgess said something about Homestead. Homestead was a strong union town, dominated by the Amalgamated Association of Iron and Steel Workers. The Amalgamated was an archetypal craft union, with its roots among the puddlers and rollers of the older iron mills, but now strongly entrenched as well among the skilled tonnage workers in the steel industry. Of the thirty-eight hundred employees in the Homestead mill, only eight hundred were permitted into the Amalgamated lodges. The excluded workers, the common laborers and furnacemen, consisted mainly of Slovaks, part of the first wave of eastern Europeans who would come by the millions to America in the years before World War I. In Homestead, as elsewhere, their arrival provoked a fierce nativist reaction, orchestrated locally by the politically active Junior Order of United American Mechanics. Craft unions often succumbed to nativism, but in Homestead the universalist principles of the Knights of Labor still held sway. McLuckie, in fact, ran against nativist candidates and, by resoundingly defeating them, redeemed the Knights' pledge of working-class unity. Despite the craft divisions, there existed among Homestead steelworkers strong ties of sympathy and solidarity. And with its government in labor's hands, Homestead came as close as any place in America to being a workers' republic.

But Homestead's economy was not in labor's hands, and the owner, the Carnegie Steel Company, was bent on expelling the Amalgamated from the Homestead works. There was no real secret on that score. McLuckie himself had been in the thick of the union's earlier wars with the company. He had been a striker at Carnegie's Edgar Thomson mill when the Amalgamated had been beaten there in 1882, and it may have been for that reason that he had left Braddock for Bellaire. In 1889, when the company had tried to dislodge the Homestead union, McLuckie had taken charge of the pickets policing the shut-down plant. The Amalgamated won that battle, but as the contract came up for renewal in 1892, prospects looked bleaker. For one thing, much new machinery had been installed that could be operated by inexperienced workers. For another, the market for steel was now slack. And it was an ominous sign that plate was being feverishly stockpiled for the company's big armor contract with the navy.

The great imponderable, however, was Andrew Carnegie. Carnegie was formidable in business—a ferocious competitor, an implacable driver of his subordinates. He loved making money and detested the crimp placed on his profits by collective bargaining. (He had, unbeknown to the Homestead workers, already decided on a break with the union.) But Carnegie also fancied himself a public figure and benefactor. He was proud of his radical Chartist origins, boasted of his sympathies for the workingman and trade unionism, and had famously pronounced it immoral for an employer to replace striking workers with scabs. This last was of the highest importance to the Homestead workers, for they knew that everything in the impending battle would turn on whether scabs came in. They thought they could wait the company out if the plant stayed down. They had some faith in Old Andy and, at any rate, doubted that he had the stomach to spill blood for the sake of profits.

The man actually in charge most certainly did have the stomach. This was Henry Clay Frick, a coal baron who had become Carnegie's partner and was now operating head of the firm. Frick still answered to Carnegie, but in April Carnegie left for Scotland, where he secluded himself on the remote Loch Rannoch until the storm blew over. Frick and his associates were glad to see Carnegie go; now they could handle the affair with the gloves off. Frick's first move was to have erected around the mill a high wooden fence, with portholes suitable for rifles. Then he engaged with the Pinkerton National Detective Agency for three hundred operatives, who at the right moment would be brought in by boat under cover of darkness to secure the mill and prepare it for strikebreakers. Frick's stance toward the union was not, as Carnegie had proposed, to announce an open break, but rather to take so implacatory a bargaining position that there could not fail to be a strike.

In Homestead the workers girded for battle. At a packed rally at the opera house on June 19, McLuckie spoke: "It is Sunday morning, and we ought to be in church, but we are here to-day to see if we are going to live as white men* in the future. The constitution of this country guarantees all men the right to live, but in order to live we must keep a continuous struggle."

Contract negotiations, as Frick had planned, broke down, and on June 28, after posting notices that henceforth it would deal only with individual workers, the company shut down two departments operated by union tonnage workers, so that the dispute technically began as a lockout. Many unskilled workers followed the union men out, and the next day, June 29, the entire works closed down. The strike was on.

With McLuckie's willing collaboration, the government of Homestead effectively passed into the hands of a union-appointed Advisory Committee, which immediately stationed patrols at the entrances to the town and on the river, posted pickets around the works, and warned the saloons to discourage drunkenness on pain of being closed down. McLuckie was informed that as many men as he needed to preserve order would be available to him. On July 5, at Frick's request, the sheriff of Allegheny County attempted to take possession of the mill on behalf of the company. His deputies were met that afternoon by McLuckie and Hugh O'Donnell, the chairman of the Advisory Committee and, in the company of a great crowd of steelworkers and their wives, escorted out of town. In thus resisting constituted authority, McLuckie believed he was upholding a higher authority: "We have our homes in this town, we have our churches here, our societies and our cemeteries here. We are bound to Homestead by all the ties that men hold dearest and most sacred." In that cause, the strikers prepared themselves for the Pinkertons they knew were coming.

During the night of July 6, a lookout in Pittsburgh spotted two barges being pushed upriver toward Homestead. By 4 a.m., the townspeople were out in force, shooting sporadically at the barges making their way along the shore to the mill, and smashing through Frick's fence at the river's edge to confront the Pinkertons as the barges came aground at the company landing. At this point, the Advisory Committee gained some control over the crowd, holding them back and pleading for calm. There was a tense parley

---

* Modern readers will be jarred by McLuckie's racism. They should bear in mind that it reflected the racism ingrained in nineteenth-century culture, but also, in this particular instance, McLuckie's expectation that blacks would be brought in as strikebreakers, which, in fact, they were.

with the Pinkertons. An escorted committee might be permitted to make an inspection, O'Donnell shouted, but under no circumstances could the Pinkertons come ashore and take forcible possession of the works. That was his intention, responded the captain, directing that the gangplank be put down for his men to disembark. There was a melee; shots rang out, wounding the Pinkerton captain and a union leader confronting him, and then a murderous barrage from both sides. After ten minutes, the firing ceased, and an uneasy calm descended, but at least a dozen on each side lay wounded or dead (O'Donnell himself escaping with a grazed thumb). Burgess McLuckie issued proclamations closing the saloons and calling on the citizens to help him preserve order, which, in the circumstances, did not mean they should lay down their arms. The union headquarters was now in a frenzy of activity, distributing donated weapons to strikers, and at the battle scene a barricade of steel scrap was hastily being erected.

At 8 a.m., the Pinkertons made a second foray and were again driven back, with more casualties on both sides. For the rest of the day, the firing continued, interspersed with ineffectual efforts by the strikers to blow up or burn the barges. Late in the afternoon, the beaten Pinkertons raised a white flag and surrendered to O'Donnell. Despite his promise of safe passage, their escorts could not shield the Pinkertons from a gauntlet of blows and curses as they made their way to the opera house. At the entrance there was a tense standoff with a crowd of Slovak men and women bent on vengeance for a fallen compatriot, which was resolved only by McLuckie's arrival with assurances that the Pinkertons would be locked up and tried for murder. That, in fact, was the general expectation among Homesteaders. Instead, the Pinkertons, many of them temporarily hired without knowing what they had signed on for, were put on trains and shipped out of state. It seemed not to have occurred to the strikers that, when it came to the question of murder, they were the ones at risk.

For the moment, however, the uppermost concern of the authorities was upholding the company's rights of property. The last thing Frick wanted was for repossession of the mill to be drawn into his dispute with the Amalgamated. The company's rights were absolute, Frick insisted; the state's duty was to enforce those rights. On July 10, the Republican governor finally obliged him and called out the entire state militia—a well-trained force of eight thousand, thoroughly revamped after the great railroad riots of 1877, and reputedly the best National Guard unit in the country. The people of

Homestead put the best face they could on this news. At an opera house rally, McLuckie welcomed the governor's decision, adding that "any man who insults the militia shall be taken to the river and ducked." To general cheers, a motion to that effect was carried unanimously. McLuckie retired to his house to compose an appropriate speech, and the town's brass bands began to prepare for the formal reception of the troops.

The commanding general, George R. Snowden, had other ideas. He regarded Homestead as hostile ground to be occupied and acted accordingly, bringing in his units unexpectedly and in force early on July 13 and deploying them rapidly on Shanty Hill commanding the town. By mid-morning, the bemused citizens of Homestead could look up and see four thousand soldiers arrayed in battle formation, and across the river, glinting in the sun, the barrels of artillery trained on the steel works. General Snowden brusquely dismissed the citizens' delegation that waited on him. The best thing they could do was go home and behave themselves, he said. From that moment, Burgess McLuckie's authority effectively ended. And ended too was the Amalgamated's battle to keep the mill down. With the town under military rule and the works closely guarded, the company began to bring in nonunion workers and slowly resume production.

The union's only hope now was the Republican party. It was 1892, an election year, with President Benjamin Harrison locked in a tight race against the Democrat, Grover Cleveland. The big issue of the day was the protective tariff, which Republicans espoused as the protector of the American wage earner. McLuckie, addressing his fellow workers, castigated them for their foolishness: "You men who voted the Republican ticket voted for high tariff and you get high fences, Pinkerton detectives, thugs and militia!" McLuckie's charge, with its marvelously quotable line about high tariffs and high fences, made Republican leaders sweat; the vice-presidential candidate, Whitelaw Reid of the *New York Tribune*, thought the Homestead strike could cost his party the election. On July 17, the Advisory Committee sent O'Donnell to New York to seek Reid's intercession with Carnegie.

But before Reid could find Carnegie in Scotland, Frick was shot on July 23 by the anarchist Alexander Berkman. Berkman had no connection to the strike; by killing Frick, he thought he was striking a blow for the revolution. The indomitable Frick survived, staying at his desk after his wounds had been treated until he finished his work. Before being taken home, Frick issued a statement that no matter what happened to him, the company's stand against the union was irrevocable, "and it will win." Carnegie in fact wavered when he received Reid's plea for a settlement, but he could not have gone against the wounded Frick. Other union men expressed shock over the assassination attempt, but not McLuckie. "This man Frick sent a lot of thugs and cut-throats into the peaceful village of Homestead, over which I have the honor to preside as burgess, and they murdered my friends and fellow citizens."

If there was a personal edge to McLuckie's bitterness, it was with good reason. He had just emerged on bail from jail, charged, along with other members of the Advisory Committee, with the murders of the Pinkertons' T. J. Connors and Silas Wain. This was the beginning of the company's end game: a barrage of criminal charges would break the strikers' spirit and immobilize their leaders. McLuckie was not cowed. When O'Donnell, flailing about, fell for the suggestion by Republican leaders that a deal was still possible if only McLuckie shut up about high tariffs and high fences, the burgess was indignant: he was not for sale to the politicians. And he undertook to beat the company at its own game by bringing murder charges against Frick and other Carnegie officials.

But in a battle of bail bonds, it was no contest. The company kept a supply of blank forms that were filled out and sent to the court as needed. In September the arrest warrants mounted up: murder, conspiracy, aggravated assault, even, at an extraordinary session of the state supreme court, treason. With bail funds exhausted, strike leaders went to jail or into hiding. McLuckie left for Youngstown, Ohio. On November 7, as the strike was finally collapsing, he resigned as burgess. The charges against him were dropped when it became clear, after the trials of O'Donnell and two others, that no Pittsburgh jury was likely to convict the Homestead strikers. But McLuckie was jobless and blacklisted. The next year a sympathetic journalist reported him to be lecturing a bit, trying his hand at "sundry small ventures," and managing to "keep his head above water," but handicapped by being forced "from the familiar pursuits of a lifetime into new and untried fields." And then McLuckie dropped from sight.

Some years later, in 1900, a friend of Carnegie's, Professor John C. Van Dyke, was staying at a remote ranch in the Sonora Mountains. There among the Mexicans and local Indians, he encountered a lone North

American. It was McLuckie, down on his luck and looking for work in the nearby mines. He talked freely about the Homestead strike, still fixed in his conviction that he had been right to resist the invasion of his town by the Pinkertons. McLuckie declined Van Dyke's subsequent offer of money, but, evidently with the professor's help, landed a job driving wells for the Sonora Railroad. After some months, Van Dyke saw McLuckie again in Guaymas, where he was supervising the repair of his equipment at the railway yards. "He was much changed for the better, seemed happy, and to add to his contentment, had taken unto himself a Mexican wife." And there the book closes on John McLuckie.

Except for this postscript. For Andrew Carnegie, the Homestead strike had been "the trial of my life (death's hand excepted)." Nothing had "wounded me so deeply," wounded, that is, in the public's esteem for him. Carnegie was excoriated in the press, shunned by liberal friends and, altogether, regarded (in the words of one embittered Republican congressman) as "the arch-sneak of this age." Not one to crawl away, Carnegie set about repairing things as best he could. On returning home in January 1893, he traveled directly to Homestead, where he read a prepared speech to the assembled workers and, as he reported afterward, "shook hands with the old men, tears in their eyes & mine. Oh, that Homestead blunder." In 1898 he gave to Homestead a fine library (which he had withheld while it was a union town). But Carnegie sought his absolution, most particularly, from John McLuckie.

It happened that Van Dyke's offer of money to McLuckie had, in fact, been Carnegie's offer. When Van Dyke revealed this to him in Guaymas, McLuckie exclaimed (according to Van Dyke): "Well, that was damned white of Andy, wasn't it?" In his autobiography, Carnegie says that he "would rather risk that verdict of McLuckie's as a passport to Paradise than all the theological dogmas invented by man." Thus we have the irony that Carnegie, the victor, needed McLuckie's benediction, while McLuckie, the vanquished, wanted nothing of Carnegie. As Carnegie's biographer, Joseph Frazier Wall, remarked about McLuckie's refusal of Carnegie's money, McLuckie had lost everything but his pride.

Florence Kelley:
Campaigns against Sweatshops
in the 1890s

KATHRYN KISH SKLAR

"Everyone was brave from the moment she came into the room," observed Newton Baker of Florence Kelley, crusader for social justice and longtime president (1899-1932) of the National Consumers' League. Kelley typifies a generation of Progressive era women reformers, many affiliated with Jane Addams and Hull-House in Chicago, who worked heroically to raise public awareness about the terrible working conditions in sweatshops, mills, and plants and then lobbied for legislation to correct those ills. Kelley's long-term impact on labor standards suggests the role that women reformers played in laying the foundation for the modern welfare state.

SWEATSHOPS, where exploited workers toil to produce garments or other commodities under unsanitary, sometimes life-threatening conditions, continue to exist, even though such employment practices are now illegal under municipal, state, and federal regulations. That was not the case a century ago. The drive to regulate sweatshop working conditions required the cooperation of many groups and individuals, but the most prominent leader of that campaign in the United States was a forgotten hero named Florence Kelley. In Chicago in the 1890s, she devised a strategy that eventually came to dominate legislative remedies for sweatshop labor. Kelley used hours legislation for women as an opening wedge: since sweatshops depended on women's labor, she reasoned, passage and enforcement of an eight-hour day would drive sweatshops out of business because their inefficient methods could not produce profits except through longer hours.

Florence Kelley's innovation required three talents on her part: an ability to understand gender as a principle of social and economic organization, an ability to analyze the causes and consequences of sweatshop labor, and an ability to translate these two skills into a workable political program. She arrived in Chicago in 1891 with the first two skills well developed. Thanks to the community of women reformers at Hull-House, she found it possible to demonstrate the third.

Like many other girls, Florence Kelley identified with her father, a dominant and, in her eyes, heroic figure. William Darrah Kelley, reelected to the U.S. House of Representatives for fifteen consecutive terms between 1860, a year after Florence's birth, and his death in 1890, was a Radical Republican who represented a working-class district in Philadelphia. A champion of the political rights of freedmen, more than any other Republican following the Civil War he strove to create a biracial political party in the South. When his party abandoned this cause, he bolted ranks and supported free silver.

By the time she graduated from Cornell University in 1882, Florence Kelley knew that her gender prevented her from following in his footsteps, but she had developed a clear alternative: championing the interests of women and children wage earners. After the University of Pennsylvania rejected her for graduate study because she was a woman, Kelley attended the University of Zurich, the first European university to grant graduate degrees to women. When Susan B. Anthony, a close friend of her father, wrote to ask her to enlist in the cause of woman suffrage, she replied that she was "humiliated that my country does not confer upon me a responsibility to which I feel myself adequate, just as I am mortified that the universities of America are closed to me," but "when my student life is over, I shall give myself to work for the best interests of the working women of America, as my Father has given himself to work for the best interests of the country."

Kelley was not simply a female version of her father, however. She had developed her own view of social injustice, which, combined with her anger over the limitations placed on her gender, meant that upon arriving in Zurich, her conscience was "tinder awaiting a match." German socialism supplied that match. As if acting out her need to find a complete alternative to her father's political culture, in 1884 she converted to socialism and sealed the deal by marrying Lazare Wischnewetzky, a Jewish, Russian, socialist medical student. During the next three years she gave birth to three children and stopped speaking to her Philadelphia family. Translating and later publishing the first English edition of Fredrick Engels' *Condition of the Working Class in England,* she became one of the most knowledgeable American students of the writings of Karl Marx and Fredrick Engels. Her own sense of her place in the political process changed as she became dedicated to the idea that intellectuals could reduce the violence of the coming revolution by promoting an understanding of industrial capitalism and providing peaceful remedies for its injustices.

Not surprisingly, perhaps, when Kelley returned to the United States with her young family and settled in New York in 1886, she failed to find a political foothold. The Socialist Labor party, a German-speaking group with no fondness for defiant Yankee women or for the writings of Marx and Engels, expelled her and Lazare for "incessant slander" against the party's leaders. When Lazare's medical practice languished, the couple repaired their relationship with her family and sought loans. Then Lazare became abusive, once bruising her face so badly that she was confined indoors for weeks. Kelley studied state child labor laws and their enforcement by state bureaus of labor, her criticisms bringing her to the attention of Carroll Wright, U.S. commissioner of labor, but otherwise she drifted ever deeper into political, social, and personal isolation.

Shortly after Christmas 1891, Kelley responded to Lazare's abuse by borrowing train fare from a governess friend at a local park and fled with the children to Chicago, where an editor for the Woman's Temperance Press knew and respected her work on child labor. That editor advised her to seek refuge at Hull-House, the innovative social settlement founded by Jane Addams and Ellen Starr in 1889. Addams welcomed her as if she had been invited and helped her arrange to board the children—Nicholas, age seven; Margaret, age six; and John, age five—in the suburban Winnetka home of wealthy reformers and Hull-House supporters, Henry Demarest Lloyd and Jessie Bross Lloyd.

In a letter to Engels, Kelley described Hull-House as "a colony of efficient and intelligent women living in a working men's quarter with the house used for all sorts of purposes by about a thousand persons a week." She was "learning more in a week of the actual conditions of proletarian life in America than in any previous year." One activity was the formation of unions "of which we have three, the cloak-makers, the shirt makers, and the book makers." She concluded on a note that mixed personal and professional perspectives. "I have found friends and an opportunity to work for the support of my little children; and I hope to be able to resume work among the wage earners." Yet Kelley missed her children, whom she never lived with under the same roof again, "with a perennial heartache."

At Hull-House Kelley's views began to change. Her socialism became "English," meaning gradual rather than revolutionary and achieved through legislation designed to benefit working people. Being a woman suddenly seemed an advantage, as she joined a community based on the belief that women could make important contributions to solving social problems. At night she attended law school, determined to acquire the skills needed to shape public policy.

"Wirepulling" by Jane Addams gave Kelley the opportunity to put her new insights into practice. Five months after her arrival, she was appointed as a special agent of the Illinois Bureau of Labor Statistics. Responsible for researching and writing a two-part report on working women in Chicago and the city's sweatshop system, she gained a street-smart knowledge of sweatshop life. The work required her to conduct a "house to house canvass, from 9 o'clock in the morning until 7 at night," of between nine hundred and a thousand workplaces and homes.

With scientific and scholarly precision, her report documented the causes and consequences of "the sweating system" in Chicago's garment industry. The pressure of competition forced conscientious manufacturers either to contract work out or leave the business. Outwork subdivided tasks so minutely that no skills were required, making workers easily replaced and unionization impossible. Shops changed location constantly to evade city health authorities, and "cooking, sleeping, sewing, and nursing of the sick" took place in the same room. Most tellingly, wages steadily declined to the point that workers had to appeal to charity to support themselves. Payroll records showed, for example, that the wages of one woman, who had once earned $3.75 weekly, fell in successive weeks to $1.50, not enough to support herself, let alone her family.

Kelley's report recommended a wide range of legislation to remedy such conditions, all of which required strong enforcement mechanisms by the state. Her belief in the efficacy of government contrasted with the position of the Chicago Trade and Labor Assembly, which in 1891 had asked Elizabeth Morgan, British trade unionist and wife of perennial socialist candidate, Tommy Morgan, to survey Chicago's sweatshops and recommend solutions. Although Morgan's report documented shocking conditions, it offered a weak analysis of the causes creating sweatshops and proposed ineffective methods to eliminate them. Pointing to the "hordes of the offscouring of Southern Europe entering this country," her study traced sweatshops to the unscrupulous among them who planted "in this free land the industrial conditions common under the despotic governments of Europe." She recommended only the implementation of existing sanitation ordinances and, doubting that this would be done by city officials, urged the Trade and Labor Assembly to create "a Bureau of Sanitation" of its own "to which all violations of the health laws might be reported." The assembly would then inform the "general public."

Chicago labor leaders were skeptical about political solutions to labor problems. And why not? They were painfully aware that they could not retain the loyalty of elected officials who came from their own ranks. In part this was due to the ability of the Democratic and Republican parties to determine electoral outcomes through fraud. (In 1885 a grand jury investigation found that only seven of the city's 171 precincts did not show violations of election laws.) Political leaders in working-class neighborhoods were easily co-opted, ultimately remaining loyal to party officials responsible for their reelection rather than to their electoral constituencies. Moreover, by one crucial measure, ethnic representation, city government was demonstrably democratic; the first Italian was elected to the city council in 1885.

Some labor leaders disagreed with the apolitical stance of the Chicago Trade and Labor Assembly on sweatshops, however, and supported Kelley's more vigorous approach. Abraham Bisno, a young organizer in the garment industry, became one of her staunchest allies. He was part of the group that Kelley assembled at Hull-House in the spring of 1893 to draft antisweatshop legislation. Also present were Henry Demarest Lloyd and Clarence Darrow.

In one of the most remarkable developments in Illinois politics during the 1890s, a reform coalition swept to power in the election of 1892, capturing the governor's office for John Peter Altgeld and bringing new faces into the Illinois legislature. This legislature passed the Hull-House bill. In addition to prohibiting the labor of children under age fourteen and regulating the labor of children ages fourteen to sixteen, this bill included two pathbreaking measures: it limited women's working hours to eight a day, and it provided for the most effective enforcement office in the United States—a chief factory inspector, an assistant factory inspector, and ten deputies, five of whom were required to be women. Altgeld asked Florence Kelley to serve as chief factory inspector because, he explained, "the sweatshop agitation was done by women."

Nowhere else in the Western world was a woman trusted to enforce the labor legislation of a city, let alone of a large industrial region the size of Illinois. Kelley's first step was a smart one: she located her office across the street from Hull-House, symbolizing the steady support she drew from that community.

During her four years as factory inspector, Kelley developed a reform strategy that characterized her work thereafter. Aware of the systemic relationships among diverse industrial conditions affecting working women and children (such as long hours, low wages, unsanitary conditions, rapid turnover, and weak unions), she focused on key ingredients that had the power to alter the whole setting. In this way, her efforts became less like a laundry list of needed changes and more like an engine, which, once started, generated other changes.

She quickly expanded and consolidated the territory under her control by soliciting a ruling from the Illinois attorney general that the child labor and eight-hour provisions of the 1893 law be applied to every factory and workshop in the state, not just those in tenements. His decision that key sections of the law were "general in their application" brought all Illinois manufacturing under her scrutiny.

In writing the 1893 legislation, Kelley had carefully drawn on her legal training to provide for the power "to prosecute all violations . . . in any court of competent jurisdiction in this State," so she could and did sidestep any uncooperative district attorney. She closely oversaw prosecutions; her office won most of their child labor cases.

Kelley knew, however, that it would be very difficult for her eight-hour law to succeed. She knew that court rulings would overturn legislation that directly prohibited tenement manufacturing. Her indirect approach of limiting women's working hours was an experimental strategy that had to overcome two obstacles: lack of support from those the act sought to aid (young women workers) and court opposition. To recruit support from young women workers, she addressed their main complaint about the law—that shorter hours might mean reduced wages—by aiding their organization into unions. Union workers, like Abraham Bisno, negotiated a "just price" for piecework with their employers, which indirectly negotiated a "just price" for a day's work and a fair length to the working day. On the basis of their greater productivity in factories instead of sweatshops, union members could prevent shorter hours from translating into reduced wages. Therefore Kelley and her staff focused on union organizing. Three of her staff—her assistant, Alzina Stevens, Abraham Bisno, and Mary Kenney—were well-known union organizers. "Three of my deputies and my assistant are . . . active in agitation," she wrote Engels. "I was fanatical almost to blindness," Bisno later wrote. The conservative *Chicago Tribune* complained, "Most of these inspectors are trying everywhere to organize unions among employes, undertaking a general organization of unorganized labor in this city."

Ultimately, however, Kelley knew that her strategy of using laws for women as a surrogate for laws protecting all workers required approval by the courts, and in this arena she lost. In an 1895 decision, the Illinois Supreme Court ruled in favor of employers who argued that the state's hours law for women unconstitutionally deprived them of the right to work as long as they chose.

Although this most radical feature of Florence Kelley's attack on sweatshop labor was blocked by the court, her ideas found success later. In 1908 her efforts at the National Consumers' League (NCL) established the constitutionality of state hours laws for women, followed by state hours laws for men in 1917. Others built on her work by incorporating an eight-hours law for women and men in the Fair Labor Standards Act of 1938. In the long run, her strategy of using legislation covering only women as an opening wedge to win protection for all workers succeeded.

In the short run, however, Kelley was out of a job. In 1897 Altgeld was defeated for reelection, and his successor replaced the troublesome factory inspector with a man who cooperated with sweatshop employers. In 1899 Kelley moved to New York to head the NCL, a position she held until her death in 1932.

By the time she left Hull-House, Kelley had become, in the words of one resident, "the toughest customer in the reform riot, the finest rough-and-tumble fighter for the good life for others, that Hull House ever knew. Any weapon was a good weapon in her hand—evidence, argument, irony or invective." Her struggle against sweatshops was life-long, and although she lost this Chicago battle, she went on to fight again at the national level. Under her direction, the NCL became the nation's largest and most effective advocate of labor legislation for women and children.

In New York, Kelley lived at Lillian Wald's Henry Street Settlement on Manhattan's Lower East Side and applied what she had learned from her Chicago struggles to the larger national scene: the process of eliminating sweatshop labor required vigorous state enforcement, which politics-as-usual was not always able to provide. Women's voluntary organizations filled the gap left by weak labor organizations, traditions of limited government, and competitive marketplace economics.

Although attorneys like Louis Brandeis and Felix Frankfurter argued NCL cases to successful conclusions before the Supreme Court, the story of the battle against sweatshops in the United States is one that features the cooperation of thousands of women, as well as one remarkable woman: Florence Kelley.

George Dewey:
Naval Hero and Political Disaster

JUSTIN KAPLAN

*Admiral George Dewey blazed into national consciousness
with his stunning naval victory at Manila Bay in the Philippines
in 1898, a spectactular culmination to the Spanish-American
War. (Secretary of State John Hay memorably characterized it
as a "splendid little war.") On Dewey's return to the United
States the next year, he received a true hero's welcome: parades, memorials, congressional honors, tributes in song and
prose. Did all this adulation go to his head? His disastrous attempt to translate his military success into a political career suggests that it did, and reminds us that heroism can be fleeting
even for the living.*

IN SEPTEMBER 1899 the nation welcomed back to its shores the first conquering hero of the Spanish-American War, George Dewey. A year and a half earlier, from the bridge of his flagship, the cruiser *Olympia*, he had commanded an attack on an enemy fleet in Manila Bay. "Remember the *Maine*, and down with Spain!" was the battle cry of his gunners. In a four-hour engagement on the morning of May 1, 1898, without losing a ship or a man (except for an engineer who died of heat prostration), Dewey's Asiatic Squadron fired off nearly six thousand shells, destroyed ten Spanish vessels, inflicted about four hundred casualties, and captured the crucial naval station at Cavite. At one point in the engagement, Dewey ordered the squadron to cease firing, withdraw for breakfast, and then return to the attack. "I control [Manila Bay] completely," he cabled to Washington, "and can take the city at any time."

Dewey's battle order to his captain on the conning tower of the *Olympia*, "You may fire when you are ready, Gridley," immediately became as famous as David Farragut's "Damn the torpedoes!" at Mobile Bay and Horatio Nelson's signal at Trafalgar, "England expects every man will do his duty." Newspapers called the battle "The Greatest Naval Engagement of Modern Times" and compared it to Nelson's victory over the French fleet in the Mediterranean a hundred years earlier. Given the pathetic condition of the outgunned and mostly unarmored Spanish fleet, however, Dewey's victory was more like a turkey shoot. According to some accounts, the Spanish admiral, Patricio Montojo, had fully expected defeat and chose a shallow anchorage for his battle group so that his men could cling to the rigging when their ships went down instead of drowning.

A "splendid little war . . . favored by that fortune which loves the brave," as John Hay described it to Theodore Roosevelt, was off to a splendid start. Dewey's triumph at Manila Bay in effect put an end to the Spanish empire and established the United States as a major world power with farflung territorial interests. A year later, President William McKinley told a delegation of clergymen that through prayer he discovered as a God-given truth that it was America's mission "to educate the Filipinos, and uplift them and civilize and Christianize them." He ordered the chief engineer of the War Department to put the vexed Philippine Islands on the map of the United States, "and there they are, and there they will stay while I am President!" Dewey was the proconsul of this new American possession. Its ungrateful natives—William Howard Taft called them "little brown brothers"—were soon waging a guerrilla war of independence against their benefactors.

Dewey had been fortunate, he recalled fifteen years later in the opening sentence of his *Autobiography*, "to be in command on May 1, 1898, of an American squadron in the first important naval action against a foreign foe since the War of 1812." At Manila Bay he accomplished something notable in his line of work, but that had been his moment. It was the chief blunder of Dewey's life that he allowed public adulation of him as a war hero to beguile him into extending the moment to peacetime civil and electoral affairs, and so beyond the limits of his own capabilities. A literal-minded, face-value, full-speed-ahead sort of man, apparently unacquainted with self-doubt and irony, he proved to be a political ignoramus with a distinctly peculiar understanding of the American presidency.

Dewey held the rank of commodore when he led his squadron into Manila Bay. Promoted to rear admiral immediately after, he was now admiral of the navy, a rank and grade revived in his honor and designated by Congress, to be held by him alone and abolished after his death. (Only the president, as commander in chief, was his superior.) "Towns, children, and articles of commerce were named after me," he wrote. "I was assured that nothing like the enthusiasm for a man and a deed had ever been known. . . . My career as a hard-working naval officer scarcely equipped me for a role as the central figure of public applause. On the 30th of April, 1898, I had been practically unknown to the general public. In a day my name was on every one's lips." "Oh, dewy was the morning, Upon the first of May," an immensely popular song began, "And Dewey was the Admiral, Down in Manila Bay."

His entry into New York City on September 28, 1899, was like the triumphs ancient Rome granted emperors and generals returning from foreign conquests. Dewey's flagship led a naval procession two and a half miles long up the Hudson River and anchored opposite Grant's Tomb. Later, reviewing a parade of thirty-five thousand marchers through Madison Square at the intersection of Broadway, Fifth Avenue, and Twenty-fourth Street, he stood under the newly erected Dewey Triumphal Arch, "perhaps the most complex memorial ever proposed in the United States," according to architectural historian Robert A. M. Stern. The collaborative work of about thirty leading sculptors and muralists, it emulated the Arch of Titus in Rome, the Arch of Triumph in Paris, and Stanford White's Washington

Memorial Arch in New York. The creators of this imperial confection embellished it in pseudo-rococo, wedding cake style and set it off with a block-long colonnade. As yet only a full-scale temporary structure of wood and plaster, the arch was to be replaced, so the plans ran, by a permanent structure of granite and marble paid for by public subscription. The proposed fund tapped the same vein of adulation that had already yielded, from the pockets of the city's schoolchildren, seventy thousand silver dimes melted down to make a loving cup for the admiral. That night, while he was being feted at a reception at the Waldorf-Astoria, the city's premier social venue, an electric sign on the Brooklyn Bridge blazed the words, "Welcome Dewey," and fireworks traced in the sky a thousand-square-foot portrait of the hero.

In Washington a few days later, Dewey took the salute of another great parade. President McKinley and his cabinet presented him with a jeweled sword of honor voted by the Congress and commissioned from the house of Tiffany. Dewey's grateful countrymen also offered him the gift of a suitable house in Washington. No other American had been so lavishly and tumultuously honored since Ulysses Grant returned from Appomattox, but this time an entire nation, South as well as North, was united in celebrating both a victor and a dawning, glorious era of American expansionism.

For some months already, there had been fevered talk of Dewey as a candidate for president in 1900, a successor to other elected war heroes, from George Washington, Andrew Jackson, and Zachary Taylor to Ulysses Grant, although the cautionary example of Grant's inept, scandal-ridden administrations seemed to have been expunged from public memory. No one knew whether Dewey was a Democrat or a Republican, or whether he had ever voted in an election, but at this point in his career, according to the *Nation,* he could have had the nomination of either party "by simply holding his peace." Still, in a cable he dictated back in the Philippines, Dewey declared, "I would not accept a nomination for the Presidency of the United States. I have no desire for any political office. I am unfitted for it, having neither the education nor the training. . . . I have been approached by politicians repeatedly, in one way or another, but I have refused absolutely to consider any proposition whatsoever. This is final." Admiral Dewey's bluff message was longer but, as it turned out, not so definitive as General Sherman's message to the Republican National Convention in 1884: "I will not accept if nominated and will not serve if elected."

The man of the hour in 1899 was a sixty-one-year-old widower, a doctor's son from Montpelier, Vermont, where he was born the day after Christmas 1837. A career naval officer, at the end of his first year at Annapolis he stood thirty-third in his class of thirty-five but showed considerable improvement in his standing by the time he graduated in 1858. In a rare breach of discipline, Dewey thrashed a fellow midshipman "who called me a name at mess which no man can hear without redress," but otherwise his record at the Naval Academy was unblemished, if also unremarkable. He served under Admiral Farragut during the Civil War and then accumulated seniority in the peacetime navy mainly by staying alive, out of trouble, and on dry land (during the past twenty years he had seen only four years of sea duty). Not brilliant or innovative in any significant respect, he was at least reliable and sober in judgment: "in short, an ordinary naval officer," his 1974 biographer, Ronald Spector, wrote, with "nothing in [his] record up to 1897 to suggest that he was in any way extraordinary." When war with Spain became likely, especially over the issue of Cuban sovereignty, Dewey used his influence with saber-rattling Senator Redfield Proctor of Vermont, his home state, and Assistant Secretary of the Navy Theodore Roosevelt, who was even more war hungry than Proctor, and got himself appointed commander of the Asiatic Squadron.

"It was my duty," he recalled, "to make sure that the squadron was properly prepared for any emergency." On February 15, 1898, the United States battleship *Maine* blew up in Havana harbor with a loss of 260 men. "Keep full of coal," Roosevelt cabled him ten days later. "In the event of declaration of war [with] Spain, your duty will be to see that the Spanish Squadron does not leave the Asiatic coast." In Hong Kong on April 24, Dewey received his final orders from Washington: "War has commenced between the United States and Spain. Proceed at once to Philippine Islands. Commence operations at once, particularly against the Spanish fleet. You must capture vessels or destroy. Use utmost endeavors."

Dewey's descent from the pedestal was only a little less sudden than his climb. Among early signs, even before he reached home from the Philippines, that he was not cut out for public life was the prescient but indiscreet prediction he made in friendly conversation with an American he met in a hotel in Trieste: "Our next war will be with Germany." "The fellow didn't say he was a reporter," Dewey complained after the story went out on the wires and enraged Dewey's partisans in Washington and the German-American community at large. "I should never have said anything of the kind if I knew he was a member of the press."

Two months after his triumphant return, in St. Paul's Catholic Church in Washington, D.C., Dewey, whose wife had died twenty-five years earlier, married Mildred McLean Hazen, a rich forty-nine-year-old widow, daughter of the founder of the *Washington Post* and sister of its current owner. Her first husband, General William B. Hazen, had been rewarded for his successes as an Indian fighter with the post of military attaché at the American embassy in Vienna. There Mildred, who had been reared a Presbyterian, hobnobbed with members of the Austrian court and upper classes and converted to Catholicism supposedly in order to take communion with them. In her fully arrived character, she was a cross between Lady Macbeth and Mrs. Astor, a snob and social climber who flaunted her possessions ("Too many jewels cannot be worn," she said of a White House reception) as well as her disdain for company she considered "underbred and common." This included most members of McKinley's (and later Roosevelt's) cabinet and their wives.

Dewey, once a relatively obscure navy captain, was now the Hero of Manila Bay and a prime catch. "For many years during my residence in Washington Mrs. Mildred (McLean) Hazen and I had been friends," Dewey recalled. "Upon my return from the East she did me the honor to become my wife." The marriage proved to be Dewey's worst public relations blunder so far. "It was as if the American public had elected itself to be Dewey's bride," Mark Sullivan wrote in *Our Times*, "and as if the Admiral had committed bigamy; or, at best, it was as if he had procured a divorce, abruptly, and without just cause." Had the public known Mildred better, they would have liked her even less.

As for the gift house on Rhode Island Avenue in Washington that the Deweys eventually acquired, she was clearly behind the admiral's stipulation, grotesque as coming from a man trained to his profession in wardrooms and ships' messes, that it have a dining room large enough to accommodate eighteen or so guests in state. Soon the news that Dewey had conveyed title to this house to Mildred raised further resentment, along with accusations of ingratitude and even betrayal of trust. The *New York Times* reported a "sudden storm of wrath." In an era of anti-Catholicism and war with Catholic Spain, the deeding over fed dark suspicions that Mrs.

Dewey intended eventually to hand the nation's gift over to her church, which would then use it as a Washington base for further Vatican infiltration of the American commonwealth.

Finally, again most probably under prodding from Mildred, who wished to be first lady rather than admiral's lady and thus outrank every other citizen except her husband, Dewey reconsidered his political future and made a decisive course correction toward disaster.

On April 3, 1900, a few months before the nominating conventions, he gave a surprising interview to a reporter from the *New York World*:

> Yes, I have decided to become a candidate.
>
> I realize the time has arrived when I must definitely define my position. When I arrived in this country last September, I said then that nothing could induce me to be a candidate for the Presidency. Since then, however, I have had the leisure and inclination to study the matter, and have reached a different conclusion, inasmuch as so many assurances have come to me from my countrymen that I would be acceptable as a candidate for this great office.
>
> If the American people want me for this high office, I shall be only too willing to serve them.
>
> It is the highest honor in the gift of this nation; what citizen would refuse it?

Up to this point, his statement had been both unexceptionable and conventional, but his demon compelled him to go on and offer a sort of civics lesson: "Since studying this subject I am convinced that the office of the President is not such a very difficult one to fill, his duties being mainly to execute the laws of Congress. Should I be chosen for this exalted position I would execute the laws of the Congress as faithfully as I have always executed the orders of my superiors."

The following day he identified himself as a Democrat and thus a potential rival to William Jennings Bryan at the upcoming national convention in Kansas City.

"Leaders Laugh at Poor Dewey," the *Atlanta Constitution* headlined its page one account of this astonishing interview. "The Entire Capital Is Laughing at the Former Hero." Adding to the general hilarity over his version of presidential function was Dewey's admission a few days later that he had never even voted in an election. Flabbergasted, uncertain as how to distinguish Dewey's ignorance and naiveté from his egotism and arrogance, the public response was first disappointment and disbelief, followed soon after by rejection, mockery, and abuse, a cycle colorfully summed up in a popular verse of the day, "Folks chase a ball that's rolling, And kick it when it stops."

"While Admiral Dewey was a hero, he was a dangerous presidential possibility," said anti-imperialist Senator Augustus Octavius Bacon of Georgia, "but since he has become a human being and indulged his fancies as others have done, he has lost his hold upon the hero-worshippers." Overnight Dewey, the political unknown, became a political has-been, no threat at all to either McKinley or Bryan. Sounding a strangely pathetic and bewildered note for an admiral of the navy, Dewey said of his aborted candidacy, "I don't understand how I got the idea in the first place." He served out the rest of his life and career as president of the General Board of the Navy Department and head of the Joint Army-Navy Board, roles in which, according to Ronald Spector, he "was clearly out of his depth." Dewey died in January 1917, at the age of seventy-nine. Mildred lived until 1931.

The subscription drive for a permanent Triumphal Arch in New York collapsed almost instantly when Dewey announced his candidacy. The $65,000 already collected went back to the donors, while the monumental plaster and wood structure decayed in wind and weather. Its brilliant wedding cake whiteness turned to streak and grime, and what had already proved to be something of a traffic problem at a difficult intersection became an eyesore and a hazard as well. In December 1900, a month after Dewey's political vanishment and McKinley's victory in the national election, workmen tore down the great arch and hauled the wreckage off to the city dump. Today, Dewey's flagship, the cruiser *Olympia*, last survivor of the American and Spanish war fleets, rusts away in the Delaware River at Penn's Landing, Philadelphia. A full century after the splendid little war with Spain, it is the *Maine* that's remembered, not the hero of Manila Bay.

Local Hero:
J. C. M. Hanson and the
Politics of Library Classification

NEIL HARRIS

*A hero who emerges from the bowels of a library? J. C. M.
Hanson is one such character. A pioneering librarian, he developed a cataloging and classification system designed to bring
order to the explosion of material and knowledge accumulating
in turn-of-the-century research libraries. Over the course of his
long and productive career, he helped to reorganize and central-
ize four major libraries, including the Library of Congress and
the University of Chicago's Joseph Regenstein Library. This
"hero of bureaucracy" also suggests the extraordinary mobility
available to talented immigrants in the late nineteenth and early
twentieth centuries in American society.*

MONUMENTS TO HEROISM are not limited to statues and triumphal arches. They can also be found in the most pervasively ordinary arrangements by which we live. Much of what we take for granted had to be invented by individual men and women. Our street names and traffic patterns, our telephone directories and dietary standards, our weights and measures and clothing sizes owe their presence to choices. And these, in turn, often rest on endless, if hidden, hours of debate. Taking stands in such battles has called for courage and selflessness, as well as intelligence and judgment. As we live for many years with the consequences of these decisions, and the adoption of routine formulas, it is worth acknowledging the code makers. These rule makers and classifiers are at least as powerful as the judges and legislators who receive more respectful attention.

The central significance of classification is nowhere better seen than in the way we store and retrieve information. Today's designers of computer software and hardware compete vigorously to dominate this enormous market, feverishly marketing rival systems and contending brands. Fervent loyalty or determined opposition often results, for mistakes can be very costly. Such intellectual range wars, now a generation old for computers, have older precedents. A century ago, the great information machine being developed to serve the modern world was the research library. While library history possesses millennial dimensions, a striking expansion of publishing, literacy, and systematic investigation provoked dramatic expansion. Multi-million-volume libraries were, by the end of the nineteenth century, either actual achievements or reasonable aspirations across the Western world. Potential clients included not only the public authorities sponsoring the great national libraries, but also universities, corporations, museums, and hospitals, all of which required access to comprehensive collections and texts in various languages.

In some ways the acts of locating, purchasing, transporting, and housing these materials in central reading depots was less challenging than the task of arranging them. The abundance and variety of the printed word confounded the most ingenious system makers. Makers of dictionaries, almanacs, encyclopedias, and world's fairs all wrestled with the problem of organizing human experience, and came up with their own schemes. But these compendia required the aid of libraries and accessibility to the record of human thought. To meet such demands, an extraordinary generation of pioneering librarians developed a range of classifying devices, some of them with far-reaching consequences on conceptions of space, time, and knowledge itself.

From this group of paper revolutionaries, one figure may stand for dozens of others. Unsung save among his colleagues, unknown even by most of those who have benefited from his work, J. C. M. Hanson's struggle toward standardized classification and centralized facilities has special claims on our attention. Not only a participant in this great international crusade, he was part of the broad human movement that peopled the United States. His story contains elements of adventure, extraordinary ambition, and continuing devotion to an ideal.

J. C. M. Hanson (born Jens, later called by American colleagues, James) was an immigrant. Born on a Norwegian farm in the Valdres valley in 1864, and proudly conscious of his heritage for the rest of his life, he came to America at the age of nine, brought here by a childless Iowa couple, friends of his mother. Both Jens and his family fully expected his return to Norway after completing an education, but that was not to be. The next nine years he spent in Decorah, Iowa, growing up within a large Norwegian community but learning English from his playmates and adapting easily to his new life. Entering the preparatory department of Luther College at the age of ten (with instruction conducted in Norwegian), the young Hanson soon added German to his English, Swedish, Dutch, and Norwegian, and began an intensive, multiyear study of Latin and Greek, among other subjects. Luther College existed within a cocoon of Norwegian history and culture, but despite this and the rigorous work required for the classroom, Hanson became an enthusiastic college athlete, particularly as a baseball player. Sports was a primary means of socialization for many young immigrants, and Hanson's autobiography is filled with lyrical memories of team tours, visits, and intense competitions, in college and after.

After graduating from Luther College in 1882, Hanson spent two years at Concordia Seminary in St. Louis, perfecting his spoken German but otherwise finding his theological studies unrewarding. There followed several years serving as the principal of a Norwegian Synod school in Chicago, during which time he indulged his taste for music and spent summers doing farm work and playing baseball in the Midwest. In 1888 he decided to return to academic life, entering Cornell University to study European history and improve his knowledge of Romance languages. At Cornell Hanson discovered, for the first time, the resources (and frustrations) of a large library and worked with great scholars like Andrew D. White, George Lincoln Burr, and Moses Coit Tyler. In an era that still blurred the distinctions between undergraduate and graduate studies, Hanson also was able to play intercollegiate baseball, though he later regretted the study time his athletic activities cost him.

While at Cornell, Hanson's interest in library work grew. Diffident by nature and convinced he lacked fluency of speech, he decided to take a summertime apprenticeship at the recently formed Newberry Library in Chicago, attracted by its librarian, William F. Poole. Poole was a national figure, an early graduate of Melvil Dewey's new library school at Columbia University, an opinionated innovator and reformer who had gathered a bright staff around him. Hanson, multilingual, broadly trained in classics, history, and literature, was turned loose on the cataloging and classification of books in foreign languages. The Dewey decimal system was still in its infancy, with different librarians retaining their own methods or modifying it to meet specific needs. Hanson acquired on-the-job training, learning as well from a set of impressive apprentice colleagues, some of whom, like Charles Martel, a Swiss immigrant, would become influential nationally at the Library of Congress. After a brief stint at the Newberry, Hanson joined the staff of the growing University of Wisconsin Library in Madison. There then followed what Hanson recalled as the four happiest years of his life: newly married with a pleasant home, good friends, and the challenge of reorganizing a large library, the first of four he would so shape.

It was in Madison, while improving his Italian and Spanish, two of the ten or so languages he commanded, that Hanson engaged in his first creative cataloging effort: bringing under control a fifty-thousand-volume library that lacked any effective index. Dissatisfied with the options available in the Dewey decimal system, which employed only numbers, Hanson adapted a method developed by another library pioneer, Charles Cutter, assigning both letters and numbers to each book. This device would later form the basis for the Library of Congress classification system, created several years later.

But Madison was only a resting point. In 1897, still in his early thirties, Hanson was invited to become chief of the Library of Congress Catalog Division. About to move into its magnificently decorated new building on Capitol Hill, the Library of Congress was engaged in a massive effort to standardize and unify cataloging practices in American libraries, a venture that would have international implications. Friendly with a group of congressional political leaders (mainly of Scandinavian descent), host to many distinguished visitors from Norway, working with colleagues like his old friend Charles Martel, the principal designer of the new system, Hanson flourished in Washington. Generously giving credit to others for working out details of the Library of Congress scheme, Hanson's overall charge included the distribution of printed catalog cards to libraries across the country and obtaining agreements from foreign librarians about classifying rules.

This last task meant mediating fierce and prolonged disputes over usage. Trivial as they might seem, without resolution such disagreements over author and title names could confuse generations of library users. The files of the Catalog Division at the Library of Congress in the early years of the twentieth century, Hanson wryly recalled years later, demonstrated that "not only a difference of opinion on religious and political questions . . . can arouse men's souls." Librarians of the day regarded issues like the proper entry of a British nobleman's name or the capitalization of common nouns in German "as something on which their consciences would permit no compromise." But Hanson was able to encourage harmony.

In 1904 the first edition of these rules of classification began to circulate, bringing in their wake a far higher level of standardization than had ever before existed. Three years later Hanson traveled to Europe, helping to obtain, at a Glasgow meeting of librarians, an agreement for English-speaking countries on all but 8 of the 174 rules that the American committee had devised.

Happy and productive in Washington, prominent on the world library scene, Hanson had demonstrated impressive qualities of mind and temper in his first twenty years or so of professional work. But his mettle had not yet been fully tested, and the heroic, if somewhat frustrating, era of his life lay just ahead. In 1910 President Ernest DeWitt Burton of the University of Chicago persuaded Hanson to move back to the Midwest and undertake the reorganization of the largest library west of the Appalachians. In retrospect, despite his Scandinavian dislike of hot Washington summers and a set of local family connections, Hanson felt the move may have been a mistake. His Library of Congress years were, he confessed, "the most interesting and most worthwhile" of his career. The challenge at Chicago was as great, but the results he confessed "far less satisfactory." With characteristic self-effacement, Hanson suggested that his Washington accomplishments may have been a function of youthful vigor, the Chicago frustrations products of increasing age and diminishing energy. But the limits of an academic institution were more responsible for these problems than biological aging, and Hanson showed abundant courage in his later years confronting faculty opposition.

The University of Chicago library was certainly large, but its records were in great disorder. About to move into an impressive (if functionally inadequate) new building, it possessed nineteen separate locations. Reflecting a system of personal investigation that tended to be specialized in focus, scientific in ideal, and publication oriented, the library had been dominated by the university's departmental divisions. The faculty emphasized immediate research needs, meaning textual availability to themselves and their graduate students in seminar rooms and departmental offices. The central or general library contained less than 25 percent of the 300,000-volume collection. So decentralized a system was plagued by extensive duplication; since many departments considered certain texts and periodicals highly desirable, they were ordered in several copies. A prominent zoologist on the faculty insisted that the cost of duplication must be borne: "The Departmental Library should under no circumstances be weakened for the sake of a General Library." When Hanson, after his arrival, drew up a list of one hundred bibliographies and reference works belonging in a university library, he found only forty-three represented, and of these the general library contained merely six.

Moreover, without a uniform classification system (some libraries had author cards, some subject cards, some neither), a recent faculty decision had endorsed the Dewey decimal system as the institutional choice. An early critic of the Dewey scheme, Hanson quickly reversed his colleagues' judgment in favor of the Library of Congress system he had helped develop. Thus the University of Chicago, eighty years later, would be a rarity: a major university collection with a single stack organized by Library of Congress schedules. Both Dewey and Library of Congress schemes had deeply embedded Eurocentric codes within them, organizing the world according to dominant cultural categories. While never challenging these cultural values, Hanson's choice turned on issues of efficiency and anticipated the future thrust of American library policies.

But while Hanson achieved this victory with relatively little effort, he found it far more difficult establishing the culture of a centralized library.

This meant not merely standardizing the rules of ordering and classifying, but moving texts to the general library and liberalizing circulation as well, for departments preferred to restrict book circulation to faculty and graduate students. The pressing task, of course, was giving catalog numbers to several hundred thousand books, many of them still unaccessioned and physically filthy, covered by coal-based grease.

As associate director and the highest library administrator who was professionally trained, Hanson might have expected one day to be appointed director. But that would not be; his highest position was the acting directorship, just before retiring. "When I in 1912 and again in 1915 and 1917 announced my position in print with reference to the question of many and large departmental libraries," he wrote a well wisher in 1924, "I . . . sealed my doom." Such candor might be thought a blunder, Hanson admitted, but his eye was on posterity. In future years when people came to realize the impossibility of a highly decentralized system, they would ask why the best-qualified librarian had not sounded a warning. Hanson's conscience would not permit ambivalence, and he held fast to his vision.

Hanson underlined his philosophical views on every occasion and in every form, however trivial. He preferred to use the phrase "university library" rather than "university libraries," he wrote, because this "awkward and cumbersome" term emphasized decentralization. "I am a thorough believer in unity of scholarship." And he was quick to protest invasions of professional authority by academics and administrators alike. When a University of Chicago committee recommended that the director of the library continue to be a regular faculty member, "vitally interested in the facilitation and encouragement of research," Hanson added a letter of protest, objecting to the assumption that professional librarians were not as interested in encouraging research as university teachers.

As it turned out, just as Hanson was approaching retirement in the late 1920s, the University of Chicago agreed to house a graduate library school and grant degrees in library science. There were many ironies in locating this enterprise within an institution that had so energetically resisted both the professionalizing spirit of librarians and their independence from faculty control. But Hanson was, no doubt, accustomed to ironies and happily accepted appointment to the first library school faculty. His sense of disappointment at Chicago had little to do with creation of a centrally placed, uniformly classed, multidisciplinary research library; that had become a university given by the end of his life. It was, rather, his sense that opponents had belittled the contributions made by professional librarians to efficient academic research and delayed many of the reforms that would improve matters even further.

Among his fellow librarians, however, Hanson enjoyed an extraordinary reputation, valued as a pioneering giant. His quiet and understated gifts as a bringer of order achieved continuing recognition. Conferences were organized and journal issues edited to honor his work. After leaving his administrative duties at Chicago, Hanson was invited to reorganize still one more library, that of the Vatican, and he remained active as a writer, teacher, and adviser before retiring to rural Wisconsin. He died there, in Green Bay, on November 9, 1943. Immigrant polymath, skilled mediator, innovative classifier, he stands out among an extraordinary generation of organizers by reason of his stubborn defense of the kind of library today's scholars take for granted. He anticipated the trend of modern interdisciplinary research by insisting on the unity of scholarship. Like many other heroes, his true memorial was his actual accomplishment: a multimillion-volume Library of Congress–classed stack, which, in today's Joseph Regenstein Library, brings together students of all kinds in the interest of informed investigation.

William Chandler Bagley:
Dr. Know of American Education

DIANE RAVITCH

Like J. C. M. Hanson in the world of library management, William Chandler Bagley made his mark in education, a sphere that depends on daily, quiet (if sometimes contentious) heroism. Like Hanson, he often took stands that challenged prevailing wisdom or ruffled professional feathers. He did not back down, no matter how unpopular his opinions. William Chandler Bagley's heroism lay in his principled defense of what he considered the right course for American education in the twentieth century: a commitment to liberal education, skepticism about the utility of intelligence testing for sorting students, and a call for higher standards in a common national curriculum. Unlike most other forgotten heroes, his once-out-of-style ideas are now receiving a second look.

S OME ARE HEROES because of their physical courage. William Chandler Bagley (1874-1946) is an example of moral and intellectual courage. For more than three decades, he challenged popular educational fashions, risking the disdain of his peers. But the possibility of being ostracized never deterred him. By all accounts, he was always civil and reasonable when engaged in intellectual combat; he criticized ideas, not persons. Despite the significant role that he played, few educators today know his name; he is seldom mentioned in histories of American education. Yet historical retrospect suggests that he deserves recognition for his role as a dissenter and a voice of reason.

Bagley was born in Detroit in 1874. His parents were from Massachusetts and apparently moved a few times, because Bagley attended elementary school in Worcester, Massachusetts, and high school in Detroit. He graduated from the Michigan Agricultural College (later known as Michigan State College), where students were required to do farm work two and a half hours each weekday. His plans for a career in agricultural science were frustrated when he graduated in the midst of an economic depression in 1895; the only job he could find was teaching in a one-teacher school in rural Garth in the Upper Peninsula of Michigan. He was fascinated by both the challenge of the job and its lack of any scientific basis. He wrote to a friend that vastly more was known "about the raising of pigs than about the minds of children."

Determined to study the science of the mind, he earned a master's degree at the University of Wisconsin in 1898 and a doctorate at Cornell University in 1900, both in psychology, which was then a new field of study. He earnestly believed that it was possible to develop a science of education, one that would be as precise and predictable as any of the physical sciences. In February 1901, he was hired as principal of an elementary school in St. Louis, and a few months later, he married a fellow student at Cornell, Florence MacLean Winger.

Because the climate in St. Louis was not good for his wife's health, he accepted an invitation in 1902 to teach psychology at the State Normal College in Dillon, Montana, and direct the training school. From 1903 to 1906, he also served as superintendent of the Dillon public schools, and in 1904 he became vice president of the college as well. In the midst of all these responsibilities, he published his first book, *The Educative Process* (1905) and founded *Intermountain Education*, the first school journal in the northern Rocky Mountain region.

In 1906, Bagley left Dillon to teach educational theory at the State Normal School in Oswego, New York, and to direct its training school. In 1907, he published *Classroom Management,* which remained in print for the next forty years. Based on the success of his books, he was offered several university professorships, and in 1909 he became a professor of education at the University of Illinois and director of the University's School of Education.

Bagley spent nine years building the faculty of the School of Education at the University of Illinois. He also published several books, was one of the founders of the *Journal of Educational Psychology,* founded a professional honor society for educators, and was president of the National Society for the Study of Education. Although deeply immersed in profession-building activities, Bagley always preferred to be addressed as "Mister Bagley" rather than "Doctor" or "Professor."

Bagley's early career offered no hint of his future role as a dissident. Admired by his peers as a leader in the field, he tirelessly advocated a sound education for future teachers, a proposition that no one disputed. Yet as early as 1907, in *Classroom Management,* he lamented "the waves of fads and reforms that sweep through the educational system at periodic intervals," and he worried about reformers who would "leave teacher and pupil to work out each his own salvation in the chaos of confusion and disorder."

Clearly Bagley was alarmed by the espousal of untested theories by his fellow professors of education. But he was not regarded as a controversialist until 1914, when he engaged in a celebrated debate with David Snedden, commissioner of education for Massachusetts, at the annual meeting of the National Education Association. Bagley was known as a genial teacher-educator; Snedden was a national leader in the vocational education movement, which was widely recognized as the leading edge of progressive reform. Snedden advocated the creation of separate vocational schools for the vast majority of adolescents.

Bagley defended liberal education for all children. He insisted that all young people should have access to the knowledge, skills, habits, and ideals that would equip them for changing situations, not just for a particular job. He contended that young people needed the historical perspective that would enable them to rise above local, sectional, or partisan points of view; the knowledge of science that would free them from superstition and error; and engagement in literature and art to enable them to understand human motives and conduct. To denigrate liberal education as a leisure activity for the few, as so many educators did, Bagley said, "is a sin against the children of the land, and it is a crime against posterity." Bagley claimed that the American people were dedicated to "the theory that talent is distributed fairly evenly among the masses and that it is the special prerogative of no especial class or group. . . . We mean to keep open the door of opportunity at every level of the educational ladder. It is a costly process, but so are most other things that are precious and worth while."

At the next annual meeting of the National Education Association in 1915, attended by more than three thousand educators, Bagley criticized the next progressive reform: the junior high school. The U.S. commissioner of education, Philander P. Claxton, maintained that the typical eight-year course should be reduced to six years, after which children as young as twelve could begin vocational and industrial training. When the leaders of the National Education Association endorsed a resolution in support of the junior high school, knowing that its purpose was to sort children into academic and vocational tracks, Bagley dissented: "Hitherto in our national life we have proceeded on the assumption that no one has the omniscience to pick out the future hewers of wood and drawers of water,—at least not when the candidates for these tasks are to be selected at the tender age of twelve."

One positive result of Bagley's debate with Snedden was that he caught the attention of Dean James Russell of Teachers College, Columbia University, the nation's leading school of education. Russell reportedly said that Bagley should be representing Teachers College in such debates instead of fighting on the outside. In 1918, Bagley joined the faculty of Teachers College as head of the Department of Teacher Education. Having abandoned his earlier belief in the possibility of a science of education, Bagley was convinced that education is an art, dependent on an adequate supply of skillful, well-educated teachers. Most of the profession, however, endorsed the scientific movement in education, whose chief feature was mental testing.

World War I offered the mental testers a remarkable field for experimenting. Invited to help classify some 1.7 million recruits, leading psychologists developed group intelligence tests (IQ tests) to determine whether men were fit to be officers or infantry, or rejected. Prominent academic psychologists, including Robert Yerkes of Harvard, Carl Brigham of Princeton, Lewis Terman of Stanford, and Edward Thorndike of Teachers College, developed the army tests. The psychologists asserted that their instruments measured innate intelligence, which they proclaimed was fixed and un-changing. After the war, Yerkes and Brigham reported that the average mental age of Americans was only about thirteen or fourteen and that the continued influx of non-Nordic groups from Europe threatened the nation's future because of their low IQs. Their claims provided fodder in the 1920s for nativists, racists, and eugenicists, as well as for efforts to restrict immi-gration from southern and eastern Europe.

Only two men responded forcefully to the intelligence testers. One was Walter Lippmann, whose blistering attacks appeared in the *New Republic*. The other was William Chandler Bagley. The overwhelming majority of educators endorsed intelligence tests, but Bagley warned that they posed grave "educational and social dangers." He rejected the testers' assumption that intelligence is innate and unchanging; whatever they measured, he as-serted, could well be the result of environment and education. He predicted that IQ tests would be used to slam the doors of educational opportunity on large numbers of children.

Bagley feared that the IQ test, cloaked in the neutral but impressive language of science, would be an instrument of social stratification, threat-ening democracy itself. He insisted that the army test results actually proved the importance of environment and educational opportunity. He pointed out, for example, that many northern blacks scored higher than many southern whites and that the scores of immigrants increased in rela-tion to their length of residency in this country.

Bagley summarized his charges against the testers and the misuse of IQ tests in *Determinism in Education* (1925). He argued that the role of schools in a democracy is not to sort students for their future careers but to improve the intelligence of everyone who comes to be educated. He wrote:

> I make no absurd claim that if I teach a common man the principle of grav-itation, let us say, I am making the common man equal to Newton. . . . I do maintain that I have enabled this common man to participate in a very real measure in the experiences of one of the most gifted men of all time; I maintain that I have given him one control over his environment equal in a substantial way to that which this gifted man himself possessed; and I maintain that *in respect of this possession* I have made this common man the equal of all others who possess it. There are undoubtedly some men who could never grasp the principle in question, but I should wish to refine my

teaching processes far more . . . before reaching any fatalistic conclusions as to where the line is to be drawn.

As in his earlier critique of vocational education, Bagley insisted that education is powerful and that virtually everyone could become better informed and more intelligent if education aimed to make them so. His complaint against the tests was not that they were invalid but that they would be used to restrict educational opportunity to those who needed it most.

Bagley was again out of step with the field, and his arguments were ignored. Intelligence testing spread rapidly among the nation's schools and was accepted as a reliable instrument to sort children into different curricular tracks, affording different educational opportunities.

Because of his defense of liberal education in 1914 and his attack on intelligence testing in the 1920s, Bagley got a reputation among his fellow educationists as a conservative who was opposed to progressive education and hostile to modern, scientific education. His continuing insistence that all children should have access to a liberal education, regardless of their IQ, branded him as a reactionary, hopelessly behind the times.

In the 1930s, when progressive educators like Harold Rugg and William Kilpatrick—Bagley's colleagues at Teachers College—led a national movement to promote classroom methods based on children's interests instead of subject matter, Bagley was their leading critic. Kilpatrick believed that curriculum should not be set out in advance and that children were best motivated if they learned through activities that interested them; his idea, christened the "activity movement," was the hottest idea in education in the 1930s. Rugg's 1928 book, The Child-Centered School (coauthored with Ann Shumaker), described schools using Kilpatrick's methods as makers of an "Educational Revolution" that would free American society from Puritanism and authoritarianism.

In his last major book, Education and Emergent Man (1934), Bagley took issue with the central doctrines of progressive education, especially its claim that the only knowledge of value was instrumental and useful. Bagley contended that although knowledge for immediate use is important, so is knowledge for understanding and interpretation. Only a fraction of what one needs to know, he maintained, can be learned by participating in activities and solving problems; a broadly educated person also needs a large fund of background knowledge drawn from the systematic and sequential study of history, geography, science, mathematics, literature, and the arts. He did not reject the progressives' preference for activities, but he did reject their contempt for organized subject matter.

Bagley insisted on a necessary balance between interest and effort. Not everything in the classroom, he argued, should be fun and interesting; such an appeal taught students to respond only to pleasure and self-gratification instead of learning self-discipline and the value of effort. There was a good deal to be said, he thought, for teaching children to complete difficult tasks; the reward was the self-confidence that children gained by conquering challenges. Bagley believed that some children would follow the line of least resistance and not learn as much as they would have if they had been instructed in subject matter by talented, insightful, and well-educated teachers.

Over the years, Bagley consistently argued that there was so much mobility in American society that a common national curriculum in basic subjects like arithmetic, history, geography, and science was needed. He believed that the federal government should support the schools to promote "equality of educational opportunity throughout the country, and the consequent protection of the stake that the people as a whole have in a literate, informed, and disciplined population." He called ignorance "a menace to national welfare." He consistently argued that the spread and improvement of education would contribute to social progress by reducing not only illiteracy, but crime, corruption, drunkenness, divorce, and poverty.

In 1938, Bagley helped organize the Essentialist Committee for the Advancement of American Education; it issued a platform advocating rigorous standards and a common curriculum to ensure a high level of a shared culture across American society. The essentialists were promptly rebuked. Although the statement was careful to praise John Dewey and to claim that his followers had distorted his teachings, Dewey told a *New York Times* reporter, "The movement is apparently an imitation of the fundamentalist movement, and may perhaps draw support from that quarter as well as from reactionaries in politics and economics." William Kilpatrick, Dewey's chief disciple, told the same reporter, "The essentialists represent the same sort of reactionary trend that always springs up when a doctrine is gaining headway in the country. The astonishing thing is not the fact of the reaction but that it is so small and on the whole comes from such inconspicuous people." *Time* magazine reported on the contretemps between essentialists and progressives by putting the president of the Progressive Education Association on its cover, accompanied by a laudatory article about progressive education.

Bagley died in 1946, never knowing that others would carry forward his lonely crusade for higher standards, equality of educational opportunity, liberal education for all, better-educated teachers, and abundantly supported schools. Widely known as a critic of fads, the only innovation that he fought for throughout his career was, in the words of his biographer, Isaac L. Kandel, to "put a competent and cultured teacher into every American classroom." Today, as the American education system is pressed to provide higher standards for the great majority of students, William Chandler Bagley's ideas deserve a hearing. And he deserves to be recalled by the term that he himself preferred: "stalwart educator," a man of outstanding vigor and commonsense. And uncommon courage.

O. Delight Smith:
A Labor Organizer's Odyssey

JACQUELYN DOWD HALL

O. Delight Smith (what a wonderful name for a believer in women's sexual equality) dedicated her life to the twin struggles of labor activism and feminism. Her contributions encompassed both the public—the strikes she led, the workers she organized, the bosses she challenged—and the private, specifically her attempt as a modern woman to create a sexually emancipated personal life without regret or recrimination, something that had eluded Victoria Woodhull forty years earlier. O. Delight Smith's life reminds us that we can find elements of heroism and courage in both public and private deeds.

H ER FRIENDS in the labor movement called O. (Ola) Delight Smith the Mother Jones of Atlanta. A tireless advocate for working-class women's rights, she wrote a hard-hitting weekly column for the local labor journal and served as president of the national Ladies' Auxiliary of the Order of Railroad Telegraphers (ORT). In 1914, when the United Textile Workers launched its first big southern organizing drive, she helped to lead a tempestuous textile strike.

By the 1920s, this daring and passionate woman had been blotted from history. In the written record of the period, she is nowhere to be found. The forces that conspired against her ranged from personal betrayal, to political defeat, to historians' assumptions about who is significant and who is not. To be sure, her flaws made her vulnerable to both scandal and historical ne-glect. But that vulnerability marks her as a modern woman, negotiating at the dawn of the twentieth century the same minefields across which women still pick their way today. The discovery of feminists in the 1960s that "the personal is political" would have come as no surprise to O. Delight Smith, whose private and public lives were so poignantly entwined. One thing, however, would have amazed her: to find herself rescued from oblivion and hailed as a forgotten hero, after all these years.

Born in Millersburg, Illinois, in 1880, O. Delight Lloyd grew up in a family whose restless wanderings across the Midwest and the South set the tone for her peripatetic career. Her father was a lumberman, and as soon as he found a job in one town, he began reading the want ads and dreaming of opportunities down the road. The family made at least twenty-nine moves in as many years, alighting in Atlanta, Georgia, seven different times. De-light remembered Epes, Alabama, best, for it was there that she met and married a "traveling man" named Edgar B. Smith and there that she learned telegraphy, the craft that she would follow for more than fifty years.

Telegraphers straddled two social worlds. Most were village or country bred, the sons and daughters of farmers, craftsmen, and, increasingly, urban blue-collar workers. Better educated than most of their peers, they traded aprons and overalls for the shirtwaists and neckties of a new low-level white-collar sector of the working class. These "kid-gloved laborers" formed craft unions that tried to hold their own against the railroads and the tele-graph companies, the nation's first great modern corporations.

Railway telegraphy in particular was a male preserve, with its own rau-cous romance-of-the-rails mystique. Railway telegraphers passed the dispatchers' orders to the conductors and engineers, and an operator's speed, accuracy, and efficiency could spell the difference between a safe trip and a tragic crash. Male telegraphers relished their reputation as a hard-drinking, "motley group of colorful characters [who] broke every rule in the book, but always turned in a good job when emergencies arose." They were also notorious "boomers"—workers who, by choice or necessity, followed rush periods of work around the country. Female railroad telegraphers, who worked long hours in isolated railroad stations and communicated with strangers through a secret code, occupied an especially suspect position. For they epitomized the autonomy of the new "working girl," whose unsupervised sexuality caused so much consternation in a period of transition from a rural to an urban, industrial world.

In 1907, Smith and her husband moved to Atlanta, capital of the New South, and she signed on with the Commercial Telegraphers Union of America (CTUA), just in time to join a disastrous nationwide strike against Western Union. Blacklisted and thrown back on her own resources in the midst of the panic of 1907, she set out to make her way in a city whose population was mushrooming and whose white female labor force was climbing at an even faster pace. Georgia, like the rest of the South, remained overwhelmingly rural, but by the 1910s a mass exodus from the state's dying farms had already begun, and female migrants outnumbered men. As a skilled worker and a craft unionist, O. Delight Smith occupied a distinctive yet revealing place in this city of women. Her husband was a traveling salesman who was usually on the road. A thoroughly unsatisfying spouse (he was, she claimed, remote, morose, and disagreeable, and he simultaneously refused to support her and placed "every obstacle possible" in the way of her success), Edgar at least provided a mantle of respectability, and Delight projected an image of determined, if wobbly, gentility. Yet she reveled in being a "lady boomer" and moved easily through a demimonde of greasy spoons, rooming houses, and cheap hotels at a time when, in many eyes, "women adrift" symbolized all that was wrong with the entry of women into the wage economy. She had to support herself, and she saw no inconsistency in blending moneymaking with homemaking, or class loyalty with pursuit of the main chance. Among other ventures, she ran a boardinghouse, set herself up as the "Eureka Letter Company" and "The Traveling Man's Secretary" and dabbled in real estate, specializing in "homes for the working man."

At the same time, she immersed herself in women's organizations and union affairs. First, she went undercover as a volunteer organizer for the Order of Railroad Telegraphers, the CTUA's sister union. Soon afterward, the ORT chose Atlanta for its 1909 national convention and hired Smith to handle local arrangements; at the convention she pushed for the creation of a ladies' auxiliary and won election as its first president, a position she held until 1913. Just prior to her move to Atlanta, she had launched a column in the city's *Journal of Labor*, and now she offered a running commentary on everything from marriage to politics, from the need for labor unity to "The Penalty of Being a Woman." The column became her platform. In it, she explained, "I always spoke my mind, and if it hurt, why, that was what I was after."

Like most craft unionists of the period, Smith excluded blacks from the house of labor. And like other white southern women, she collaborated with the politicians who were using rape scares to justify driving blacks out of politics and imposing on the region a draconian system of racial segregation. In 1906 a white mob, enraged by rumors of black-on-white rape, rampaged through Atlanta's black community. Smith responded to the bloodshed by urging "the sons of this grand old Southland" to protect women from the "Black Peril." If they could not, she threatened, then "in the name of God, let us, who are women, arm ourselves for protection!" To most white southerners, these turn-of-the-century rape scares suggested that white women were hedged about on all sides by a "nameless horror." But for some, those panics drove home a different lesson. White men had already "failed": first as soldiers unable to shield the home front during the Civil War, then as providers in a region impoverished by war. White women could no longer cower under the umbrella of male protection; they had to watch out for themselves.

In other ways Smith pushed the labor movement to be more inclusive. She urged men to view their wives not only as fellow workers but also as integral members of the labor movement. She chose as her political weapons the women's auxiliary and the union label league, new types of voluntary organizations that arose in the 1890s. Through these groups, women tried to use their leverage, not as employees but as consumers to pressure companies into employing union labor and to make novel demands on the state.

Such working-class activism, Smith believed, could be amplified through alliances with middle-class women. She herself joined the State

Congress of Mothers, denounced prostitution, and urged the creation of a reformatory for girls. In so doing, she reinforced the fears about women's sexuality that underlay the "social control" (or the more punitive) aspects of her allies' agenda. But she gave her solutions a working-class twist. Middle-class observers often responded to the surge of white women into wage labor with pity, puzzlement, and disapproval. They assumed that black women should work and would probably be sexually active, but the independent, and possibly promiscuous, white working girl was a new and frightening phenomenon, and the anxieties she aroused helped put prostitution and juvenile delinquency at the center of the turn-of-the-century reform agenda. Smith too decried the "depravity of our boys and the ruination of our girls," but she blamed those problems on "poor wages, long hours and bad working conditions," and she proposed a bottom-up response: bring women into the labor movement, thus giving them the clout to fend for themselves. In the meanwhile, unionists should reach out to such women; they should not leave to "churches and charitable organizations" the task of saving the fallen "from the error of their ways."

It was, however, neither the housewife nor the wayward girl but the independent wage-earning woman who inspired Smith's most original and impassioned columns. The assumptions that inspired her to organize wives as consumers were summarized in a title she favored for columns on the union auxiliaries, "The Hand That Rocks the Cradle Rules the World," and she promoted women's behind-the-scenes influence rather than agitating for their right to vote. But when she turned from the "Housewife" to the "Industrial Woman," she offered a brief for autonomy that marked her as a modern feminist, a member of a small band of rebels who, in the 1910s, demanded not only influence but economic independence and sexual liberation.

In 1914, when workers at Atlanta's Fulton Mills joined the United Textile Workers (UTW) union and walked off their jobs, Smith secured a commission as a paid organizer. Equipped with that coveted imprimatur, she dove into the prolonged and hard-fought textile strike. She would soon learn, however, that it was one thing to berate craft unionists for their sexism and women reformers for their classism while building alliances with both. It was quite another to cross the line between the world of the ladies' auxiliaries and that of the South's most despised white workers. Making that leap, Smith found herself the target of a smear campaign, orchestrated by labor spies ("snakes . . . in human flesh devoid of character or con-science") hired by the company to live in the mill village and infiltrate the union. Smith had no experience in organizing textile workers, but she moved quickly to capitalize on her skills as a publicist, combining the pen with the camera in a campaign designed both to encourage collective self-confidence among the workers and to garner public support. Working closely with national UTW organizer Charles Miles, she recruited a moving picture company to film the picket line, then invited the workers to free screenings in a local theater. Sporting a hand-held "detective camera," she darted about the mill village, snapping pictures of child laborers, evicted families, defiant workers, and undercover agents. She then captioned those photographs, mounted them on cardboard, and displayed them in store windows, in order to fix in the public imagination an image of the spies' sneering arrogance and the strikers' poverty and respectability.

The spies, in turn, sought to undermine the workers' solidarity and the public's sympathy by casting the union in a disreputable light. They singled out O. Delight Smith for special vilification, using tactics that ranged from rumor-mongering to blackmail and entrapment. They staked out her house, peeping through the windows until the lights went off. They observed her drinking beer in the German Cafe "until long past midnight" and having a "jolly good time" with her fellow organizer Charles Miles. One man went so far as to claim that he saw the couple registering at a hotel under an as-sumed name but promised to keep the secret if Smith would have "inter-course" with him.

Smith's nemesis was a wily and ambitious detective named Harry Pres-ton, and the interaction between them is particularly revealing. Preston dis-liked Smith from the start, with an intensity that did not extend to the other UTW organizers. The reasons for his animus are not altogether clear, but they were certainly aggravated by frustration. Try as he might, Preston could not worm his way into Smith's confidence. Nor could he establish a stable link between her outward behavior and her inner substance; to him this boundary-crossing "new woman's" motives and character were completely opaque. It was, above all, Smith's partnership with Charles Miles that played havoc with Preston's powers of deduction. When she failed to take a back seat to the national UTW organizer, Preston decided that the two were locked in a power struggle and that Smith was trying to seize control of the union. When they continued to work together harmoniously, he jumped to the conclusion that they were entirely "too friendly." Preston shadowed Smith constantly, watching her every move and expression, hoping for signs that the spies' campaign of sexual innuendo was taking effect, predicting— prematurely, as it usually turned out—that she could not stand the strain. Early on, he reported that Smith had told him "that she was worn out . . . and was almost sick, and she could not keep it up much longer." Long before Smith actually fell from grace, Preston was gloating that "the 'cockey' walk . . . she used to have [is] all gone, and she goes around like a smacked 'a—' now, (excuse the expression, it fits so perfectly)."

Although fighting on uneven ground, O. Delight Smith proved to be an impressive adversary, and she managed quite often to give as good as she got. She prided herself on her physical courage. "These pictures were taken by myself," she boasted, "while thugs and spotters were ever around me." Several cameras were "knocked from my hand and smashed before I succeeded in collecting these." This was not O. Delight Smith's first experience with down-and-dirty attempts to use her private life to undermine her public role. As an organizer for the Order of Railroad Telegraphers, she had ridden in cabooses and handcars, stayed in hotels, and dodged efforts to "'catch me' with a man in my room." What set the Atlanta case apart—and what she couldn't fight—was the apparent collusion of her husband with those who sought to do her in.

In the midst of the strike, Edgar initiated divorce proceedings, aided by the mill's legal counsel and influenced by the spies. He claimed that Delight had befriended a dark-haired stranger named Pat Callahan. Coming home from a sales trip, he said, he had surprised the couple embracing on a couch, drunk and "about half dressed." But Edgar's main charge was that Delight refused to stay at home "where all good women ought to be." Delight countersued. In the end, the jury refused her request for a divorce with alimony and granted her husband a divorce instead. It went further, giving him but denying her the right to remarry.

Until this domestic scandal erupted, the spies' campaign seems to have had little effect on Smith's standing in the labor community. Eventually, however, the president of the UTW decided that she had to go. He fired her on November 18, 1914, despite her protests that while professional UTW organizers had come and gone, she held the strike together under extraordinarily difficult circumstances. Even after her dismissal, Smith seems to have maintained the strikers' support. Less concerned with sexual propriety or more skeptical of her detractors' accusations, they urged the UTW at least to retain and assign her elsewhere, as she would be "Superior to Many in Organising in the South."

With Smith gone, the strikers held out through the winter, but with dwindling hopes and diminishing support. By the spring, when the UTW admitted defeat, Smith had vanished from the pages of the *Journal of Labor* and the records of the Atlanta labor movement. Her departure remained unmarked and unexplained.

Vanished perhaps, but not vanquished. Smith still had her craft—she could walk into a railroad office and say, "Here you fellows, I can deliver the goods[,] now put me on your payroll"—and she found a job handling "train loads and train loads of boys" once World War I broke out. In the meanwhile, she traveled back and forth to Atlanta trying to convince the court to remove the disabilities that prevented her from remarrying.

This she did with growing urgency. For within a few months after she lost her job and left Atlanta, Delight had plunged into a passionate and clandestine love affair. Almond A. (Lon) Cook was the man's name. He was a painter by trade, and the moment and means of his entry into her life are a mystery. It is possible that "Pat Callahan" was an alias for Lon Cook. In any case, Delight and her lover now found themselves in a floating world populated by a ragtag army of the unemployed, the rebellious, the declassé. They lived apart, always on the move, compelled by longings that could not be "put into words and can only be explained in unspoken words from the heart." When they were finally able to marry in 1918, Lon's brother summed up the force of their romance: "Yours is the happiness that is complete. The kind that is read about, to be envied—a paradise on earth."

These were, like Delight's hopes for more inclusive labor and women's movements, utopian expectations, but this time stripped of their political meaning. They were also expectations that were bound to be disappointed, kindled as they were by adversity, secrecy, and the drama of a courtship on the lam. What could not have been predicted—what was, at least for Delight, literally unimaginable—was the breathtaking rapidity with which her marriage fell apart.

Two years after their wedding, on a trip across the West, Lon left her in a rooming house in a small town outside Portland, Oregon, while he went into the city. He never returned, and she never saw him again. She stayed in Portland, penniless and sick, condemned to wearing a veil in public after cancer disfigured her face. Desperately lonely, she struck up an unhappy ménage à trois with Lon's first wife and his daughter, who showed up in Portland with nothing but the clothes on their backs. Fearing that she could not hold a job if her political background were known, Smith lived what was essentially an underground existence until the late 1930s, when New Deal labor policies encouraged her to come out of hiding. She got a job at Western Union, became a charter member of the Portland local of the Commercial Telegraphers Union, and threw herself heart and soul into the labor movement once more. By the time she died in 1958, she was known as the "first lady of Oregon labor." "I have 'cast my bread on the waters' all through my half-century in the LABOR MOVEMENT," she exulted. "It has 'returned to me ten fold.'"

O. Delight Smith was a warrior, embroiled simultaneously in what she saw as a "Mighty Conflict" between capital and labor and in a struggle for sexual equality. She fought on two fronts, with workingmen against their bosses and with women against the "petty prejudices of the present day." She also joined forces with middle-class women reformers who presented themselves as asexual protectors of working-class girls. Delight too adopted that public persona, but in reality she subscribed to a more complicated moral code—a bohemianism that was blossoming most spectacularly in Greenwich Village, but that was also inspiring sexual rebels across the country to assert a new, more public and provocative brand of comradeship and sexual experimentation.

The attack on Smith's sexual reputation, the collapse of her marriage, her banishment from Atlanta's craft community, and her wager on the bright promise of romantic love all helped to ensure that in the written accounts of the period her name could not be found. By recovering the lives of such forgotten people we do more than honor heroes who gave much and got little in return. We are reminded of our own limitations and losses, and confronted with the wonders of resiliency and the wayward politics of love.

"Brave about Words":
Margaret Anderson and the *Ulysses* Trial

CHRISTINE STANSELL

It isn't far from O. Delight Smith's struggle for personal and political liberation to Greenwich Village "new woman" Margaret Anderson, founder of a literary magazine called the Little Review. Both were feminists who insisted on economic independence and sexual liberation alongside political equality and justice. Free speech, not labor politics, was the backdrop of Margaret Anderson's heroism. In 1918 she risked reputation and livelihood by publishing sections of James Joyce's Ulysses *in the* Little Review, *which led to her indictment and prosecution on charges of criminal obscenity. She lost her case, but she was right about* Ulysses.

MARGARET ANDERSON was a brilliant modernist editor and defender of free speech in the 1910s. Almost entirely on her own between 1918 and 1920, Anderson defied the U.S. censors and a censorious literary establishment to publish in her journal, the *Little Review*, substantial pieces of James Joyce's masterpiece *Ulysses*, the first appearance of the book anywhere. Anderson's championship of Joyce subjected her magazine to continual police action and finally, in 1920, landed her in court on criminal obscenity charges. A consummate ironist and a profoundly happy person, Anderson never counted herself a hero; with the insouciance that was her trademark, she deflected attention from the high emotional and professional price of the *Ulysses* trial, which ruined her as an editor and indirectly led to her expatriation to Europe. Yet a hero she certainly was: steely in her determination to uphold deeply held beliefs, unyielding in the face of superior force.

Like most other heroes, Anderson underwent a long preparation for her moment of courage. Her first act of heroism was her determined self-transformation in the early 1910s from a midwestern debutante—born in 1886 in Indianapolis to the higher life of country clubs and bridge, as she put it acerbically—to a feminist, radical, and aesthete of amazingly fine judgment. In 1908, Anderson wrenched herself out of Indiana and rode early-twentieth-century currents of young women's ambition and rebellion (sexual and social) to Chicago to become a journalist. Cut off from her family, she lacked money, but her lyrical sense of a dramatic encounter between herself, the "new woman," and the great city sustained her. She found friends and matched spirits in Chicago's small but vibrant bohemian community. In 1914, she pressed beyond her role as "girl reporter" to create something new for herself and the literary world, her *Little Review*, conceived amid the close bohemian circle and funded on a shoestring of contributions from fellow artists and intellectuals devoted to the "new" taste in literature, the onrushing tide of the modern. A new lover, the painter Jane Heap, became a coeditor; in a milieu where lesbianism still seemed a matter of genteel "Boston marriages," the two presented themselves—again in the modern manner—as a forthright couple to their peers and supporters.

The *Little Review* was a journal in the modern manner. Its poetry was unrhymed free verse (seen as revolutionary at the time); its literary and art criticism combined aesthetic sophistication with meditations on political radicalism, a chemistry effected in part through Anderson's friendship with the anarchist firebrand Emma Goldman. In an eclectic American manner, Anderson mixed avant-garde writing with the political preoccupations that swirled around her in a time brimming with feminist and labor insurgency. She made her journal a free speech soapbox, publishing articles on Nietzsche, classical music, and postimpressionism, along with defenses of radical labor organizations and birth control. Readers, ranging from middle-class art lovers to eager working-class socialists, responded with passion—sometimes enthusiastic, sometimes disdainful—to Anderson's presentation of the new in all realms of thought.

It took grit and determination to keep the magazine going. The culture, a few years earlier so receptive to the new literature, had begun to turn against radical writing of any kind and antipathy mounted. In the rumblings of mounting war sentiment, the radicals and the left-wing trade unions blended in the public imagination into a diffuse mass of pacifist quislers, immigrants of shaky loyalties, and anarchist saboteurs. Undeterred, Anderson continued to lend journal space to the defense of radical causes. The Boston doyenne of free verse, Amy Lowell, offered to support the journal on the condition that Anderson leave out the support of labor and Emma Goldman, but Anderson refused.

In 1917, with their financial situation dire, Anderson and Heap made a risky bid to catapult the journal into the big time by moving it to New York. The move was not propitious. The wartime political chill had already set in in Greenwich Village, where they took up residence. The censors were gearing up; editors and newsstands were newly wary of radical publications; once-sympathetic wealthy liberals were not returning calls. The Village writers who were the *Little Review*'s natural allies were preoccupied with their own troubles; the editors of the *Masses*, the centerpiece of downtown modern radicalism, had been regularly harassed by the censors and by summer were on trial for their antiwar writing under the newly passed Espionage Act. Financial duress, compounded by loneliness, plagued the New York adventure from the start. The subscription base eroded as readers turned away from a literary revolt that once looked psychologically tantalizing but now smacked of political sedition. From 1917 until 1922, Anderson remembered, "There was almost never a week when the morning coffee was assured."

To keep the journal going, Anderson took on as foreign editor Ezra Pound, the avant-garde Philadelphia poet now living in London. Pound brought with him a guarantee of a solid sum per year from his friend and backer John Quinn, a New York lawyer and crusty patron of modern art. Pound and Quinn were looking for an American forum for their cranky views, and the *Little Review* seemed ripe for a takeover. Anderson and Heap were young, broke, and lacking in New York literary connections. Yet the two women held their own with the rescuers. Ezra Pound got his two pages of editorial space and the satisfaction of seeing his English friends' work published in the United States, but he failed to take control and even came, one senses from his letters, to respect Anderson's savvy and judgment. He supplied the journal with stunning writing—his own poems as well as new work from Eliot and Yeats. Anderson, for her part, was fortified in her dealings with Pound by a distinct set of alliances and commitments on the left as well as by her unflappable self-confidence.

Both Pound and Quinn were devoted to James Joyce, who was knocking around the Continent in a penniless state not dissimilar to Anderson's. In 1918, Joyce was scarcely published. In Europe, his work received publishers' responses that ranged from censorious to frightened. In the United States, *Portrait of the Artist* had appeared in 1916, to indifferent critical response. Now Joyce was finishing off great chunks of *Ulysses*, and his publishing prospects seemed, if anything, dimmer.

In New York, even the "new" publishers who prided themselves on taking modern work—Joyce's first publisher Ben Huebsch, Horace Liveright, and Alfred Knopf—were anxious. The thickening atmosphere of government surveillance in the war crisis had given energy and renewed authority to John Sumner, head of the quasi-government Society for the Prevention of Vice and heir to Victorian moral reformer Anthony Comstock. Comstock had harassed the New York literary scene for years, seizing and suppressing copies of books and journals under an obscenity law that he had secured in 1871. Sumner was now seeking to fill the shoes of the giant. Alfred Knopf, a man who moved at the edges of radical circles and a contributor to the *Little Review* as well as a publisher, had just capitulated to Sumner's demands, not only pulling all copies of an offending novel from the stores but going so far as actually to burn the plates. The years 1917 and 1918 were rip-roaring ones for censorship; "political" literature was virtually guaranteed to be prosecuted under the Espionage Act, and "art" that was not liable to suppression under the act was vulnerable to obscenity prosecutions from John Sumner. The two forms of surveillance also interacted, a point seldom grasped by historians of the war and free speech. Thus the *Little Review* first ran afoul of the Comstock law with a Wyndham Lewis short story that had little to do with sex but was steeped in antiwar sentiment.

Publishing *Ulysses* was without question a dangerous proposition. Ben Huebsch would not even touch the manuscript unless Joyce agreed to excise scatological and sexual sections. Quinn, a man who, whatever his sophisticated tastes in art, prided himself on his social respectability, was leery of the book from the beginning. He hated all the language of body fluids and saw an inevitable tangle with the police looming in the not-too-distant future. Pound was excited over the chance to sponsor the publication of a masterpiece, but wary lest he offend Quinn; he tried to mediate by asking Joyce to edit out some of the offending lines, a request Joyce adamantly refused. Only Anderson and Heap were unambivalent. They found a printer, a Serbian immigrant who was the son of a distinguished poet. His lack of English and commitment to great literature combined to make him impervious to the threat of being shut down by the censors. In spring 1918 they went to press with the first of twenty-four installments of the then-unknown *Ulysses*, printed virtually as Joyce finished writing each section and mailed it off to them.

In taking the risk Anderson went on her own instincts, undergirded by Heap. Support, applause, acclaim—even respect—were lacking. Writers in New York were uninterested. The New York literary critics were indifferent. The publishers looked the other way. Joyce himself was too involved with the writing to be grateful; publication as he saw it was his due. But Anderson and Heap were enchanted with the beauty and the comedy of the book, so much so, Anderson confessed at one point to Joyce, that they could barely lay out one episode because they laughed so hard. The censors seized one issue after another for burning—four thousand copies at a swoop—driving the journal's finances into the ground. Finally, in fall 1920, Sumner brought up Anderson and Heap on criminal charges of purveying obscenity through the mails. The offending matter was the "Nausicaa" episode in which Leopold Bloom engages in "some erotic musings"—Anderson's delicate phrasing—and masturbates while watching Gertie McDowell lean back and bare her legs.

At this pass Anderson had no choice but to turn to Quinn, an eminent lawyer and, theoretically, a man committed to Joyce and the cause of modern literature. Indeed, faced with the disinterest of liberal and left New York literary circles, Quinn was the only ally within reach. But Quinn, who disliked women to begin with, harbored a particular contempt for Anderson and Heap because they were lesbians. "I have no interest at all," he had already written Pound when he saw trouble brewing, "in defending people who stupidly and brazenly and Sapphoisticaly and pederastically and urinally, and menstrually violate the law, and think they are courageous." If Anderson and Heap faced ruin because of *Ulysses*, it was only what they deserved. Lesbians and litigation went hand in hand. "All pederasts want to go into court. Bringing libel suits is one of the stigmata of buggery. The bugger and the Lesbian constantly think in terms of suits and defenses."

Margaret Anderson went to trial on criminal charges with a lawyer who detested her and her magazine and had only lukewarm convictions about the rightness of her cause. If it had not been for his devotion to Pound and his fellow Irishman Joyce, Quinn would have had no truck with what he called "sex literature." He tried to reach a gentleman's agreement in a series of lunches with Sumner, but Anderson, who knew well the tactics of publicity, militant defense, and legal appeal that Emma Goldman, the Industrial Workers of the World, the editors of the *Masses*, and other feminist and labor radicals and their lawyers had used to turn courtrooms into theatrical defenses of the right to free speech, insisted on going to trial. As to the conduct of the defense, Quinn, who had his own sympathies with censorship, insisted on sticking to the narrowest possible grounds. He brought in a panel of male experts who testified variously that *Ulysses* was incomprehensible, not obscene; loathsome and disgusting, not obscene; and Freudian, not obscene. In his summation, he apologized for Joyce, agreeing with John Sumner that the book was indeed "disgusting in portions but not maliciously so" and prompting one judge, in gentlemanly agreement, to observe, "Yes, it sounds to me like the ravings of a disordered mind. I can't see why anyone would want to publish it!" Anderson and Heap remained silent, on counsel's orders.

Yet the two were not cowed. In a pretrial hearing, Jane Heap horrified Quinn by standing up to give a lyrical speech, defiant in its lovely matter-of-factness, on the relations of literature and life. "Girls lean back everywhere," Heap observed memorably of the example of Gertie McDowell, "showing lace and silk stockings, wear low-cut sleeveless blouses, breathless bathing suits; men think thoughts and have emotions about these things everywhere—seldom as delicately and imaginatively as Mr. Bloom—and no one is corrupted." Outside the courtroom, they published a running denunciatory account of the trial accompanied by diatribes against the suppression of free speech.

The verdict was, unsurprisingly, guilty. Quinn succeeded in having the sentence reduced from a jail term to a fine, although not in preventing his clients from being hauled off to be fingerprinted like common felons. Incredibly, in the light of later litigation over *Ulysses*, he gave no thought to an appeal. The trial stirred some mild interest in the press, although to the detriment of both the *Little Review* and *Ulysses*; the *New York Times* led the pack, sneering at "a decadent art magazine that delights in publishing the filth of diseased contemporary writers" and voicing genteel pleasure that the legal defense had fizzled before the matter became a free speech fracas. Anderson returned to publishing the journal, although its financial and intellectual health was broken; in 1922 she and Heap left the country for more congenial milieus, Anderson to Paris and Heap to London.

Not too much later, the tables would turn. With all publication blocked in the United States, the American expatriate Sylvia Beach, owner of a bookstore in Paris, in 1922 published Joyce's book under her shop's imprint. Backed now by leading French critics, the novel in its French venue quickly garnered acclaim through the Atlantic world as a modernist masterpiece. In the United States, critics and writers circulated underground copies from Paris and filled newspaper columns lamenting the puritanism of an American culture that forebade legitimate publication in this country. Perhaps out of embarrassment, perhaps from ignorance, the latter-day defenders did not mention Margaret Anderson except to denigrate her efforts. When a critic for the *New York Tribune* was challenged on his past evaluation, he replied he had misjudged *Ulysses* because the *Little Review* installments contained so many spelling errors.

Anderson refused the self-pity that can result from the thwarted act of courage. Her only regret was that she had not pressed for a jail term to make the case more flamboyant and public. In the mid-1920s, she did allow herself to mock publicly the American papers and literary critics who, now that the winds had turned in Europe, were rising to defend James Joyce, critics who had once denounced him. But mostly she had other fish to fry. Heap took the journal to London, and Anderson went on to another kind of life in Paris, returning to the classical music she loved and establishing herself as an elegant artistic presence in the avant-garde lesbian world there until the war. She died in 1973.

Anderson's courage was a cheerfully oblivious kind. She was uncalculating and bold, buoyed by an absolute confidence in her judgment in public matters. She risked her livelihood and, in essence, destroyed her journal by making a political defense of the right of artists and editors, not police and magistrates, to judge the value of artistic work. Once the Serbian printer, alert to the tremors of trouble that reading Joyce's language set off, told Anderson he had grown up believing that "words are good for people" but that in America, "people are not brave about words." In Margaret Anderson, he met an American heroine—dashing, beautiful, fashionable, and lighthearted—who was brave about words.

Ned Cobb: He Stood His Ground

JACQUELINE JONES

Sometimes a single book can rescue a historical character from obscurity. Such was the case with Theodore Rosengarten's All God's Dangers: The Life of Nate Shaw *(1974), the pseudonym for Alabama sharecropper Ned Cobb. Cobb's whole life was a series of small but powerful protests against the oppression of a southern agricultural system that treated blacks like second-class citizens and a political system that denied them their rights entirely. In this grinding, daily struggle for respect, even buying a pair of shoes became a heroic act.*

ONE MONDAY morning in December 1932, in Tallapoosa County, Alabama, a forty-seven-year-old farmer named Ned Cobb arrived at the home of a friend who was scheduled to lose all of his livestock to a white creditor that day. There Cobb found six other black men, all of them members of the recently formed Sharecroppers Union; together they intended to take a stand against the predatory practice of "cleaning out" households deemed debt ridden. In the Depression-era rural South, foreclosure proceedings were hardly a novelty, but on this day sheriffs' deputies must have been taken aback to encounter Cobb, attired in a brand new pair of Big-8 overalls, a white cowboy hat, and knee-high Red Wing boots, and fortified with the courage of his convictions. Recalled Cobb many years later, "From my boy days comin along, ever since I been in God's world, I've never had no rights, no voice in nothin that the white man didn't want me to have— even been cut out of education, book learnin, been deprived of that. How could I favor such rulins as have been the past?"

Cobb watched silently as the arrival of carloads of deputies prompted his friends to flee into the nearby swamp. Another black man he knew, hired by the lawmen, set to rounding up the mules that were to be hauled away. Describing the confrontation half a century later, Cobb told an interviewer, "I just stood right on and I was standin alone," facing down four armed white men. When he turned around to enter his friend's house, one of the deputies opened fire and shot Cobb in the back: "Blood commenced a flyin—." At that point Cobb whipped out his own .32 Smith and Wesson pistol and began shooting just as the deputy ducked behind a tree.

When the smoke cleared, Cobb managed to limp a mile to his own house, but he was later arrested and convicted for his part in the confrontation. Despite receiving legal counsel from the International Defense Fund, a communist-backed organization that provided legal assistance for southern black defendants, Cobb served twelve years in prison (from 1933 to 1945), with his wife, nine children, and one adopted nephew forced to piece together a living without him. In prison, Cobb was sustained by his religious faith (he underwent a conversion in April 1933) and by the knowledge that he was worth more alive to his family than dead. Essentially Ned Cobb lived out his prison years the way that many other southern black men and women lived out their entire lives: holding dear the ties with friends and family rather than risk life and limb in retaliation for denying the color-caste system.

The shoot-out that cold morning in the winter of 1932 forms the moral center of Theodore Rosengarten's book, *All God's Dangers: The Life of Nate Shaw*, published in 1974, the year after Cobb died. Throughout the book, Rosengarten used pseudonyms for all the persons and most of the places he mentioned in order to protect the privacy and identity of Cobb and his family. In a note at the beginning of the paperback edition of the book (published in 1975), Rosengarten confirmed what several articles in newspapers and magazines had by that time already revealed—that Nate Shaw was in fact Ned Cobb.

Based on 120 hours of interviews conducted over thirty-one sessions, the book chronicles Cobb's life, from his birth in 1885 to his death in 1973, and in the process provides a gripping narrative detailing one man's refusal to yield to the brutalities of the Jim Crow South. Nevertheless, this particular incident in 1932 represented but the culmination of Cobb's resistance to the code of passivity and deference imposed by whites on virtually all blacks during this period. Indeed, he lived a whole life marked by everyday acts of heroism as he attempted to provide well and proudly for his family. It is the accumulation of these seemingly modest achievements that gives Cobb the stature of a true American hero.

Ned Cobb was a hardworking man. Throughout his long life as a farmer, he achieved the near impossible; he was dependent on white landlords for only four years, when he was a young husband and father just starting out. Released from slavery without the cash or land that would have enabled their households to achieve a modest self-sufficiency, most freed people and their descendants in the rural South remained landless, beholden to white property owners and arrogant white creditors who routinely engaged in fraudulent practices. In contrast, Cobb paid his own way each year, avoiding the tangle of indebtedness and crop liens (mortgages on a farmer's harvest) that ensnared his neighbors season after season.

The Sharecroppers Union (SCU) included both black and white members who were "tired of the rich man gettin richer and the poor man gettin poorer." The group traced its origins to 1931, when declining cotton prices devastated landless families of both races in the Alabama black (cotton) belt. In the spring of that year, local farmers, working with an organizer sent by the Communist party, met together to draw up a list of demands that would ease their plight; they demanded that sharecroppers have the right to plant small gardens, that day laborers be paid cash wages, and that black children receive a public education equal to that provided to white children. In the summer of 1931, law enforcement agents raided a meeting of the fledgling SCU; one black farmer was killed, and thirty-five others were arrested and jailed. This incident formed the backdrop for the December 1932 shoot-out.

In 1935, the SCU managed to sponsor wage strikes among Alabama farm laborers and gained a measure of influence as a mediator between New Deal farm agencies and Alabama tenants and sharecroppers. Later in the decade, now called the Farm Laborers and Cotton Field Workers Union, it merged with the American Federation of Labor.

Throughout the Great Depression, the SCU suffered from violent repression at the hands of individual white landlords and their agents representing the legal and judicial systems. Cobb himself believed that, in the eyes of the white judge who sentenced him, his real crime was not self-defense but "bein a member of this organization," one that posed an implicit threat to a series of southern social hierarchies—rich over poor, white over black, creditor over debtor.

"The colored man was used to havin the white man lookin over his shoulder all the time; that was the main way of life in this country since slavery days," but, Cobb stressed, no white man ever had to cajole or force him to work; he took seriously his responsibilities to his family and refused to let whites get in his way. He declined to join his kinfolk who were moving north. Possessing unique talents as a farmer, he early in his life had decided to ease his lot with a life on the land. Within the circumscribed limits of rural southern society, he made a good living and was not afraid for the whole world to know about it. It was Cobb's own love of the land that spurred his commitment to social justice: "And who is the backbone of the world? It's the laborin man, it's the laborin man."

Ned Cobb pursued prosperity in a way that set him at odds with other black farmers in the area. He "scuffled" so that he would not be entirely reliant on any single crop of cotton. Together with his wife, Viola Bentley Cobb, and his children, he grew cotton and raised hogs, kept honeybees, and peddled milk, butter, syrup, and eggs. He raised watermelons and whittled ox handles, operated a blacksmith's shop, wove baskets and caned chair bottoms, and hauled lumber. Yet Cobb engaged in a kind of domestic consumption that was dangerous just because it was so conspicuous. He kept his mules well fed and fat. It was not even the size of the mules that attracted the attention of suspicious white folks for miles around; "it was the *vim* of the mules I had." In the early 1920s, he bought a brand-new Ford and over the next few years traded in outdated models for new ones. In the Jim Crow South, where whites equated blackness with impoverishment, for a man like Cobb to buy things, or even to aspire to own things, was a bold act in itself.

Close to home, both his father and his brother, Peter, eschewed the hard work that seemed to benefit only white landlords and creditors; these black men preferred to spend their days hunting, leaving the hard field work to their wives and children. Cobb remembered Peter as an indifferent worker, who early in his life decided not to want much of anything of material value. By refusing to hope for or want too much, these men, and many others like them, shielded themselves from bitter disappointment; they abided by the lesson of Jim Crow labor economics: "it weren't no use in climbin too fast; weren't no use in climbin slow, neither, if they was goin to take everything you worked for when you got too high."

From the Civil War until well into the twentieth century, the crop lien system was among the most effective instruments of white supremacy. Under this system, one poor harvest provided white creditors with the license to seize the lifetime fruits of a farmer's labor. Cobb understood that by controlling the rural credit system, white men controlled the labor and circumscribed the lives of black men and women. Yet, referring to the boll weevil plague around the time of World War I, Cobb admitted that "all God's dangers aint a white man."

Still, whites had the power to make or break any black farmer. As a young man, Cobb encountered merchants who refused to sell him supplies. Later, when he accumulated a pretty homestead "and was makin somethin of myself, then they commenced a runnin at me, wantin to make trades with me." Many years later he recalled a turning point, the day when he successfully resisted the demands of a white creditor. Referring to a bank note that entitled a bank to strip the Cobb homestead of all its worldly possessions at the end of the year, the white man, a Mr. Watson, assured him, "Oh, it's just a paper, it don't amount to nothin." Cobb turned down Watson, and other white money lenders, "flat as a griddlecake."

In order to keep the upper hand, white men were as likely to put a pen in the hand of an illiterate farmer as to put a gun to his head. Cobb himself often had to rely on his wife, Viola, who could read, write, and reckon; he understood full well that his lack of schooling was a considerable hindrance in a system that revolved around the annual, end-of-the-year credit accounting. Cobb loved his wife and appreciated her hard work as a mother and helpmate; unlike most sharecroppers, he could afford to insist that his wife attend exclusively to duties inside their home, rather than work in the fields and thus increase her vulnerability to white men of all kinds.

It is revealing of the white South's peculiar, and peculiarly perverse, value system that the black man who sought to buy his son or daughter a decent pair of shoes had to demonstrate extraordinary persistence, not to mention raw physical courage. For Cobb as a young father, his wife's seemingly innocuous request one day—"'Darlin, you goin to town, I want you to get Rachel and Calvin some shoes'"—set in motion a series of hair-raising encounters with a number of white people. Of his mission, Cobb later recalled, "Well I was fully determined to do it—and that was some of my first trouble."

In town, at Mr. Sadler's general store, Cobb was initially waited on by a white woman clerk, incurring the wrath of one of her male co-workers, a man named Henry Chase. Enraged that Cobb insisted on buying nice shoes and would not settle for some broken-down brogans for his children, Chase grabbed a big old shoe and tried to strike the black man with it, but Cobb deflected the blow. At that point, Chase ran to the other side of the store, seized a new shovel, and came back to threaten Cobb with it. Cobb yelled at him, "'Don't you hit me with that shovel!'—told him to his head, didn't bite my tongue—'don't you hit me with that shovel.'"

Taken aback by Cobb's verbal bravado, Chase screamed, "Get out of here, you black bastard." The commotion prompted the appearance of another white clerk, who also began to menace Cobb. Standing his ground, Cobb declared that he would not leave unless forcibly removed. As Chase reached for a gun off the rack and loaded it with shells, Cobb could hardly believe his eyes. Surely this agitated white man was not going to shoot him dead, right there and then in the store, in front of so many witnesses. By this time, the woman clerk had delivered to Cobb the two pairs of shoes that he had picked out, and he left the store.

Henry Chase soon caught up with him, a policeman in tow. The policeman accused Cobb of carrying a concealed weapon, a notion that Cobb ridiculed ("I had no gun, I didn't tote no gun around thataway"). The two whites escorted Cobb to the office of the town mayor, a man who already knew that Cobb possessed a sterling reputation and never went looking for trouble. Waving Chase and his accomplice away, the mayor advised Cobb to leave town quietly as soon as possible, advice that was echoed by one of Cobb's elderly kinfolk whom he met while walking back to his mules and wagon. Uncle Jim counseled, "Things are hot here, son," and suggested that the younger man quickly and quietly retrieve his mules and wagon before Chase decided to come after him again. Uncle Jim urged Cobb not to embark on his journey home by coming back down the main street, but to take a back way and get out of town as soon as possible.

Cobb chose to ignore this seemingly reasonable piece of advice and instead sauntered down the street, in full view of Uncle Jim and everyone else, taking his time and "defiant as a peacock." He later recalled, "I didn't run nowhere. I stood just like I'm standin today—when I know I'm right and I aint harmin nobody and nothin else, I'll give you trouble if you try to move me."

Cobb was a man of principle and contended not only with high-handed whites, but also with some of his own neighbors—black people who resented him for his proud ways and claimed that he was too attached to his mules and wagon and other kinds of property that he had accumulated, that he "worshipped it all." Cobb expressed his contempt for blacks who were just as greedy as white men, and he also called to account kinfolk who would or could not live up to his own standards of righteous living—a whisky-besotted brother-in-law, the son-in-law who was physically abusive toward Cobb's daughter. Of his cellmates in prison who scorned him for his defiance of whites, he noted, "Really, they had no respect for theirselves so they picked at me."

In prison, Cobb drew upon the lessons he had learned earlier about outwitting Jim Crow. He decided to work hard and keep his thoughts to himself. He "played dumb" and kept his own counsel, knowing that the worst sin a black man could commit in the eyes of whites was the sin of self-understanding. He had "to humble down and play shut-mouthed in many cases to get along." He survived. Cobb refused to accept early release, rejecting the condition that he never return to his home. He served the full twelve years of his sentence.

Cobb left prison in 1945 and went back to a world that was changing; his kinfolk were scattered, many of his white adversaries were dead, tractors were replacing mules. He relinquished his blacksmith shop; the tools that had served as the lifeblood of his livelihood now fetched a white dealer some cash as antiques.

Cobb remained an astute student of history to the very end. Of the contradictions inherent in American democratic ideology, he observed, "I've had white people tell me, 'This is white man's country, white man's country.'" But living through two world wars taught him that "they don't sing that to the colored man when it comes to war. Then it's all *our* country, go fight for the country." Black soldiers died for the United States, but black veterans endured the humiliation of Jim Crow.

Nevertheless, Cobb was hopeful at the time of his death. Among the more dramatic developments in his neighborhood, he pointed to "somethin I never thought I'd see—school buses travelin every day through the settlement. Change is on, and everything that aint changed goin to be changed." His one regret was that after a lifetime of hard work, he possessed nothing tangible to bequeath to his children. But on this last score, Ned Cobb was wrong; he left to his children, and, via Theodore Rosengarten, all of us an epic story of one man's struggle against the historic forces of poverty and injustice.

Carlo Tresca,
a drawing by Eliena Krylenko

Carlo Tresca: "Every Inch a Fighter"

JOHN PATRICK DIGGINS

Carlo Tresca had a lot of enemies, but he had even more friends. They did not always agree with his political priorities, but they found his passion for life irresistible. Even before he left southern Italy for America, he had been drawn to revolutionary politics. From then on he continued to preach anarchism on street corners, in strikes, in newspaper editorials—wherever he found an audience. Tresca's heroism lies in his willingness to speak out, at two key moments in twentieth-century history, against fascism and then communism. It cost him his life.

N O ONE EXPECTED him to die peacefully in bed. When news spread through New York's Greenwich Village on the evening of January 11, 1943, that "Tresca has been gunned-down," his acquaintances were saddened but hardly surprised. As much as Carlo Tresca had many friends and admirers, he also had, to use the title of Dorothy Gallagher's valuable biography, "all the right enemies."

It has been said of Tresca that if there was a political cause to fight, he was the man for it (*Ci volveva un uomo come lei*). With gusto he took on both the antifascist and the anti-Stalinist causes and moved them from the shop floors and political halls out into the streets, and it was in the streets that a hit man stepped out of a car to shoot him from behind, one bullet piercing his back, another lodging in his skull. Tresca died instantly. The murder remains unsolved.

Perhaps, as Max Eastman observed at the time, "Carlo had to die a violent death" at the "hands of a tyrant's assassin. He had lived a violent life. He had loved danger. He had loved the fight." Years earlier, in a profile titled "Troublemaker" in the *New Yorker*, Eastman gave readers a taste of Tresca's "moral philosophy": "'Everybody likes me. I like everybody,' he says. 'Jeez Christ, I canna keep no enemy.' And then he adds 'I t'ink beautiful to have frien's and be frien's. But when de fight comes, an' my closest frien' he on de wrong side, I give no quarter, I make no pity for my frien.'"

Had Tresca learned English well, he could have been, Eastman observed, the "most powerful" figure in the American labor movement. Possibly so, but it is impossible to classify Tresca politically. In the early part of the century, he joined forces with the anarchosyndicalist Industrial Workers of the World (IWW) and led the textile strikes at Lawrence, Massachusetts, and Paterson, New Jersey. But Tresca shunned organizations and rarely identified with an established political party. "Individual liberty," John Dos Passos said of him, "was his daily passion." Sidney Hook saw him as "a kind of Renaissance figure" whose "sunny enthusiasms" for ideas, people, and freedom flowed from an "enormous appetite for life." Leon Trotsky told Tresca that he had the "deepest esteem for you, as for a man who is every inch a fighter." An undaunted freedom fighter, Tresca's very fearlessness struck fear in the minds of his adversaries. "One felt," wrote Hook, "that a lost cause always had a chance, that it was never a dead cause, if Carlo were part of it."

"Who ever saves us is a hero," wrote Hook in *The Hero in History*, published the year of Tresca's death. A hero appears in situations of urgency and crisis, the setting in which he or she can play a decisive role in acting on events and influencing the course of history. Tresca played such a role in the 1920s when his valiant opposition to Mussolini's dictatorship denied fascism the legitimacy of unanimity and hegemony. He played a similar role in the late 1930s and early 1940s when he exposed the atrocities of Stalin in Spain and elsewhere, thereby denying communism its claim, widely accepted among left factions in America, to be a progressive force moving toward political freedom. With Tresca, alternative visions of political possibility remained alive. Edmund Wilson saw in Tresca the "antique virtue" of the ancient Romans, the heroic quality of individuals who are willing to fight and die for ideas. Tresca is also Emersonian in the way he carried out the depth of his convictions and thus gave political causes an unswerving confidence of purpose and passion. When Ralph Waldo Emerson tells us why we should "profoundly revere" the heroic, he could have been describing Tresca:

> Self-trust is the essence of heroism. It is the state of the soul at war, and its ultimate objects are the last defiance of falsehood and wrong, and the power to bear all that can be inflicted by evil agents. It speaks the truth and it is just, generous, hospitable, temperate, scornful of petty calculation. It persists; it is of an undaunted boldness and of a fortitude not to be wearied out.

Tresca's political activism began in southern Italy, where he was born in 1879. As a youth, he became involved with the socialists in his hometown of Sulmona and started a little revolutionary paper, called *The Seed*. The scion of one of the big landlord families, Tresca fell afoul of the law when he was indicted for libeling his father's friend, the town's political boss. Sentenced to a year and a half in jail, Tresca forgot to file his appeal, and so had no choice but to go into exile. On his way to America in 1902, he stopped off in Geneva and ran into the town's celebated socialist agitator. Tresca spent all night with the radical poseur arguing over religion and revolutionary strategies. When they parted the next morning, the local celebrity uttered his last words: "Well, comrade Tresca, I hope America will make you over into a real revolutionist." Tresca responded: "I hope, comrade Mussolini, that you'll quit posing and learn how to fight."

In his first years in America, Tresca lived in a coal-mining town in Pennsylvania and edited *La Plebe* (The Common Man), the journal of the Italian Socialist Federation. He joined Big Bill Haywood, Arturo Giovannitti, and Joseph Ettor in staging Wobbly strikes and sharing the dreams of workers' syndicates and the tactics of "direct action." Tresca then moved to New York and became editor of *L'Avvenire* (The Future). Like the rest of the left, Tresca opposed America's entry into World War I, and with his comrades he was hounded by government officials during the war and in the hysterical red scare that followed. After *L'Avvenire* was suppressed by postal authorities, Tresca started his own paper, *Il Martello* (The Hammer), which he would publish and edit the rest of his life.

In the 1920s, together with Aldino Felicani, the gentle Boston anarchist and another forgotten hero in American history, Tresca rescued the Sacco-Vanzetti case from obscurity through early organizational and publicity work. Later Tresca would somehow discover evidence that suggested that both suspects, accused of murder in a bank holdup, needed to be separated since it appeared that only Sacco was guilty.

Benito Mussolini, who marched on Rome and seized power in 1922, became an enormously popular figure in America, the first publicity-conscious dictator in modern history. The American press depicted him as the proper answer to the threat of communism, and the J. P. Morgan Company lent his regime sufficient money to avoid bankruptcy. For two decades Tresca devoted almost all his energies to the antifascist struggle in America, maintaining close contact with Italian-American labor unions and with the *fuorusciti*, Italian exiles, mainly intellectuals and scholars, who arrived in America in the 1930s. Norman Thomas claimed that "Carlo Tresca blocked the rise of blackshirted fascists who terrorized the streets of Italian-American districts. This was a great and too little appreciated service to American democracy."

In reality, neither Tresca nor the exiles succeeded in checking the influence of the fascists, who were popular among Italian-Americans as well as with certain segments of the American government. The struggle between the fascists and antifascists was often violent and bloody, with raids on each other's headquarters, shootings, bombings, and killings.

The flamboyant Tresca became the prime target of the fascists. Legendary were the attempts made upon his life. In championing the cause of labor and antifascism, he had been arrested thirty-six times, "had his throat cut by a hired assassin, been bombed, been kidnapped by the Fascisti, been shot at four times . . . been marked for death by the agent of Mussolini, and snatched from death's jaws by the magic power of the Black Hand," wrote Max Eastman in 1934.

Many intellectuals and journalists admired the combative Tresca. Both the labor struggle and the antifascist causes benefited from his love of adventure, talent for agitation, and sense of social justice. Tall, with thin-rimmed glasses, a shock of hair, and a gray beard grown to conceal a gaping scar down his cheek and throat, he often wore the broad-brimmed black hat of the Italian anarchists, which made him look like a cross between Leon Trotsky and Wyatt Earp. Tresca's lust for the life of political struggle made him a hero in the eyes of those who knew him. "Big, bearded, boastful, life-loving," was journalist Eugene Lyons's description of him. Feminist Suzanne La Follette remembered him as "a most impressive looking man" with "the kindest blue eyes twinkling through his glasses."

The anticlerical Tresca had no use for priests but got along well with the police; even the district attorney of New York (who publicly denounced him as an enemy of law and order) would drink at his table. Tresca had passions for women as well as politics, and he became the common-law husband of Elizabeth Gurley Flynn, a dark haired, blue-eyed "East Side Joan of Arc" who combined beauty with radicalism.

Although Tresca did not seek publicity, it often sought him. In 1924, after he had been released from Atlanta prison on a birth control charge, he stopped off at Washington for a look at the capital. Standing outside the gates of the White House, he was soon surrounded by touring children eager to enter the regal building. When the attendant signaled the children to come inside, they insisted on taking the affable stranger along arm-in-arm. At the end of the tour, the children and Tresca shook hands with President Calvin Coolidge. The press could not resist this incongruous sight. "Tresca at the White House," headlined the papers the next day. "Criminal Anarchist Released from Atlanta Makes Peace with the President."

To the antifascists Tresca remained an irrepressible presence. He wrote and directed a ribald play attacking Mussolini and planned and directed guerrilla tactics against the Blackshirts in the back alleys of New York City and elsewhere. His scurrilous barbs against Il Duce, the Vatican, and the monarchy were so unsparing it is no surprise that the fascists would try to eliminate him. On one occasion, the attempt was bungled when the car carrying the bomb blew up outside his office, killing three passengers, two later identified as members of the Fascist League of North America. Tresca told the police that earlier that evening he had received a phone call: "You people tried to kill Mussolini," the voice protested, referring to an assassination attempt in Rome. "We are going to get our revenge tonight."

Although Tresca hardly shrank from violence, he himself was too humane to instigate it and perhaps too inept to employ its instruments. Once, out of need for protection, he bought himself a revolver, but when he proceeded to put it in his pocket, he shot himself in the foot. Eastman, noting that the press usually began a story with the title, "Tresca, the Troublemaker," responded: "This is a slander. Tresca never makes trouble. He merely goes where it is, cultivates it, cherishes its fine points, props up its weak ends, nurtures and nurses it along, so that from being a little, mean, and measly trouble it becomes a fine, big, tumultuous catastrophe approaching the proportions of a national crisis." Eastman had often been with Tresca and could speak from experience. "That is what he did in Paterson, Lawrence, Westmoreland, Mesabi Range, Calumet, the great hotel workers strike of 1913, and many other less memorable battlefields. There is hardly a major industrial conflict, a genuine revolt of the workers, in the last twenty years of our history in which Carlo Tresca has not joined in the vanguard and stood in the front line under fire."

In the late 1930s and the early years of World War II, Tresca again joined in the vanguard in another struggle that was just as perilous. Part of the antifascist struggle had been carried out by Italian and Italian-American communists. Political leaders like Congressman Vito Marcantonio advocated America's noninterference in England's war with Nazi Germany. But with Hitler's invasion of Russia in June 1941, communists called for a united front, not only with other elements of the noncommunist left but with fascists and former fascists, most of whom were proclaiming their sudden conversion to the principles of liberal democracy. Tresca believed, as did many Italian-American labor leaders, that collaborating with communists would be treacherous and a betrayal of the antifascist cause. Not only had the Soviet Union supported fascist Italy during the Ethiopian war, Stalin's agents had ordered the killing of anarchists, some of whom Tresca knew personally, in Spain during its civil war.

"I see you have added a new job . . . that is to show up the long arm of Stalin," Emma Goldman wrote to Tresca in 1938. "Well, I do not envy you!" Russia, Goldman warned, had poisoned all the wells of decent public opinion and one cannot hope to get a hearing even in the so called liberal press. In the second place you will become a target for the rotten Communist gang not only to besmirch your character but also to endanger your life. For they are capable of murder open and underhand as they have proven. . . . All in all I do not envy your job . . .

Tresca had the guts of a gladiator. In 1938 he was the first American courageous enough to come straight out and indict the Russia OGPU in the kidnapping of Juliet Poyntz, a former communist who was never heard from again after her disappearance. Tresca had also accompanied Suzanne La Follette, the philosopher John Dewey, and others to Mexico City to conduct a "countertrial" for Trotsky, which cleared him of the charges the Stalinists had been making.

In his new struggle against the Stalinists, Tresca's bête noire was Enea Sormenti (aka Vittorio Vidaldi). The two had been friends in the 1920s when Tresca help Sormenti in his fight against deportation. But Tresca's discovery of Sormenti's murder of the anarchist Andres Nin during the Spanish Civil War, as well as his possible connection with the assassination of Trotsky in 1940, made him a furious antagonist. Tresca also accused Stalinists of trying to take over the Mazzini Society, an organization of Italian intellectual exiles who had democratic aspirations for Italy after the fall of fascism.

Tresca remained a thorn in the side of the Stalinists who sought to take up leading positions in Italy's liberation. The Italian National Commission of the Communist party printed a statement in its paper maintaining that "Tresca's isolation is a measure of elementary defense for all anti-Fascism." In his pamphlet, *The Moral Suicide of Carlo Tresca*, the communist Pietro Allegra described Tresca as "politically dead," referred to his "elimination from society," and advised that "it is a duty to put a stop to his deleterious, disgusting work."

After his assassination in 1943, Tresca's friends gathered together information; few had doubts that communists were involved in the murder. The labor leader Luigi Antonini informed the New York district attorney's office that two weeks before the murder, Tresca had told him he had seen Sormenti in town. "Where he is, I smell murder," Tresca whispered to Antonini. "I wonder who will be his next victim." Such suspicions led Antonini to advise Norman Thomas that the Stalinists were "95 percent" responsible for the murder.

Yet the fascists as much as the communists also had good reason to eliminate Tresca, who made every effort to keep former fascists and fascist sympathizers off the various committees that had been planned for the future of Italy after the war. And the recent research of Nunzio Pernicone indicates that there may even have been a personal rather than a political dimension to the affair. It turns out that Tresca had insulted a girlfriend of a mafia member in a restaurant and that he said of another gangster who entered the room, "The gunman is here."

The outpouring of emotion at the news of Tresca's murder testifies to his place in history. "Can you name any man," Lewis S. Gannett asked, "who lived in the midst of so many quarrels of every scale and dimension, who loved so many different kinds of people, and was so universally loved in return?" When Tresca died, John Dewey praised a warrior who always fought the right causes and left history with a legend larger than life: "We have all lost a wonderful lover of all mankind. But the world is much richer because of his life."

The novelist Mary McCarthy had further reflections on the murder some years after the event. The early religious wars, and even some of the atrocities of the Nazis, she observed, pale before the crimes that have emerged from a radicalism that supposedly knows no evil yet commits it:

> On the Left . . . a new set of values seems to have appeared. On the Left, it is Gandhi who can be killed or Trotsky or Tresca, men *integri vitae scelerisque puri* [of pure lives of integrity inside and out] while Stalin remains invisible to assassin's bullets. In Gandhi's death, as in Tresca's and Trotsky's, the very amiability and harmlessness of the victim appears to have formed part of the motive: Gandhi on his way to a prayer meeting, the Old Man in his study, Tresca stepping out from a spaghetti dinner . . . to the murderer, the serenity of the victim comes as the last straw.

The final tribute should come from Tresca's lover, Elizabeth Gurley Flynn:

> Even to see your name in today's papers
> Evokes the memory of your smile
> The violence of your tragic end—alone.

The awareness that you are no more
Creates a somber void within my heart.
There like a battered ikon you remain.
Memories, like candles, light the backward years
That twist the long road to our glorious youth. . . .
Farewell dear love of yesterday.
Farewell.

Alice Paul:
Friend and Foe of the
Equal Rights Amendment

JOAN HOFF

*Alice Paul drafted the first version of the Equal Rights Amend-
ment in 1923. Shouldn't this make her a beloved hero of modern feminism? The story is more complicated than that,
because not all feminists agreed with Paul's priorities, especially
her willingness to jettison protective labor legislation for women
in favor of legal equality. Paul's demanding and uncompromising personality also alienated many potential followers, including younger feminists who rediscovered the ERA in the 1970s.
Paul died in 1977, and the Equal Rights Amendment died in*

1982, the victim of a conservative backlash and, as Paul un-compromisingly asserted before her death, mistakes of the very movement that was promoting it.

I F ALICE PAUL is remembered at all, it is because, as a quiet, sickly New Jersey Quaker, she led militant, direct action tactics on behalf of women's suffrage, which landed her in jail in 1917. Fifty-nine years later, confused memories of being forcibly fed during hunger strikes while imprisoned in England and the United States for participating in pro-suffrage demonstrations led the ninety-one-year-old Paul to refuse to eat food delivered by uniformed personnel in a nursing home. But her true claim to fame as a forgotten hero is that she perceived that suffrage was only the beginning and not the end of the battle to obtain full citizenship rights for women. This led her to draft the original Equal Rights Amendment introduced in Congress in 1923 as the logical next step after women could vote. She doggedly supported that amendment before it was taken up by the revitalized women's movement in the 1970s. When in her opinion its subclauses were hopelessly compromised through rewording by the National Organization for Women, she refused to support passage of the amendment she had originally authored and correctly predicted why it would be defeated.

The eldest of four children born to William M. and Tacie (Parry) Paul on January 11, 1885, Paul came from a long line of Quaker rebels on her mother's side stemming back to William Penn. Her father, a successful business man in the Quaker community of Moorestown, New Jersey, could trace his lineage to another line of religious reformers, the Winthrops of Massachusetts. Raised in the Quaker tradition of sex equality, Paul remembered attending suffrage meetings with her mother as a child. After entering Swarthmore, the college founded by her mother's family, she quickly shed the strictness of her Quaker upbringing by taking dance lessons and becoming a tennis player. Despite Paul's life-long interest in literature, she majored in biology at Swarthmore, graduating in 1905. By 1907 she had obtained an M.A. in sociology with minors in economics and political science from the University of Pennsylvania and ultimately a Ph.D. in 1912. Her doctoral dissertation was presciently entitled "Towards Equality," a study of the legal status of Pennsylvania women.

Between her M.A. and Ph.D., Paul dabbled in social work at the New York School of Philanthropy and in England, but finally came to the conclusion that "you couldn't *change* the situation [of women] with social work." Her adult interest in suffrage began when she heard the militant British suffragette Christabel Pankhurst speak at the University of Birmingham; she participated in her first suffrage demonstration in London in 1908. By 1910 she was a seasoned member of the English Women's Social and Political Union, complete with an arrest and hunger strike record.

Although she addressed the National American Woman Suffrage Association (NAWSA) convention about the battle for the vote in England the year she returned, Paul did not become an active member until 1912. Appointed to chair NAWSA's Congressional Committee, she immediately began to question the tactics followed by the established—and older—American suffragists. In her battle to perk up the campaign for votes for women, Paul counted on the support of her close friend and alter ego, Lucy Burns. The two had met in a London police station and were studies in contrast: the wealthier Paul suffered from bouts of mysterious illnesses requiring hospitalization and looked "as though she were a Tanagra carved from alabaster," according to one biographer. Compared to the robust, red-haired, Brooklyn-born Burns, Paul was businesslike at best, but mainly quiet and shy. Burns's lower-class volatility and vitality played second fiddle, however, to Paul's ailing prima donna persona. Yet supporters like Inez Haynes Irwin perceived them to be perfectly compatible leaders: "Alice Paul had a more acute sense of justice, Lucy Burns a more bitter sense of injustice. Lucy Burns would become angry because the President or the people did not do this or that. Alice Paul never expected anything of them." And yet together, for almost ten years until Burns withdrew exhausted from all reform activity in February 1921, they formed an unbeatable suffrage team.

By 1914 Paul and Burns had transformed the Congressional Committee into the Congressional Union and formally separated themselves from NAWSA. This split in the women's movement marked a turning point in Paul's career as a radical suffragist. Her decision to go her separate way in pursuing voting rights for women propelled her into establishing the National Woman's party in 1917 and eventually led her to write the proposed Equal Rights Amendment (ERA) to the U.S. Constitution in 1923. Disagreements over how best to win woman suffrage would carry over to the ERA and last for over half a century.

What was at stake in that moment of separation? The facts seem some-what obtuse today, but were very important at the time. In March 1914, over Paul's objections and without consulting its membership, NAWSA leaders decided to support a long-since-forgotten piece of congressional leg-islation known as the Shafroth amendment. This states' rights approach to enfranchising women, which mandated a state referendum if 8 percent of voters signed a suffrage petition, directly contradicted the pending Susan B. Anthony amendment, which gave women the right to vote nationally in all elections. NAWSA's action prompted Paul, as head of the Congressional Union, to come out in public opposition.

As late as the 1970s Paul recalled in two different sets of interviews a profound sense of betrayal over NAWSA's support of the Shafroth amend-ment and especially of Ruth Hanna McCormick's role in that affair. "We had this constant conflict because we [the Congressional Union] would use the 'we demand an amendment to the United States Constitution enfran-chising women,' and they [NAWSA leaders] would say, 'we demand the passage of the Shafroth-Palmer giving women to [a] referendum. . . . It was the *acme* of the complicated for the congressmen and for the women of the country." Paul insisted that she had not been consulted by McCormick, a NAWSA officer, beforehand about the Shafroth amendment and that Lucy Burns had to call her back from a holiday in New Jersey to tell her. "You know what it would have done?" she practically shouted in a 1976 inter-view at the age of ninety-one. "It would have required a long petition of men's names in any given state before there could have been a referendum. Of course, it would have increased the number of state referenda on suf-frage, but it wouldn't have given the vote to a single woman!" When asked if this was the key to the division between NAWSA and the Congressional Union, she straightened up in her wheelchair and insisted: "Oh, it was. That's what it was all about. Never anything else." NAWSA's position on the Shafroth amendment led Paul to believe that it was now the duty of the Congressional Union to concentrate exclusively on obtaining the Anthony amendment through whatever means necessary.

The means she drew on came from the three years she had spent in London between 1907 and 1910, and her new direction split the suffrage movement even more deeply. Such tactics as launching state campaigns against Democratic antisuffrage candidates, picketing in front of the White House, burning the words of President Woodrow Wilson at "watch-fires" in nearby Lafayette Park, and arranging public suffrage pageants and parades were all nonviolent compared to the window smashing and rock throwing that she had witnessed in England, but they nonetheless resulted in incarceration, hunger strikes, and forced feedings for the suffragists. Ironically Paul and her followers were arrested for relatively moderate forms of civil disobedience such as picketing with banners that asked, "Mr. President, How Long Must Women Wait for Liberty?" Once the United States entered World War I, however, even peaceful protests were no longer tolerated by authorities or a patriotic public. A June 1917 banner that read, "Tell Our Government That It Must Liberate Its Women Before It Can Claim Free Russia as an Ally," drew especially virulent patriotic opposition.

Like so many other rigidly dedicated political leaders, Alice Paul was a difficult person to deal with. Her cause and her life were seemingly inseparably locked within a fragile and demanding body that was always on the verge of breaking under the strain of her single-minded pursuit. She simply refused to pay attention to the daily details of life, relying on others to take care of her monetary, physical, and psychological needs. Even before she courted martyrdom through her hunger strikes, some of her opponents within NAWSA viewed her as a devious hypochondriac who was incapable of steady leadership. "Miss Paul is an anaemic fanatic," wrote Ruth Hanna McCormick in 1914, who did not "believe in spending more than 30 cents a day on food." She is "well intentioned and conscientious from her point of view, but almost unbalanced because of her physical condition . . . [and] she will become a *martyr*, whether there is the slightest excuse for it in this country or not, and I am really convinced that she will die for the cause, but it will be because of her 30 cent meals." That same year Dr. Anna Howard Shaw compared the Congressional Union to Judas Iscariot and condemned the young women following Paul because of their refusal "to work unless they could work in their own way, even though that method was entirely contrary to the principles of the whole association." Their purported desire for unity was that of a lion's which is "perfectly willing to unite with the lamb provided the lamb unites inside of it."

By the time Carrie Chapman Catt replaced Shaw as head of NAWSA and reestablished the organization's middle-of-the-road, nonpartisan support of the Anthony amendment, Paul had moved implacably into a collision course with the traditional, older generation of suffragists. When NAWSA belatedly proposed that the Congressional Union become an affiliate once again in December 1915, it offered only terms of surrender as part of the reunion. After Paul categorically rejected restrictions on Congressional Union activity, Catt turned to her and said prophetically: "I will fight you to the last ditch." Several generations of women activists would continue to battle Paul—not just over woman suffrage (which was adopted in 1920) but also over the ERA.

Former suffragists who ended up opposing the ERA largely came from the social justice wing of the Progressive movement. Long before winning the vote, these women had fought through litigation and legislation to protect working women and children. (Only rarely could they win such protections for men.) Their opposition to the ERA came partly from their belief that it was based too much on an individual, rather than a group or social, approach to reform. There was also a partisan dimension to this dispute. Paul was viewed as a friend of the Republican party, especially for her role in drawing up a blacklist of Democratic candidates targeted for defeat in the 1916 election. Moreover, financial support for the National Woman's party came in the early years almost exclusively from wealthy women with Republican ties such as Alva Belmont, and the Republican party was officially the first to endorse the ERA in the 1940s. Only in the 1970s did Democrats become the major source of partisan support for the proposed constitutional amendment.

Both pro- and anti-ERA feminists tended to be middle- and upper-middle-class women who claimed that they were acting on behalf of all women. What is usually not said about those in the National Woman's party was that they were, or they were perceived by their married elders as being, too openly woman oriented, especially during the heterosexual revolution of the 1920s. Their homosocial bonding became a source of controversy as Freudian ideas began to place a greater stigma on close relationships among women. Dorothy Detzer, national secretary of the Women's International League for Peace and Freedom (WILPF), once said in an interview that she believed that young members of the National Woman's party displayed their sexual preference in a way that she found more offending than the "blue-stocking" arrangements that characterized the lives of so many of the older generation of reformers. A few disillusioned former members of the National Woman's party also complained about the "weird goings on at Wash. hedquts. wherein it was clear she thought Paul a devotee of Lesbos & afflicted with Jeanne d'Arc identification." Paul, who never married but also apparently never formed an intimate long-term relationship with any one woman, denied these charges. The fact that Paul and Detzer, who dropped out of reform activity when she married after World War II, were still privately disagreeing with each other in the 1970s over this sensitive issue shows another level of the depth of the split between the two groups.

In the 1920s only a handful of feminists, led by Paul, Anne Henrietta Martin, and Burnita Shelton Matthews, focused on the limitations of woman suffrage. All the inequalities in the law pertaining to jury service, property, custody and guardianship rights, marriage, divorce, and work had to be eradicated before women could truly exercise the right to vote in any meaningful manner, they argued. Paul appointed a committee of women lawyers to survey discriminatory law in all the states and to write individual legislative packages geared to eliminate discrimination. The results of this survey convinced National Woman's party leaders that another national amendment was necessary, and so Paul wrote the one that was formally submitted to Congress on December 10, 1923. It originally read: "Men and women have equal rights throughout the United States and every place subject to its jurisdiction. Congress shall have the power to enforce this article by appropriate legislation." By 1943 she agreed to the more familiar wording: "Equality of rights under the law shall not be denied or abridged by the United States or by any State on account of sex."

From the beginning Paul realized that her amendment would face serious opposition over the question of protective legislation, states' rights, and women's traditional domestic role. At first she tried to remain neutral on all three issues. She created an Industrial Council within the National Woman's party that lobbied against female employment discrimination and tried to work through other national organizations rather than build up a larger national membership for her own group. But by 1922 it was clear that labor and women's groups, including the Women's Bureau headed by Mary Anderson within the Department of Labor, would not budge on the protective legislation issue even when Paul offered to include a "construing clause," which would exempt the amendment from changing any industrial protection for women. Consequently, her "blanket" amendment did not include such a clause. On the states' rights question, she tried to placate southern opposition to the ERA by agreeing to an enforcement subclause that stated, "Congress and the several States shall have power, within their respective jurisdictions, to enforce this article by appropriate legislation.

This amendment does not require uniformity of legislation among the several States." This compromise did not produce the support she hoped for. As far as the question of women as primarily homemakers, Paul agreed that women were different from men because they were the nurturers and peacemakers, but she argued that these traditional distinctions were irrelevant to the question of equality in a democracy.

Undeterred by numerous inconsequential Senate hearings throughout the 1920s and 1930s on her amendment, Paul took the ERA into the international arena by presenting it to the League of Nations and at major international conferences. She also created a National Woman's party–dominated Inter-American Commission of Women, which became part of the Pan American Union. Then she directed a research project of all nationality laws in the Western Hemisphere and succeeded in getting an Equal Nationality Treaty signed by the participating governments in the 1933 Pan-American Conference. At this same conference, four Latin American nations actually signed an Equal Rights Treaty. In 1938 the League of Nations agreed to appoint a committee to conduct a comprehensive, worldwide survey on the status of women and even to discuss an equal rights treaty, and Paul led an effort to create a World Woman's party. These early victories at the international level came to abrupt halt in 1938 when Eleanor Roosevelt and other women within the Democratic administration conspired to eliminate National Woman's party members from the Inter-American Commission of Women.

The outbreak of World War II also contributed to ending international efforts on behalf of equal rights for women, but did little to mitigate the hostility between anti- and pro-ERA supporters in the United States. Nonetheless, on the eve of World War II, Paul's blanket amendment had garnered the support of the National Business and Professional Women's clubs, the National Federation of Colored Women, and even the Women's International League for Peace and Freedom. Only Eleanor Roosevelt could have persuaded Democratic women to unite with Republican ones and take advantage of the war to obtain the ERA as a reward for female wartime efforts, just as women had overcome their differences to achieve the vote as a result of World War I. But she did not. The National Woman's party and its international allies were able, however, to persuade Eleanor Roosevelt when she chaired the U.N. Human Rights

Commission after the war to substitute the words *human beings* for *men* in the phrase, "All men are created equal," when drafting the Universal Declaration of Human Rights.

Paul accomplished all this with an aging and small band of first-generation supporters of the ERA who had been her young colleagues in the 1920s and who now took care of Paul's economic and emotional needs at Belmont House, the national headquarters across from the Supreme Court in Washington, D.C., where she lived off and on until the early 1970s. National Woman's party membership had declined precipitously from its peak of sixty thousand in 1920 to four thousand in 1945, and the tight leadership rein Paul exercised erupted into major internecine battles in 1947 and again in 1953. In each case Paul and her ever-protective group of allies emerged victorious, but the organization became more closed, exclusive, and financially strapped as a result. By 1965, party membership had slipped to fourteen hundred. Now it was she who was considered out of date, even though initially the leaders of the second women's movement paid lip-service to her past efforts on behalf of her own amendment.

By 1972 when the ERA was sent by Congress to the states for ratification, Paul was estranged from many in her own National Woman's party and perplexed by the many organizations and splintered goals of a new generation of feminists. That same year Paul left Belmont House for the last time over a dispute with the party president, Elizabeth Chittick. Despite the independent role Paul played in modern feminism, her dependence, especially in financial matters, became an almost tragic liability just before her death, when a nephew she scarcely knew took advantage of her to "waste her estate" and to profit from selling her private papers. Paul died on July 9, 1977, at the age of ninety-two, convinced that the ERA would not be passed because the tactics employed by both the National Woman's party and the National Organization for Women were too timid and because of increased conservatism in the South and other parts of the country following the end of the war in Vietnam. Once again, Alice Paul found herself at odds with the mainstream women's movement. This time, her age prevented her from successfully taking up the challenge to achieve equal rights for women as she had earlier helped achieve suffrage for them.

Alice Paul remains a forgotten hero in part because she helped to create—and then became a victim of—a split among women reformers that lasted over half a century. By the time this split was healed in the 1970s, her recommendations for how to achieve ratification of the amendment she brought to life a half-century before were ignored. In this sense she has been twice forgotten: first as a friend and then as a foe of the Equal Rights Amendment, which she originated and then ended her life opposing.

Samuel Seabury:
The Man Who Rode the Tiger

HERBERT MITGANG

Tammany Hall met its match in crusading idealist Judge Samuel Seabury, whose investigation into widespread corruption in New York City municipal governance from 1930 to 1933 drove Mayor Jimmy Walker from office and set the stage for the election of Fiorello La Guardia. Sensational revelations of graft, bribery, and influence peddling shocked New Yorkers and made Seabury a national figure with aspirations to higher political office. But it was another player in this drama, New York governor Franklin D. Roosevelt, not the crusading judge, who won the 1932 Democratic nomination for president. As Raymond Moley, the Columbia law professor and future New Dealer, later said: "Samuel Seabury lived a massive consis-

tency, no sure qualification for great political success." Some-
times, although not often, such lives of massive consistency
take on heroic dimensions, as in Seabury's crusade for honest
governance and unassailable ethics in public life.

I F EVER A New Yorker could claim membership in that amorphous elitist group known as the establishment, it was Samuel Seabury (1873–1958). All his life, he bore the Protestant ethic and Anglo-Saxon legal traditions of his ancestors, not as a burden but as an escutcheon. He was proud that he carried the famous name of his great-great-grandfather, Samuel Seabury, the first Episcopal bishop in the United States. As a wealthy Wall Street lawyer, with a town house on the Upper East Side of Manhattan and hundreds of acres surrounding his mansion in East Hampton, he had no reason to want to rock the boat, set aside his comfortable life for several years, and take on the biggest enemy of clean government in the country: the sachems of Tammany Hall who ruled New York City and whose political influence extended to Albany and Washington.

And yet it was Citizen Seabury who rode the Tammany tiger into the ground. In the early 1930s, he heroically conducted the greatest investigation of city government in the history of the United States. He was opposed by the most powerful political machine in the Democratic party. In the course of his investigations, Seabury challenged the practices of every department in the city, deposed Jimmy Walker, Tammany's popular but corrupt mayor, and enabled Fiorello H. La Guardia, the half-Jewish, half-Italian ex-congressman from East Harlem, to become the legendary mayor of New York under the Fusion party banner.

At heart, Seabury was a "goo-goo"—a term of derision used to describe those who worked for good goverment before and after the first half of the twentieth century. From his youthful days as a lawyer in Manhattan in the early 1900s, Seabury was the very image of a Progressive party reformer and anti-Tammany Democrat. Early in his career, he represented indigent clients in human rights cases. His pro-labor speeches and reform positions in various political clubs brought him to the attention of the unions. The tough longshoremen on the West Side docks of the Chelsea District—the neighborhood where Sam Seabury was born in the rectory of the Church of the Annunciation on West Fourteenth Street—found a champion in the lawyer who did not condescend but who talked of their ideals, sought recognition for their leaders, and understood the needs of the rank and file. Seabury defended the right of the longshoremen to organize, including the rights of assembly and free speech in the streets. In an era when the average working day was at least twelve hours, Seabury spoke up at public meetings for an eight-hour day for employees in every field.

Although he would later become a wealthy lawyer representing corporate clients, his fiery language on behalf of ordinary citizens foretold the Seabury investigations that he undertook when he was in his early sixties. In one speech calling for enactment of labor laws, he said: "City employes are forced to work on Sundays without pay. Laws are grossly violated in the interest of large corporations. Public officials purposely violate the law. Resort to the ballot is the remaining weapon in the hands of labor."

Seabury's reputation grew as an attorney because of his knowledge of and respect for the law. Strongly supported by labor unions, he was first elected to the state supreme court in 1907 and then was elevated to the court of appeals in 1914. But after a few years in Albany, even the highest bench in the state was not exciting enough for a reformer with his own private political ambitions. Judge Seabury resigned in 1916 and returned to private practice. In the 1920s, he became an affluent lawyer, but he always kept an eye on Democratic party politics, especially the unchallenged rule of Tammany Hall.

When Seabury was summoned to look into municipal corruption in 1930, he could not resist. For nearly three years, he practically shut down his private practice and concentrated all his energies on saving the city. As a result, there were three linked Seabury investigations between 1930 and 1933: the first into corruption in the magistrates' courts, the second into the district attorney's office, and the third into all the departments and affairs of the City of New York. It was this inquiry that inevitably led into Mayor James J. Walker's office.

Under Jimmy Walker, the Tammany district leaders flourished. When former governor Alfred E. Smith opposed John F. Curry as head of Tammany Hall, hoping for someone with his own personal integrity, he in turn was opposed by Mayor Walker. "The political history of our organization," Walker glibly declared, "shows that the successful leaders of Tammany Hall were once district leaders. There is nothing too big for a Tammany leader that democracy can give. They are the outstanding benefactors of this town." Mayor Walker failed to mention Boss Tweed (1823–1878), the great symbol of nineteenth-century corruption. After deducting their cut, the Tweed Ring had sold and resold the city to the highest bidders.

Crime and corruption reached such proportions in New York City that the Citizens Union and other civic organizations demanded a clean-up. The murder of Arnold Rothstein pointed up the state of decay. Rothstein was the gambling czar of New York whose wires reached across the country. He was the banker for fixes in baseball and at the racetrack, and he also handled stolen and smuggled goods—a real-life personality who served as the inspiration for the fictional character Meyer Wolfshiem in F. Scott Fitzgerald's *The Great Gatsby*. "Rothstein is a man who dwells in doorways," one of his own lawyers said of him. "He's a gray rat, waiting for his cheese." On Election Day in 1928, Rothstein was gunned down during a floating card game in the Park Central Hotel. The Damon Runyon crowd whispered that had he lived, Rothstein would have collected a million dollars in bets on Al Smith's loss to Herbert Hoover for president.

The unsolved Rothstein murder dogged the Walker administration. A little more than a year later, the presiding judge of the Appellate Division of the State Supreme Court, Edward R. Finch, informed Seabury that he had been appointed referee to conduct an investigation of the magistrates' courts of New York City. Judge Finch's appointment order had come after consultation with Governor Franklin D. Roosevelt, who had requested a broad formal investigation. FDR himself named Judge Seabury as commissioner to study the conduct of the Manhattan district attorney. Finally, a joint state legislative committee was created to look into citywide corruption, with Judge Seabury as its counsel.

The political paths of Samuel Seabury and Franklin D. Roosevelt ran parallel for a few exciting years. The Hudson River patrician and the Episcopal bishop's descendant from the Chelsea area of Manhattan could meet on common ground. Early in 1930, a group of distinguished Americans started an organization called the Anglo-American Records Foundation. The aim was to establish a fund for research into the official British records from the colonial era. Seabury was named president; Roosevelt was a director. Although they worked together during the Seabury investigations, there was a great personal distance, even a political rivalry, between the two patricians.

Politically, Roosevelt was flexible enough to work with the Democratic machines in the big cities and bend to the new directions of the nation. Seabury could do so only on the municipal level. He was considered too much of a straight arrow and lacked the magical Roosevelt name and style. With the country in the midst of the Great Depression, a genius for recognizing the public weal would lead one of these men to the presidency; the other would gain moral respect but meet political disappointment. As the press covered the investigations, Seabury's name became nationally known and assumed heroic proportions.

Corruption flourished in the 1920s. Prohibition helped to link politicians to gangsters and businessmen. Tammany clubhouse leaders regularly divvied up the city, and every service had a price: $50 to make a cut in a sidewalk for a gasoline station, $10,000 and up for a seat on the judicial bench, $50,000 to lease a pier to berth an ocean liner on the Hudson River. Having handpicked legislators and judges, the Tammany bosses thought they were immune from testifying and prosecution. The wags in the tabloid press summed up the situation in a song:

> Tammany Hall's a patriotic outfit,
> Tammany Hall's a great society,
> Fourth of July they always wave the flag, boys.
> But they never, never waive immunity!

The magistrates were the center of a system of political payoffs, quashing of indictments, bribery, and false imprisonment. Judge Seabury found that as mayoral appointees, the magistrates delivered when called to do so by their patrons, the county political bosses who had arranged for their positions in the first place. Seabury and his staff of eager young lawyers looked into the rulings by the magistrates and discovered links with criminal elements in the city. A number of the magistrates were dismissed or forced to resign in disgrace for reasons of "ill health."

The Manhattan district attorney, Thomas C. T. Crain, was then punished for his puerile investigation of the magistrates and inability to halt unscrupulous bail bondsmen and police officers, some of whom were on the take during prohibition and the running-board, getaway-car gangster era.

Judge Seabury and his investigative staff, made up of two dozen lawyers whose average age was twenty-eight, began to dig deeply into city records. They turned up the case of Dr. William ("Horse Doctor") Doyle, who gave up his veterinary practice to become a lobbyist for builders, contractors, and landlords in cases before the Board of Standards and Appeals. He split fees with public officials. The board had the discretionary power to permit building variances, a power providing a rich source of graft.

The department-by-department investigation of the Walker administration put Judge Seabury into direct confrontation with the grand sachems of Tammany Hall. They protected their trough-feeding roles by holding down jobs as sheriffs and county clerks. Eighty-five district leaders received salaries of about $7,000 each for no-show positions as keepers of various seals and records. Beneath the leaders were clubhouse fixers who killed traffic tickets, served as the links to corrupt city departments, and got out the vote for Tammany candidates.

The Seabury investigations were not devoid of public entertainment. Long afterward, they would lead to the musical *Fiorello!* and a hit tune about "little tin boxes." The subject of greatest ridicule was the sheriff of New York County, the Honorable Thomas A. Farley, who testified during the citywide investigation. On a salary of $8,500 a year, the sheriff had managed to accumulate nearly $400,000 in six years. Judge Seabury personally cross-examined him and elicited this testimony:

Seabury: Where did you keep those moneys you had saved?

Farley: In a safe-deposit box at home in my house.

Seabury: Whereabouts at home in the house did you keep this money that you had saved?

Farley: In the safe.

Seabury: In a little box in a safe?

Farley: A big safe.

Seabury: But a little box in a big safe?

Farley: In a big box in a big safe.

Seabury: Was the box crowded or very full?

Farley: Well, it was full and plenty in it.

Seabury: Now, Sheriff, was this big box that was safely kept in the big safe a tin box or a wooden box?

Farley: A tin box.

Seabury: Giving you the benefit of every doubt on sums from your official vocation, the $83,000 extra you deposited in 1929 came from the same source that the other money came from?

Farley: It did. Same tin box.

Seabury: Kind of a magical box?

Farley: It was a wonderful box.

Seabury: A wonderful box. What did you have to do—rub the lock with a little gold, and open it to find more money?

Farley: I wish I could.

At the beginning of the investigations, Governor Roosevelt remained aloof, knowing that what happened in the New York County courthouse could affect his chances for the presidental nomination in 1932. His advisers told him that he needed Tammany Hall and the other big-city machines. At the same time, they were aware that he could not give the appearance of being soft on corruption.

Governor Roosevelt personally presided as judge at the removal proceedings against Mayor Walker in Albany. Although he had limited experience as a lawyer and none as a jurist, FDR surprised and impressed New Yorkers and the rest of the nation. Future voters for the presidency admired the impartial and intelligent way that he conducted the trial of Jimmy Walker, the most prominent and popular Tammany mayor. Governor Roosevelt had done his homework, a fact that Seabury acknowledged, and recognized that the evidence against Mayor Walker was overwhelming.

Records unearthed by Judge Seabury's staff showed that a slush fund was maintained for Walker by a group of politicians and businessmen seeking contracts with the city; a $10,000 letter of credit in his name for a European trip was discovered; a brokerage account for him was found, bearing the initials J.J.W., to which he contributed nothing but which magically kept growing.

Using Seabury's evidence, Governor Roosevelt deftly exposed Walker's secret accounts and business ties. Facing Seabury on the witness stand, the glib mayor complained that he was being persecuted—"transported back to Russia." Walker's mentor, Alfred E. Smith, the former governor and unsuccessful Democratic candidate for president, tried to save the mayor but finally asked him to resign "for the good of the party." Mayor Walker eventually did so, but without going to jail. Franklin P. Adams cracked in his newspaper column, "The old gay Mayor, he ain't what he used to be."

After the investigations, Judge Seabury emerged as a national personality, and there was talk of his running for president. He attended the 1932

Democratic convention in Chicago, dreaming that in case of a deadlock, he might capture the nomination for himself—in effect, stealing it from Roosevelt. But lightning did not strike. He declined invitations to run for mayor and insisted that the candidate be a fiery reformer on a Fusion ticket who despised Tammany as much as he did—Fiorello H. La Guardia, the Little Flower.

After La Guardia's victory, Judge Seabury became known as the mayor's "bishop." They were a strange, unlikely pair: Seabury, whose ancestors were proud names in old New York, and La Guardia, whose immigrant parents were among the millions of non-Anglo-Saxons who flourished despite their ethnic names and backgrounds. La Guardia, who served as mayor from 1934 to 1945, gave the city an honest and exciting government through the years of depression and World War II. All this time Seabury stood behind him as a private citizen, not telling La Guardia what to do but serving as his conscience and guide.

Historically, the Seabury investigations underscored the central point that the renowned journalist Lincoln Steffens made in *The Shame of the Cities* in 1904: "Politics is business—that's what's the matter with it. The corruption that shocks us in public affairs we practice ourselves in our private concerns." Steffens found that corruption was not merely political. "It was financial, commercial, social; the ramifications of boodle were so complex, various and far-reaching that one mind could hardly grasp them." He saw a system where corruption existed in banks and labor unions and dummy corporations as well as in political machines.

The lessons of the Seabury investigations remain.

Tammany is hardly mentioned in Democratic circles nowadays. But once it was an instrument of bribery and skulduggery. The Seabury investigations can still be studied profitably by students of city and state government. Conscience—the exercise of a private, unwritten code of ethics—can be found in the life of such public servants as Samuel Seabury, a fighting reformer for a civilized city. He believed that to overcome tyranny, public ethics must be guarded; to prevent corruption, private ethics must be lived.

Edwin L. Godkin had once written in the *Nation*: "The three things a Tammany leader most dreaded were, in the ascending order of repulsiveness, the penitentiary, honest industry, and biography." After the Seabury investigations were concluded, Walter Lippmann wrote in the *New York Herald–Tribune*, "Samuel Seabury is the most terrifying biographer that Tammany has had in modern times." And Heywood Broun, the crusading columnist, wrote in the *World-Telegram*, "I'd have my son know Seabury instead of Cicero."

As an investigator, Samuel Seabury was the right man in the right place at the right time. He was like a Roman candle, brilliant and steady and slowly sputtering out—a dedicated son of the Empire City who might be forgotten but for an investigation that bears the name Seabury in the annals of municipal history.

Edward Prichard:
Forgotten New Dealer

ARTHUR SCHLESINGER, JR.

Edward Prichard was one of the idealistic young lawyers who flocked to Washington in the heady days of Franklin Roosevelt's New Deal. Less than ten years later, his brilliant career lay in ruins, the result of a conviction on a charge of ballot stuffing in his native Kentucky. Prichard fought back, emerging as an influential figure in Kentucky politics, especially in the field of education. When he died in 1984, four Kentucky governors and the state's leaders from the press, the bar, and academe paid their respects at his funeral. Through tragedy and triumph, he remained an unrepentant New Dealer.

ONE KNEW OF PRICH by reputation. He had made a powerful impression when he was at the Harvard Law School. He was Felix Frankfurter's adored protégé, the coeditor at the age of twenty-four with Archibald MacLeish of *Law and Politics: Occasional Papers of Felix Frankfurter*. When I first met him in 1941, he was the Wunderkind of the New Deal. He was enormously fat, enormously well read, enormously funny. Bursting with legal ideas, political insight, administration gossip, and intrigue, he seemed to know everything that was going on, mimicking the mighty with immense relish. Prich dominated partly because of extraordinary personal brilliance and charm, partly too because he mingled two basic streams of New Deal energy, one political, one intellectual—the Kentucky side and the Frankfurter side.

Edward F. Prichard, Jr., was born in 1915 in Paris, Kentucky, in the bluegrass region. His father, Big Ed Prichard, was a local personality, a rough and convivial man, who had served a couple of terms in the state legislature and made his living as a beer distributor. Sonny, as young Prichard was known, was a precocious little fat boy. He wore a broad-brimmed Panama hat. He read voraciously, skipped several grades, and, after school, he hastened not to the playground but to the Bourbon County courthouse.

Kentuckians are famous storytellers, and Prich learned the art. Sometimes a county judge invited him up on the bench to hear a case. He soaked up Kentucky history, politics, and law and seemed to forget nothing. Already certain characteristics were evident: his habit of closing his eyes while he absorbed information, his passion for books, his passion for the law, his impudent humor, his remarkable memory.

Kentucky was still a southern state, where the past was a living part of the present. Politics remained a road to status as well as a source of entertainment long after the North had given itself over to moneymaking. But Kentucky was also a border state, the "dark and bloody ground," which made it sensitive to northern and national preoccupations. The Kentucky instinct for accommodation went back to the Great Compromiser, Henry Clay. Kentuckians were natural politicians.

Democratic politics in Kentucky had a liberal and cosmopolitan cast, owing in part to the presence of a great newspaper, the *Louisville Courier-Journal*, and Kentuckians were a disproportionately large presence in FDR's Washington. Alben Barkley of Paducah, Truman's vice president, was then Senate majority leader. Fred M. Vinson of Ashland was perhaps the most effective New Dealer in the House before becoming secretary of the treasury and chief justice under Truman. Stanley Reed of Mason County was solicitor general before he went to the Supreme Court. The erratic and egotistical Albert B. "Happy" Chandler of Versailles, after a term as governor, crashed into the Senate in 1939. Paul A. Porter of Lexington, one of the keenest of the younger New Dealers, helped to found the law firm of Arnold, Fortas and Porter. Arthur Krock had worked for the *Louisville Courier-Journal* and was now the chief Washington correspondent of the *New York Times*.

Prich grew up in this most political of cultures. But he added to it a first-rate analytic mind and broad intellectual interests. He was only sixteen when, in 1931, he entered Princeton. In freshman English, a professor, seeing Prich sit through class with his eyes closed, denounced him for sleeping. Prich responded with a verbatim summary of the lecture just delivered. He quickly became a renowned figure on campus.

Graduating summa cum laude in 1935, he went on to the Harvard Law School, where his friendship with Frankfurter began. As a professor, Frankfurter was effervescent and combative. He delighted in irreverent young men. Prich, a special favorite, stayed on an extra year as his research assistant. One day in 1939, shortly after Roosevelt nominated him to Benjamin N. Cardozo's seat on the Supreme Court, Frankfurter set forth an argument in administrative law. Prich said, "That is the most tenuous legal proposition I have ever heard." "I hope, Mr. Prichard," Frankfurter said, "that your capacity for surprise has not been exhausted." "No, it has not," said Prich, "and I'll tell you why. You can never tell what one of these new justices may decide."

Justice Frankfurter inherited his first law clerk, Joseph L. Rauh, Jr., from Justice Cardozo. Rauh was followed by Adrian Fisher, who was followed by Prich, who was followed by Philip Graham (later publisher of the *Washington Post*), who had spent a year clerking for Stanley Reed. These Frankfurter clerks, a high-spirited, iconoclastic group, took full advantage of their license to challenge their principal. Once when the justice was holding forth, Prich could be seen slumped down at the end of the table, counting on his fingers. Felix interrupted himself and said, "Prich, what are you doing?" Prich said, "Oh, nothing, Mr. Justice. Just counting your digressions."

For living arrangements, Prich and a group of New Deal bachelors rented an old Virginia mansion called Hockley, overlooking the Potomac.

One day roommate John Oakes, later editor of the *New York Times* editorial page, brought along Katharine Meyer, the daughter of Eugene Meyer, the owner of the *Washington Post*. Both Prich and Phil Graham became interested in this lively and attractive young woman, but Graham won and Prich was best man at the wedding. To everyone's surprise, given his unreliable habits, he appeared on time and with the ring. The wedding lunch was disrupted by a violent argument when Frankfurter (this was at the time of the Soviet-Nazi Pact and of vehement communist opposition to the Roosevelt policy of aiding Britain) proposed outlawing the American Communist party. Prichard and Graham accused him of betraying the Bill of Rights. There was much shouting, and Frankfurter finally took Kay Graham for a walk in order to cool off.

On the Court, Frankfurter became more conservative, more possessive, more insistent on agreement. Though nothing interrupted their personal affection for him, Ben Cohen (a more senior New Dealer), Rauh, and Prichard felt in the end that his reputation would have been brighter had he never gone on the Court. In 1975, after the publication of the Frankfurter diaries, Prich recalled Mrs. Mark Howe's opinion that Felix was an intellectual and spiritual vampire sucking the blood of his protégés. "While I must agree that there is some truth in this contention," Prich wrote, "it is also true that he, at the same time, pumped their blood full of life, giving oxygen, so that it was really Felix's giving and Felix's taking away."

Once Prich was having his hair cut at the Carlton Hotel when a telephone call came for him from the White House. Frankfurter was on the line and in an urgent voice asked him to get to the Oval Office as fast as he could. Prich shot out of the barber chair, his hair half cut, and tore over to the White House, wondering what crisis had caused the summons. He entered the office to find Roosevelt and Frankfurter sitting in somber silence. "Ah, Prich," Frankfurter said. "We have been waiting for you. The President would like to hear your imitation of John L. Lewis."

The stories should not obscure Prichard's immense abilities. In 1941, at the age of twenty-six, he became a key figure in solving problems and overcoming bottlenecks in the nation's preparation for war, from lend-lease agreements with Britain and Russia to the reconversion of the economy to defense production. There were many able lawyers in Washington, but, in Rauh's words, "Prich outshone all the rest in his innovativeness and determination." In 1942 he went to the White House to work for James F. Byrnes at the Office of War Mobilization. With a small staff, including Prich, Ben Cohen, Paul Porter, and Samuel Lubell, Byrnes did a masterful job of settling interagency disputes and bringing a measure of coherence to the domestic front. John Kenneth Galbraith, who was running the Office of Price Administration, said of Prich, "He was, I think, the most brilliant lawyer I ever knew." For a time, he shared an apartment with Isaiah Berlin, the Oxford philosopher then attached to the British embassy. They vied in brilliance and became lifelong friends.

There was a fine but dangerous carelessness about Prich in those days. The young men of Franklin Roosevelt's Washington were not deficient in willfulness and presumption. Judge Learned Hand, who liked the New Deal but not the New Dealers, confided to Justice Harlan Stone, "The Filii Aurorae make me actively sick at my stomach; they are so conceited, so insensitive, so arrogant." Prich was notably spoiled. He could be irresponsible and outrageous. His friends were constantly protecting him, forgiving him, and picking up the pieces after him.

Prich frequently leaked stories to the press. Leaking is always a temptation to young men in government, partly to demonstrate their self-importance, partly to advance or repel bureaucratic intrigue. Like all other presidents, Roosevelt was irritated by leaks. One day he called in the White House staff to announce he would tolerate no more leaks. "He put the fear of God into us," Prich told the story in later years. "Then he tossed his head back and, with that Roosevelt grin, said, 'Of course there comes a time occasionally when there should be a leak. Now there's a certain matter that I'm going to make a decision on that needs to be leaked and,'" looking at Prichard, "'I guess you're the one that ought to leak it. Will you tell Drew Pearson about it?'" Prich said, "Well, Mr. President, I already have."

Hockley in time was reclaimed by its owner. The young New Dealers were drawn into the war. As medical standards fell, Prich was drafted into the army, all three hundred pounds of him. "They have scraped the bottom of the barrel," he said. "Now they are taking the barrel." He spent most of his brief military career in the hospital, received a medical discharge, and returned to the White House for the duration. When the war ended, he prepared to go back to Kentucky, secure his political base, and, in time, run for governor. "We all felt then," Joe Rauh said in later years, "that of all the young men in Washington the two most likely to become president were Ed Prichard and Phil Graham."

Prich began law practice in Lexington. In 1947 he married Lucy Elliott, the daughter of a patrician bluegrass family, a striking woman with a strong personality. He attached himself to the New Deal wing of the Kentucky Democratic party, led by Earle Clements, who was elected governor later that year. Prich was not unanimously welcomed by the state political establishment. Some resented his Washington success, his high-handedness, and his vaulting expectations. They felt he had not paid his local political dues. But others saw him as the most promising man to come out of Kentucky since Henry Clay.

In 1948 Virgil Chapman, an undistinguished congressman, won the Democratic nomination for senator. His opponent was the intelligent and liberal Republican John Sherman Cooper. On Election Day in Paris, before the polls opened, workers found ballot boxes already stuffed with 254 ballots, all but one marked for the Democrats. When the news appeared on the ticker, the newspaperman Joseph Alsop, another of Prich's close Washington friends, noting that the ballots had been stuffed in Prich's home town and knowing of Prich's contempt for Chapman and admiration for his opponent, sent off a jocular telegram saying he assumed Prich was responsible for the Cooper ballot.

Alas, it was no joke. In May 1949 Prich and his law partner were indicted by a grand jury for ballot stuffing. Why had he done it? It was partly his recklessness. It was partly, he told a reporter in 1979, the "heady wine" of his days in the New Deal: "I got to feeling, perhaps that I was bigger than I was, that the rules didn't always apply to me." It was probably also out of an impulse to prove that, despite his associations with powerful people in Washington, he was still one of the boys in Bourbon County.

"We have two natures," Prich told Charles E. Claffey of the *Boston Globe* in 1983:

> We all have conflicting forces in our lives. I was raised in a country where monkeying with elections was second nature; my father did it; my grandfather did it. . . . I was raised to believe that was just second nature. There I was on the one hand with all those great moral and intellectual principles, believing I ought to stand for the good, the true and the beautiful; on the other hand, thinking it's perfectly all right to stuff a ballot box. Now that's the kind of dichotomy I got into, and it's absolutely unforgivable.

The Kentucky side of Prich clashed with the Frankfurter side, and in that fatal moment Bourbon County won. He told John Ed Pearce of the *Courier-Journal*, "It was as common in Bourbon County as chicken-fighting, and no more serious. I . . . thought of it as something you did for fun. It was a moral blind spot. . . . It was wrong, and I know it was wrong, and I think you may grant that I paid for it."

Prichard and his partner pleaded not guilty, but Prich privately admitted his guilt when he sought the counsel of a Kentucky judge, William Breckinridge Ardery, the father of a former law partner, who later testified against him in court. Prich's lawyers tried to stop Judge Ardery's testimony as a violation of the lawyer-client privilege, but the plea was rejected, an arguably dubious ruling. In July 1949 Prich was found guilty. His partner was acquitted. Washington lawyers mobilized to fight the case on appeal, and Hugh Cox of Covington & Burling prepared the brief. The court of appeals sustained the conviction. The Supreme Court refused to hear the case, sufficient justices disqualifying themselves on the grounds of personal friendship. Access to people in high places was not a total blessing.

Prich was sentenced to two years in the federal penitentiary. He missed the annual dinner of the Frankfurter law clerks, and sent a telegram: "Dear Mr. Justice, You are greatly appreciated by the criminal classes." President Truman pardoned him on Christmas Day 1949 after he had served five months. A brilliant career seemed utterly shattered.

Once out of prison, Prich sank into depression. These were dark years. He and his family were living now in Heartland, Lucy's handsome old family house in Versailles. Prich had resigned from the bar before his trial, but he was soon readmitted to practice. Still, he could not bring himself to deal with his problems. Washington friends like Paul Porter and Joe Rauh threw briefs and clients his way. He failed them. His financial matters were a mess. He often did not pay his bills or taxes and had to hide out from bill collectors and Internal Revenue agents. His friends despaired of him. He took refuge in books, spending long hours reading in the library at Heartland.

But Kentucky politics, having broken Prich, offered a chance of redemption. Earle Clements was now senator, and in 1955 the Clements wing ran Bert T. Combs, a staunch liberal, for governor. The demagogic A. B. "Happy" Chandler, returning to politics after five years as commissioner of baseball, opposed Combs in the Democratic primary. One day Prich appeared without invitation at Combs's headquarters. Combs knew from Clements of Prich's talents and set him to work. Prich remained in the backroom, but the Chandler people denounced Combs for using an ex-convict. Combs publicly defended Prich, praising his abilities and saying he had paid his debt to society. Prich said, "It is true that I was an inmate at the federal penitentiary. I lived with rapists, murderers, thieves, and embezzlers. But I tell you, my friends, that every one of those men was the moral superior of A. B. Chandler."

Chandler won in 1955, but Combs took the governorship four years later. By this time Prich was one of his closest advisers. His life was not yet under control, however. Politics seemed at times almost an escape from responsibility. Lucy had stood by him; they now had three children; but Prich was still, as Combs said, "wandering in the wilderness." On occasion he would disappear. He would send a friend to a library with a list of books and then, hiding out in some boardinghouse, read for days. He would, Combs said, "go without notice and return without explanation."

As governor, Combs put through a reform program that did much to change the face of the state. Prich functioned as legislative strategist, policy analyst, and speechwriter. His knowledge of Kentucky was encyclopedic. Saturated in its history, he knew every county and courthouse and crossroads. Combs called him "philosopher": "Well, philosopher, what should we do about this?" In 1963 Combs's friend Edward T. Breathitt ran for governor. By now Prich had recovered sufficiently in the public eye to emerge from the shadows and go out and make speeches. They sent him to eastern Kentucky, perhaps figuring that his jail sentence would not greatly bother the mountaineers.

Prich was as close to Governor Breathitt as he had been to Governor Combs and a constant liberal influence on issues of civil rights, poverty, and education. In 1966 Breathitt appointed him to the State Council on Higher Education, the policymaking body for the public universities and colleges of Kentucky. Education now became Prich's absorbing cause. Kentucky had no serious research university. It ranked last among fourteen southern states in a composite index of state support for higher education. His objective was to coordinate the competing elements in the state system, improve their quality, and make education a prominent issue. The aim of education, he used to say, was "opening the way for a larger life," and he propagated the gospel tirelessly in speeches around the state. After fourteen years on the council, he became chairman of a citizens' committee, soon re-baptized officially as the Prichard Committee on Higher Education in Kentucky's Future. The Prichard Committee's first report, In Pursuit of Excellence, became a model for other states.

By the late 1960s, his rehabilitation seemed complete. He maintained an unpretentious law office in Frankfort. Visitors climbed steep, dark stairs to a large room where he sat behind a huge desk, leaning back in his chair and smoking cigars, his eyes often closed, while he chatted about politics and law and education. His law firm at last was prospering. He had his share of corporate practice but always had time for the poor and the mountain people. "When they wanted a big-shot lawyer," a Kentucky judge said, "they would call Mr. Prichard." He knew their towns, families, genealogies, and he talked with the same unaffected ease and enjoyment to folks from the hollows as he had to Felix Frankfurter and Isaiah Berlin.

By the 1970s he was much revered. For all his joy in partisan combat, he had a basic disinterestedness and delicacy of mind. When he spoke seriously, he spoke with notable fairness and objectivity. In 1976 this ex-convict was offered, and declined, appointment as a judge on the Kentucky Court of Appeals. He had triumphed.

But now new adversities struck him. Prich suffered from diabetes, which led to glaucoma. He lost the sight in one eye, then in the other—an inconceivable blow for a passionate reader. He was uncomplaining, indomitable, without a trace of self-pity. Friends read aloud to him: legal briefs, judicial decisions, newspapers, magazines, books. He miraculously seemed to know everything that was going on, not just in Kentucky but in Washington and New York, Cambridge and London. More affliction was to come. Lucy and one of their sons had operations for cancer. Prich's kidneys failed, and for the rest of his life he had to undergo dialysis three times a week, five hours at a time. Blindness and dialysis did not stop his legal practice, his educational crusade, his advice to governors, did not stop his brilliant mind or subdue his high humor. Rather, affliction seemed to give him new self-discipline and strength of purpose and responsibility.

In 1979 he came to New York to speak at a fund raiser for his young protégé Harvey Sloane, the mayor of Louisville who was seeking the Democratic nomination for governor. Muhammad Ali and Colonel Sanders were the other speakers, but Prich, as usual, stole the show. Prich, no longer the fat boy, was now gaunt and gray, with a huge Roman head and furrowed face. "His sightless eyes were closed when I first saw him," his old friend, the editor and columnist James Wechsler, later wrote. "There was an aspect of tragic old age about him, and I almost flinched from the encounter. I could not have been more wrong. Within moments . . . he was talking as spiritedly, entertainingly—and thoughtfully—as he did when I first met him in that long-ago Washington era." It was often said of Prich, Wechsler continued, that he was the brightest of the young men whom FDR had attracted to Washington. "Amid unbearable ordeals, he has also ultimately proved to be the bravest."

He made his peace with himself and with life. During his dark years, he had found great consolation in reading Reinhold Niebuhr. Though he faithfully attended the Episcopal church in Versailles, he described himself as at best a "believing unbeliever," borrowing the phrase Frankfurter had once used to Niebuhr (who had replied by describing himself as an "unbelieving believer"). With Heraclitus, Prich concluded that character was fate. He had a diverting fancy about Judgment Day. When the last trumpet sounded, he would say, the Lord isn't going to send people to heaven or to hell. "He's just going to take away their inhibitions, and everybody's going to go where he belongs."

Character was fate. "What good does it do not to be at peace with oneself?" Prich said. "I don't know anything to do but submit to the inevitable. You know, I've had a lot more joy out of life than I have sorrow, a lot more fun than pain." His life ended, on December 23, 1984, in serenity and wisdom.

To the end he remained a New Dealer. Underneath the wit and the Kentucky anecdotes and the detached, drawling irony, he was a deeply serious and radical man, more radical than he publicly admitted. He cared in age even more fiercely than he had in youth about the powerless, the dispossessed, and the humiliated. He believed in the potentialities in every child, and he wanted an America in which every child, however poor, of whatever race or with whatever disabilities, had a reasonable chance for education, work, and happiness.

Prich rose, and fell, and rose again. He carried in his bones the comedy and anguish of the dark and bloody ground. To those who had known him since his New Deal days, he was by way of being a hero of his times.

Caroline F. Ware:
Crusader for Social Justice

THOMAS DUBLIN

The cause of civil rights produced many heroes, both black and white. Caroline Ware was one of the white ones. Born into an old New England family with abolitionist roots, she received a doctorate in history from Harvard and served (like Edward Prichard) in Washington, D.C., during the New Deal, in her case as a consumer advocate. In the 1940s Ware found herself teaching at the predominantly black Howard University in Washington, D.C. Soon she was joining her students on picket lines and at sit-ins to protest segregation in public accommodations. Ware's stature as one of history's forgotten heroes comes not from a single action but from a lifelong commitment to social justice and political activism.

As a historian and an activist, Caroline F. Ware saw a "common thread" that united her life's work. She summed it up in an interview when she was eighty-two, as her "belief in participatory democracy and the ability of people that needs to be tapped and can be tapped, and the benefit to society as a result." This conviction, she continued, "has led me to be interested in workers' education, it has led me into the consumer movement, it has led me into my concern with the integration of racial and ethnic groups, . . . into the civil rights field, and . . . into the women's field." This conviction, and the ways that Ware acted on her beliefs, made her one of the twentieth century's unsung heroes in the struggle for social justice.

Remarkably attuned to the times she lived in and the opportunities posed by dramatic social change, Caroline Ware drew on patrician roots to fashion a life committed to political, economic, and social democracy. Her commitment to racial equality had strong familial roots. Her abolitionist grandfather and great-aunt had participated in the Port Royal experiment, an effort to aid freed slaves after the Union occupation of the Sea Islands of South Carolina in November 1861. Charles Ware served as a labor superintendent of cotton plantations, while his sister, Harriet Ware, taught at a school for freedmen and women.

Their experiences, as filtered through her parents, no doubt influenced Caroline Ware as she was growing up. Later in life she compared her forebears' idealism to that of the Peace Corps during the 1960s. That same idealism was evident in all of her adult political commitments. In the 1930s and the 1960s, two periods characterized by conflict and polarization, she knew where her loyalties lay. She recalled, again in her 1982 interview, "From the time I became politically conscious at college, I identified with the underdog and always expected to be in the minority. I had a great sense that the establishment was the establishment and it was not the side that I was on."

What is most striking is how Ware drew on her privileged life to shape a life committed to issues of social justice. Born in 1899 in Brookline, Massachusetts, she attended the Winsor School in Boston and then Vassar College, where she studied under the historian Lucy Maynard Salmon and graduated in 1920. She undertook graduate study at Oxford, Radcliffe, and Harvard, earning her doctorate in 1925 for a dissertation on the cotton textile manufacture in New England between 1790 and 1860. Had she been a man, such training would no doubt have fitted her for a career at a major graduate institution—Columbia, Wisconsin, or perhaps Johns Hopkins. As a woman Ph.D., however, Ware found her first employment in the history Department of her alma mater, Vassar College. In 1927 she married Gardiner C. Means, a textile entrepreneur and graduate of the Harvard Business School; they had no children. While Ware taught at Vassar, her husband did economic research at Columbia Law School, work that earned him a Harvard doctorate. Ware's tenure at Vassar lasted until 1934 and included a two-year leave, when she directed a community study of Greenwich Village at Columbia University.

From the outset, her scholarship showed evidence of a commitment to studying the lives of ordinary Americans. In *The Early New England Cotton Manufacture* (1931), Ware devoted considerable attention to the Yankee farm daughters who worked in the cotton textile mills, as well as to the wealthy Boston investors who founded those mills. In her 1935 study, *Greenwich Village, 1920–1930*, much influenced by Robert and Helen Lynd's community study *Middletown* (1929), she examined the interaction and conflicts of diverse cultural traditions within an urban setting. She was far more interested in the varied immigrant and working-class groups in the neighborhood than in the minority who gave Greenwich Village its bohemian reputation. Her work in these two books anticipated by a generation the call for "history from the bottom up" that emerged out of the student movement of the 1960s and led to the growth of the "new social history," so prominent in American historical scholarship today. In concluding her own contribution to an edited volume of essays, *The Cultural Approach to History* (1940), Ware sketched out this perspective: "In the still unexplored history of the non-dominant cultural groups of the industrial cities lies the story of an emerging industrial culture that represents the dynamic cultural frontier of modern America."

History proved to be only a small part of Ware's calling. When the New Deal brought Gardiner Means to Washington, D.C., Ware sought work with the federal government. By 1937 she was working full time in Washington as a consumer advocate within the New Deal. She also taught at American University and served as a lobbyist for the American Association of University Women, testifying before Congress on numerous pieces of legislation of interest to consumers.

Ware coupled her work as a consumer advocate in the federal government with a continuing interest in women's labor education. She taught

five summers between 1922 and 1944 at summer schools for women workers, including the Bryn Mawr Summer School and the Southern Summer
School. In 1946 she authored a study that surveyed a major portion of this
field, *Labor Education in Universities*.

The balance between government service and teaching shifted in 1942
when Caroline Ware began teaching history and social work at Howard
University. By this point in her life, she had published three significant historical works yet remained on the margins of a male-dominated historical
profession. Some of that status resulted from her decision to move to Washington and her involvement with the New Deal. Still, gender played a significant part in her distance from the mainstream of the profession. Her
decision to take a full-time position at a predominantly black institution
signaled Ware's commitments beyond the historical profession.

At Howard, Caroline Ware became a source of strength and support for
the most politically active and committed black students. Pauli Murray, a
law student at Howard during World War II and later a noted feminist
lawyer, activist, and Episcopal priest, came to know Caroline Ware well in
the 1940s. In her autobiography, *Song in a Weary Throat* (1987), she described Caroline Ware's farmhouse in Vienna, Virginia (still well outside
the ring of Washington, D.C., suburbs), as "a sanctuary for city-weary students and government workers, intercontinental travelers on diplomatic
missions, writers, professionals, and leaders of various humanitarian
causes." She commented on the hospitality that Ware and her husband provided Howard students, making "the Farm . . . an extension of Dr. Ware's
classroom." It was in that atmosphere, in numerous conversations with
Caroline Ware, that Murray "began to develop a broader perspective on
[her] minority status and to see the parallels between racism and sexism."
Ware made the connections herself and was sensitive to the defensiveness
and sense of inferiority that students and faculty at these institutions developed toward the dominant white-male institutions of higher education.

Both Caroline Ware and Gardiner Means made important contributions to the emerging civil rights movement at Howard. Ware picketed the
Little Palace Cafeteria with students and supported student sit-ins at neighborhood restaurants in 1943 and 1944. She acted not simply on behalf of
others—that is, blacks denied service at local lunch counters—but to defend her own civil rights: "'My constitutional rights are being violated . . .
when I am prohibited by segregation laws from associating with my friend

and am compelled to sit in a separate car!'" This reasoning underlay Ware's unwavering commitment to civil rights.

Caroline Ware became still more actively involved in the early civil rights efforts when four Howard students who had attended a picnic at her home in May 1944 were arrested as they returned home from the event by public bus. The students refused to move to the back of the Virginia bus that had picked them up not far from Ware's farmstead. When policemen came to arrest the young women, one of them quoted chapter and verse from the interstate commerce clause as her authority. Travel between Virginia and the District of Columbia was, after all, interstate commerce and, hence, subject to federal rather than state authority. Perhaps this Howard student had learned the lesson in Caroline Ware's undergraduate course on constitutional law. In any event, when arrested and taken to Fairfax County jail, the students' first phone call was to Ware asking for her help in raising bail.

Ware, though not aware in advance of her students' decision to test Virginia's Jim Crow laws, was an enthusiastic supporter of their efforts and sprang into action. After calling National Association for the Advancement of Colored People (NAACP) attorney Charles Houston, Ware went about raising bail for the students, while other attendees at the picnic made sandwiches for the "jailbirds." The mood was jubilant in large part because the Howard students had been charged with violating the state's Jim Crow law rather than being charged with disorderly conduct, the common Virginia subterfuge to avoid direct challenges to segregation in public transportation and accommodations. The students had thus set the stage for a possible test case before the courts.

Ware picked up the students at the jail, helped arrange for NAACP attorneys to handle the case, and provided strong personal support throughout the trial. The atmosphere that surrounded the case and Ware's central role are revealed in an incident described by Pauli Murray, who attended the picnic at Ware's home that day but had not been one of those who engaged in civil disobedience: "Riding in Dr. Ware's car on the way back from the trial, the group circled the Lincoln Memorial, paused in front of the steps to wave at the statue of Abraham Lincoln, and someone called out, 'Abe, here we are, still at it!'" Caroline Ware must have smiled as she steered her car through the traffic.

Eventually the state prosecutor realized the mistake that had been made in charging the Howard students and rather than face a test case on appeal, he dropped the charges and let the women go free. Within two months, however, another test case developed that did go all the way to the Supreme Court. In its 1946 decision in *Morgan v. Virginia*, the U.S. Supreme Court overturned Virginia's Jim Crow law for public transportation, vindicating the Howard students' efforts.

Ware's decision to teach at Howard during the 1940s reflected her broader commitment to racial equality in American society. Throughout her career, she made conscious efforts to contribute to the advancement of African Americans in American society. During World War II, for example, she worked for the Consumer Advisory Committee of the Office of Price Administration. While there, she supported efforts to hire and train black women for secretarial positions, one of the federal government's first steps to improve the position of black women in government office work.

Ware lent support to other African American pioneers. Maida Springer Kemp, a local business agent in the International Ladies' Garment Workers Union, served in 1945 as an American Federation of Labor representative on a labor delegation sent to Great Britain. That trip began with a week's orientation in Washington, D.C., where the Panamanian-born Kemp was rudely introduced to that city's Jim Crow system. Despite the public feting of the group, Kemp could not stay at a local hotel with the others of the delegation, could not be served at most restaurants, and was not accepted as a passenger by white taxicab drivers. Thirty-six years later, Kemp recalled the trials of that orientation period and commented on Ware's crucial support: "Had it not been for that Saturday afternoon with Caroline Ware, on the Ware-Means Farm, just prior to going overseas, I think I would have snapped." After the war, Kemp moved into increasingly important union positions, joining the staff of the Department of International Affairs of the AFL-CIO in 1959. Over the years, Caroline Ware supported several of Kemp's activities. She provided financial support to African students in the United States and also supported financially and wrote an afterword for a pamphlet that Kemp put together, *Negro Pioneers in the Chicago Labor Movement*.

From personal and financial support for Howard students, African American trade unionists, and African students, it was a natural progression for Caroline Ware to become involved in the postwar decades in issues of decolonialization and Third World economic development. She taught social work four successive summers at the University of Puerto Rico and later at schools of social work in Chile, Colombia, and El Salvador. This teaching launched a twenty-five-year period in which she was active in Latin American development issues. She was an articulate advocate for community education and community participation in the development process, working as an adviser to a range of international organizations: the Organization of American States, the United Nations, the Pan American Union, the Overseas Education Fund of the League of Women Voters, and UNESCO. She wrote a Spanish-language manual for community study and action that "for years was the Pan American Union's most popular publication." She participated in numerous regional and international conferences on development, taking extensive notes in Spanish and Portuguese, and was described at one United Nations seminar as "the foremost Latin American worker in community development and organization." Ware's consulting in Latin American development built on her earlier interests yet offered ample room for continued personal growth.

Another area of growth for Caroline Ware after 1960 involved her participation in the rebirth of the women's movement in this period. She had always been interested in women's issues, perhaps influenced by having been fired from a summer teaching job at the University of Wyoming in 1935 because she was married. She had unsuccessfully fought that action, gaining a good deal of support from women's organizations and generating considerable publicity. However, like so many other socially committed women of her generation, she had not supported the Equal Rights Amendment out of a concern for its impact on protective labor legislation. Still, her work with UNESCO beginning in the mid-1950s on the twentieth-century volume of the *History of Mankind* led her to see connections between issues concerning colonial people, racial minorities, and women. With others in Washington, she had discussed the need to reexamine the status of women.

This discussion led to the idea of a presidential commission, and in 1961 Ware was asked to serve as a member of the President's Commission on the Status of Women, chaired by Eleanor Roosevelt. Following the commission's report, Ware continued to serve through the end of the Johnson administration on the Citizens' Advisory Council on the Status of Women. As a member of the commission, Ware succeeded in avoiding a direct vote on the Equal Rights Amendment and helped to craft a position that supported women's legal equality without explicitly taking a stand on the amendment itself. In 1966 Ware became a founding member of the National Organization for Women, and as changing federal policies eased her concerns about protective labor legislation, she became a strong supporter of the Equal Rights Amendment.

Caroline Ware was a committed multiculturalist long before that term came into common usage. She pioneered in the development of what a later generation called "history from the bottom up," and fought numerous battles on behalf of the underdog. Like the abolitionists of her grandparents' generation, Caroline Ware became an advocate for a variety of social justice causes, supporting workers' education, New Deal protective legislation, consumers' rights, civil rights, economic development in the Third World, and women's rights. She remained a committed activist right up until her death in 1990. Her last major published writing, in fact, provided a history of consumer action in the twentieth century. Activist and historian, Caroline Ware, like those she wrote about, made a difference in the world around her.

Lew Ayres:
Conscience in Hollywood

BERNARD A. WEISBERGER

Most Hollywood heroes appear on the screen, but Lew Ayres was a hero in real life: he took an unpopular stand that jeopardized his career and won over the moviegoing public with his quiet heroism in support of his convictions. In 1942 the actor who had first won fame for his leading role in the antiwar classic All Quiet on the Western Front *(1930) and then gone on to star in a series of successful Dr. Kildare films startled industry executives by announcing that he would seek conscientious objector status rather than be drafted into the army. Most saw this as an act of professional suicide, but defying the odds, Ayres's principled stand (he was the only Hollywood actor to*

*take it) did not cost him his career. After serving with great dis-
tinction as a chaplain's assistant in the Pacific, he returned to
star in such films as* Johnny Belinda *(1948).*

PROBABLY THE LEW AYRES best remembered by filmgoers of the 1930s is on display in a powerful still shot from *All Quiet on the Western Front* (1930), his greatest picture. Playing a youthful German infantryman, he is crouched in a shell hole next to a Frenchman whom he has mortally wounded. His eyes swim with remorse and pain as realization claws at him that he has murdered not merely an "enemy," but a man like himself.

Twelve years after that photo was taken, in an eerie instance of life imitating art, Ayres flung himself against the patriotic tidal wave sweeping the nation just after Pearl Harbor, and declared that he could not serve in the armed forces if it meant killing another human being.

That any movie star should seek conscientious objector status under the draft law—and Ayres was the only one who did—was remarkable in itself when Hollywood was shouldering arms with maximum fanfare. Even more astonishing was the potential cost of the actor's gesture. After a post–*All Quiet* career lull, he had broken through to the ranks of big-time box office draws in a series of movies about Dr. Kildare, Everyperson's favorite healer. Now he threw aside this golden gift for any actor and, on behalf of a principle, skidded into popular rejection.

Ayres's life story sparkles with fairy-tale touches. As one biographical dictionary of film says, the career was "sweet with youthful salad days, but bitter with public fickleness." But this player did not submit passively to either storms or doldrums. In Hollywood, a universe of permitted illusions and the constant courtship of the public's love, he insisted on defining his own reality, setting his compass by it, and following that course. When that kind of integrity involves personal sacrifice, it can fairly be called heroic.

Ayres was part of the early-twentieth-century trek to golden California. Born in Minneapolis on December 28, 1908, as Frederick Lewis Ayres (or Ayers, according to some sources), he was taken to San Diego by his mother after a divorce from her cello player husband. There the boy finished high school and learned to play the banjo and guitar. There was a stint at the University of Arizona, reportedly as a pre-med student, but it must have been brief, since at age nineteen Ayres was already playing professionally with a traveling dance band.

Then came the first improbable wave of the entertainment fairy's wand. Ayres had movie ambitions—as did thousands of other young men and women, to whom the Hollywood of 1928 opened a fantasy: to win overnight stardom without acting experience, merely by virtue of some intangible attraction that a trained scout could spot. Screen-struck youngsters flocked to the movie capital and as their savings dwindled, replayed the imaginary scenario over and over: the "discovery," the screen test, the makeover by drama coaches and costumers and makeup artists, the ultimate riches and fame. It was the stuff of moonbeams, and it happened to Ayres. A scout spotted him circling the floor with actress Lili Damita at a tea dance in a Hollywood hotel, and at age twenty he found himself playing in one of the last silent films, *The Kiss,* opposite no less a queen of the screen than Greta Garbo. Two years and two uncelebrated films later, he was cast in *All Quiet on the Western Front* as its central character, Paul Baumer, the disillusioned warrior barely out of teens who serves as narrator of Erich Maria Remarque's somber antiwar novel.

The movie touched a resounding chord in the young actor suddenly raised to the heights. It is still one of the best antiwar films ever made. Director Lewis Milestone gave it multiple novelties. It portrayed the Germans sympathetically for the first time on American screens, but dialogue coach George Cukor insisted on neutral accents, and thereby universalized his group of numb and battered veterans and made it possible for American viewers to identify with them. The combat scenes unsparingly showed the terror, filth, and brutality of the trenches, while those of Baumer on leave ripped at the ignorant cheerleading of home-front superpatriots. One could believe that these soldiers were left in the end with nothing but faith in each other's comradeship, a concept that must have infused the cast, since a 1942 newspaper story noted that several of its members were still among Ayres's few intimates at the time.

In spite of *All Quiet's* success, Ayres found himself enmeshed in the next eight years in a string mainly of B-movies for major studios. Rarely did they give him a chance to be more than a good-looking foil for leading ladies. It was steady and well-paid work, but Ayres was in something of a rut, personally and professionally. A pair of movie colony marriages had fallen through. The first, to Lola Lane in 1931, lasted just two years. In 1934 he married Ginger Rogers, on her way up the ladder, but they separated in two years and divorced in 1941. Thereafter his private life became withdrawn. He lived alone with his books, his music, a hobby of astronomy, and a few companions. But in 1938, the magic wand was waved again by Metro-Goldwyn-Mayer.

Louis B. Mayer, the studio's chief, had struck gold with a succession of Andy Hardy movies starring Mickey Rooney as a mischievous but clean and lovable adolescent who lived in a neat home on a tree-lined street, had an upright father (a judge), a gentle mother helped out by a black cook, and a sweet, long-suffering girlfriend. This was life as Depression-stricken America quite consciously wanted to see it and as Hollywood was glad to show it. The relationship was symbiotic. The box office take was impressive, and Mayer asked his writers to find another such bonanza. They came up with a set of novels by Max Brand involving a young and courageous physician's adventures in a big hospital. Mayer had recently seen Ayres's work opposite Katharine Hepburn in *Holiday*, and found in his clean-cut looks just the combination of gentleness and intelligence that he wanted for Dr. Kildare. *Calling Dr. Kildare* was made and released in 1938, showed a profit, and was followed almost immediately by *The Secret of Dr. Kildare* and then by seven more Kildares in three years. The plots were boilerplate; Kildare would confront and overcome some baffling ailment aided by rough-edged old Dr. Gillespie (Lionel Barrymore) and faithful nurse-sweetheart Mary Lamont (Laraine Day), who was resigned forever to play second fiddle to medicine in Dr. Kildare's heart. He was just the kind of dedicated physician whom the American Medical Association hoped the public would see as typical.

By 1941 Ayres had nine Kildare films under his belt and a tenth in production, and if he had not exactly achieved thespian immortality, he had something more bankable: instant recognizability and affection for his on-screen persona. But meanwhile the world had been drifting toward war, and Lew Ayres had, uncharacteristically for a celebrity, been seriously thinking. What would he do when, under the draft that began to function in 1940, his number came up?

"I thrashed it all out with myself," he told writer Irving Wallace in a postwar interview. "To me, war was the greatest sin. I couldn't bring myself to kill other men. Whatever the cost, I decided to remain true to myself." This conviction might have come from what he would call (in 1956) his "liberal Protestant upbringing." Or from a train of thought begun with *All*

Quiet on the Western Front. Or from reflective reading in works by distinguished pacifists like Tolstoy and Romain Rolland, as well as "the Bible . . . and every religious book I could find." Whatever the sources, by the time that he confronted Selective Service Board 246 early in 1942, his mind was made up. On the official form for claiming conscientious objector (1-AO) classification, he wrote that his personal religious convictions would make it impossible for him to bear arms. However, he requested exemption A, which expressed a willingness "to participate in noncombatant service or training therefor under the direction of military authorities." Ayres wanted to serve in the Medical Corps. He had, in fact, taken Red Cross training and become an instructor on the MGM lot, and now he begged to "be of service . . . in a constructive and not a destructive way."

Had Selective Service Board 246 listened to him, Ayres and his employers would have been spared considerable turmoil, but they insisted that his only alternative was to take exemption B, which refused "participation in any service . . . under the direction of military authorities." So it was that on March 31, 1942, reporters followed Ayres, already in dungarees and work boots, aboard a sleeper bound for Oregon and Cascade Locks work camp, maintained by the Brethren and Mennonite churches. There, he and other conscientious objectors would put in 6 a.m. to 10 p.m. days felling trees, clearing brush, and doing other forestry work. The news was out at last: "Dr. Kildare" would not pick up a gun to defend his country, still reeling from the sneak attack on its navy, and still fearful of a possible invasion of its West Coast.

The news could hardly have come at a more worrisome time for the film industry, so tightly concentrated that its leaders could usually speak on public issues with a single voice. They had been riding high, becoming the mirror and teacher of the American way for as many as 80 million viewers a week earning, according to *Variety*, half a billion dollars in 1941. Their star performers were a curious democratic royalty, theoretically "regular" guys and gals, actually living in unattainable luxury, with their every move (real and invented) reported to millions by columnists to be devoured, envied, and emulated. Stars and studios together were an enormous cultural force. How should it fuse itself with the nation on new terms? How would it speak the language of war?

There were practical issues for the government and the industry to settle. Was it in the best national interest for Hollywood to crank out diverting fictions to sustain morale? Or to focus on propaganda actions? Or lend its technical expertise to instructional films? What scarce materials should be allotted to the moviemakers? How much profit should they be allowed? And what of the male stars? From a hard-boiled point of view, a Clark Gable or a Henry Fonda cheerleading at war bond rallies or bucking up tired factory workers might be more useful to Washington than a Gable or a Taylor in uniform. Yet if democracy meant equality, would it present a better image if such men took their chances in the ranks? (As it worked out, the latter road was taken. Of leading men who donned uniforms, some, like Jimmy Stewart, compiled combat records; some, like Gable, became officers with administrative duties; some, like Robert Montgomery, organized entertainment for the navy; some, like Ronald Reagan, made training films; and some, like John Wayne, stayed out.)

These questions of participation tugged at leaders not known for boldness—the same movie moguls who, in 1934, under threat of boycott from the Legion of Decency, had conferred unlimited self-censorship powers on a Production Code Authority under Will Hays, and the same who, in 1947, would bow their necks to the House Un-American Activities Committee and other cold war communist hunters. Early in 1942 they might be unsure of whether their stars should join the colors, but conscientious objection was not an option! In their almost unanimous view, Ayres had thrown a stick of dynamite into MGM's public relations office and every other studio's too. What would the country say?

Most nervous were the exhibitors, at that time tied monopolistically to the studios. They would be the gas-testing canaries in the mineshaft, the first to live or die economically by the public reaction and so cue the next moves of the producers and distributors. The immediate impact was frightening, for as usual the outraged struck first and noisily. A theater in Hackensack, New Jersey, showing *Dr. Kildare's Victory*, the latest in the series, registered a hundred hostile calls and pulled the film. The American Legion of New Bedford, Massachusetts, demanded that theaters there do likewise. Panicked, entrepreneurs Barney Balaban and Sam Katz ordered their hundred movie houses in the Chicago metropolitan area alone to show no Ayres films. A downstate Illinois chain followed suit, and in Canada, the Famous Players Corporation banned Ayres in its 150 theaters.

Reactions like these account for the statements in some dictionaries of film that Ayres "suffered a fierce boycott" or "became an object of derision . . . abandoned by his fans." The facts are somewhat less melodramatic. Within days, the industry had taken a quick survey of audiences and found, as Variety put it in mid-April, that "film players' personal war record or service has had little bearing on their box-office draw." There was some "sporadic hissing" at a Los Angeles house showing Dr. Kildare's Victory but neither rings of pickets nor the flames of burning effigies outside the marquees. Balaban and Katz and the other chains that had rushed to purge Ayres rebooked Dr. Kildare showings as early as April 26.

By then, the situation was already on the way to partial solution. On appeal to Washington, Ayres was granted his request to join the Medical Corps. Before May was over, he was undergoing basic training at Camp Barkeley in Abilene, Texas, and soon disappeared from the headlines and into the routine of army life as Private Ayres, receiving no favors and compiling excellent reports from his commanders. Yet even before that happened, Ayres's quiet but unapologetic defense of his beliefs had won him some support. Few journals of public opinion scolded him or even paid attention. The New York Times editorialized that while widespread adoption of Ayres's creed of nonviolence would mean that "the Nazis could do whatever they wished, in this country," the public should not "hold back an honest tribute to a man who gives up a rich career and faces public ridicule and contempt because he will not hide the faith that is in him." The timing was in fact better for the handful of conscientious objectors in 1942 than during the manufactured hysteria of World War I or the cruel divisiveness of the Vietnam War.

The reaction of picture business executives was different. Their religion was always to do the acceptable thing, with minor deviations allowed the stars in such matters as divorce or conspicuous consumption. Why would someone destroy his own property value without searching for a way out? Doing otherwise, however honorable, was self-immolation. Hollywood columnist John Chapman recorded a general feeling among movie men he talked to: "All thought him [Ayres] foolish, all regretted the end of a career and the fatal damage to the popular 'Dr. Kildare' series; all thought he could have found some war work that would fit his conscience." A Miami newspaper broke the story that Nicholas Schenk, a major Loew's-MGM executive, had, at a private dinner, called Ayres "washed up." This provoked an "Open Letter" from Schenk to Variety. He said he had been misquoted, lavishly praised Ayres's sincerity, vegetarianism, charitable gifts, and Red Cross work, and added with undoubted truth: "At no time did I . . . express agreement with the stand you have taken. . . . It is a peculiarity beyond my personal comprehension."

The command decision at MGM finally turned out to be this: Ayres's pictures already shot or showing—a million-dollar investment—would be left alone, but the Kildare film in progress, tentatively titled *Born to Be Bad*, would be remade with another actor and the Kildare character eliminated. The good doctor vanished, to reappear years later on television as played by Richard Chamberlain. But in the spring of 1942 he was presumed dead, along with Lew Ayres's professional future.

But there was to be a Hollywood fairy-tale ending. Ayres was in fact not through. His military record turned out to be exemplary. He served nearly two years in New Guinea jungles (where he contracted dengue fever) and in the Philippines, where he landed with U.S. invasion forces in October 1944. Carlos P. Romulo, the Philippine writer and statesman, ran into him on the beachhead-bound transport, feeding records into a phonograph to entertain fellow GIs. "No man on that shipboard was more popular," Romulo reported, or, he might have added, braver. By then Ayres had become a chaplain's assistant who had helped to calm wounded men under fire. On Leyte, he volunteered to assist in treating civilian casualties during heavy aerial bombardment. A *Life* photographer snapped an unforgettable shot that ran full page in the Christmas issue. Inside a church converted to a hospital, Ayres, gaunt and moustached, kneels in fatigues and woolen cap over a Japanese prisoner whom he is tenderly bandaging—the essential Ayres putting faith into practice.

And as in fairy tales, goodness was rewarded. In January 1946, Ayres, back home, was signed by International Pictures to play the lead in *The Dark Mirror* opposite Olivia DeHavilland. Next came a contract with Warner Brothers, and Ayres was back in business, resuming life in a house on a Hollywood hill, with two thousand phonograph records and booklined walls. His career revved up anew in 1948 when he was nominated for a best actor Oscar for playing, in *Johnny Belinda*, a sympathetic doctor (what else?) who teaches speech and the power of love to a deaf-mute girl impregnated by a local bully's rape.

Then, once more, Ayres danced to his private tempo and turned his back on success. In 1953 he left picture making for an extensive trip to film religious practices around the world. The result was a book and a television documentary, *Altars of the East*. His goal, he wrote, was to advance world peace through tolerance and understanding, to "ultimately help usher in the long-dreamed of Brotherhood of man."

In 1964 he reappeared in a major movie role in *Advise and Consent*, playing the president of the United States, the same year in which he married a much younger woman, Diana Hall. Four years later he recorded his joy at becoming, aged sixty, a first-time father (of a son, his only child). For the remaining twenty-nine years of his life, the graying and still gentle-looking Ayres did small parts for a hugely changed movie industry (*Battle for Planet of the Apes* and *Battlestar Galactica* being prime examples) and made dozens of appearances in every kind of television show. He was simply a working actor tending to business, enjoying life, his battles behind him.

In *John Brown's Body* Stephen Vincent Benét wrote a poetic tribute to a man who performed a quietly courageous act of rescue during Brown's raid. He said, in paraphrase, that if there were writers out there seeking to tailor literary clothes for heroes, that man would be a first-rate candidate on which to drape them. The same applies to Lew Ayres, who died on December 30, 1997, two days after his eighty-eighth birthday.

The Trials of Miriam Van Waters

ESTELLE B. FREEDMAN

In 1949 Miriam Van Waters's reputation as one of the country's leading prison administrators was on trial. The Massachusetts commissioner of corrections had dismissed Waters, the well-respected superintendent of the Massachusetts Reformatory for Women in Framingham, for supposed leniency in dealing with the female prisoners in her charge. To protect her institution, and her career, Van Waters successfully fought efforts to replace her in a widely publicized two-month trial, which led to her reinstatement to her position. Fighting for one's job is not normally considered heroic, but when a woman becomes an overnight cause célèbre and she maintains her principles throughout, it becomes a very modern form of heroism.

TODAY FEW AMERICANS recognize the name of Miriam Van Waters (1887–1974), once the country's leading woman penologist. In 1949, however, when she fought her dismissal from office as superintendent of the Massachusetts Reformatory for Women, Van Waters's name filled the media. Banner headlines in Boston's newspapers popularized sensational charges that her leniency had led to rampant perversion in prison. The national media followed closely the crisis in Van Waters's career, for her name had become synonymous with the liberal reform tradition. Even Hollywood capitalized on the publicity over her struggles with conservative state officials, producing the first major women's prison film, *Caged* (1950), in which actress Agnes Moorehead created a remarkable facsimile of the heroic, dedicated, but beleaguered prison superintendent.

Since 1932, Miriam Van Waters had directed the Massachusetts Reformatory for adult female offenders in Framingham, treating it more like a progressive school than a prison and bucking national conservative trends in prison management. On January 7, 1949, however, the new, hard-line commissioner of corrections, Elliott E. McDowell, dismissed Van Waters from office. A series of investigations and newspaper exposés claimed that she had hired former inmates, condoned homosexuality in prison, and allowed the women she insisted on calling "students" to work for pay outside the reformatory. To defend her actions, Van Waters demanded the hearings to which she was entitled. The Massachusetts State House on Boston's Beacon Hill provided the setting for the opening round in a series of well-attended public hearings on "The Matter of the Removal of Dr. Miriam Van Waters."

During the first months of 1949, Van Waters's liberal supporters flocked to witness firsthand the compelling events being daily reported in the press and on the radio. On the opening day of the hearings, so many spectators arrived at the State House that the proceedings moved to the six-hundred-seat Gardner Auditorium. Overflow audiences continued for the next two months, as local housewives, off-duty reformatory staff members, college students, and workers on their lunch breaks filled large auditoriums each day. Some traveled from New York to witness the hearings; those who could not gain entrance weathered the winter cold as they gathered around windows and doorways to catch a glimpse of the proceedings.

Daily headlines in all the Boston newspapers highlighted both sensationalistic charges of rampant sexual perversion in prison and the effective strategies of Van Waters's attorney, Claude Cross (who would later defend accused communist Alger Hiss but always considered the Van Waters case his favorite). The national liberal press strongly supported Van Waters. The *Nation* linked her case with the defense of progressive underdogs in a story that began: "Not since the Sacco-Vanzetti affair has the collective stability of Massachusetts been jolted so violently as by the current Van Waters episode." According to the *Progressive*, the Van Waters hearings were part of a "national epidemic of investigation," referring to the anti-communist hysteria that would target liberals as well as communists for many years. Eleanor Roosevelt wrote about the case in her newspaper column, pointing out that she missed hearing President Truman's inauguration on the radio because she was giving a talk to a women's club deploring the ouster of Miriam Van Waters.

The center of this attention, sixty-one-year-old Miriam Van Waters, certainly cut a heroic figure at the hearings. Elegantly attired, the short, trim, white-haired reformer remained quietly in her seat until questioned, and then she insisted on standing, like a prisoner in the dock, throughout hours of interrogation. Usually calm and composed, only rarely did she show an uncharacteristic "outburst of emotion," as when she demanded that inmate names be suppressed at the hearings. "Sir, in my opinion, it is very cruel and unnecessary that this woman, completely rehabilitated, should have this incident brought up here," she effectively asserted to a round of cheers from the audience. Another time, when an accuser introduced evidence from inmate records, Van Waters visibly "wept in her chair." A special connection formed between Van Waters and the responsive gatherings at the hearings. As one spectator described the scene, "Her audience, of an unbelievable variety of types just rise right up and take her to their hearts." They also responded to attorney Cross as if on cue, laughing when he prodded Commissioner McDowell and vocally censuring the introduction of lurid testimony concerning homosexuality.

After two months of testimony, a gubernatorial committee chaired by Harvard Law School dean (and later U.S. solicitor general) Erwin Griswold overruled her dismissal, and on March 11, 1949, Miriam Van Waters triumphantly returned to her position as superintendent of the Massachusetts Reformatory for Women. The national press highlighted her reinstatement as a moral victory. According to the *New York Times*, Van Waters's dismissal "would have meant a serious setback to the cause of prison reform throughout the world." Privately, U.S. Supreme Court justice Felix Frankfurter wrote of his relief at Van Waters's vindication.

What was so significant about Miriam Van Waters's reinstatement as superintendent of the Massachusetts women's reformatory in 1949 to elicit this national sigh of relief? In part, the liberals who rallied to her defense recognized the importance of women's reform to a larger progressive coalition that was on the defensive. Just as attacks on contemporary feminism fueled a conservative political movement after the 1970s, so too did attacks on the female reform tradition represent an entering wedge against New Deal liberalism in the late 1940s and the 1950s. Van Waters's triumph represented a small victory for liberalism, although in the long run it proved to be an illusory one. In addition to Miriam Van Waters's heroic personal stand, her dramatic hearings reveal a great deal about American reform at midcentury, especially its relationship to religious liberalism, maternalism, and women's institutions.

Like many other women reformers before and during her lifetime, Miriam Van Waters had been raised within a liberal Protestant tradition. Born in 1887, she grew up in the rectory of her father's Portland, Oregon, Episcopal church, where she first learned that a "social gospel" obligated Christians to rectify the glaring inequalities wrought by industrialism. Van Waters practiced the social gospel through her commitment to prison reform, which for her rested on a belief in the redemption of all sinners. Although she earned a doctorate in anthropology in 1913, she chose to enter social service rather than academia in order, she wrote, to be of "constructive" use to the world. First in juvenile justice and then women's prison reform, Van Waters drew on her spiritual moorings for inspiration.

At the Massachusetts Women's Reformatory in Framingham, both inmates and staff members were moved by Van Waters's faith in individual redemption. Her own charismatic personality appealed in an almost spiritual way to the alcoholics, drug addicts, prostitutes, and petty criminals who filled the institution, women who had so often been considered, and considered themselves, lost souls. To Van Waters, no student had strayed beyond the reach of what she called "Christian penology." Her ability to reach deeply into the hearts of her students, implant a germ of self-worth, and cultivate a devoted following represented her most important and unique contribution. In an era of professionalized social work and welfare bureaucratization, her religious outreach sustained the historical link between Protestant spirituality and progressive reform.

Not surprisingly, when Van Waters faced dismissal from office, local clergy of all faiths rallied to her side, as did local churchwomen. Religious organizations endorsing Van Waters included the Rabbinical Association of Greater Boston, the Massachusetts Council of Churches, and the Universalist church. At her hearings, numerous clergy testified to her ability to rehabilitate her charges. Perhaps most compelling, though, was public testimony from former inmates during the hearings. As one woman explained:

> Dr. Van Waters has been my life saver. She has given me a new life. I was all finished, I thought, when I first came to the Reformatory, and only that she believed in me, I think I'd be dead now. She felt that I could make it, as they say. Her confidence in me gave me confidence in myself, and hence I am happy today, working, happy and a different person.

Another former inmate wrote that an eminent psychiatrist had concluded "that *I was a hopeless alcoholic.* Dr. Van Waters doesn't know the meaning of the word hopeless and I have never heard it used in this institution." Such human testimony counteracted the evidence about Van Waters's clear violation of administrative procedures by appealing to spiritual rather than bureaucratic values.

Closely related to her faith in individual salvation was Miriam Van Waters's belief in the power of maternal love. Personally she considered her own mother, Maud Van Waters, a model "of all Christian beautiful living . . . an inspiration and a saint," and credited her, along with Jane Addams, for her decision to enter social service. Her father referred to Miriam as "the mother of us all" because of her maternal role in the family, helping to raise her four younger siblings and caring for her parents as well. Although Van Waters chose not to marry, while serving as a "referee" (or female judge) at the Los Angeles Juvenile Court in the 1920s, she "fell in love" with an eight-year-old ward of the court, whom she brought home, renamed Sarah Ann Van Waters, and eventually adopted.

In her efforts to reach out to women prisoners, Miriam Van Waters drew on a tradition of maternalism. Historians have used this term to refer to the transformation of motherhood from a private duty to a public responsibility, a shift that contributed to the emergence of state welfare structures in Europe and America from approximately 1880 to 1920. Maternalist policies included protective labor legislation for women workers, child welfare measures ranging from juvenile courts to the creation of the U.S. Children's Bureau, and the maternal and infant health care movements. Although maternalism seemed to be waning in the United States by the 1920s, in Van Waters's case it survived within the unlikely arena of women's prison reform.

From the beginning of her career before World War I, Miriam Van Waters had tried to create "homelike" juvenile detention institutions in Portland, Oregon, and Los Angeles, California. As referee for girls' cases at the Los Angeles juvenile court in the 1920s, she combined a hard-hitting professional style with an effort to become a surrogate mother to troubled girls. But her work at Framingham from 1932 until 1957 best illustrates the persistence of maternalism, for there she consciously tried to create a "child-centered institution." Over half of the inmates had living children; like the unwed mothers, who received two-year sentences for fornication or lewdness, they brought their young children to prison. Van Waters's response to their plight was "to glorify motherhood" through a training program for mothers and babies, the creation of a model nursery, and a weekly Mothers' Club for parent education. Politically, she successfully lobbied to defeat a bill that would have prevented inmates from keeping their babies with them and, with the help of Eleanor Roosevelt, she won federal grants to build a special open-door residence for mothers and children.

At the hearings on her dismissal, Van Waters and her staff defended their child-centered approach against state claims that inmates should give up their children for adoption. As Van Waters's protégé Ann Gladding explained, Framingham inmates deserved to be mothers, and many were "criminals" only by virtue of their pregnancies; they "might never have come to the Reformatory if they had had financial resources to provide for themselves and for their infants." Even those convicted of neglect, she argued, might never again neglect another child. For the good of the child, mothers should be encouraged to create homes for their children. Once mothers left the reformatory and completed parole, "our answer to them should not be, 'No, we won't let you try because it might be too much for you,' but, 'Yes, it will be difficult, and we'll try to get outside help for you.'" Even nonmothers benefited from the maternal emphasis. A former inmate, who had once been suicidal, testified at the hearings: "I was given charge over a difficult group who called me 'mother' and to them I became as a mother . . . my cure had been effected." Such affirmations of the benefi- cence of maternalism helped consolidate public opinion in favor of Van Waters. An attack on her administration was tantamount to an attack on motherhood.

Miriam Van Waters's career also shows the importance of women's net- works as a reform strategy. In Los Angeles in the 1920s, Van Waters had worked and lived within a circle of women lawyers, judges, and social work- ers who staffed the juvenile court and participated in an elaborate commu- nity of professional women. When Van Waters adopted her daughter, members of her communal household helped raise Sarah Ann Van Waters. First in Los Angeles and later in Massachusetts, Van Waters mobilized women's organizations, including the state federation of women's clubs, the Colored Women's Federation, and the local Council of Jewish Women, to support reform legislation. She also brought women's church and service or- ganizations into the life of the reformatory to offer classes, social services, and jobs to students.

In addition, close personal relationships with older women patrons fa- cilitated Van Waters's reform efforts. During the 1920s, Chicago's Ethel Sturges Dummer, a wealthy benefactor of juvenile court reform, provided material and emotional support so that Van Waters could write her influen- tial books on juvenile delinquency, *Youth in Conflict* (1925) and *Parents on Probation* (1927). After 1930, Van Waters's main emotional and political sustenance came from her "dearest love," Geraldine Morgan Thompson (1872–1967), a former suffragist and Republican national committeewoman from New Jersey who devoted her life, and her considerable wealth, to the cause of charitable institutions. By 1930, Miriam Van Waters and Geraldine Thompson had become romantic partners, as well as reform allies.

Geraldine Thompson supported Van Waters' reform efforts at Framing- ham in many ways. She often visited the institution and addressed staff meetings and student assemblies; thanks to Thompson, her ally Eleanor Roosevelt also spoke at the institution. Thompson's philanthropy provided stipends for reformatory interns, funded a part-time psychiatrist, and sup- plemented the educational and nursery budgets at Framingham. Thompson also provided a physical and emotional refuge for Van Waters. When the superintendent felt overwhelmed by institutional responsibilities, she could recuperate at Brookdale, the Thompson estate near Red Bank, New Jersey.

The two friends would take early morning horseback rides and long walks, talk of their work and their spiritual beliefs, and take comfort in each other's love. Although neither woman self-identified as a lesbian, a term which to them connoted psychopathology, underground rumors about Van Waters' personal life contributed to the public charges that she condoned homosexuality.

Thus, when Commissioner McDowell sought grounds to dismiss Van Waters from office, he claimed that the superintendent knew of and tolerated lesbianism in prison and that homosexual inmates received special favors from the staff. At her dismissal hearings, Van Waters invoked scientific authority to counteract these claims, resisting the labeling of women as homosexuals. Although she publicly denied all charges of homosexuality in prison, privately Van Waters recognized the power of these accusations to sabotage her career. "In the hands of malevolence, the character assassin, has turned gossip into guilt," she wrote in her journal, mourning that "all the pleasant kindly innocent ways of Framingham" had been "turned into weapons against our policy." So many of her methods for empowering dispossessed women—fraternization of staff and inmates, hiring of former students on staff, trips for movies, concerts, and ice cream—now carried the taint of homosexuality.

If her strong ties to women made Van Waters politically vulnerable, they also proved critical in the defense of her administration. Geraldine Thompson provided funds and handled Republican politicians, Eleanor Roosevelt worked behind the scenes to influence the Democrats, and club- and churchwomen wrote letters to the editors of Massachusetts newspapers and flocked to the public hearings. Like the inmates who testified to Van Waters's charismatic appeal, local club women felt personally vindicated by her reinstatement. "What a victory has been won," one letter read. "I am writing especially to tell you what you have done for women in general."

Religious liberalism, maternalism, and the power of women's networks helped Miriam Van Waters sustain the female reform tradition. By the time of her retirement in 1957, however, each of these was at risk. Although Van Waters had maintained a child-centered institution, her successors dismantled the nursery; almost all women prisoners now face the additional punishment of loss of contact with their young children. Although the revival of the women's movement since the 1960s has encouraged women's networks, second-wave feminism has been uneasy about both maternalism and organized religion. As both gentle and harsh critics have recently pointed out, maternalism and spirituality have been co-opted by a conservative right-wing movement that well understands the rhetorical power of these concepts.

Why has the older tradition exemplified by Miriam Van Waters become obsolete, so much so that it has almost vanished from historical memory—as has her name? Despite her popularity as a writer in the 1920s, her local fame, and her national notoriety during her dismissal in the late 1940s, Van Waters has remained historically significant largely to those who knew her personally. Perhaps her choice of penology, a small and marginal arena even within reform circles, kept her from gaining a lasting reputation. Equally important is the fact that Miriam Van Waters' unique contribution consisted not in the leadership of a social movement but rather in her exceptional ability to touch individuals deeply. Although she campaigned nationally for her beloved causes—improved treatment of juvenile delinquents, the abolition of capital punishment, the rehabilitation and the rights of women inmates—it was her personal charisma, her spiritual power to heal lost souls, that most impressed others. Thus it has been in individual memory, not in political history, that until now her legacy has endured.

Pauli Murray
and the Killing of Jane Crow

ROSALIND ROSENBERG

Pauli Murray has already appeared in this book as one of the young black Howard University students in the 1940s who was influenced by Caroline Ware. Fifteen years later, both women found themselves serving on John F. Kennedy's President's Commission on the Status of Women, where they confronted the divisive issue that Alice Paul had pushed since the 1920s—the Equal Rights Amendment. Pauli Murray's unique contribution centers on her formulation of a legal strategy for women's rights based on the equal protection clause of the Fourteenth Amendment and her lifelong commitment to eradicating both "Jim" and "Jane Crow." Her personal odyssey was not over. In 1977 Pauli Murray was ordained as the first Black female priest of the Episcopal Church. She died in 1985.

I N THE FALL OF 1941 Pauli Murray entered Howard Law School with the intention of becoming a civil rights lawyer, but the thirty-year-old writer and activist soon broadened her agenda. On the first day of classes, one of her professors announced that he did not know why women came to law school, but since they were there, the men would have to put up with them. Murray sat in shocked silence, as her mostly male classmates laughed. Soon after, another professor, Leon Ransom, put up a sign inviting "all male students of the First Year Class" to a smoker at his house to be considered for admission to Sigma Tau, a male legal fraternity. When Murray objected that she was being excluded from a group that could advance her career, Ransom suggested that she set up a legal sorority. Stunned that men who were dedicated to abolishing Jim Crow could be so insensitive to the unfairness of discrimination based on sex, she responded by working her way to the head of her class. Then, in Professor Ransom's famed civil rights seminar, she took on the entire civil rights establishment by crafting a fifty-nine-page critique of the standard approach to civil rights litigation.

For over a decade, Ransom and others had been chipping away at *Plessy v. Ferguson*, the 1896 Supreme Court monument to legally sanctioned segregation. Case by case, they had challenged states to live up to *Plessy*'s "separate but equal" standard by making separate public facilities truly equal. Nowhere had they succeeded in winning equality for blacks. Nor could they, Murray believed, until they attacked segregation head-on. A full decade before the Supreme Court struck down state-imposed segregation in *Brown v. Board of Education of Topeka, Kansas* (1954), Murray laid out the basic argument on which the Court would ultimately rely in her paper for Ransom. State-imposed segregation, she argued, violated the Fourteenth Amendment's guarantee of "equal protection of the laws" in two ways. By using race as a basis for assigning legal rights, states resorted to "arbitrary and unreasonable classification." In addition, segregation harmed Negroes by doing "violence to the personality of the individual affected." When Murray finished her paper, she attached a cover letter to Ransom, which, in addition to outlining her general approach to killing "Jim Crow," posed a pointed question: "Now, how do I go about killing '*Jane Crow*'—prejudice against sex?"

When Murray graduated from Howard in 1944, few jobs existed for an ambitious, black, female lawyer committed to both women's rights and racial justice. For seventeen years, she eked out a living, for the most part as a writer and solo practitioner. Then an opportunity opened up with the election of President John F. Kennedy. Esther Peterson, a long-time Kennedy adviser and the new head of the federal Women's Bureau, persuaded the president that he should investigate ways to improve the status of American women. Having won the 1960 election by a scant 100,000 votes, Kennedy saw the wisdom of an initiative that would appeal to female voters, and he authorized the creation of the President's Commission on the Status of Women (PCSW). He appointed Eleanor Roosevelt to head the commission, and Roosevelt, who had come to know Murray in the 1930s as a result of their common interest in civil rights, recruited her to serve on the Committee on Civil and Political Rights. Murray agreed to serve, though she knew that she would be entering a battle that had divided the women's movement for four decades.

Ever since the 1920s, advocates for women had warred over whether to endorse an Equal Rights Amendment (ERA) to the Constitution. Supporters of the ERA, led by the National Woman's party, were mostly affluent, business oriented, and politically conservative. They viewed the world as a place populated by competitive individuals, all of whom shared the same basic nature, values, and aspirations—whatever their sex. Believing that men and women were essentially the same, they predicted that equal treatment would lead to equal achievement. Opponents of the ERA, by contrast, were more likely to be poor, union oriented, and politically liberal. Led by the Women's Bureau of the Labor Department, these working-class women and their advocates stressed the value of interdependence over individualism and cooperation over competition. Believing that women were more vulnerable and heavily burdened by domestic responsibilities than men, they argued that equal treatment would simply ensure women's continuing economic disadvantage.

Behind the battle over the ERA lay a bitter disagreement over state protective labor laws that applied to women but not to men. When Progressive era reformers had first tried to regulate working conditions in the United States, the Supreme Court had struck down laws for male workers. Shifting tactics, reformers argued successfully that women deserved protection, even if men did not, because they were physically weaker and more vulnerable to exploitation. ERA supporters deplored both the argument and the result of reformers' efforts. Protective legislation, they argued, restricted women's ability to compete with men for high-paying jobs. ERA opponents believed, however, that these laws helped women and offered a model for what the state might one day provide for all workers.

Roosevelt could not have chosen a better arbiter of the ERA dispute, for Murray's unique background drew her powerfully, if inconsistently, to both sides. Her commitment to civil rights, as well as her intense personal ambition, inclined her toward support of an Equal Rights Amendment. Even more so did her personal struggles with racial and sexual identity, which made her suspicious of categories into which she never comfortably fit. Like many other African Americans, Murray was confronted by the absurdity of racial classification. Darker than other members of her family but much lighter than African Americans in the larger community, she experienced a sense of "in-betweenness" with respect to race, which made her feel like "a nobody, without identity." At home she was reminded, "Brush your hair child, don't let it get kinky! Cold-cream your face, child, don't let it get sunburned! Don't suck your lips, child, you'll make them look niggerish." At school, however, children taunted: "You half-white bastard! You dirty-faced Jew baby! Black is honest! Yaller is dishonest!"

The whipsaw of color prejudice heightened Murray's sensitivity to arbitrary classifications, but what turned that sensitivity into a preoccupation was her extreme confusion over issues of gender and sexuality. Though briefly married at nineteen, Murray confided in notes to herself that she felt physical attraction only to "very feminine and heterosexual women." Moreover, she liked "wearing pants," wanted "to be one of the men," and enjoyed "doing things that fellows do." Having grown up in the sexually repressive atmosphere of a deeply religious African American household, Murray found it difficult to embrace what friends were labeling her homosexuality. She preferred to think of her sexual orientation and gender as another example of her "in-betweenness," and further evidence that classification based on physical characteristics was arbitrary, not to say limiting. No ERA supporter opposed treating women as a class more than she did.

And yet anti-ERA forces exercised a powerful attraction, because they included two of Murray's closest and most admired friends: Eleanor Roosevelt and labor historian Caroline Ware. Following college in the early 1930s, Murray had found it impossible to find a steady job. Only through the efforts of Roosevelt, who helped create a camp for unemployed women outside New York City in 1933, did she recover from malnutrition brought on by joblessness. In 1936 she found a job teaching workers through the

Roosevelt administration's Works Progress Administration, and from there she became involved in both labor and civil rights work. As part of that work, she came to know Roosevelt well and to gain faith in the power of government to protect workers, especially women workers, from hardship.

Even more important than Roosevelt to Murray's thinking about arguments over the ERA was Caroline Ware. Murray met Ware at Howard University in 1942, when she audited the latter's undergraduate course in constitutional history and was deeply influenced by her approach to equal rights and workers' welfare. While Ware agreed with Murray that the law should not discriminate on the basis of sex, she persuaded the budding lawyer that protective laws did not, in general, discriminate. Rather, they offered protection from exploitation to the country's most vulnerable workers, who happened to be women. Moreover, the labor historian regarded these laws as the first step toward universal coverage. In 1961, Ware, like Murray, joined the PCSW, and she helped Murray formulate a plan that would circumvent the bitter ERA debate. To support the ERA, they agreed, would risk invalidating all laws that distinguished between the sexes, both the good and the bad. A better approach would be to develop the ideas on race that Murray had first explored in her final law school paper on Jim Crow and apply them on a case-by-case basis.

With this goal in mind, Murray's first act on joining the PCSW's Committee on Political and Civil Rights was to offer to write a memorandum on the equal protection clause of the Fourteenth Amendment. Throughout her memorandum, Murray stressed the analogy between sex and race. Like Negroes, women were an easily identifiable group, who had long been stereotyped as naturally inferior to white men. As in the case of race, this discrimination brought psychological damage by preventing women from developing their full human potential. Murray wanted to challenge laws that barred women from jury service, denied them employment benefits, limited their access to credit, and in other ways restricted their opportunities. By working case by case, she believed, lawyers could strike down laws that limited the rights of women as a class, without either jeopardizing desirable protective legislation or undertaking the wasteful, and probably futile, effort to win a new amendment.

Having identified the principle under which equal protection should be extended to women, Murray concluded her memorandum by laying out a plan of action. Lawyers and social scientists should form a team, like the one organized by the Legal Defense Fund of the National Association for the Advancement of Colored People (NAACP) to select the cases for which the strongest constitutional argument could be made. Lawyers should write law review articles on sex discrimination. Social scientists should investigate sex prejudice. And women's leaders should organize the public on behalf of equal rights.

Esther Peterson looked on Murray's proposal as a real breakthrough. "You must know how grateful I am to you for this work," she wrote. "I feel in my bones that you are making history." Not all women leaders agreed. Members of the National Woman's party resented what they saw as an effort to derail their Equal Rights Amendment campaign. One party officer charged that Murray was a stalking horse for civil rights groups, which wanted to use the ERA struggle "as a springboard for their own propaganda." But far from attempting to hitch the cause of civil rights to the Equal Rights Amendment struggle, Murray was trying to hitch women's struggle for legal equality to the newly successful arguments of civil rights lawyers. After months of debate, the Committee on Civil and Political Rights finally endorsed Murray's position and recommended that the PCSW "not take a position in favor of the equal rights amendment at this time."

Putting together the legal team necessary to turn the Fourteenth Amendment into a vehicle for advancing women's rights posed a far greater challenge than did articulating the idea behind it. The NAACP Legal Defense Fund, which was Murray's model, had been in existence for over two decades. Lawyers had been writing law review articles about race discrimination, and social scientists had been publishing studies about the consequences of race prejudice for many years. As of 1963 there was no law review article on how to attack sex-based discrimination, no team of lawyers working on a legal strategy, no NAACP for women. Moreover, there was no group of social scientists prepared to present the kind of evidence that Murray thought necessary to show that discrimination caused women, as she believed it had caused African Americans, specific harm.

In the absence of an established feminist organization, Murray turned to the American Civil Liberties Union (ACLU). With a staff of lawyers in New York and offices throughout the country, the ACLU was uniquely positioned to put Murray's litigation strategy to work. Known principally for its work on behalf of free speech, the organization had won some scattered victories for women in the area of employment rights under the leadership of board member Dorothy Kenyon. But major advances had foundered on the refusal of the Supreme Court to extend the equal protection clause to cover women. As recently as 1961, in the jury case of *Hoyt v. Florida*, the Court had found women's domestic responsibilities a reasonable ground for limiting their jury service. When the PCSW asked the ACLU to review Murray's Fourteenth Amendment memorandum in 1963, Kenyon recognized its promise. Two years later she recruited Murray to the ACLU board, and almost immediately a case in Alabama presented an ideal opportunity to test Murray's sex-race analogy.

The case of *Gardenia White* (a black woman) *v. Bruce Crook* (a white male member of the Lowndes County [Alabama] Jury Commission) grew out of the murder of a civil rights worker in Lowndes County in August 1965. The county was 80 percent black and over 50 percent female, but juries in Lowndes were invariably 100 percent white and male—and hostile to civil rights workers. Convinced that an all-white, male jury would never find a white defendant guilty of the murder of a civil rights worker, the ACLU immediately filed suit against the county jury system. With the help of Murray and Kenyon, it persuaded a three-judge district court in Montgomery that both race and sex discrimination were based on unreasonable classifications that violated the equal protection clause of the Fourteenth Amendment. The ACLU attorneys eagerly awaited Alabama's appeal, but when the state attorney general decided to let the district court's ruling stand, Murray and Kenyon had no alternative but to find another case that might take them to the Supreme Court.

As a long-time activist, Murray knew that waiting for the right case to come along would not be enough. She therefore followed her own advice about educating the public. With Mary Eastwood, a Justice Department attorney with whom she had worked on the PCSW, she published a law review article, "Jane Crow and the Law," and whenever the opportunity arose, she lectured about the need to put pressure on the government to grant women equal rights. One such lecture brought her to the attention of Betty Friedan, who had gained national prominence with her publication of *The Feminine Mystique* in 1963. Through Murray, Friedan met a number of women in key governmental positions, including Mary Eastwood in the Justice Department, Catherine East at the Women's Bureau, and Sonia Pressman at the Equal Employment Opportunity Commission (EEOC). Together they began to build support for an organization that would serve as an NAACP for women. In June 1966, their efforts paid off with the founding of the National Organization for Women (NOW).

Murray had great hopes for NOW, but those hopes were dashed the following year, when, over her vigorous objections, the organization voted to mount a campaign for the Equal Rights Amendment at its 1967 conference. To Murray, the sight of mostly young, overwhelmingly white, professional women railroading a resolution through a body she had hoped would be responsive to the concerns of all women—young and old, black and white, rich and poor—was a crushing blow. Murray had come to sympathize with women workers who objected to state laws because they effectively barred them from the possibility of promotion into jobs that paid overtime. But she remained concerned about others who continued to value laws that protected them from being pressured into working long hours. The possibility of earning time-and-a-half for overtime was fine, these latter workers conceded, *if* one had a choice in the matter, but increasingly employers were treating overtime as a requirement, not an opportunity. As the cost of benefits packages increased, employers found it less expensive to force employees to work longer hours (even at time-and-a-half pay) than to hire additional workers. Before endorsing a campaign that threatened to jettison what few protections existed for the country's most vulnerable workers, Murray wanted to give those concerned a chance to air their grievances and, if possible, reach a consensus on a uniform code of labor laws that applied to all workers.

Immediately following the NOW conference, Murray wrote to her friend, and fellow labor law advocate, Kay Clarenbach of Wisconsin. She asked Clarenbach, who chaired NOW's National Board, to withdraw her name from consideration as a board member. "If I were merely a professional woman, or a white woman, or a young woman, perhaps I would be more in tune with the view which prevailed on the issue of the Equal Rights Amendment at the Conference," Murray wrote. "But I hold the status of several minorities." As a result, she objected to what seemed to her the high-handed efforts of NOW leaders to force the ERA on a membership many of whose members still harbored doubts about its wisdom.

Disappointed in NOW, Murray redirected her attention to the ACLU. Her efforts finally paid off in 1970 when a group of younger women lawyers forced the creation of the Women's Rights Project. Granted independent funding and led by Ruth Bader Ginsburg, the future Supreme Court justice (then a law professor at Rutgers Law School), the Women's Rights Project was finally able to carry through the strategy that Murray had first articulated. In 1971 Ginsburg won the first breakthrough in *Reed v. Reed* (1971) in which the Supreme Court struck down an Idaho law that gave men preference as executors in estates. At long last the Supreme Court had found that a state could not engage in arbitrary classification on the basis of sex. In recognition of Dorothy Kenyon's decades of preparatory work and Pauli Murray's crucial addition of the race-sex analogy, Ginsburg placed their names alongside her own as authors of the ACLU brief in *Reed*.

Soon after *Reed* was decided, Congress sent the ERA to the states, but a decade later it was defeated, having fallen three states short of ratification. While NOW struggled unsuccessfully to pass the ERA, lawyers from the Women's Rights Project gradually persuaded the Supreme Court of Murray's basic argument: that classifying on the basis of sex, if not exactly the same as classifying on the basis of race, is almost always as harmful. This triumph came at a cost. Despite Murray's initial hope that protective labor laws for women could be extended to cover men, these laws fared no better in court challenges than did other laws that classified by sex. By the mid-1970s state protective labor laws had all but disappeared. The benefits won for women by Murray's Fourteenth Amendment strategy were nonetheless substantial. By the end of the 1970s, neither the federal government nor any state could discriminate against women in employment, deny them equal pension benefits, or limit their right to serve on a jury. Today most women take these gains for granted, but it took the work of unheralded heroes like Pauli Murray to make them a reality.

Sam Phillips:
Southern Visionary

JOEL WILLIAMSON

*Forgotten heroes lurk not just in politics, law, and social re-
form, but also in popular culture, as Lew Ayres demonstrated.
Let us add the name of Sam Phillips in the field of popular
music. As a young radio announcer and producer, Phillips introduced new sounds to the airwaves—women's voices, working-class voices, black voices. He anticipated the appeal of
what were then called "race records" and along the way discovered Elvis Presley. Sam Phillips hastened a transformation in
commercial musical tastes in postwar America that was truly
revolutionary.*

S AM PHILLIPS will surely be forever remembered for his part in discovering Elvis Presley and shaping his early career. What might be lost to collective memory if we did not stop, look, and listen is that he was not only an innovator in music whose work had cultural import nationally and internationally; he was also a highly significant actor in the transition of southern culture from a rural order to one that was increasingly urban, industrial, and commercial. Indeed, in that process he was a revolutionary force in all three areas in the mantra that describes the South: race, class, and sex. In all of this he wrestled with precisely the same vital and essential elements that William Faulkner grappled with in a highly celebrated fashion a generation before. Faulkner's medium was literature. Sam Phillips's medium was music, but it was music electronically transmitted and vastly multiplied. Through this powerful new medium, Sam's message was that African Americans, working-class white southerners, and women have something to say—to communicate—that all the rest of us need to listen to and hear.

If Sam had been in politics or journalism, or perhaps even possessed a Ph.D., scholars would have called him "a southern white liberal" and placed him in the hagiarchy of such movers and shakers as Ralph McGill, the nationally famous and highly influential editor of the *Atlanta Constitution*, and Frank Porter Graham, long-term president of the University of North Carolina at Chapel Hill, assistant secretary general of the United Nations, aristocrat and democrat. Had Sam chosen a more conventional career such as the law and politics, we would have at least one book on him by now, if not two or three.

While Sam Phillips's rebellion covered a remarkably wide spectrum, he opened fire on his carefully selected targets sequentially: race, class, and gender.

We have not yet given Sam Phillips his just deserts as a self-conscious racial revolutionary who played a substantial role in bringing down the thick wall between the races in the South and the rest of America. He did not wait for the U.S. Supreme Court's desegregating *Brown* decision in 1954 to begin the deliberate undermining of the seemingly invincible biracial establishment in the South.

Sam was one of those relatively rare southern whites who saw beauty across the race line in African American culture and moved to understand and embrace it. Such folks are keenly aware, too, of racial injustice. Often they seem to begin as patricians and paternalists and end by recognizing the equal humanity of black people and relishing elements of black culture. C. Vann Woodward did it as a writer, historian, and scholar. Harry Ashmore did it as a journalist and editor of the *Little Rock Arkansas Gazette*. Lillian Smith did it as both a writer and as a lay leader among southern Methodists. Sam Phillips did it with electronics and music.

Why these fairly few people crossed over and others, their very own brothers and sisters, did not remains a mystery—same gene pool, same family environment, yet children as different as the night differs from the day. Why do some look over the wall and listen and others do not? In every southern community, there are a few white people who are like that. Atticus Finch in *To Kill a Mockingbird*—Gregory Peck in the film—was perfectly historical.

Born in 1923, Sam Phillips was reared on a two hundred-acre farm in northwestern Alabama where he had full access to the broad stream of black culture, and he drank thirstily of its waters. There was an African Methodist Episcopal church just down the road from his own church. As a boy, he would stand outside to listen while the congregation sang and music poured out of the open doors and windows. More personally, there was an older black man, Uncle Silas Payne, who worked for his father. Silas would tell him stories about mythical sausage and buttercake trees in Africa, about the Molasses River, and, highly relevant to Sam's own future, about the real Beale Street in Memphis. It was almost as if both man and boy had taken their script from Joel Chandler Harris. Uncle Silas was Uncle Remus, comfortably settled in his doorway, smoking his pipe, telling stories to Mars Tom. Young Tom thereby acquired a mission in life to carry the wisdom and richness of black life (e.g., Br'er Rabbit and the Tar Baby) to white people. Uncle Silas also played the guitar and the harmonica.

Twenty-two-year-old Sam came to Memphis in 1945 with a wife, a son, and four years' experience in radio in northern Alabama and, briefly, Nashville, Tennessee. He went to work for station WREC where his older brother Jud sang with the Jolly Boys Quartet. Soon Sam became the engineer for the regular nationwide broadcast over CBS of the big bands that played in the rooftop Skyway Room of the Peabody Hotel. Increasingly, he was irritated by the formulaic, stilted, stiff manner of the big bands he broadcast—the Dorseys, Glen Miller, Ted Weems. He was bothered by the sight of the made-up, evening-gowned girl singers sitting sedately on the bandstand and the rows of identically dressed musicians all mechanically turning the pages of their music at the right moment even though they had played the same song thousands of times and could have written it out from memory. It was all too bland, too narrow, and boringly predictable. He wanted a music that communicated real and spontaneous feeling.

In January 1950, Sam established his storefront Memphis Recording Service at 706 Union Avenue, several blocks east of WREC's studios in the Peabody. His company would record anything to make enough money to survive, but Sam put it there, as he said, to give some of the "great Negro artists" a chance to be heard. He said that he wanted "genuine, untutored Negro" music. He wanted "Negroes with field mud on their boots and patches in their overalls . . . battered instruments and unfettered techniques." As he recalled forty years later, "I was shooting for that damn row that hadn't been plowed."

Sam survived, but barely. He was working eighteen-hour days. In the studio, he was recording "cotton patch blues" as well as rhythm and blues. Sometimes he sent his work on to a "race" label such as Chess in Chicago or RPM operating out of the Watts area in Los Angeles, which would market the record through its well-established network. One of his records, appearing in late 1951, was B. B. King's "Three O'Clock Blues." Another, "Rocket 88" by Ike Turner and his saxophonist and sometimes singer Jackie Brenston, held first place on the nationwide rhythm and blues (R&B) chart for seventeen weeks. Seminal in the R&B movement, it has become a classic. All in the same day, Sam might wire a baseball stadium for sound, go to the studio to record that primal blues man Howlin' Wolf (Chester Burnett), then go on to the Peabody for the late-night Skyway broadcast.

Respected by his fellow workers for his obviously high skills, Sam nevertheless had to pay for his unorthodox interest in black people. At the Peabody, someone might say to him, "Well, you smell okay. I guess you haven't been hanging around those niggers today." Frank Porter Graham and Ralph McGill encountered precisely that attitude, though no one would have expressed it so crudely to them. White southerners who manifested too much respect for black people earned epithets and paid a price in the white world for their lack of conformity. No one tampered with established race relations lightly.

In June 1951, after Sam's employer remarked on his frequent absences from the station, he quit his job at WREC. Now he was on his own. But not quite. Marian Keisker was there.

Marian was an amazing woman. Born in 1917, she herself was first heard on WREC in 1929 on a children's weekly show, "Wynken, Blynken, and Nod." In 1938, she graduated from Memphis's prestigious private college, Southwestern, with a degree in English and medieval French. She married, gave birth to a son, and continued her career in radio. In 1946, she began to host the "Meet Kitty Kelly" talk show on WREC five days a week. While she was becoming a well-known and very popular radio personality, she was writing, producing, and directing as many as a dozen other shows, including the nightly "Treasury Bandstand" from the Peabody Skyway. She first met Sam Phillips in the offices of WREC, located in the basement of the Peabody just beneath its lobby.

"He was a beautiful young man," Marian said in describing to writer Peter Guralnick how it all began in 1950. "Beautiful beyond belief, but still that country touch, that country rawness. He was slim and had those incredible eyes; . . . with touches of real elegance, beautifully groomed, terrible about his hair."

Marian was with him when he discovered the empty store in just the right location, several blocks east of the Peabody, only two hundred yards north of Beale Street. She helped him remodel the store into a studio. Then she quit her job at WREC and single-handedly staffed the business while Sam continued his multiparted life. She was receptionist, typist, secretary, bookkeeper—everything up front. Sam, when he was in, either worked in back in the studio or took his current visitor to what was laughingly called "the conference room," actually the third booth on the window side in Miss Taylor's restaurant next door.

African American artists had learned that Sam Phillips was the man in Memphis who understood their music, who was fair, and who might record and sell their work. They came to his little studio on Union Avenue, and he recorded a lot of them: Howlin' Wolf, B. B. ("Blues Boy") King, Ike Turner, first husband to singer and actor Tina Turner. Like Ike and Tina and pioneering bluesman Muddy Waters, a striking number came out of that wellspring of musical creativity in the delta, Clarksdale. Interestingly, it was also the childhood home of Tennessee Williams. In early 1952, encouraged by the success of recordings he had produced for others, Sam established his own label, Sun Records. By the summer of 1953, he had scored a big hit with blues man Rufus Thomas's "Bear Cat." Two others, "Feeling Good" by Little Junior Parker and "Just Walkin' in the Rain" by the Prisonaires, rose

into the charts in the fall of that year. The latter were, literally, black prisoners in the state penitentiary in Nashville brought to Memphis under
guard to make their record. Both the warden and Governor Frank Clement
were into rehabilitation.

I t was Marian who was there, up front at her desk one Saturday in the
  summer of 1953, when young Elvis Presley, age eighteen, walked in. He
was white and blue collar. He drove a truck for Crown Electric Company
delivering supplies to electricians at job sites.

Elvis became the great star of Sun Records, but well before Elvis walked
in the front door of the Memphis Recording Service, Sam was already into
broadening his search for talent to include whites in the lower social orders.
One person he recorded was Scotty Moore, whose daytime job was blocking
men's hats in his brother's dry cleaning establishment on McLean Boule-
vard, near Southwestern College and Overton Park. His other job was as
guitarist with the Starlite Wranglers, a country and western band that
played honky-tonks on the edge of town with improbable names like the
Bon Air or the Eagle's Nest. Also in the band was Bill Black, a worker in the
huge Firestone plant north of town. Other Wranglers were also Firestone
people. The Wranglers and their audiences were very much "country come
to town," literally from the cotton patch to the production line. Sam, who
often drank coffee and consulted with Scotty in "the conference room" in
the restaurant next door, chose to put Scotty and Bill to work with Elvis on
Sunday, July 4, 1954. It was he who chose the team that in the next two
years would launch Elvis's career.

"I saw—I don't remember when," Sam told Elvis biographer Peter Guralnick, "I thought to myself: suppose that I would have been born a little
bit more down on the economic ladder. I think I felt from the beginning the
total inequality of man's inhumanity to his brother."

Sam did not stop with Elvis. Even as Elvis's star was rising, Sam was
bringing forth a stream of talent that is no less than astounding. They were
fully as untutored and spontaneous as he could have wanted. They were
also ambitious. Out of that tiny storefront studio in Memphis came Carl
Perkins ("Blue Suede Shoes"), Johnny Cash ("Folsom Prison Blues"), Jerry
Lee Lewis ("Great Balls of Fire"), and a host of others. It was as if they all
came out of "the same womb," Sam said. Hat blockers, truck drivers, appli-
ance salesmen (Cash), youthful ne'er-do-wells (Jerry Lee), they went on to

achieve great fame at home and, often, for better or for worse, to represent American culture abroad.

L ess known—virtually unknown, in fact—but equally intriguing was Sam Phillips's extraordinarily revolutionary move in the area of gender. He created the first radio station in America to have an on-the-air staff made up entirely of women. Its call letters, WHER, were marvelously appropriate to its sound and its mission: to communicate with the women in and around Memphis. Soon it had a woman as its general manager and a majority of women on its off-air staff.

On Saturday morning, October 29, 1955, WHER Memphis came on the air. On that same day, Sam sat in a booth in the restaurant of the newly opened Holiday Inn in downtown Memphis and agreed to sell Elvis Presley's contract to RCA for $35,000 and the $5,000 he owed Elvis in back royalties.

By industry standards, it was a high and unprecedented price. Sam needed the money to support his new radio station and the new talent he was developing. But it was a major shift in the configuration of his business, and he wondered if he had done the right thing. He consulted his very good friend Kemmons Wilson. Kemmons was just then beginning to reach flight speed in executing his own revolution in the hotel industry—a chain of "Holiday Inns" offering in locations everywhere the same highly dependable, moderately upscale, quality motel accommodations. Kemmons was giving Sam free office space in his downtown Holiday Inn while he was launching WHER. The hotel man had no difficulty making a judgment. "Jesus Christ!" he exclaimed. "Thirty-five thousand dollars? Hell, he can't even sing, man. Take the money!"

Elvis could sing, of course, and that voice possibly saved an ailing RCA from bankruptcy. But the sale also worked for Sam. He did not have the capital and the organization to market Elvis's explosively lucrative talent. RCA and Colonel Tom Parker, Elvis's new manager, a "carney" who might well have rivaled P. T. Barnum in showmanship, did. Sam emerged from the transaction with money that he immediately put to work.

An audibly all-woman radio station was shockingly new. Always there on the dial at 1430, it was conspicuous, and it did not go away if you frowned. Memphis did not quite know what to do about it. One way to relieve the tension generated by the new and the different was to poke fun at it. When the station was several days late coming on the air, the *Commercial Appeal* called it "lady-like tardiness." The staff itself rolled into the humor, promoted it, and played to it. Getting attention was their business, their goal, and their bread and butter. "No other station loses so many announcers to pregnancy and marriage," one staffer boasted in an interview with the press. She heightened the humor by hastily adding, "not necessarily in that order." The women proudly broadcast the image of their studio—located in Kemmon Wilson's Third Street Holiday Inn just south of downtown—as tastefully done in pastel colors and loaded with mirrors ("Vanity is thy name"). They also delighted in the gender plays they made on ordinary radio jargon. "This is WHER, the all-girl station," announcer Jeanie Botto would say in conventional style, and then conclude, "Now it's time for the news from a-broad." It was stereotypical, it was tacky, but it was also the 1950s. It was there to make money for owners, managers, and staff, but it was also women talking.

From sunrise to sunset seven days a week, there were women—and only women—on the air at 1430 on the dial. They were all, in one or more ways, "breakaway women." They might be married and they might have children, but they might also be divorced, and they all had a profession, a public persona, and a salary. Some used their salary to establish their independence.

Commercial radio is a never-ending and highly competitive quest to find the market, and WHER was in that business. The feminine touch began in 1955 as a plus in the search; it ended, in 1980, twenty-five years later, as a minus.

After 1965, WHER was always managed by males and had more and more males on the staff, both on and off the air. In late 1971, a new manager, Bill Thomas, brought his highly successful Dallas, Texas, radio experience to WHER. The press understood that he was shifting the format from popular songs and "the soft-talking, familiarly honey pace of the station's distaff deejays to a new brisker image featuring what the trade calls the 'adult-contemporary sound.'" It meant down with Glenn Miller and up with the Carpenters to target the eighteen- to forty-two-year-olds. Thomas also brought in his protégé Bill Reeves as news director. Bill would spearhead WHER's now hard-driving commitment to information and news. One female announcer who had always used simply the name Jaine was advised to add another. No loose, unattached women allowed. Listeners protested the changes loudly and threatened desertion, but the new hard-edge sound stuck.

The end of WHER really came in early 1973 when Thomas canceled a highly popular three hour, 9 A.M. to noon, keystone show called "Feminine Forum." Described as a "sex radio" phone-in talk show, the male host would announce topics, sometimes have guests, and talk with the radio audience by phone. Patterned after a successful Los Angeles show, the idea, Thomas said, was "to provide stimuli for one's own conclusions on questions having to do with sex." After being on the air for ten months, WHER's ratings doubled for the morning time period. On the day before the cancellation, Margaret Dichel of Family Planning was the guest on the "Feminine Forum" show. She said that since she had appeared there a few months earlier, Family Planning in Memphis had more referrals from the show than from any other single source. Women were using the airwaves to network in an area vital to their lives.

Ratings doubled, but from the beginning, the manager explained, there had been "consistent disapproval" from some quarters. The source of disapproval was always vague. Thomas had heard that petitions against the show were being circulated by "church groups and others." Complaints were lodged with the Federal Communications Commission. Boycotts of sponsors were threatened. Thomas concluded that "the atmosphere in Memphis simply does not seem to welcome the show." On the other hand, with ratings doubled for the time when the "Feminine Forum" was on the air, a lot of people in Memphis obviously loved it.

No petition ever came to Thomas. In personal communications he encountered as much positive as negative response. The power to cancel lay with sponsors. Yet again the opposition was vague. Only one sponsor defected totally; others asked that their advertising be moved to other times. Finally Thomas gave up. "The show has not been a super-financial success," he told the *Press-Scimitar* on February 20, 1973, "so we're taking it off and we're doing it tomorrow." Sex talk was out on WHER, but Sam kept the gender label for the station—WHER—on the air for seven more years.

Formally, WHER came to an end in 1980. "We're all talk and all news all the time," Bill Thomas, still manager, announced forcefully. No more music. Further, and more decisively, they were changing the call letters to

WEEE. The emphasis, the manager said, was on the "We" part. The inclusive pronoun masked a management and staff that had become heavily male.

"We feel our call letters, WHER, have hurt us," Thomas explained. "It still gives us the image of an all-girl station, when we haven't been that for a long time. A lot of people have a stigma about listening to an all-girl station."

Stigma? Stigma. Sam Phillips perceived that a lot of people in 1950 saw a stigma about listening to black music. He also saw a lot of people attached a stigma to listening to lower-class country and western, hillbilly, and "redneck" music. He guessed that there were a lot of people who could overcome those stigmas, and he was right.

WHER, on the other hand, faced an enemy that had no name, no clearly discernible shape, and yet possessed the power to erase the symbol from the air waves. It was a minor miracle and a tribute to his commitment that he was able to keep the call letters WHER conspicuously on the air for a quarter of a century. It was also in his character that even as he gave up the symbol of an all-woman station, he worked to retain and improve the substance. WEEE, for example, soon featured an interview with Jackie Cash, a young woman who fought for admission to the local chapter of the Jaycees, traditionally a heavily male institution. In a typically Phillipsian move, Sam also flanked the enemy and attacked. He hired an African American woman, Gwen Sneed, as an announcer on WEEE. At 6 p.m. every weekday evening, Gwen, who had a master's degree in broadcasting, came on WEEE for an hour of talk. "Her show will deal with racial matters," the station manager declared, "but it won't be a black-oriented show. It is for everybody." Sam Phillips, too, is for everybody.

Sam is alive and well in Memphis, turning seventy-five in 1998. B. B. King goes on still. Johnny Cash and Jerry Lee Lewis—in their very separate ways, holy and unholy—go on. And so too Elvis, though the King is dead. They were all boosted by, if not launched in their careers by, this man: twenty-seven years old when he opened his recording service, thirty-one when he recorded Elvis, thirty-two when he started WHER. He was a self-conscious, broad-gauged revolutionary against the crippling, smothering categories and stereotypes of his culture, a man who understood the deeply conservative nature of his people so well that he knew he must be stealthy in order to promote his subversion. He mined the thick walls of race, class, and gender orthodoxy, and where he mined them, he blew them up. Sun Records goes on too, now run by Sam's sons Knox and Jerry, still bringing up the young and talented, the folks who don't have friends and kin in Nashville, artists who might otherwise end their creative lives unheard, stillborn.

Hazel Brannon Smith:
White Martyr for Civil Rights

KATHLEEN BRADY

Sometimes heroic acts can make a person practically an outcast in her own community. That happened to crusading white newspaper editor Hazel Brannon Smith for her controversial support of the emerging civil rights movement in the 1950s and 1960s. Rejection by her Mississippi peers hurt her personally, but she never backed down from her support for the movement that was reshaping the South and the nation. In 1964 she won the Pulitzer Prize for editorial writing.

A T THE TIME she became a hero, Hazel Brannon Smith was forty
years old. She was tall and buxom with fair skin and hair that she
worked to keep light brown. She was the owner and editor of two small
newspapers in the Mississippi Delta and the wealthiest self-made woman in
the state. While she did not hesitate to crusade against gambling, social disease, and even Joe McCarthy, Hazel enjoyed nothing more than wearing
showy, costly hats, driving the latest model Cadillac, and basking in her
final acceptance into the white society of Lexington, Mississippi, an ante-
bellum town of Greek Revival mansions that was the seat of languid, fertile
Holmes County.

In her youth, Hazel had cared more about achievement and adventure
than about approval. She was born in Gadsden, Alabama, in 1914 to an
electrical contractor and his wife. She graduated from high school at sixteen, too young for college, and so worked as a reporter for the local paper,
where she became so successful at selling advertising that its editor put her
on salary because her commissions were costing him too much. At the University of Alabama, she was woman's editor of the campus newspaper and
beauty queen of her sorority. After graduation, with a $3,000 bank loan
cosigned by her boyfriend, she bought a failing newspaper in Durant, Mississippi, some three hundred miles away on the edge of the cotton-growing
delta. By focusing on chatty local news of marriages, arrests, and family re-
unions, she doubled circulation and paid off the debt in four years.

She bought a second paper in Lexington and as she prospered, she took
long trips to foreign countries, mailing weekly reports from various cities
that were printed in her papers. She wore mink in winter and in summer
sped through the county in an open white Cadillac. She was glamorous and
racy and, given that she was still single at age thirty-five, not quite respectable. "Honey," she told a journalist forty-five years later, in describing
her ability to claim a beau in whatever town she worked in, "I had the most
eligible bachelor in Durant and the most eligible bachelor in Lexington,
and my only trouble was that I couldn't have them both. That's true. I was
something."

Wives found her shocking, and husbands insisted they bought advertising space from her simply because she owned the only newspapers in the
county. As Hazel prospered, her five-foot six-inch frame became plumper,
graced by well-cut clothes and Hattie Carnegie hats. Sailing to Europe in
1949 after a romantic disappointment, she married the ship's purser, Walter

D. Smith, who was two years her junior and as small and slight as Hazel was sturdy. He had traveled the world, and even though he was a Yankee, her friends found him as charming as a true native-born southern gentleman.

The Smiths built a simple home on wooded acreage at the far end of the finest street in Lexington. In the evenings, Hazel Brannon Smith set aside the role of editor and publisher and took up the task of southern lady. She began inviting a few couples over for dinner, and then a few others, and as people reciprocated, she and Smitty were accepted by Lexington's social arbiters.

It was an era when blacks were Negroes and women were ladies, and these concepts were fields of force. Blacks did not drink at water fountains used by whites, or sit with them to eat, or attend schools where they would learn white children's education and sit in close and consistent contact with them. Blacks and whites sat in different churches where the same Christian message of "love thy neighbor" was taught, but the idea of neighbor was defined by race.

In the beginning, Hazel Brannon Smith doubted none of this. She never questioned that at the courthouse that dominated the town square, white people sat on the main floor and blacks crowded into the balcony. Yet in her view, all persons stood on equal footing before the law. She broke with southern journalistic tradition and covered the trials of whites who had committed crimes against blacks with the same attention with which she covered crimes against whites.

Like most other white southerners, Hazel Smith was effectively a segregationist. She had never editorialized for Negro suffrage or for better schools for black youth. Then on May 17, 1954, ninety-one years after the Emancipation Proclamation, the Supreme Court ended official federal tolerance of segregation. In *Brown v. Board of Education of Topeka*, it ruled "separate schools are inherently unequal" and outlawed separation of the races in public schools. Equality of education and social opportunity, this race mixing, was the triumph of everything the white South had battled against during the Civil War and Reconstruction, indeed ever since.

In publicly supporting the decision, Hazel Smith allowed American law to defeat her sense of tradition and the rightness of things as they had always been, but she revealed her agony over the decision in her column "Through Hazel Eyes:" "This is probably the most complex problem we have ever had to solve in our lifetime. It is going to require the best that is in us to do it. But solve it we must. Perhaps if we had done as much as we should to improve our Negro schools throughout the South in the past ten years, we would not have these lawsuits in the Courts today. . . . Unless our leaders in both races do better in the future than they have in the past ten years, we are doomed to oblivion."

As she counseled obedience to the new law of the land, others mobilized to thwart it. White Mississippi businessmen formed the Citizens' Councils to circumvent integration. Her one-time friend, Wilburn Hooker, a civic leader who set up the Citizens' Council in Holmes County, explained years later, "We felt like the blacks were organized, they had the NAACP, so the white people ought to have some organization to tell them what was going on. The Citizens' Councils were more an educational process than anything else to keep the people informed on how to maintain segregation. After a while we saw that wasn't happening, so we tried to figure out ways to cope with the situation."

The Citizens' Council did not use the flaming, night-raiding violence of the Ku Klux Klan, but its pressure was lethal nonetheless. Councilmen asked Hazel to support them, but she refused. In July 1954, when the sheriff shot a black man in the back of his leg for making noise on a highway outside town, Hazel insisted that the sheriff should be fired. She wrote: "The vast majority of Holmes county people are not rednecks who look with favor on the abuse of people because their skins are black. Mr. Byrd as Sheriff has violated every concept of justice, decency and right in his treatment of some of the people of Holmes County." She continued to editorialize, even after he sued her for libel damages of $60,000 and a jury returned a $10,000 verdict against her. "This will all blow over in a few weeks!" she predicted when a young woman who worked for her begged her to take care.

At Christmas, Hazel gave a party for sixty people. Only four of scores of invited guests showed up. Her friends say that was when she saw what her crusade was costing her. Still, she refused to back down. Hers was not the heroism of one outstanding moment, but the valor of enduring through a long and grinding process. She spoke up for law and showed the enlightened face of a new, emerging South that would see all races work together.

Not only did Hazel become a social pariah; she became the target of people determined to bring her to ruin. Members of the Citizens' Council stopped advertising in her papers. Whites who were interested in what she was doing sent their black employees out to buy copies. Besides this boycott, Wilburn Hooker had the hospital board fire Smitty from his job as administrator, despite the written support of the entire medical staff. Hooker, who by then had been elected to the state legislature, said, "Hazel had gotten so involved in politics and had gotten crossed up with the county, whereas before she was in such good standing with them, that at the first meeting the new board fired Smitty."

But as Lexington tried to freeze out Hazel, America awakened to the civil rights struggle and began to hear about her. When the Mississippi Supreme Court overturned the libel judgment against her in 1955, national papers and magazines carried the story. The proud community of Lexington resented the attention she was bringing on them. In 1957, when she failed to protest President Eisenhower's sending troops to Little Rock to integrate Central High School, feelings ran against her even though she did not support his action either. But although whites stopped advertising in Hazel Smith's newspapers and cancelled subscriptions, she remained solvent because she owned the only printing press in the county. There was no one else to print local government documents and supermarket handbills, so she was able to keep these accounts. Still, the Smiths mortgaged their property and continued to write columns and editorials supporting civil rights. In a daring innovation, she began to report on weddings, graduations, and other social events of the black community just as she covered social news of white society.

Mary Younger, a white woman who worked at the *Advertiser*, recalled, "Sometimes she would have Willie Wylie, our black printer who had worked for Hazel for years, and me read over her copy. We would say, 'Don't print this! More people will dislike you,' but she would go ahead."

If Hazel Smith was stoic in the face of large troubles, she grew shrewish over petty matters. Younger said, "The funny thing about her losing her temper was it would be over nothing. Big things she would take very calmly."

No one who knew Hazel Brannon Smith doubts she would have preferred to avoid the fight, that she would have preferred to have the money to trade in her Cadillac each year and be in the thick of the best parties in town. Still, she felt compelled to speak out.

She herself was now subject to the viciousness that had been meted out to blacks. Having failed to intimidate her into silence by the boycott of her newspapers, the Citizens' Councils decided to ruin her completely by setting up the rival *Holmes County Herald* with a printing plant that took over all the county printing business on which she had relied. Her employees were lured away, except for the loyal Willie Wylie.

"At that point, they had done all the boycotting they could possibly do," recalled Robert Smith, a black businessman in the state capital of Jackson. "They had taken all the advertisers away and finally they took away the printing business. All the fear left Hazel because there was nothing else they could take away from her." Attempting to earn money elsewhere, she and Smitty took out loans and acquired two more newspapers—the *Outlook* in Flora and the *Northside Reporter* in Jackson—and ran her weekly crusading columns in all of them.

By 1960, she financed her papers largely by printing coupons and handbills for Robert Smith's thriving grocery business. She also printed the *Mississippi Free Press*, a pet project of Medgar Evers that chronicled the civil rights movement in the state. Hazel helped Evers lay out the paper and organize the volunteer staff, and also wrote many *Free Press* editorials. "We had no sad moments," Robert Smith said. "When you attend mass rallies, as we did, and you hear speakers that make you feel that one day you will unshackle the chains, you have happiness."

Still, the Citizens' Councils did not let up. Knowing she was winning financial supporters around the country and that people were sympathizing with her, they contacted corporations with national brands and threatened to boycott any product advertised in her paper. Only monopolies like the Mississippi Power & Light Company and Southern Bell dared advertise with her. She filled the empty advertising columns with public service announcements boosting the Peace Corps and promoting the use of seat belts.

Unlike the days when she wrote at length about her travels around the world, she was silent about her trips across the country to speak on the civil rights struggle in Mississippi. Her lecture fees and funds raised by journalists like Ralph McGill, Turner Catledge, and that other crusading Mississippi newspaper editor, Hodding Carter, paid her bills. Local people learned she was having national impact only on the day in 1964 when network television crews drove around the square and turned down Yazoo Street. They entered the *Lexington Advertiser* offices to interview her because she had won the Pulitzer Prize for editorial writing for "steadfast adherence to her editorial duty in the face of great pressure and opposition."

Later in that summer, NBC hired her to do off-camera reporting at the Democratic Convention in Atlantic City. She covered the two rival Mississippi delegations, one white, the other integrated, each of which claimed to be the legitimate representatives of the party in the state.

Two days after Hazel Smith explained the intricacies of her state's political problems to the nation on the *Today Show* and NBC's *Nightly News*, a bomb was tossed into the empty offices of the *Northside Reporter* outside Jackson. It exploded with such force that it destroyed printing equipment and blew the rest room door into the opposite wall two hundred feet away.

Still she published. As lunch counters were desegregated, as James Meredith enrolled at the University of Mississippi and students poured into the South from the rest of the country to register black voters, Hazel Brannon Smith wrote editorials supporting them all. The civil rights movement triumphed.

Blacks gained electoral power in Holmes County, but political influence was never Hazel Smith's again. She was one of a handful of white southerners who fought to bring racial justice to her region and the country. Her side was victorious, but her battles cost her everything.

In 1967 she ran for state senate. When she lost, she accused the black community of not supporting her. The same tenacity and sense of mission that had made her noble also made her an irritant. In the era of Black Power, blacks disliked her call for moderation as little as whites had liked her call for justice years before.

Relentless pressures took their toll on the Smiths and their life together. Smitty found a job in Jackson with a federal program for the children of migrant workers, and he helped print and manage Hazel's newspapers, but his bouts of drinking and lack of formal religion troubled her. Although friends say he had the better financial judgment of the two, she began to resent his role in her business. She became shrill and so forgetful that she lost her car after parking it in the town's main square and lost her engagement ring, which someone later found in her purse. Confusion did not lessen her determination. Deciding to fulfill the one dream that remained to her, without Smitty's knowledge she mortgaged their property to renovate their small house into Hazelwood, a Tara-like mansion with fourteen rooms, a heated pool, and an elevator. In 1982, soon after Hazelwood was completed, Smitty fell off a ladder while working on the roof. A rib punctured his spleen, and he bled to death.

Almost three decades had passed since she began her stand for racial justice. In the face of tragedy, her past was forgiven her. When Smitty was buried from the First Baptist Church, Lexington turned out to support her in her grief. As people walked to the front of the church to pay their respects, Hazel broke down and wept. An old friend said, "The first thing that she said to me after the funeral was 'Everybody came. Even after all the anger, everybody came.' It made her so happy. If people in Lexington had known how much they meant to her, things might have been different. The thing is, Hazel was right, you know."

Hazel Smith's woes might have ended with the "forgiveness" she found at her husband's funeral, yet they did not. She grew disorganized to the point that doctors suspected she had Alzheimer's disease. She was obliged to return to her home town of Gadsden, Alabama, where her sister took her in. Hazelwood was auctioned to pay her debts even as black leaders in Mississippi tried to establish a fund to help her.

Popular entertainment encourages the idea that stories of heroes have happy endings. Usually they do not. In Hazel Brannon Smith's life, where lines of right and wrong are drawn so clearly, one can choose to believe she received a kind of blessing in the end. Before Hazel Smith died in 1994, she was moved to a home for the infirm. When she took her place amid strangers in wheelchairs, she felt restored to her glory days. Her muddled mind led her to believe she was sitting down in her office in Lexington—prosperous, merry, and writing the kind of editorials that would improve her world.

Gertrude Ederle:
"America's Best Girl"

SUSAN WARE

The world of sports has given America a disproportionate share of its twentieth-century heroes, but most of these athletes have been men. Gertrude Ederle was the rare woman who used her athletic prowess—in this case, long-distance endurance swimming—to become one of the best-known sports celebrities of the 1920s by swimming the English Channel in 1926. She was the first woman to do so, and she did it in record-breaking time. But Ederle found it difficult to capitalize on her fame, and she spent the rest of her life as a swimming instructor, far from the limelight that she so briefly enjoyed.

WHEN GERTRUDE EDERLE waded ashore near Dover on August 6, 1926, after swimming the English Channel in the record time of fourteen hours and thirty-one minutes, she went from being the unknown daughter of a German-American butcher to a worldwide celebrity overnight. Foreshadowing Charles Lindbergh's experience by more than a year, she had the right stuff for a sudden rise to fame in 1920s America, as the *New York Times* realized: Gertrude Ederle "has all the qualities that go to make up the kind of heroine whom America will ungrudgingly and freely worship and honor for her splendid achievement. The record of her 19 years shows her to be courageous, determined, modest, sportsmanlike, generous, unaffected and perfectly poised." Moreover, she was blessed with "beauty of face and figure" and "abounding health." After the largest and most enthusiastic ticker-tape parade ever given to an individual in New York City's history, Trudy, as she was called both out of affection and the need for punchy headlining, was showered by commercial offers approaching $1 million.

It might seem strange that the mere fact of swimming the English Channel qualified this young woman, who never graduated from high school, for all this fame and fortune, but the 1920s was a sports-crazy era. Babe Ruth, Jack Dempsey, Bobby Jones, and Red Grange were household names. Sportswriter Paul Gallico noted that heroes' welcomes used to be reserved for admirals, generals, and visiting royalty, but the 1920s "produced a new royalty, the kings and queens of sport, as a vivid and thrilling demonstration of the workings of this unique democracy, where the poorest and the humblest could instantly become national heroes and heroines." Gertrude Ederle was the first swimmer, and one of the first women, to join this elite crowd.

Her channel swim had definite feminist implications. Not only was Ederle the first woman to complete the swim, she did it faster than any of the previous men. In other words, this young American girl had proved herself to be men's better in the water, thereby undermining, if not demolishing, rationales about women's being the weaker sex. Pity the London newspaper that by chance had chosen the very day of her channel swim to run an editorial that baldly stated, "Even the most uncompromising champion of the rights and capacities of women must admit that in a contest of physical skill, speed and endurance they must remain forever the weaker sex." That is, until Trudy proved them wrong. She saw her individual triumph as a victory for her sex, saying prophetically to a New York sports editor, "All the women of the world will celebrate, too." At a time when women were embracing dramatically expanded roles in public and private, Ederle's accomplishment became part of this larger story. As Will Rogers quipped, "Yours for a revised edition of the dictionary explaining which is the weaker sex."

By the 1920s a certain degree of athleticism and competence at sports was considered desirable, even necessary, for young American women, in striking contrast to just several decades before, as suffrage leader Carrie Chapman Catt recalled: "It is a far cry from swimming the channel to the days to which my memory goes back, when it was thought that women could not throw a ball or even walk very far down the street without feeling faint." Catt was one of many to make the link "that women's freedom would go hand in hand with her bodily strength." Golfer Glenna Collett seconded this view: "The tomboy ideal is far more healthful than that of the poor little Goldilocks . . . who was forbidden vigorous activities lest she tear her clothes." And yet although sports and physical activity were encouraged for girls and young women, they rarely held the central role in girls' lives that sports did for the American male—except, of course, for Gertrude Ederle.

People wanted to swim the English Channel for the same reason they wanted to climb Everest or the Matterhorn: it was there. The feat had first been accomplished by an Englishman, Captain Matthew Webb, in 1875; so amazing was his epic twenty-three-hour swim that it was not duplicated for another thirty-six years. After the second successful swim in 1911, there was another gap until 1923, when three men made it, lowering the time to around sixteen and a half hours. Ederle herself had tried and failed in 1925, done in not by physical exhaustion but by seasickness in the rough seas. And just the week before Ederle's second try, another American woman, Clarabelle Barrett of New Rochelle, New York, had come within several miles of succeeding, before being forced to turn back by the tides and poor weather. As Charles Lindbergh would find the next year when he made his solo transatlantic flight, luck and timing were often just as important as skill and preparation in becoming a hero.

Gertrude Ederle was born in 1906 in New York City to parents who had recently emigrated from Germany. Her father ran a small butcher shop and delicatessen on Amsterdam Avenue on Manhattan's West Side. The third of six children, she learned to swim at the age of nine on the New Jersey shore at Highlands, where her family vacationed. Her sister, Margaret, was also a competitive swimmer. Both girls received their swimming instruction at a remarkable institution called the Women's Swimming Association (WSA) of New York, which had been founded in 1917. In its tiny indoor pool on the Lower East Side, the WSA trained several generations of female swimmers who went on to national and Olympic success, including backstroker Eleanor Holm and future Hollywood star Esther Williams. At age thirteen, Trudy began serious training under WSA supervision. She benefited from a farsighted coach named L. B. de Handley, who revolutionized women's swimming by changing the leg action of the crawl stroke from a conservative four-beat flutter kick to a more powerful six- to eight-beat kick.

At this point swimming was just emerging as a serious competitive sport, and Ederle excelled. In 1924 she held eighteen world records for distances from fifty yards to a half-mile, and won three medals at the 1924 Paris Olympics: bronze medals in the 100- and 400-yard freestyle and a gold for the 4 × 100 relay. As early as 1922 she began to move into the endurance swimming that would be her claim to fame, beating the world's top female swimmers, American Helen Wainwright and Liverpool's Hilda James, in the prestigious three-and-a-half-mile Day Cup race in New York Bay as an unheralded fifteen-year-old. The next year she established a new record (seven hours, eleven minutes, thirty seconds) for the swim from the Battery to Sandy Hook, New Jersey.

Ederle's success in open-water endurance swimming is an example of the advantage that women have in this athletic area. Because of women's lower center of gravity and higher percentage of body fat, they are anatomically better fitted for cold-water swimming over the long haul than men. Also critical to her success was the development, and popular acceptance, of one-piece bathing costumes for women that allowed them to swim, rather than just bob in the water weighted down by the pounds of waterlogged stockings, shoes, bloomers, and blouses demanded by Victorian modesty. This was part of a general revolution in women's clothing that freed female bodies from unnecessary constraints. As Tom Robinson, a swimming instructor at Northwestern, noted of Ederle's triumph, "A woman could not possibly have accomplished this same feat thirty years ago, for corsets and other ridiculously unnecessary clothing hampered her physical condition and deprived her of the muscular effort so necessary in the development of a good swimmer."

Australian swimmer Annette Kellerman is credited with developing the first one-piece suit, which she proudly displayed in swimming exhibitions throughout the United States in the 1910s and 1920s. Even her early bulky versions were liberating compared to the bathing costumes of old; by the 1920s, a trim one-piece suit was standard apparel for most young women. Paul Gallico's childhood memory of seeing Kellerman perform in a vaudeville routine well captures the intersection of swimming, sexuality, and women's bodies: "It made the question of how ladies were put together no longer a matter of vague speculation."

Newspapers and newsreels were finding out that swimming had sex appeal. Whereas editors would be barred from running photos of skimpily dressed showgirls in family magazines, they were free to run pictures of wholesome, fresh-faced American girls in their bathing costumes. Soon the bathing beauty would be as important as the girl athlete. It is no coincidence that the early 1920s saw both the launching of Ederle's competitive swimming career and the Miss America pageant.

Ederle did not present herself as glamorous, nor did the press feel the need to press her into that mold. Competitive swimming demanded hefty bodies, and Ederle carried close to 150 pounds on a frame of about five feet five inches. Because she did not have a heavily muscled body, however, and because slimness had not yet been established as an all-encompassing cultural norm, her appearance drew favorable comment from the press. Observed the *New York Times*, "In her street dress she looked like a healthy girl, a little on the bouncing order, but her dimensions were not very large." Paul Gallico noted that "her somewhat Teutonic chubbiness, round, dimpled face, and fair-brown bobbed hair, were offset by agreeable features and an extraordinarily sweet expression."

It was Ederle's wholesomeness that proved most appealing to the press. Even though she was once called a "bob-haired, nineteen-year-old daughter of the Jazz Age," she was no flapper. News coverage approvingly noted that she did not drink or smoke, and was not excessively interested in boys. In short, she was an excellent model for American girls. "American Girlhood Triumphs," headlined the *Syracuse Herald*. "The American girl is all right," said the *Washington Star*. It was President Calvin Coolidge himself who called her "America's best girl."

Although Ederle amassed an amazing amateur record, competitive swimming cost money, especially expensive undertakings like channel swims. The Women's Swimming Association had helped underwrite Ederle's unsuccessful 1925 attempt, but they could not finance a second try, so Ederle made the difficult decision to give up her amateur status and turn professional: she accepted commercial backing from the *Chicago Tribune* syndicate and the *New York Daily News*. In return for exclusive access to her story, she would receive a salary, her training and coaching expenses would be paid, and she would be eligible for a bonus if she succeeded. As with most exploits in fields like aviation and exploration, such commercial backing was absolutely necessary, but the public often conveniently overlooked those aspects and instead celebrated the accomplishment as that of a supreme individual, acting alone. That is certainly how the public reacted to Trudy's heroic battle against the elements on her record-breaking swim.

At 7:08 on the morning of August 6, 1926, Ederle, heavily greased against the chilly sixty-one-degree water, waded into the surf off Cape Gris Nez and began to swim at the steady rate of twenty-eight strokes to the minute. She wore a red bathing suit, cut deeply under the arms to free her powerful shoulders, goggles to protect her eyes from the sting of the saltwater, and a skull cap. She was accompanied by the tug *Alsace* containing her father (her mother was too nervous to make the trip), sister, trainer, and several fellow swimmers, who sometimes kept Ederle company in the water while she swam; a second boat filled with reporters and photographers followed closely. Both boats were equipped with wireless radio, so that reports of her progress could be relayed ashore, including back to a waiting America. Ederle took little sustenance during the swim, just some beef extract, chicken broth, chocolate, and sugar blocks, and luckily she escaped the seasickness that had plagued her earlier try. At times she sang "Let Me Call You Sweetheart" to keep up her rhythm; other times she was serenaded with songs from her supporters in the boat. If her spirits sagged, she could look up at the banner draped over the side of the tug, which said, "This Way, Ole Kid!" with an arrow pointing straight ahead.

The Ederle entourage had chosen the date of August 6 because of a favorable forecast, but the weather soon deteriorated into squall conditions and a heavy, rolling sea typical of the severe conditions that characterize that uncompromising body of water. After almost eleven hours in the water and with the weather still worsening, it was suggested that she give up and come out of the water. "What for?" she replied, to the cheers of the reporters in the press boat, who were understandably eager for a good story.

Ederle kept swimming. In the end, her speed as well as her endurance won the day, because she caught the favorable tide that would take her into the English shore by only ten minutes.

When she waded ashore near the cliffs of Dover, she was greeted by bonfires and an enthusiastic crowd, plus an overzealous police officer who demanded to see her passport. After straightening out that bureaucratic snafu, she was free to relax in a hot bath, her first since her arrival in France in June to train. (She hadn't wanted to spoil herself for the chilly channel water.) She wasn't sore, she told reporters, adding that her only injury was a tender right wrist from shaking the hands of so many admirers.

Perhaps as the telegrams poured in, and the requests for interviews piled up, and the crowds thronged outside her hotel, she began to realize that she wasn't just little Trudy Ederle from Amsterdam Avenue anymore. She was on the front page of every newspaper in America, indeed throughout much of the world, an overnight sensation. The *New York Daily News*, a tabloid paper heavily dependent on photos, organized the fastest and most expensive relay in the history of journalism to date to get photographs of her actual swim back to an eager American public. All the major news syndicates had placed sets of their developed photographs onboard express liners leaving Southampton for New York that day, but the *Daily News* trumped them by sending their pictures on a steamer bound for Montreal, which cut one day off the trip. From there, with a combination of sea and land planes, a racing car, a train, and even an ambulance for the last leg, the *News* got the packet showing Ederle emerging from the water near Dover into print twelve hours before its competitors. But their scoop was short-lived, since a rival paper simply photographed its front and back pages and reproduced the pictures in its next edition.

Two weeks later Ederle received a hero's welcome from her hometown of New York. Her ocean liner from Europe was met by Grover Whalen, the city's official greeter, who escorted her to the Battery in a city tug. From there she went by motorcade up Lower Broadway to City Hall, the streets lined with supporters and ticker tape showering out the windows of the skyscrapers. She was dressed in a lavender hat, a blue serge coat suit, a scarf from Paris, and gray silk stockings. A police officer noted the larger than usual number of women in the crowd, symptomatic of how Ederle's individual achievement meant something special to the nation's women. Ten thousand people and the mayor awaited her at city hall. The only slightly

sour note to the whole celebration was a dispute about how much prominence should be given to her German-American roots. At that point
World War I was less than a decade old, and wounds were still fresh. The
event was pointedly portrayed as an American, not a German-American,
triumph. Ederle herself reinforced the patriotic theme by telling the crowd,
"It was for my flag that I swam and to know that I could bring home the
honors, and my mind was made up to do it."

Once the formal ceremony was over, Ederle was free to go home to her
own neighborhood at 106 Amsterdam Avenue (between Sixty-fourth and
Sixty-fifth streets), where waiting for her outside her father's butcher shop
was a bright red roadster, a gift from her backers. The newspapers quoted
her agent, lawyer Dudley Field Malone, as saying that almost $1 million of
potential endorsements and opportunities had been offered to Ederle, so
she must have thought that the car was just the first of many riches that
would flow her way. It did not turn out that way, and within that tale lies
the downside to sudden celebrity: how hard it is to capitalize on sudden
fame and how quickly the public forgets.

In retrospect, it is clear that Ederle's finances were badly handled by
Malone: instead of accepting offers while she was still hot property, he held
out for more. But she was also hurt by a combination of factors that rein-
force how ephemeral heroic status can be. Instead of hurrying home to
America after her swim, she took time to visit her grandmother in Germany. In that period, an Englishwoman, and the mother of two children at
that, swam the channel, although not as fast as Ederle. She was still the first
woman, and the fastest human, but her salability was tarnished just a bit.

Most of Ederle's potential offers were in the area of entertainment. She
traveled for a while with a vaudeville show, giving swimming exhibitions, and
even auditioned for a part in Hollywood. (The studios quickly realized that
her bulky frame, so necessary to long-distance swimming, was the antithesis
of the steamlined, lithe look movie cameras wanted.) But Ederle found the
strain of public performance unbearable, and there was talk that she might
have had a nervous breakdown. Her lack of ease in public was exacerbated by
the partial loss of hearing she had suffered as a result of the battering her body
took during her swim. Very little of the money she made actually got to her,
certainly not enough to make a difference for the rest of her life.

Since she had turned professional in order to make her channel swim,
Ederle could not return to amateur swimming, which precluded participat-

ing in the 1928 Olympics. She eventually took a job as a swimming instructor, and that was how she supported herself in the years to come. At one point she injured her back in an aquatic performance and spent many months in a cast. And her deafness grew worse. She did make a small appearance at Billy Rose's Aquacade at the 1939 New York World's Fair, but by then she had been long forgotten by the public.

Gertrude Ederle spent the rest of her life living in a small house in Flushing, Queens. She never married, and for many years shared her home with two other women. She never complained about her deafness or expressed bitterness about how she had lost out on the opportunities to cash in on her success. "Don't write any sob stories about me," she told a reporter in 1966. Although each August 6 there was usually some mention of her record-breaking channel swim, she made only infrequent public appearances. As a reporter put it in 1976, "In effect, Miss Ederle has gone from a legend in her own time to a relic in everyone else's, trotted out on anniversaries of her triumph to bask in the glow of an America that used to be."

In 1936 reporter Ishbel Ross captured the fleeting nature of Ederle's fame: "She flashed through the news columns, made the headlines, tasted the heady wine of extravagant publicity; then went out of sight with the speed of an expiring rocket." That is how the twentieth century has often treated its popular heroes, especially from the world of sports and entertainment. One day they are front-page news, the talk of the town. The next, they are practically forgotten, reduced to a single line in the record books and perhaps a few faint memories of a ticker-tape parade.

Gertrude Ederle didn't set out to be a hero; she just wanted to swim the English Channel. As she put it simply, "I knew I could do it. I knew I would, and I did."

"Manila John" of Guadalcanal:
Hero of the Pacific War

KENNETH T. JACKSON

*A book on forgotten heroes would be incomplete without a dec-
orated combat veteran, and World War II Marine Corps
sergeant John Basilone fits the bill. Growing up poor in a working-class family in Raritan, New Jersey, he joined the peacetime army to escape the devastating impact of the Great
Depression. When war came, he was ready. Basilone's examples of extraordinary bravery and patriotic service to his country in the Pacific earned him medals, honors, marriage
proposals, and the admiration of his hometown and the country
at large. And then, like so many other war heroes, he dropped
from our historical memory.*

Tens of thousands of motorists every day race along the New Jersey Turnpike, one of the busiest highways in the world and the main north-south corridor connecting Washington, Philadelphia, and New York City. Most drivers focus on the pavement in front of them, and few notice that one of the service areas is named for John Basilone. The purpose of those who stop is refreshment and relief, not reflection or remembrance. Few pause by the side of the main building to read a rusting bronze plaque about "Manila John," the home town boy who won the nation's two highest awards for valor in World War II: the Congressional Medal of Honor and the Navy Cross.

Few would have predicted from John Basilone's early life that he was heroic material. He was born in Buffalo, New York, on November 4, 1916, and grew up in Raritan, New Jersey, a working-class community thirty-five miles southwest of New York City. His parents, Angelina and Salvatore Basilone, struggled to get by on their income from a small tailorshop, a task made more difficult by the fact that they had ten children, all of them crowded together in a modest house at 113 East First Avenue. John, a skinny kid, was often into mischief. He attended St. Bernard's parochial school before ending his formal education at age fifteen, when he dropped out of school to drive a laundry truck. He grew to be tall and handsome, with black hair, a strong chin, and a barrel chest. Except for his pug ears, he was almost movie-star handsome.

The Great Depression was in full swing throughout John's teenage years. Jobs were scarce, and no one John knew in Raritan ever seemed to have enough money. At age nineteen he joined the army. The pay in uniform was lousy too, but military life at least offered three square meals per day, as well as clothes, lodging, and adventure. John adapted quickly to peacetime soldiering, winning a Golden Gloves tournament as a light-heavyweight before being sent to the Philippines, then an American possession. In Manila, the capital city, he acquired his nickname, "Manila John," as well as large tattoos on both arms—a woman on the right and an unsheathed sword on the left, with the legend "Death before Dishonor." More important, he developed such a fascination, even a love, with automatic weapons that before long, he could break a machine gun down and reassemble it, all the time blindfolded.

When his army hitch was up in 1939, John returned to Raritan, where his mother urged him to get married and raise a family. Economic conditions were better, and he found work in a nearby chemical plant. But World War II had already begun in Europe, and although the United States was technically at peace, its armed forces were expanding rapidly. So in 1940 "Manila John" enlisted again, this time in the Marine Corps. His specialty remained the same: machine guns. And because of his previous military experience, he was quickly promoted to private first class, and then to sergeant.

Basilone's peacetime life ended on December 7, 1941, a Sunday morning when Japanese carrier pilots without warning attacked the great American naval base at Pearl Harbor in the Hawaiian Islands, destroying most of the huge battleships docked there. Over the next six months, Japan's soldiers and sailors ran roughshod in the Pacific, conquering the Philippines (where resistance finally ended on Corregidor), Malaya, Burma, Indonesia, and many Pacific islands. By June 1942, the Empire of the Rising Sun reached its farthest points of advance in the Aleutian Islands and New Guinea.

That month, June 1942, Japan experienced its first major defeat when American cryptoanalysts broke the top-secret Japanese naval code. As a result, the commander of the United States Pacific Fleet, Admiral Chester Nimitz, knew the intentions of his counterpart, Admiral Isoroku Yamamato, at the crucial Battle of Midway, and the Japanese attackers lost all four of their biggest aircraft carriers in the span of a few days.

Meanwhile, John Basilone and the First Marine Division had been undergoing grueling amphibious training in March 1942 at the prophetically named Solomons Islands, Maryland. Their equipment was not impressive. While Army divisions received the excellent M-1 Garand semiautomatic rifle in 1936, their Marine counterparts carried the same M-1903 Springfield bolt-action rifle that their fathers had used in World War I. Basilone and his comrades were anxious to get into the fight. Basilone's unit crossed the country by rail to San Francisco before it sailed in June to an unknown destination across the vast Pacific Ocean. By mid-July, Sergeant Basilone was in Wellington, New Zealand.

The Marines did not have time to see the sights, however. Because of the great American naval victory at Midway in May, the United States went over to the offensive in the summer of 1942. The first target was the Solomon Islands. At that time, few people had ever heard of Guadalcanal, and for good reason. From the air, it seemed a quiet and peaceful paradise, with lush green mountains, abundant waterfalls, and glorious beaches. On the ground, however, Guadalcanal was a tropical hell. Ninety-two miles long and thirty-two miles wide, it was mostly dense jungle, infested with ferocious ants, poisonous snakes, and malarial mosquitoes, not to mention lizards, crocodiles, spiders, leeches, and scorpions. Anyone traversing the island had to cross precipitous ravines, wade through swamps rank with the smell of rotting vegetation, and hack through stout vines. "If I were a king," author Jack London once remarked, "the worst punishment I could inflict on my enemies would be to banish them to the Solomons."

Both the Japanese and the Americans wanted Guadalcanal, not because it was paradise, or anything close to that, but because it was strategic. Located northeast of Australia, ten degrees below the equator, it would be Japan's southernmost and easternmost outpost, an important staging area for offensive action in the Southwest Pacific region, as well as the first line of defense for the far-flung empire. For the United States, taking Guadalcanal would protect the Australian continent and represent the first clear sign that America's growing air, sea, and land forces were going over to the attack.

On August 7, 1942, eight months to the day after the Pearl Harbor attack and only weeks after it had arrived in New Zealand, the First Marine Division and John Basilone went ashore on Guadalcanal. A few thousand Japanese construction workers were already there, busy building an airstrip on the north coast. They put up little resistance and conveniently abandoned their new runways. The Marines promptly named the airstrip Henderson Field, after Major Lofton Henderson, who had been killed at Midway. Everything seemed to be going well for the Americans.

In the early morning hours of August 9, 1942, however, the U.S. Navy suffered the worst defeat on the high seas in its history. In the Battle of Savo Island, which took place entirely at night, Vice Admiral Gunichi Mikawa skillfully outmaneuvered his Allied opponents, sinking four modern heavy cruisers and killing 1,023 American and Australian sailors. Although he did not attack the vulnerable Marine transport ships along the beaches, Admiral Mikawa had caused such destruction that every Allied ship—destroyers and cruisers as well as cargo vessels, troopships, and minesweepers—fled the area. The Marines on Guadalcanal, short of ammunition and food, had been abandoned, and Japanese reinforcements, ordered by Tokyo to retake Henderson Field at any cost, were already on their way.

Over the next five months, the struggle for Guadalcanal was as savage and merciless as any in all of World War II. For its part, the U.S. Navy recovered from the disaster at Savo Island and took a horrible toll of the Japanese destroyers and transports trying to support and supply their hungry troops on land. But even without adequate food, medical supplies, and military equipment, Nippon's soldiers were tough, resourceful, and determined, and almost to a man, they were willing to fight to the death in the service of their emperor. Hand-to-hand fighting was common, and neither side took many prisoners. Sergeant Basilone and his men understood that Henderson Field and its vital runways were the key to the battle. As the American commander, Marine General Arthur Vandergrift, told his staff, "We're going to defend this airfield until we no longer can."

Although fighting was continuous over a period of many weeks, the Japanese made three major efforts to overrun Henderson Field. The last and most desperate came during the night of October 24–25, 1942. At half past midnight, the Sandai Regiment rushed forward toward Lunga Ridge, only a thousand yards south of the airstrip. Screaming through a torrential rain and hurling grenades toward the Marine foxholes and gun pits, the Japanese used the bodies of their dead comrades to climb over the barbed wire ten feet in front of the American positions. Sergeant Basilone, in charge of two heavy machine guns, was at the center of the attack and in the midst of the most desperate fighting. When one of his gun crews was wiped out, Basilone rolled back and forth over the ground, firing first one, then the other. When one of the guns jammed, he repaired it in the darkness. When the guns got too hot, he used his pistol. When he ran out of ammunition, he raced through hostile lines for more. The fighting went on through the night. At dawn, more than a thousand dead Japanese soldiers lay before the American positions. Marine officers counted thirty-eight enemy bodies piled up around "Manila John," who had been forced to move his guns because he could not shoot over them. Miraculously, he had suffered only superficial wounds. He had helped save Henderson Field. Three months later, all the Japanese were gone from Guadalcanal.

On January 19, 1943, John Basilone received the Medal of Honor, the first Marine in World War II to win the nation's highest award for bravery. The official citation from President Franklin D. Roosevelt proclaimed in part: "For extraordinary heroism and conspicuous gallantry in action against enemy Japanese forces, above and beyond the call of duty, while serving with the 1st Battalion, 7th Marines, 1st Marine Division in the Lunga Area, Guadalcanal, Solomon Islands, on 24 and 25 October 1942. . . . His great personal valor and courageous initiative were in keeping with the highest traditions of the U.S. Naval Service."

After the pale blue ribbon with the medal, inscribed simply with the words "For Valor," was draped around his neck at a Division Review, Basilone was brought home to a hero's welcome. The government wanted to use him to sell war bonds and to boost morale on the home front. Characteristically modest, he shared the honor with his dead comrades. "Only part of this medal belongs to me." he said. "Pieces of it belong to the boys who are still on Guadalcanal." No matter. The adulation for "Manila John" was extraordinary. In New York City on September 4, 1943, Mayor Fiorello La Guardia gave him the key to the city and said: "I know you have plenty of guts, because that medal is awarded only for conduct above and beyond the call of duty. That is something for all of us at home to consider. In the coming bond drive we must all do something above and beyond the call of duty; make some sacrifice and do a 'Basilone.'"

The celebration continued in "Manila John's" home town of Raritan, where the community shut down for a day as the local hero rode in an open convertible through the familiar streets. His portrait was hung in the town hall, and marriage proposals poured in. And at the two-thousand-acre New Jersey estate of heiress Doris Duke Cromwell, various governors, mayors, judges, and even a movie starlet (who reportedly kissed him on the mouth) joined twenty thousand in paying tribute.

The war was over for Sergeant Basilone. He had fought his share of the war and paid his dues; he had earned the right to sleep in a safe bed in a snug house. It was time for someone else to take a turn in the killing fields. All the United States asked was that John make public appearances, shake hands, and accept congratulations.

Even though Basilone married Lena Riggi, herself a member of the Marine Corps Women's Reserve, on July 10, 1944, he was restless giving speeches, especially when the news every day was of battles across the sea. As he told one reporter, "That war bond drive was worse than fighting Japs." Finally he asked for reassignment to combat duty. He wanted to rejoin his buddies, to get back to the Philippines, and ultimately to march in victory up Dewey Avenue in Manila. "I ain't no musuem piece," he said. The Marine Corps offered Basilone a commission as an officer, but he turned down the bars of a second lieutenant. "I'm just a plain soldier," he said. "I want to stay one."

So John Basilone returned to danger, this time as a member of the Twenty-seventh Regiment of the Fifth Marine Division. But he never made it back to the Philippines. Instead, he was in the first attack wave at Iwo Jima on February 19, 1945. A tiny, disgusting, rancid, and volcanic island, Iwo Jima, if anything, was worse than Guadalcanal. Alive with boiling sulfur pits, it was only six miles long and two miles wide, a third the size of Manhattan and too small to appear on most maps. Its value lay in its critical location 625 miles north of Saipan and 660 miles south of Tokyo. With an airfield on Iwo Jima, Americans could provide a safe haven for crippled B-29 bombers, and they could intensify their aerial assault on Japan.

The twenty-one thousand Japanese defenders on Iwo Jima knew perfectly well what was at stake. They knew that there was nothing between them and their home islands. They knew that if they failed, their families and their emperor would be in peril. They knew that there would be no compromises, no quarter, no half-measures, and no prisoners. They would repel the American invaders or die. As Lieutenant General Tadamichi Kuribayashi told his commanders, "Once the enemy invades the island, every man will resist until the end, making his position his tomb." Just before the battle, he wrote to his only son: "Once Tokyo is raided it means that Iwo Jima has been taken by the enemy. It means your father is dead. . . . Therefore, you must be the central figure of our family and help Mother."

For the United States, too, Iwo Jima would become a legend, comparable to Valley Forge in the American Revolution, Gettysburg in the Civil War, and the invasion beaches of Normandy in World War II. Iwo Jima was a place of trial, sacrifice, heroism, and death, and it took the lives of 6,821 Americans, most of them not yet old enough to vote. Considering the size of the battlefield, the length of the struggle, and the relatively small number of men involved, Iwo Jima was singularly awful in World War II. Indeed, the most famous American image of the entire war was of six Marines raising the stars and stripes, while the battle still raged, over Mount Suribachi.

Intense Japanese resistance began even before the first sixty-nine amphtracs, each carrying about twenty men, made it to shore. But it was only after the Marines were on the beach and struggling through black volcanic ash that offered no cover from mortars, rifles, machine guns, and artillery that they realized how difficult their task would be. American tanks proved to be almost useless, either because they could not move in the soft ash or because Japanese antitank guns destroyed them before they could maneuver. Dead bodies were everywhere. Sergeant Basilone, caught in the fury of Red Beach II, saw that the only hope for anyone to escape the murderous crossfire was to get off the beach and toward the sand dunes a bit inland. Unfortunately, a Japanese machine gun emplacement, protected by a concrete blockhouse and almost hidden in the sand, controlled the open field. It had to go. Ordering his assault team to burrow into the sand, Basilone jumped up and ran alone through intense rifle and machine-gun fire, zigzagging his way through the sand. No one knew how he made it to the top of the blockhouse, but once there, he tossed grenades through the openings, killing everyone inside and silencing the enemy machine gun.

With the Japanese pillbox out of the way, Basilone shouted, "C'mon you guys! Let's get these guns off the beach." At that, he stood up and was leading his men across the dunes toward the edge of Motoyama Airfield when a Japanese mortar shell exploded directly in front of him, opening up his body from his head through his knees. Although medical corpsmen reached him within minutes, his extensive wounds were obviously fatal, and he died from massive internal injuries without leaving the beach.

In the short run, John Basilone was not forgotten. Because of his earlier fame on Guadalcanal, his death was reported in newspapers across the nation. And for his heroism on Iwo Jimo, he was honored again, this time posthumously with the Navy Cross, the Marine Corps' second highest decoration for bravery, after the Medal of Honor. The town of Raritan put up a statue of its hero, bare-chested, a machine gun cradled in his arms, ammunition belts around his neck, and a fierce look in his eyes. In December 1945, the U.S. Navy named a destroyer the USS *Basilone* and the Marine Corps named a road at Camp Pendleton in his honor. And of course New Jersey named a rest stop for him.

But memories are short, even national ones, and John Basilone is a forgotten hero at the end of the twentieth century. The USS *Basilone* is no longer in commission, the Basilone statue is ignored, and his grave site in Arlington National Cemetery (his body was moved from Iwo Jima in 1949) is rarely visited.

Why should John Basilone endure in national memory? Even if he had not been on Lunga Ridge on the night of October 24–25, 1942, the Japanese would probably not have taken Henderson Field. And even if they had taken the Guadalcanal airstrip, they lacked the strength to defeat the United States in a titanic war of attrition. Even if John Basilone had never lived, the Empire of Japan would have been ground to powder by 1945.

There is, moreover, an increasing American tendency to believe that military history is irrelevant and unimportant, that no one who kills should be honored, and that the world would somehow be better off if everyone would simply refuse to fight. This is true in the same sense that we would be better off without laws, without police, without prisons. Why not have a society in which everyone loves and no one hates? Until human beings move much closer to the perfection that has eluded them over the last few thousand years, until nations renounce aggression, until everyone simply accepts the status quo, there will be conflict and there will be war.

And wars are not won simply by guns or ships, however numerous, however large, however sophisticated. Rather, victory comes only because of individual effort and individual sacrifice, when ordinary people perform extraordinary deeds, sometimes at the obvious risk and obvious cost of life itself. Somebody has to do it; somebody has to die. As the *New York Times* editorialized after "Manila John's" death:

> Being a marine fighting man, and therefore a realist, Sergeant Basilone must have known in his heart that his luck wouldn't last forever. Yet he chose to return to battle. When it has needed them the United States has always had men like him. The tragedy of their deaths is that it ever should have become necessary for their country to ask them to make the sacrifices they have made and must continue to make until the war is won. The finest monument they could have would be an enduring resolve by all of us to this time fashion an enduring peace. If it had been done the year John Basilone was born he would not have had to die last month on an alien beach so far from home.

Frederick Funston: A Song of Rage

MARK C. CARNES

Frederick Funston, who proved his mettle in the Philippines forty-five years before Guadalcanal and Iwo Jima, was an old-fashioned war hero. Showing daring and not a little hubris, Funston's actions almost singlehandedly led to the suppression of a nasty guerrilla war. But unlike John Basilone, the nation soon turned against its home-grown hero, perhaps rightly so, and he dropped from history. Funston's story provides a final note of caution to our collection: while heroes emerge in all times and places, heroism can be fleeting. Norms of heroism change over time, and what one era celebrates may be precisely what another wants to forget.

Sing, Goddess, of Achilles' maniac rage: ruinous thing! It roused a thousand sorrows and hurled many souls of mighty warriors to Hades.

Homer, *The Iliad*

O N THE NIGHT of March 22, 1901, as fierce rains battered his camp site in the wildest reaches of Luzon Island, Frederick Funston pondered what awaited him the next day. Ten miles to the north lay his prey, Emilio Aguinaldo, leader of the Filipinos. Aguinaldo had gone to war against the United States two years earlier, a bizarre consequence of the momentous events of 1898. In April of that year, President McKinley had declared war against Spain over Cuba. In May, Admiral George Dewey destroyed the Spanish fleet in Manila Bay and invited Aguinaldo's Filipinos to join American forces against the Spanish army in the Philippines. By August, the American army had crushed the Spanish army in Cuba, and Spain sued for peace, ceding Cuba and the Philippines to the United States. When McKinley decided to annex the Philippines, tensions mounted between the Filipino and American soldiers who remained entrenched in adjacent positions outside Manila.

Funston had been there when American sentries first fired on Aguinaldo's troops. The skirmish ignited an all-out war that turned into a rout, as the untrained and ill-equipped Filipino army repeatedly collapsed before the furious American assaults. On March 1, 1899, with the fall of Malolos, the capital, the main Filipino armies dispersed. Funston had been the first American soldier into Malolos, spurring his horse past the burning buildings, racing into the town square, and cleaning out the final barricade with his revolver. But since then, Aguinaldo directed a bitter guerrilla campaign that for two years had bedeviled the U.S. expeditionary army of some sixty thousand men. McKinley had replaced the American commander with General Arthur MacArthur, who publicly stated that while the Filipino rebels could be defeated, the war would cost $100 million and thousands of American lives, a sobering prognostication that inflamed critics of the war. But Funston knew that if he could capture Aguinaldo, Filipino resistance would collapse and the war would be over.

During the past two years, however, Aguinaldo had proved elusive, and now that he was securely ensconced in his remote jungle hideout, the prospects for catching him were even worse. Long before an American army sufficient to seize his stronghold could make it through the intervening jungles, swollen streams, and mountain ranges, Aguinaldo and his army could slip away to even more inaccessible outposts. That Funston had made it this close was proof that his ruse was working—unless, of course, Aguinaldo was luring him into a deadly trap.

It was a wild idea, something out of a boy's adventure story. Funston came up with it after his men had captured a Filipino courier in possession of coded documents. Several bore the signature of Colon de Magdalo, which Funston recognized as the secret Masonic name of Aguinaldo. Funston's interrogation of the courier had been successful. (It was later said that Funston had subjected him to the "water torture," an effective new aid to military intelligence whereby several gallons of water were forced down a suspect's throat; his painfully distended belly was then beaten with logs. Funston later admitted that he had interrogated the courier "forcefully," but declined to elaborate.) For whatever reasons, the courier saw fit to confirm that Aguinaldo had authored the despatches; after further questioning, he revealed that Aguinaldo's secret redoubt was located at the inaccessible village of Palanan. Working feverishly through the night, fortified by coffee and whiskey, Funston deciphered the courier's documents. One he found particularly intriguing. In it Aguinaldo demanded that the recipient send reinforcements back with the courier.

Funston decided to oblige Aguinaldo, but instead of providing the Filipino *insurrectos* Aguinaldo desired, Funston would disguise and send his Macabebe scouts, inveterate foes of Tagalogs such as Aguinaldo. The Macabebes would escort five American "prisoners," including Funston, directly to Aguinaldo's headquarters at Palanan. The entire entourage would be guided, as Aguinaldo had ordered, by his erstwhile courier, whose enthusiasm for the Filipino cause diminished by the hour. Once planted at the heart of Aguinaldo's compound, the Macabebes and the American "prisoners" would overpower the startled Filipino defenders, seize Aguinaldo, race him back to Manila, and thereby bring the war to an immediate end.

When Funston outlined his scheme to his superior, General MacArthur had deep misgivings. Sitting on his desk was a cable from Washington ordering Funston's recall; he was to be mustered out of the service immediately. Quite apart from his orders, MacArthur saw that Funston's venture was a tissue of implausibilities. Surely Aguinaldo or at least some of his Tagalogs would see through the disguises of the Macabebes or overhear them speaking their own dialect. Or the Macabebes, on approaching the insurgent stronghold, would panic and open fire too soon. And even if they got inside Aguinaldo's compound, the Filipino army would doubtless obliterate Funston's greatly outnumbered troupe of actors. On the other hand, MacArthur had boldly promised decisive results and so far had little to show for his efforts. He finally agreed to allow his headstrong subordinate to give it a try. "Funston, this is a desperate undertaking," he said as they parted. "I fear I shall never see you again."

Funston knew that the top brass wanted to be rid of him and that this would be his last chance. He had attracted far too much attention: his colorful comments had played into the hands of critics of the war, and his headline-grabbing exploits had irritated the regular officers. Time and again Funston had been told to keep his mouth shut, but every corpuscle in his blood impelled him to the heart of the action and then obliged him to comment on what he did or saw. The truth of the matter was that Funston had always wanted to be a hero. He wanted to be acknowledged as a great warrior, someone whose martial prowess and courage could determine the outcome of a war: David bringing down Goliath and routing the Philistines; Achilles wading into the Trojans and breaking the siege, or Napoleon working his will upon all Europe. His was the dream of boys who play soldier: of charging ahead of the others into the teeth of enemy fire; of seizing the ramparts and dispatching the enemy into oblivion; of sustaining dreadful (but not disfiguring) wounds; of being publicly feted by a grateful nation; and of receiving, in private, the adoring ministrations of some sweet young thing. Most men, on easing into manhood, redefine heroism in more prosaic terms: of providing for a family despite being laid off; of preserving scruples or friendships when to do so is unpopular; of walking nobly, at the close of life, toward the abyss. Funston would have none of this. He craved pristine glory of the classical kind, a type of glory to which the industrial world, with its behemoth battleships and monstrous cannon, had nearly blasted into oblivion. He wanted not just to win battles, but to reclaim a type of heroism that had already become old-fashioned.

Funston had undertaken such a quest out of fear that he did not measure up. Partly this was because his father had set so daunting a standard. Edward Funston was six feet two and two hundred pounds. Known as "Foghorn" Funston, he had a deep, bellowing voice and a sharp, scathing tongue that suited him to leadership. During the Civil War, he worked his way through the ranks to become an officer in the artillery. After the war, he set up a homestead in Kansas, became prominent in Republican circles, and was repeatedly elected to Congress. Nearly always he plunged into whatever frays he could find. At sixty-nine, he gave a fiery speech on a street corner and came to blows with a law officer who tried to arrest him for disturbing the peace. Foghorn Funston was a veritable exemplar of late-nineteenth-century manhood.

But not his first son, Frederick, born in 1865, a boy who was always much smaller than his friends and effeminate in appearance. His school-mates teased him. At an early age Funston resolved to compensate for his appearance with bravado displays of martial manliness. He soaked up his father's war stories, and read all that he could about war in dime novels and frontier tales; he also read Carlyle's biographies of Cromwell and Napoleon, as well as Macauley's and Plutarch's celebrated essays on heroes and heroism.

Funston craved a military career, but though his father was a congress-man, the boy was rejected by West Point: his grades were mediocre, and he was too small. In 1886 he went instead to the University of Kansas at Lawrence, but there proved something of a misfit. The professors and classes held no interest for him, and he instead read war novels and biographies of military figures. But most of his energies were devoted to his highly visible and wholly unsuccessful pursuit of the most desirable women on campus, all of whom spurned him on account of his size. His fraternity brothers at Phi Delta Theta called him "Little Timmie Funston." Jokes about his size followed him into the army. Behind his back, his men called him the "Bantam General." Even his father, when asked to comment on his son's activities, responded with wry humor, as if he were amused rather than inspired at his boy's exploits. Worse still, the New York Times, in its cover-age of a battle after Malolos that led to his winning the Congressional Medal of Honor, ran the headline: "Daring Little Colonel Funston." The opening paragraph attributed Funston's courage to the fact that, at five feet five inches and 115 pounds, he was too small to hit.

His fear of humiliation had made him wary of people. Increasingly he retreated from social gatherings, preferring to drink alone in his room, or periodically to fly out of it in a drunken rage, tearing up the wooden board-walks in Lawrence and screaming obscenities at the top of his lungs. Some of his friends worried that he was becoming an alcoholic.

Then he withdrew from college—and, emphatically, from human contact. First, he explored an unmapped section of Death Valley. Then he volunteered to gather botanical samples in northernmost Alaska for the Department of Agriculture. When the department proposed that he head an entire expedition for the purpose, he flatly turned them down. "I do not need anybody to take care of me, and I do not want to take care of anybody." Alone, he trekked into the frigid wastes of northern Alaska and remained there for the better part of a year. When he ran out of food, he ate his sled dogs.

During those excruciatingly long, hollow nights at the top of the world, Funston would read aloud the only book he had lugged beyond the Arctic circle: Kipling's *Three Soldiers,* a collection about British army life in India. It was a curious choice. In thickly accented dialogues, each soldier attempts to get the better of the others with lewd tales and sharp banter; what keeps their rivalry from destroying their friendship is a shared conviction that as English fighting men, they were destined to prevail over the native peoples of India. Perhaps during one of these evenings it came to Funston that he could hardly prove that he measured up if no one was around to take the measurements. War plainly provided an ideal stage for proving one's manhood.

Funston returned from Alaska longing for life as lived by Kipling's heroes. He wanted to experience war and didn't much care whom or for what he fought. In 1895, he went to New York City to sell accounts of his adventures to the newspapers and magazines. While there, he happened upon a rally for the Cuban insurgents who were trying to rid the island of its Spanish overloads. Almost instantly Funston volunteered to serve with the Cuban rebels; though he had never fired a cannon, he was offered—and accepted—a commission as an artillery officer. Within weeks, he had slipped into Cuba and was at war with the Spanish, one of a handful of Yankee *guerrilleros* fighting for the Cubans. He made up for his lack of gunnery skill by sneaking his Hotchkiss cannon absurdly close to Spanish fortifications at night, often within four hundred yards, while a gang of nervous Cubans frantically threw up a protective parapet. As the sun rose, the Spaniards, aghast at what was sitting on their doorstep, fired everything they had at the cannon. Time and again, Funston calmly adjusted the sights, pulled the lanyard, and climbed on the parapet, shouting, "Viva cuba libre!" During that year he was repeatedly wounded, once when a bullet pierced both lungs. An even more serious hip wound became badly infected, for which Funston sought permission to seek medical treatment in the United States. The Cubans refused to allow him to do what they could not, so Funston simply sneaked out of camp. On the way to the coast, however, he was apprehended by a Spanish patrol and brought before a court-martial, which threatened him with execution. He managed to talk his way out and was released to the American consulate in Havana.

He was not yet done with war. In 1898 Funston, age thirty-two, lobbied for and was given command of the Kansas regiments that volunteered to fight against Spain. To his dismay, however, the Kansans were sent not to Cuba, where Teddy Roosevelt and others were acquiring the fame Funston believed he had earned, but to the Philippines, where the Spaniards were hopelessly trapped in a fortress at Manila, surrounded by Filipino nationalists and the U.S. Army. The Spanish garrison eventually surrendered without giving battle. Then, to Funston's delight, hostilities broke out in the trenches between the Filipino nationalists and the Americans, and he finally got the war he craved, with plenty of sweeping charges, glorious victories, and newspaper and magazine feature stories, and just ten miles ahead was the greatest one of all. Captive would become captor, and the little man a great one. Dead or alive, Funston would become his nation's biggest hero ever.

On the afternoon of March 23, 1901, eighty-one Macabebes wearing Filipino uniforms and their five American "prisoners," including Funston, met up with a contingent of Aguinaldo's army, which escorted them to the banks of the Palanan River. The Filipinos held the Americans on the far bank and ferried the Macabebes across and into town, where the houses were festooned with garlands and wreaths of flowers. Aguinaldo's lieutenant explained that the townspeople had been celebrating the thirty-second birthday of el presidente. He apologized that most of the festivities were over. "But," he added, "we still have music, and I believe you can still have some fun." He led them to a bandstand in the town square, where they were presented to an honor guard of some sixty soldiers wearing the blue tunics and white hats of the Filipino army. Aguinaldo watched from a window in his headquarters. One of his officers grew uneasy and requested permission to disarm the newcomers. Aguinaldo angrily refused to countenance such behavior toward his "brothers and allies."

A few minutes later, a shout came from outside. "Now is the time, Macabebes! Give it to them." Shots rang out.

Aguinaldo ran to the window, thinking the troops were firing a salute. "Stop that foolishness," he cried out. "Don't waste ammunition!"

Below was chaos. Some of his men lay dead. Others were fleeing the square, trying to load their guns as they ran.

On the other side of the Palanan River, Funston and the other American "prisoners" snatched their hidden guns and began firing. They leaped into a boat and paddled madly across the river. By the time they stormed *el presidente's* headquarters, Aguinaldo had been seized.

"I am General Funston, commander of the expedition. You are a prisoner of war of the Army of the United States of America. You will be treated with due consideration and sent to Manila at the first opportunity in a steamer, which is coming to take us on board."

Dazed, Aguinaldo replied: "Is this not some joke?"

Before Aguinaldo's army could regroup to save their leader, Funston and the Macabebes dashed him to the awaiting steamer. Weeks later, after being subjected to intense pressure by U.S. military officials, Aguinaldo renounced the Filipino revolution, swore allegiance to the United States, and called on his followers to do the same. Most did, and the Philippine-American war was over, though pockets of opposition persisted in isolated islands for several years. Frederick Funston had in fact won the war, and almost single-handedly. Because of him, more than anyone else, the United States became a formal empire and the Philippines its first colonial possession.

Back home, Funston was a sensation. Instead of being mustered out of the army, he was promoted to brigadier general, the youngest in the nation. Newspaper editors and politicians championed him for governor of Kansas, or for vice president on a ticket headed by Teddy Roosevelt in 1904. Publishers offered big advances for his memoirs, and he was the hottest speaker on the lecture circuit. If not the bravest soldier in the annals of American warfare, he was the only one whose actions in the field had decided an entire war. Funston had realized his fondest dream.

Funston's name streaked across the national consciousness, but within a few years all but vanished. In 1902 President Teddy Roosevelt ordered

Funston to cease giving speeches, and Funston was subsequently given in-consequential commands. In 1906 he was stationed in San Francisco when the earthquake struck; Funston took it upon himself to blow up buildings to create a firebreak. Grateful citizens of San Francisco named a park after him. He died of a heart attack in 1917, at the age of fifty-one.

Why was Funston so quickly forgotten? Part of the explanation is that immediately after Aguinaldo's capitulation, Funston was subjected to sharp criticism. Anti-imperialist members of the Senate, perhaps fearful of Funston's political prospects, launched an inquiry into disturbing rumors concerning his behavior. One of his captains told the Senate committee that Funston had routinely administered the water torture and had ordered his men "to take no prisoners." The hearings were quickly shut down, but some of Funston's men revealed that they had set entire villages ablaze, incinerating women and children. One Kansas private swore that Funston had ordered the execution of twenty-four Filipino prisoners; several reporters confirmed that Funston claimed to have killed the prisoners to avenge American deaths. Another of Funston's men reported that after seizing a Catholic church during a battle, Funston had donned vestments and performed a mock mass in the ruins.

The manner in which Aguinaldo was apprehended also proved unsettling. Critics noted that Funston and the Americans had fired their weapons *after* they had surrendered and that the Macabebes were wearing enemy uniforms; both actions violated international law. The underhanded manner in which the Filipinos were defeated raised further doubts about whether the imperial venture subverted the ideals on which the American nation was founded.

There was something else too. Though he embodied a heroic ideal as old as history itself, Funston's stark lust for martial glory, unsoftened by the haze of time, disconcerted those who chose to look closely. There was no point in blaming Funston for his deeds, wrote Mark Twain, "because his conscience leaked out through one of his pores when he was little."

Shame has always impelled young men to battle, and to do things great and gruesome. Tim O'Brien, our foremost novelist of the Vietnam War, explained that he participated as a foot soldier in that war "out of a kind of personal terror—fear of censure, fear of humiliation, fear of exile, fear of jail, fear of ridicule, fear that my reputation might be damaged among my friends and family, fear of blushing before the stolid folks in my little hometown. . . . in short, I capitulated to an overwhelming fear of *embarrassment*. . . . We kill out of embarrassment. We die of embarrassment."

Aggression is necessarily synonymous with military success, and both are essential to the survival of peoples and nations. Yet aggression often takes root in the darkest recesses of the soul, wherein lurks, among young men especially, an immense fear of humiliation. Funston's life, so familiar in its basic outlines, so heroic in its wild trajectory, so inspiring in its determined assault on adversity, on closer inspection provided a disturbing glimpse into that darkness.

Sometimes we forget our heroes because there is too much to remember: the press of new events inevitably crowds out the old. But sometimes it's best that our heroes remain forgotten, lest they remind us of things we do not wish to know.

Suggestions for Further Reading

JOHN QUINCY ADAMS

Paul C. Nagel, *John Quincy Adams: A Public Life, a Private Life* (1997)
Samuel F. Bemis, *John Quincy Adams and the Union* (1956)
George Dangerfield, *The Era of Good Feelings* (1952)

MARGARET ANDERSON

Margaret Anderson, *My Thirty Years' War* (1969)
Holly A. Baggett, "Aloof from Natural Laws: Margaret C. Anderson and the *Little Review*, 1914–1929" (Ph.D. dissertation, University of Delaware, 1992)
Edward de Grazia, *Girls Lean Back Everywhere: The Law of Obscenity and the Assault on Genius* (1992)
Steven Watson, *Strange Bedfellows: The First American Avant-Garde* (1991)

LEW AYRES

Irving Wallace, "The Amazing Comeback of Lew Ayres," *Coronet* (November 1948)
Lew Ayres, *Altars of the East* (1956)
Garth Jowett, *Film: The Democratic Art* (1976)
Clayton Koppes, *Hollywood Goes to War* (1987)

WILLIAM CHANDLER BAGLEY

Isaac L. Kandel, *William Chandler Bagley: Stalwart Educator* (1961)
Lawrence A. Cremin, David Shannon, and Mary Evelyn Townsend, *A History of Teachers College, Columbia University* (1954)
Walter H. Drost, *David Snedden and Education for Social Efficiency* (1967)

JOHN BASILONE

New York Times, June 24, 25, September 20, 1943, July 9, 1944, March 9, 1945, December 22, 1945; *Life*, October 11, 1943; *Time*, March 19, 1945; *New York Herald-Tribune*, September 5, 1943; *Collier's*, June 24, 1944
Richard B. Frank, *Guadalcanal* (1990)
Bill D. Ross, *Iwo Jima: Legacy of Valor* (1985)

ROBERT BASSET

New Haven, *New Haven Town Records, 1649–*, in *Ancient Town Records*, vol. 1 (1917); *Records of the Colony and Plantation of New-Haven from 1638–1649* (1857); *Records of the Colony or Jurisdiction of New Haven, from 1653 to the Union* (1858)

Isabel M. Calder, *The New Haven Colony* (1944) and *Letters of John Davenport, Puritan Divine* (1937)

JAMES A. BAYARD

Morton Borden, *The Federalism of James A. Bayard* (1954)

Elizabeth Dorman, ed., "Papers of James A. Bayard, 1796–1815," *American Historical Association Annual Report for 1913*, vol. 2 (1915)

Stanley Elkins and Eric McKitrick, *The Age of Federalism: The Early American Republic, 1788–1800* (1993)

MYRA BRADWELL

Myra Bradwell Collection, Schlesinger Library, Radcliffe College

Jane Friedman, *America's First Lawyer: The Biography of Myra Bradwell* (1993)

Chicago Legal News, 1868–1894

JOHN CHAPMAN (JOHNNY APPLESEED)

Robert Price, *Johnny Appleseed: Man and Myth* (1954)

Howard Fast, *The Tall Hunter* (1942)

Dixon Wecter, *The Hero in History* (1941)

Works Progress Administration, *The Ohio Guide* (1940)

NED COBB

Theodore Rosengarten, *All God's Dangers: The Life of Nate Shaw* (1974)

Donald H. Grubbs, *Cry from the Cotton: The Southern Tenant Farmers' Union and the New Deal* (1971)

Jacqueline Jones, *The Dispossessed: America's Underclasses from the Civil War to the Present* (1992)

Robin D. G. Kelley, *Hammer and Hoe: Alabama Communists during the Great Depression* (1990)

GEORGE DEWEY

Ronald Spector, *Admiral of the New Empire: The Life and Career of George Dewey* (1974)

George Dewey, *Autobiography* (1913)

Frank Freidel, *The Splendid Little War* (1958)

David Haward Bain, *Sitting in Darkness: Americans in the Philippines* (1984)

GEORGE DROUILLARD

M. O. Skarsten, *George Drouillard: Hunter and Interpreter for Lewis and Clark and Fur Trader, 1807–1810* (1964)

Robert M. Utley, *A Life Wild and Perilous: Mountain Men and the Paths to the Pacific* (1997)

Stephen E. Ambrose, *Undaunted Courage: Meriwether Lewis, Thomas Jefferson, and the Opening of the American West* (1996)

MARY DYER

Edward Burroughs, *A Declaration of the Sad and Great Persecution and Martyrdom of the People of God, Called Quakers, in New-England, for the Worshipping of God* (1661)
Mary Dyer, *Quaker: Two Letters of William Dyer of Rhode Island, 1659–1660* (1903)
Philip F. Gura, *A Glimpse of Zion's Glory: Puritan Radicalism in Seventeenth-Century New England* (1984)

GERTRUDE EDERLE

"How a Girl Beat Leander at the Hero Game," *Literary Digest*, August 21, 1926
Paul Gallico, *The Golden People* (1965)
Paul T. Carter, *Another Part of the Twenties* (1977)
Doris H. Pieroth, *Their Day in the Sun: Women of the 1932 Olympics* (1996)

FREDERICK FUNSTON

Frederick Funston, *Memories of Two Wars: Cuban and Philippine Experiences* (1911)
David Haward Bain, *Sitting in Darkness: Americans in the Philippines* (1984)
Stuart Creighton Miller, *Benevolent Assimilation: The American Conquest of the Philippines, 1899–1903* (1982)
Thomas W. Crouch, "Frederick Funston of Kansas: His Formative Years, 1865–1891," *Kansas Historical Quarterly* (Summer 1974)

J. C. M. HANSON

Olvind M. Hovde, *J. C. M. Hanson, What Became of Jens: A Study in Americanization Based on the Reminiscences of J. C. M. Hanson, 1864–1943* (1974)
Papers in Honor of the Seventieth Birthday of James Christian Meinrich Hanson (1934)
Arthur T. Hamlin, *The University Library in the United States: Its Origins and Development* (1981)
John Richardson, Jr., *The Spirit of Inquiry: The Graduate Library School at Chicago, 1921–51* (1982)

DUMMY HOY

L. S. Ritter, *The Glory of Their Times* (1966)
J. L. Reichler, ed., *The Baseball Encyclopedia* (1985)
Bill James, *The Bill James Historical Baseball Abstract* (1986)

FLORENCE KELLEY

Kathryn Kish Sklar, *Florence Kelley and the Nation's Work: The Rise of Women's Political Culture, 1830–1900* (1995)
Eileen Boris, *Home to Work: Motherhood and the Politics of Industrial Homework in the United States* (1994)

Kathryn Kish Sklar, ed., *The Autobiography of Florence Kelley: Notes of Sixty Years* (1986)

HENRY KNOX

North Callahan, *Henry Knox: General Washington's General* (1958)
Noah Brooks, *Henry Knox: A Soldier of the Revolution* (1900)
George Athan Billias, ed., *George Washington's Generals* (1964)

JOHN McLUCKIE

Paul Krause, *The Battle for Homestead, 1880–1892* (1992)
Arthur G. Burgoyne, *The Homestead Strike of 1892* (1893)
Joseph Frazier Wall, *Andrew Carnegie* (1970)

PAULI MURRAY

Jack Greenberg, *Crusaders in the Courts: How a Dedicated Band of Lawyers Fought for the Civil Rights Revolution* (1994)
Cynthia Harrison, *On Account of Sex: The Politics of Women's Issues, 1945–1968* (1988)
Pauli Murray, *Proud Shoes: The Story of an American Family* (1956)
Pauli Murray, *Song in a Weary Throat: An American Pilgrimage* (1987)

ALICE PAUL

Amelia R. Fry, *Conversations with Alice Paul* (oral history prepared for the Regional Oral History Office, Bancroft Library, University of California, Berkeley, 1976)
Amelia R. Fry, "Alice Paul and the ERA," in Joan Hoff, ed., *Rights of Passage: The Past and Future of the ERA* (1986)
Christine A. Lunardini, *From Equal Suffrage to Equal Rights: Alice Paul and the National Woman's Party, 1910–1928* (1986)
Leila Rupp and Verta Taylor, *Survival in the Doldrums: The American Women's Movement, 1945 to the 1960s* (1987)

THOMAS PETERS

Gary B. Nash, "Thomas Peters: Millwright and Deliverer," in David G. Sweet and Gary B. Nash, eds., *Struggle and Survival in Colonial America* (1981)
James W. St. G. Walker, *The Black Loyalists: The Search for a Promised Land in Nova Scotia and Africa* (1976)
Sylvia R. Frey, *Water from the Rock: Black Resistance in a Revolutionary Age* (1991)
Robin Winks, *The Blacks in Canada: A History* (1971)

SAM PHILLIPS

Howard A. DeWitt, *Elvis, The Sun Years: The Story of Elvis Presley in the Fifties* (1993)
Peter Guralnick, *Last Train to Memphis: The Rise of Elvis Presley* (1994)
Jerry Hopkins, *Elvis: A Biography* (1971)

EDWARD PRICHARD

Tracy Campbell, *Short of the Glory: The Fall and Redemption of Edward F. Prichard, Jr.* (1998)
John Ed Pearce, *Divide and Dissent: Kentucky Politics, 1930–1963* (1987)

Lowell H. Harrison and James C. Klotter, *A New History of Kentucky* (1997)

Katharine Graham, *Personal History* (1997)

SAMUEL SEABURY

Herbert Mitgang, *The Man Who Rode the Tiger: The Life and Times of Judge Samuel Seabury* (1964)

Oliver E. Allen, *The Tiger: The Rise and Fall of Tammany Hall* (1993)

Arthur Mann, *La Guardia: A Fighter against His Times* (1950)

Gene Fowler, *Beau James: The Life and Times of Jimmy Walker* (1949)

HAZEL BRANNON SMITH

Hodding Carter III, *The South Strikes Back* (1959)

Mary King, *Freedom Song: A Personal Story of the 1960s Civil Rights Movement* (1987)

Howard Raines, *My Soul Is Rested: Movement Days in the Deep South Remembered* (1983)

Juan Williams, *Eyes on the Prize* (1986)

O. DELIGHT SMITH

Edwin Gabler, *The American Telegrapher: A Social History, 1860–1900* (1988)

Gary M. Fink, *The Fulton Bag and Cotton Mills Strike of 1914–1915: Espionage, Labor Conflict, and New South Industrial Relations* (1993)

Jacquelyn Dowd Hall, "O. Delight Smith's Progressive Era: Labor, Feminism and Reform in the Urban South," in Nancy Hewitt and Suzanne Lebsock, eds., *Visible Women: New Essays on American Activism* (1993)

Jacquelyn Dowd Hall, "Private Eyes, Public Women: Class and Sex in the Urban South, Atlanta, 1913–1915," in Ava Baron, ed., *Work Engendered: Toward a New History of American Labor* (1991)

SUSIE KING TAYLOR

Catherine Clinton and Nina Silber, eds., *Divided Houses: Gender and the Civil War* (1992)

Joe Glatthar, *Forged in Battle: The Civil War Alliance between Black Soldiers and White Officers* (1991)

Susie King Taylor, *Reminiscences of My Life in Camp with the 33rd U.S. Colored Troops, Late 1st South Carolina Volunteers* (1902), edited by Patricia Romero, *A Black Woman's Civil War Memoir* (1988)

CARLO TRESCA

Dorothy Gallagher, *All the Right Enemies: The Life and Murder of Carlo Tresca* (1988)

John P. Diggins, *Mussolini and Fascism: The View from America* (1972)

Elizabeth Gurley Flynn, *I Speak My Own Piece: Autobiography of "The Rebel Girl"* (1955)

NICHOLAS TRIST

Robert Ketchum, "The Thankless Task of Nicholas Trist," *American Heritage* (August 1970)

Louis Martin Sears, "Nicholas P. Trist, a Diplomat with Ideals," *Mississippi Historical Review* (June 1924)

Odie B. Faulk and Joseph A. Stout, Jr., eds., *The Mexican War—Changing Interpretations* (1973)

Paul H. Bergeron, *The Presidency of James K. Polk* (1987)

MIRIAM VAN WATERS

Estelle B. Freedman, *Maternal Justice: Miriam Van Waters and the Female Reform Tradition* (1996)

Papers of Miriam Van Waters and the Anna Gladding-Miriam Van Waters Papers, Schlesinger Library, Radcliffe College

CAROLINE F. WARE

"Maida Springer Kemp on Dr. Caroline F. Ware," supplement to the Black Women Oral History Project, Schlesinger Library, Radcliffe College

Papers of Caroline Farrar Ware, Franklin D. Roosevelt Library, Hyde Park, New York

"Women in Federal Government Project: Interview with Caroline Ware, January 27–29, 1982," Susan Ware, interviewer, Schlesinger Library, Radcliffe College

EMMELINE B. WELLS

Carol Cornwall Madsen, "A Mormon Woman in Victorian America" (Ph.D. dissertation, University of Utah, 1985)

Jill Mulvay Derr, Janath Russell Cannon, and Maureen Ursenbach Beecher, *Women of Covenant: The Story of Relief Society* (1992)

Claudia L. Bushman, ed., *Mormon Sisters: Women in Early Utah* (1976)

Carol Cornwall Madsen, ed., *Battle for the Ballot: Essays on Woman Suffrage in Utah, 1870–1896* (1997)

VICTORIA WOODHULL

Emanie Sachs, *The Terrible Siren: Victoria Woodhull* (1928)

John C. Spurlock, *Marriage and Middle-Class Radicalism in America, 1825–1860* (1988)

Madeleine B. Stern, ed., *The Victoria Woodhull Reader* (1974)

Lois Beachy Underhill, *The Woman Who Ran for President: The Many Lives of Victoria Woodhull* (1995)

About the Contributors

LEONARD J. ARRINGTON is the former historian of the Church of Jesus Christ of Latter-day Saints and the Redd Professor of Western History Emeritus at Brigham Young University. He is author, among others, of *Brigham Young: American Moses* and co-author with Davis Bitton of *The Mormon Experience: A History of the Latter-day Saints*.

JEAN HARVEY BAKER is Professor of History at Goucher College, and the author of several books, including *Mary Todd Lincoln: A Biography*, *The Stevensons: A Biography of an American Family*, and the newly republished *Affairs of Party*.

JAMES M. BANNER, JR., an independent scholar and writer in Washington, D.C., has written many books and articles about the early republic, the humanities, and public affairs, and is most recently the coauthor, with Harold C. Cannon, of *The Elements of Teaching*.

PATRICIA U. BONOMI is Professor Emerita of History at New York University. Her writings include *Under the Cope of Heaven: Religion, Society, and Politics in Colonial America*, and *The Lord Cornbury Scandal: The Politics of Reputation in British America*.

KATHLEEN BRADY is the author of *Ida Tarbell: Portrait of a Muckraker*, the biography of the crusading investigative journalist who wrote the classic expose of the Standard Oil Company, and of *Lucille: The Life of Lucille Ball*.

DAVID BRODY is professor emeritus of history at the University of California, Davis and the author of *In Labor's Cause: Main Themes on the History of the American Worker* and other books on American labor history.

MARK C. CARNES is Professor of History at Barnard College and author or editor of numerous books, including *Secret Ritual and Manhood in Victorian America*, *Mapping America's Past*, and *Past Imperfect: History According to the Movies*.

CATHERINE CLINTON, the Douglas Southall Freeman Visiting Chair at the University of Richmond for 1997–1998, is the author of *Tara Revisited: Women, War and the Plantation Legend* and, most recently, *Civil War Stories*.

JOHN PATRICK DIGGINS is Distinguished Professor at the Graduate Center, City University of New York. Among his recent works are *The Promise of Pragmatism* and *Max Weber: Politics and the Spirit of Tragedy*.

THOMAS DUBLIN is Professor of History at the State University of New York at Binghamton and the author of *Women at Work: The Transformation of Work and Community in Lowell, Massachusetts, 1826–1860* and *Transforming Women's Work: New England Lives in the Industrial Revolution*.

THOMAS FLEMING, a novelist and historian, wrote *Liberty! The American Revolution*, the companion volume to the PBS series of the same title. He is the author of eighteen novels and almost as many nonfiction books, such as *The Man from Monticello* and *West Point: The Men and Times of the U.S. Military Academy*.

ESTELLE B. FREEDMAN is Professor of History at Stanford University, where she chairs the Program in Feminist Studies. She is the author of *Their Sisters' Keepers: Women's Prison Reform in America, 1830–1930* and *Maternal Justice: Miriam Van Waters and the Female Reform Tradition*, and the co-author of *Intimate Matters: A History of Sexuality in America*, 2nd ed.

STEPHEN JAY GOULD is the Alexander Agassiz Professor of Zoology and Professor of Geology at Harvard University and is curator for invertebrate paleontology at Harvard's Museum of Comparative Zoology. His most recent books are *Questioning the Millennium, Full House*, and *Dinosaur in a Haystack*.

JACQUELYN DOWD HALL is Julia Cherry Spruill Professor of History and the Director of the Southern Oral History Program at the University of North Carolina at Chapel Hill. She is the author of *Revolt Against Chivalry: Jessie Daniel Ames and the Women's Campaign Against Lynching* and coauthor of *Like a Family: The Making of a Southern Cotton Mill World*.

NEIL HARRIS is Preston and Sterling Morton Professor of History at the University of Chicago. His publications include *Humbug: The Art of P. T. Barnum* and *Cultural Excursions: Marketing Appetites and Cultural Tastes in Modern America*.

JOAN HOFF is Professor of History at the Contemporary History Institute, Ohio University. She is the former editor of the *Journal of Women's History* and *Presidential Studies Quarterly*. A specialist in U.S. foreign policy and politics, and women's legal history, her latest books are *Law, Gender, and Injustice: A Legal History of U.S. Women* and *Nixon Reconsidered*.

HELEN LEFKOWITZ HOROWITZ is Professor of American Studies and History at Smith College. She has written *Culture and the City, Alma Mater, Campus Life*, and *The Power and Passion of M. Carey Thomas* and has edited *Love Across the Color Line* and *Landscape in Sight*.

KENNETH T. JACKSON is the Jacques Barzun Professor of History and the Social Sciences at Columbia University and the author or editor of many books, including *Crabgrass Frontier: The Suburbanization of the United States* and *The Encyclopedia of New York City*.

JACQUELINE JONES teaches American history at Brandeis University, and is the author of *American Work: Black and White Labor Since 1600* and *Labor of Love, Labor of Sorrow: Black Women, Work, and the Family from Slavery to the Present*.

JUSTIN KAPLAN, General Editor of *Bartlett's Familiar Quotations*, is the author of *Mr. Clemens and Mark Twain, Walt Whitman: A Life*, and other books, including *The Language of Names* (with Anne Bernays).

ALFRED KAZIN was Distinguished Professor (Emeritus) of English, City University of New York Graduate Center, and the author of many books on American literary and cultural history, from *On Native Grounds* to *God and the American Writer*.

WILLIAM E. LEUCHTENBURG, William Rand Kenan, Jr. Professor of History at the University of North Carolina at Chapel Hill, has served as president of the American Historical Association, the Organization of American Historians, and the Society of American Historians. His many books include *The Perils of Prosperity, Franklin D. Roosevelt and the New Deal, 1932–1940*, and *In the Shadow of FDR: From Harry Truman to Bill Clinton*.

DAVID MCCULLOUGH, historian and biographer, is the president of the Society of American Historians. His books include *Truman, The Great Bridge, The Path Between the Seas, Mornings on Horseback*, and *The Johnstown Flood*.

WILLIAM S. MCFEELY, author of *Grant: A Biography, Frederick Douglass*, and, most recently, *Sapelo's People: A Long Walk into Freedom*, lives in Wellfleet, Massachusetts.

HERBERT MITGANG, author and critic, is a former member of *The New York Times* Editorial Board. Among his fifteen books in the fields of literature, reportage, history and biography is *The Man Who Rode the Tiger: The Life and Times of Judge Samuel Seabury*, winner of the American Bar Association Silver Gavel Award and runner-up for the Pulitzer Prize in biography. His writing prizes include the George Polk Career Award.

GARY B. NASH is Professor of History at the University of California, Los Angeles and Director of the National Center for History in the Schools. He is a former president of the Organization of American Historians and a member of the American Academy of Arts and Sciences.

DIANE RAVITCH is Research Professor at New York University, and a Senior Fellow at the Brookings Institution, where she holds the Brown Chair in Education Studies. She is author and editor of numerous books, including *The Great School Wars: New York City, 1805–1983*; *The Troubled Crusade: American Education, 1945–1980*; and *The American Reader*.

ROSALIND ROSENBERG is Professor of History at Barnard College, Columbia University, and author of *Beyond Separate Spheres: Intellectual Roots of Modern Feminism* and *Divided Lives: American Women in the Twentieth Century*.

ARTHUR SCHLESINGER, JR., Emeritus Schweitzer Professor in the Humanities at the Graduate School of the City University of New York, is the author of many books, including *The Age of Jackson*, three volumes of *The Age of Roosevelt*, *A Thousand Days: John F. Kennedy in the White House*, *Robert Kennedy and His Times*, *The Imperial Presidency*, and *The Cycles of History*. He served as special assistant to President Kennedy in 1961–1963.

KATHRYN KISH SKLAR is Distinguished Professor of History at the State University of New York, Binghamton. She is the author or editor of many books, including *Florence Kelley and the Nation's Work: The Rise of Women's Political Culture, 1830–1900*, and *Catharine Beecher: A Study in American Domesticity*.

CHRISTINE STANSELL is a Professor of History at Princeton University and author of *City of Women: Sex and Class in New York, 1789–1860*. Her new book, *American Moderns*, will be published by Metropolitan Books of Henry Holt in 1999. Her reviews and essays about women, feminism, and American culture appear in *The New Republic* and the *Boston Globe*.

ROBERT M. UTLEY is a former Chief Historian of the National Park Service and author of thirteen books on the history of the American West, including *A Life Wild and Perilous: Mountain Men and the Paths to the Pacific* and *The Lance and the Shield: The Life and Times of Sitting Bull*.

SUSAN WARE has been named the editor of volume five of *Notable American Women: A Biographical Dictionary* at Radcliffe College. Her books include *Letter to the World: Seven Women Who Shaped the American Century* and *Still Missing: Amelia Earhart and the Search for Modern Feminism*.

BERNARD A. WEISBERGER is a former professor and current freelancer who has written history for young and adult readers and scripts for television documentaries. He is a Contributing Editor to *American Heritage* and writes its column, "In the News." His most recent book was *The LaFollettes of Wisconsin: Love and Politics in Progressive America*.

TOM WICKER, a retired columnist for the *New York Times*, has written several books of fiction and nonfiction, including *Unto This Hour*, a novel about the Civil War.

JOEL WILLIAMSON is Lineberger Professor in the Humanities at the University of North Carolina at Chapel Hill. He is the author of a number of books, including *William Faulkner and Southern History*, *The Crucible of Race*, *A Rage for Order*, *New People*, and *After Slavery*.

Acknowledgments

MARK CARNES came up with the original idea for *Forgotten Heroes*, and I am grateful to him for his help and advice at all stages of the project. I would also like to acknowledge the support of the Society of American Historians, especially president David McCullough and vice-president Kenneth T. Jackson, who stood behind the book from the start. Early on we had the good fortune to link up with Bruce Nichols at The Free Press, whose enthusiasm, excellent critical judgment, and never-failing sense of humor facilitated the book's timely completion. Thanks, too, to Albert DePetrillo for his editorial assistance.

A colleague once compared the process of editing a book to "herding hummingbirds" and there is a certain truth to that characterization. But I must salute my authors for making the whole process far more pleasant than I could have ever dreamed possible. In the course of editing this book, I worked with old friends and made many new ones, some of whom I have never met in person. Thank you all for making this such a rewarding undertaking.

Susan Ware
Hopkinton, New Hampshire

Index

CHAPTER OPENING PHOTO CREDITS

2. Independence National Historical Park
3. Courtesy Commonwealth of Massachussets, Massachussets Art Commission. Photo by Douglas Christian.
6. St. Memin, "James Asheton Bayard" (1767–1815), Engraving, In the Collection of the Corcoran Gallery of Art, Washington, DC
7. Courtesy Mead Art Museum, Amherst College
8. Library of Congress
9. Courtesy of William E. Loechel
11. Illinois State Historical Library
12. Collection of The New York Historical Society
13. Courtesy Historical Department, The Church of Jesus Christ of Latter-Day Saints
14. National Baseball Hall of Fame Library & Archive, Cooperstown, NY
15. Borough of Homestead
16. Library of Congress
17. Naval Historical Foundation, Washington, DC
19. Blackstone Studios
20. Jacquelyn Dowd Hall
24. The Schlesinger Library, Radcliffe College
25. AP/Wide World Photos
26. Courtesy of Philip Burling
27. The Schlesinger Library, Radcliffe College
28. The Library of Congress
29. Courtesy of Gordon N. Converse
30. The Schlesinger Library, Radcliffe College
31. Courtesy of Howard DeWitt
32. AP/Wide World Photos
33. AP/Wide World Photos
34. Town of Raritan Archives